More information about this series at http://www.springer.com/series/10099

Springer Texts in Busin

More infor

Peter Zweifel · Aaron Praktiknjo ·
Georg Erdmann

Energy Economics

Theory and Applications

Peter Zweifel
Bad Bleiberg, Austria

Aaron Praktiknjo
E.ON Energy Research Center
RWTH Aachen University
Aachen, Germany

Georg Erdmann
Department of Energy Systems
Berlin University of Technology
Berlin, Germany

ISSN 2192-4333 ISSN 2192-4341 (electronic)
Springer Texts in Business and Economics
ISBN 978-3-662-53020-7 ISBN 978-3-662-53022-1 (eBook)
DOI 10.1007/978-3-662-53022-1

Library of Congress Control Number: 2017934524

© Springer International Publishing AG 2017

This work is subject to copyright. All rights are reserved by the Publisher, whether the whole or part of the material is concerned, specifically the rights of translation, reprinting, reuse of illustrations, recitation, broadcasting, reproduction on microfilms or in any other physical way, and transmission or information storage and retrieval, electronic adaptation, computer software, or by similar or dissimilar methodology now known or hereafter developed.

The use of general descriptive names, registered names, trademarks, service marks, etc. in this publication does not imply, even in the absence of a specific statement, that such names are exempt from the relevant protective laws and regulations and therefore free for general use.

The publisher, the authors and the editors are safe to assume that the advice and information in this book are believed to be true and accurate at the date of publication. Neither the publisher nor the authors or the editors give a warranty, express or implied, with respect to the material contained herein or for any errors or omissions that may have been made. The publisher remains neutral with regard to jurisdictional claims in published maps and institutional affiliations.

Printed on acid-free paper

This Springer imprint is published by Springer Nature
The registered company is Springer-Verlag GmbH Germany
The registered company address is: Heidelberger Platz 3, 14197 Berlin, Germany

Preface

Access to energy resources, energy supply security, high and increasing prices of energy, lack of competition, slow market entry of renewables, insufficient investment in energy efficiency, and sluggish progress in reducing greenhouse gas emissions are all well-known issues and concerns characterizing energy markets. Yet, what are the possibilities of finding effective, efficient, and sustainable solutions to these problems? The fundamental claim of this book is that solutions cannot be found without an in-depth analysis of energy markets that acknowledges not only their physical and technological constraints but also their structural idiosyncrasies and the behavior of market participants.

This text is the result of 30 years of teaching and research performed by the authors at both German- and English-speaking universities in Europe. It therefore adopts a distinctly European approach, yet without neglecting developments worldwide. While firmly anchored in economic theory, it also presents empirical evidence enabling readers to assess the relevance of predicted relationships. For instance, it is certainly of interest to know that the so-called elasticity of substitution is a crucial parameter for answering the question whether man-made capital can replace energy quickly enough to assure sustainability in terms of consumption in spite of the fact that energy constitutes an ultimately limited resource. In addition, it is also important to see whether the estimated elasticities of substitution are typically below one (making sustainability questionable) or above one (suggesting sustainability can be attained).

Debates about energy policy tend to be short-lived, reflecting the interests of governments who wish to demonstrate to their electorate that they are "on top of things." By way of contrast, this text focuses on the basic conditions and mechanisms that all public interventions in the energy sector have to deal with. It provides readers with the tools enabling them to assess the chance of these interventions reaching their objectives. Turning to the private sector, one condition is that management decisions concerning energy are economically viable, lest they fail to contribute to the economic survival of the company. This book is therefore also of interest to business practitioners who may be confronted with the question whether investment in an energy-saving technology has a sufficiently high return to be worthwhile. Analysts of the energy industry, energy traders, and other professionals acting in and on behalf of the energy sector will benefit from this text as well. Like the makers of public policy, they are confronted with shocks of all sorts impinging on energy markets with unprecedented frequency, exposing them to increasing business risks.

Finally, this work also targets future researchers with an interest in energy. The distinct properties of energy sources (ranging from coal to solar) need to be taken into account when modeling the behavior of businesses and consumers. The corresponding markets are distinct to a sufficient degree to warrant a partial (rather than general-equilibrium) approach for their analysis, at least as a first approximation. The statistical documentation of energy is excellent both at the national and international level, paving the way for empirical research. Moreover, an important motivation may be that research revolving around the economics of energy is met with considerable interest by society and public policy.

Students at the Swiss Federal Institute of Technology ETH Zurich (Switzerland), the University of the Armed Forces in Munich (Germany), the Technical University of Berlin (Germany), the RWTH Aachen University (Germany), and the Diplomatic Academy of Vienna (Austria), as well as participants in international conferences, have all contributed to this volume through their suggestions and criticisms. Its original German version has been well received by both Engineering and Economics students (future leaders and decision-makers in energy markets), thus motivating our attempt to make this work accessible to English-speaking readers.

This text is somewhat voluminous because in addition to expounding the theoretical groundwork, it also addresses each of the several energy sources. However, individual chapters are self-contained, with cross-references to other topics. This broad approach has the advantage of providing a reference especially for business practitioners who need to obtain insight into a particular market. At the same time, readers never lose sight of the consequences of public regulation and liberalization, which frequently cut across sectors (not least caused by substitution processes that depend on the elasticity of substitution alluded to above). At a time when energy markets change and develop at an unprecedented pace, this guidance through the maze is particularly valuable, and when new market developments challenge received wisdom, new economic insights develop. We will therefore provide on our website www.energy-economics.eu additional material reflecting new data sources and the scientific progress in the field.

This joint effort would not have been possible without the support of many colleagues and collaborators, which is sincerely acknowledged. Of course, the authors remain responsible for all remaining errors.

Bad Bleiberg, Austria	Peter Zweifel
Aachen, Germany	Aaron Praktiknjo
Berlin, Germany	Georg Erdmann
October 2016	

Contents

1 Introduction 1
   1.1 Philosophical and Evolutionary Aspects of Energy 1
   1.2 Why Energy Economics? 4
       1.2.1 Price Mechanism and Market Coordination 5
       1.2.2 Particularities of Energy Markets 7
       1.2.3 Energy Policy 9
   1.3 History of Energy Economics 12
   References 13

2 Energy in Science and Engineering 15
   2.1 Energy and the Natural Sciences 16
       2.1.1 Physics 16
       2.1.2 Chemistry 18
       2.1.3 Biology 18
   2.2 Engineering and Energy 19
       2.2.1 Energy Units 20
       2.2.2 Energy Conversion 21
   2.3 Energy Balance 23
       2.3.1 Gross Energy (Primary Energy) 23
       2.3.2 Final Energy Consumption 26
       2.3.3 Data Sources 26
       2.3.4 Useful Energy (Net Energy) and Energy Services ... 27
   2.4 Cumulated Energy Requirement 28
   2.5 Energy Input-Output Analysis 29
   References 34

3 Investment and Profitability Calculation 37
   3.1 Basics 38
   3.2 Interest Rate and Price of Capital 44
   3.3 Inflation-Adjusted Interest Rate 45
   3.4 Social Time Preference 47

		3.5	Interest Rate and Risk	49
			3.5.1 Capital Asset Pricing Model (CAPM)	50
			3.5.2 New Asset Pricing Methods	53
		3.6	Real Option Valuation	54
			3.6.1 Energy Investments as Real Options	55
			3.6.2 Black-Scholes Model	58
			3.6.3 Application to Balancing Power Supply	60
		References		63
4	**Bottom-Up Analysis of Energy Demand**			65
		4.1	Process Analysis	66
		4.2	Stock of Appliances, Buildings, Vehicles, and Machineries	68
		4.3	Energy Efficiency	77
			4.3.1 Definitions	77
			4.3.2 Determining Energy Efficiency Potential	81
			4.3.3 Energy Efficiency: A Case of Market Failure?	82
			4.3.4 Contracting	85
		References		87
5	**Top-Down Analysis of Energy Demand**			89
		5.1	Population Growth	90
		5.2	Economic Growth	92
		5.3	The Price of Energy	94
			5.3.1 Short-Term and Long-Term Price Elasticities	95
			5.3.2 A Partial Energy Demand Model	96
			5.3.3 Substitution Between Energy and Capital	102
		5.4	Technological Change	107
		References		110
6	**Energy Reserves and Sustainability**			111
		6.1	Resources and Reserves	112
			6.1.1 Resources	113
			6.1.2 Static Range of Fossil Energy Reserves	115
		6.2	Profit-Maximizing Resource Extraction	117
			6.2.1 Hotelling Price Trajectory	117
			6.2.2 Role of Backstop Technologies	120
			6.2.3 Role of Expectations and Expectation Errors	122
		6.3	Optimal Resource Extraction: Social Welfare View	123
			6.3.1 The Optimal Consumption Path	126
			6.3.2 The Optimal Depletion Path of the Reserve	128
			6.3.3 Causes and Implications of Market Failure	129
		6.4	Sustainability	131
			6.4.1 Potential of Renewable Energy Sources	131
			6.4.2 Hartwick Rule for Weak Sustainability	132
			6.4.3 Population Growth and Technological Change	137
			6.4.4 Is the Hartwick Rule Satisfied?	138
		References		140

7 External Costs ... 143
- 7.1 The Coase Theorem ... 144
- 7.2 Aggregate Emissions ... 147
- 7.3 Instruments of Environmental Policy ... 150
  - 7.3.1 Internalization Approaches ... 150
  - 7.3.2 Standard-Oriented Approaches ... 152
- 7.4 Measuring External Costs of Energy Use ... 154
- References ... 157

8 Markets for Liquid Fuels ... 159
- 8.1 Types of Liquid Fuels and Their Properties ... 160
  - 8.1.1 Properties of Crude Oil ... 160
  - 8.1.2 Reserves and Extraction of Conventional Oil ... 161
  - 8.1.3 Peak Oil Hypothesis ... 163
  - 8.1.4 Unconventional Oil ... 166
  - 8.1.5 Refineries and Oil Products ... 167
  - 8.1.6 Biogenic Liquid Fuels ... 168
- 8.2 Crude Oil Market ... 171
  - 8.2.1 Vertically Integrated Monopoly ... 171
  - 8.2.2 Global Oligopoly of Vertically Integrated Majors ... 174
  - 8.2.3 The OPEC Cartel of Oil-Exporting Countries ... 176
  - 8.2.4 State-Owned Oil Companies ... 180
- 8.3 Oil Price Formation ... 182
  - 8.3.1 Oil Spot Markets and the Efficient Market Hypothesis ... 183
  - 8.3.2 Long-Term Oil Price Forecasts and Scenarios ... 185
  - 8.3.3 Prices of Crude Oil Futures ... 190
  - 8.3.4 Wholesale Prices of Oil Products ... 192
- References ... 195

9 Markets for Gaseous Fuels ... 197
- 9.1 Gaseous Fuels and Gas Infrastructures ... 198
  - 9.1.1 Properties of Gaseous Fuels ... 199
  - 9.1.2 Reserves and Extraction of Natural Gas ... 200
  - 9.1.3 Biogas and Renewable Natural Gas ... 202
  - 9.1.4 Hydrogen ... 203
- 9.2 Natural Gas Economy ... 204
  - 9.2.1 Transport by Pipeline ... 205
  - 9.2.2 LNG Transport and Trade ... 211
- 9.3 Gas Markets and Gas Price Formation ... 213
  - 9.3.1 Long-Term Take-or-Pay Contracts ... 214
  - 9.3.2 Natural Gas Spot Trade ... 216
- 9.4 Third Party Access to the Gas Infrastructure ... 221
- References ... 224

10 Markets for Solid Fuels and CO_2 Emissions 227
    10.1 Solid Fuels and Their Technologies 228
        10.1.1 Biomass 228
        10.1.2 Coal Reserves 230
        10.1.3 Surface and Underground Coal Mining 231
        10.1.4 International Coal Market 232
    10.2 The Greenhouse Gas Problem 234
    10.3 Markets for Emission Rights 237
        10.3.1 Prices for CO_2 Emission Rights 239
        10.3.2 Clean Dark Spread 242
        10.3.3 Coal Perspectives 244
    References 245

11 Uranium and Nuclear Energy 247
    11.1 The Foundations of Nuclear Technology 248
        11.1.1 Radioactivity 249
        11.1.2 Uranium as the Dominant Fuel for Nuclear Power ... 251
        11.1.3 Nuclear Waste 252
    11.2 Uranium Market 254
    11.3 Risk Assessment of Nuclear Energy 256
        11.3.1 Probabilistic Safety Analysis of Nuclear Power Plants 258
        11.3.2 Risk Assessment According to the (μ, σ^2) Criterion ... 260
        11.3.3 Risk Assessment Based on Stated Preferences 264
    References 267

12 Markets for Electricity 269
    12.1 Features of Electricity Markets 270
        12.1.1 The Consumer Surplus of Electricity 271
        12.1.2 Non-storability of Electricity 272
        12.1.3 Power Market Design Options 273
    12.2 Electricity Generation 275
        12.2.1 Types of Power Generation Technologies 275
        12.2.2 Power Plant Dispatch in Liberalized Markets ... 278
        12.2.3 Properties of Day-Ahead Power Prices 280
        12.2.4 Intraday Markets 282
        12.2.5 Portfolio Management 283
        12.2.6 Market Power 285
    12.3 Power Plant Investments 288
        12.3.1 Power Plant Investments in Regulated Markets 288
        12.3.2 Power Plant Investment in Competitive Markets ... 291
        12.3.3 Capacity Markets 293
    References 295

13 Economics of Electrical Grids ... 297
13.1 Grid Properties and System Services ... 298
13.1.1 Electrotechnical Aspects ... 298
13.1.2 Services to Be Provided by Electrical Grid Operators ... 300
13.1.3 Markets for Control Power ... 301
13.2 Regulation of Grid Fees ... 302
13.2.1 The Grid as an Essential Facility ... 303
13.2.2 Optimal Grid Fees ... 303
13.2.3 Incentive Regulation ... 307
13.2.4 Unbundling ... 309
13.3 Economic Approach to Transmission Bottlenecks ... 310
References ... 312

14 Epilogue ... 315
References ... 317

Index ... 319

List of Figures

Fig. 1.1	Market price coordinating supply and demand	5
Fig. 1.2	Magical triangle of energy policy goals	10
Fig. 2.1	Principle of a steam engine	21
Fig. 2.2	Energy flow chart	23
Fig. 3.1	Net present value as function of the interest rate. Assumptions: Investment outlay $Inv_0 = 5500$ EUR; variable cost $c_{var} = 200$ EUR/a; sales revenue 850 EUR/a; operation period $T = 20$ years	43
Fig. 3.2	Energy cost as a function of lifetime and interest rate. Assumptions: investment cost $Inv_0 = 2000$ EUR/kW; variable cost $c_{var} = 0.01$ EUR/kWh; capacity factor $\nu = 0.2$	43
Fig. 3.3	Aggregated capital demand and supply	45
Fig. 3.4	Net present value of future financial flows at different interest rates	47
Fig. 3.5	Value of a call option	56
Fig. 3.6	Option value as a function of the expected contribution margin	62
Fig. 3.7	Option value as a function of volatility (Vega)	62
Fig. 4.1	Process analysis for modeling energy demand	67
Fig. 4.2	Logistic function for modeling ownership probability	70
Fig. 4.3	Structure of a nested logit model (example)	74
Fig. 4.4	Energy efficiency: engineering and economic definitions	80
Fig. 4.5	Theoretical and achievable efficiency potentials	81
Fig. 4.6	Waiting as a real option	85
Fig. 5.1	Lorenz curves of the global energy consumption and income distribution. Data source: World Bank (2014)	92
Fig. 5.2	Sample exchange rate and purchasing power parity. Data source: OECD	94
Fig. 5.3	Short-term and long-term effects of a reduction in energy supply	96
Fig. 5.4	Efficient and inefficient technical processes	102

Fig. 5.5	Isoquants with different elasticities of substitution	104
Fig. 5.6	Isoquants reflecting technological change	108
Fig. 6.1	Logistic path of cumulative global resource discoveries	114
Fig. 6.2	Discovery of conventional oil resources over time. Source: Erdmann and Zweifel (2008, p. 125)	115
Fig. 6.3	Static range of conventional oil and natural gas reserves. Data source: BP (2014)	116
Fig. 6.4	Optimal extraction trajectories of an exhaustible resource	121
Fig. 6.5	Prices in the presence of capacity shortages and market power	130
Fig. 6.6	Ramsey and Hartwick consumption trajectories	133
Fig. 6.7	Production function with alternative elasticities of substitution	137
Fig. 7.1	Pareto-optimal output given negative external effects	145
Fig. 7.2	Marginal profit and marginal external cost	145
Fig. 7.3	Impact of emission reductions on the market outcome	150
Fig. 7.4	Consequences of underestimated marginal profit	152
Fig. 8.1	Properties of crude oil varieties. Sources: American Petroleum Institute; Erdmann and Zweifel (2008, p. 173)	161
Fig. 8.2	Marginal cost of crude oil production (source: Oil Industry Trends)	163
Fig. 8.3	Crude oil extraction in the United States (source: EIA, CGES)	164
Fig. 8.4	Crude oil prices between 1900 and 2013 (data source: BP)	175
Fig. 8.5	Extraction and refinery capacities of oil companies. Data source: www.energyintel.com	176
Fig. 8.6	Crude oil price and OPEC market share (data source: BP)	177
Fig. 8.7	OPEC revenues from oil exports (data source: EIA 2014)	181
Fig. 8.8	Histogram of $\Delta \ln p_t$ for 420 days, 2005–2006	184
Fig. 8.9	Crude oil price forecasts published by the U.S. Department of Energy	188
Fig. 8.10	Perspectives of crude oil supply. Source: Erdmann and Zweifel (2008, p. 207)	189
Fig. 8.11	Oil forward curves between 1993 and 2006. Data source: Centre for Global energy Studies (CGES)	191
Fig. 8.12	Refinery margins (data source: BP 2014)	193
Fig. 8.13	Gasoline prices relative to heating oil prices in the United States. Data source: EIA (2014)	195
Fig. 9.1	Long-distance transportation costs of oil and gas. Source: Erdmann and Zweifel (2008, p. 233)	212
Fig. 9.2	German natural gas border prices (data source: BAFA (2014))	215
Fig. 9.3	Gas and heating oil prices on the U.S. spot market. Monthly price averages; data source: Energy Information Administration EIA	218

List of Figures

Fig. 10.1	Classification of solid biomass fuels	229
Fig. 10.2	Monthly coal and gas prices in Germany (data source: EEX). Note: 'cif. ARA' denotes inclusion of cost for insurance and freight for delivery to the ports of Amsterdam, Rotterdam, or Antwerp	233
Fig. 10.3	Global CO_2 emissions (data source: BP 2014)	235
Fig. 10.4	GHG emission trajectories	237
Fig. 10.5	Marginal emission abatement costs for two companies	238
Fig. 10.6	Prices of CO_2 emission rights (data source: EEX)	240
Fig. 10.7	German (clean) dark spread between 2001 and 2014	243
Fig. 11.1	Uranium supply and demand (source: Gerling et al. 2005)	255
Fig. 11.2	The feasibility locus $E[D] = 1$ and two indifference curves	260
Fig. 11.3	Willingness to pay for reducing exposure to nuclear risks (Switzerland, 2003)	266
Fig. 12.1	Daily electricity load profiles	272
Fig. 12.2	Wind speed and electricity generation from wind turbines	277
Fig. 12.3	Levelized costs of electricity depending on capacity utilization	278
Fig. 12.4	Price formation on the electricity spot market	280
Fig. 12.5	Histogram of adjusted day-ahead power prices. Data source: EEX (May 2003 to December 2005)	282
Fig. 12.6	Load duration curve and planning of power plant investments	289
Fig. 12.7	Optimal investment in generating capacity	290
Fig. 12.8	Annual price duration curve	291
Fig. 12.9	Scarcity rent for capacities	294
Fig. 13.1	Control power and balancing power	302
Fig. 13.2	The electrical grid as a natural monopoly	304
Fig. 13.3	Reverse flow and the elimination of a grid bottleneck	311

List of Tables

Table 2.1	Metabolic rate for continuous physical labor, humans vs. work animals	19
Table 2.2	Conversion table (based on IEA data)	19
Table 2.3	Energy conversion processes (examples)	21
Table 2.4	Energy balance of the European Union 2011	25
Table 2.5	Global commercial primary energy supply	27
Table 2.6	Cumulated energy requirement (CER) in 2012	29
Table 2.7	Sample input-output table of a country (in monetary units)	31
Table 2.8	Sample energy input-output table of a country (in energy units)	31
Table 2.9	Leontief multipliers corresponding to the input-output Table 2.7	33
Table 3.1	Sample present value factors (PVF) of an annuity	41
Table 3.2	Variables used for financial and real option valuation	60
Table 3.3	Value of the real option 'power plant' according to the Black-Scholes formula	61
Table 4.1	Indicators of energy demand	69
Table 4.2	Income elasticities of probability of car ownership (Norway, 1985)	75
Table 4.3	Marginal effects of decider-specific variables on probability of ownership	76
Table 4.4	Sample calculation of an investment into energy efficiency	84
Table 5.1	Population and per-capita primary energy supply	91
Table 5.2	Development of population, per-capita income, and energy intensity	93
Table 5.3	Income and price elasticities of crude oil demand	101
Table 5.4	Elasticities of substitution between capital, labor, and energy	107
Table 6.1	Ultimately recoverable resources	113
Table 6.2	Global fossil energy reserves and resources 2013	114
Table 6.3	The role of expectations: a crude oil example	122
Table 6.4	Worldwide potential of renewable energy sources	132

Table 7.1	External costs of power generation in Germany	157
Table 8.1	Standardized conversion factors for crude oil	161
Table 8.2	Quality levels and prices of crude oil	162
Table 8.3	Reserves and extraction rates of crude oil, 2013	162
Table 8.4	Expert views on the production maximum of crude oil	165
Table 8.5	Properties of crude oil and oil products	167
Table 8.6	Product portfolio of modern oil refineries	168
Table 8.7	Properties of liquid fuels	169
Table 8.8	Yields of energy plants	170
Table 8.9	Mega mergers between oil majors	176
Table 8.10	Payoff matrix for OPEC members in mn USD/day (example)	179
Table 9.1	Conversion factors for natural gas (at upper heating value H_s)	199
Table 9.2	Properties of gaseous fuels	200
Table 9.3	Storage properties of hydrocarbons	201
Table 9.4	Reserves and extraction of conventional natural gas	201
Table 9.5	Indicators for natural gas and heating oil spot market prices	219
Table 9.6	Capacity utilization by final users of natural gas	224
Table 10.1	Properties of solid fuels	229
Table 10.2	Properties of solid energy biomass	230
Table 10.3	Coal reserves and coal mining 2013	231
Table 10.4	Indicators of the greenhouse gas problem	235
Table 10.5	Energy wholesale prices in Germany given a CO_2 price of 10 EUR/tons	241
Table 11.1	Milestones for the development of nuclear power	249
Table 11.2	Radioactivity units	250
Table 11.3	Unit cost of uranium fuel production	252
Table 11.4	Inventory of 100 tons uranium fuel after 3 years in a light-water reactor	253
Table 11.5	Radioactivity of 100 tons uranium fuel and waste	253
Table 11.6	Global uranium demand for power generation in 2014	254
Table 11.7	Accident scenarios for the Mühleberg nuclear power plant (Switzerland)	258
Table 11.8	Expected loss of nuclear power plants	259
Table 12.1	Typical properties of generating technologies	276
Table 13.1	Average power transmission and distribution losses in Germany, in percent	299
Table 13.2	Unbundling concepts	310

Table of Abbreviations

ADF	Augmented Dickey–Fuller test
ARA	Ocean harbors of Amsterdam, Rotterdam, and Antwerp
BAFA	German *Bundesamt für Wirtschaft und Ausfuhrkontrolle* (Federal Office for Economic Affairs and Export Control)
bbl	Barrel (159 L)
BGR	German *Bundesanstalt für Geowissenschaften und Rohstoffe* (Federal Institute for Geosciences and Natural Resources)
bn	Billion
BtL	Biomass to liquid
BTU	British Thermal Unit (=1.055 kJ)
cif	Price including cost, insurance, freight
CER	Cumulated energy requirement
CGES	Centre for Global Energy Studies (London)
CCGT	Combined cycle gas turbine
CCS	Coal capture and storage
CFC	Chlorofluorocarbons
CHP	Combined heat and power (cogeneration)
CNG	Compressed natural gas
CtL	Coal to liquid
DOE	Department of Energy (Washington, DC)
EPEX	European Power Exchange
EIA	Energy Information Administration (DOE)
ENTSO-E	European Network of Transmission System Operators for Electricity
ETS	European emission trade system
EUA	EU Allowances (CO_2)
EUR	Euro
fob	Prices free on board
GDP	Gross Domestic Product
GHG	Greenhouse gases
GtL	Gas to liquid
IAEA	International Atomic Energy Agency (Vienna)
IEA	International Energy Agency (Paris)
IMF	International Monetary Fund

IGCC	Internal Coal Gasification and Combustion technology
IPCC	International Panel for Climatic Change
LCOE	Levelized cost of energy
LNG	Liquefied natural gas
mn	Million
NBP	National Balancing Point (wholesale gas market in the United Kingdom)
NPV	Net present value
OECD	Organisation for Economic Cooperation and Development (Paris)
OPEC	Organization of Petrol Exporting Countries (Vienna)
pkm	Passenger kilometers
PP	Phillips–Perron test
ppmv	Parts per million by volume
PV	Photovoltaics
SLP	Standard load profile
tce	Tons of coal equivalents
TFC	Total final consumption (final energy consumption)
toe	Tons of oil equivalents
ToP	Take-or-pay contract
TPA	Third-party access
TPES	Total primary energy supply
TSO	Transmission system operator
TTF	Title transfer facility (Dutch natural gas wholesale market)
UCTE	Union for the coordination of Transmission of Electricity
UNEP	United Nations Environment Programme
USD	U.S. dollar
CHP	Combined heat and power
WTI	Crude oil of West Texas Intermediate quality
WTP	Willingness-to-pay

Introduction

1

This chapter seeks to answer a few questions of general interest:

- Why has energy economics developed as a separate discipline of economics?
- Why does energy economics cover more than the straightforward application of standard economic methods and models to energy markets?

What are the reasons for politicians to have a particular propensity to intervene in energy markets?

The variables used in this chapter are:

- C Annual production cost
- Π Annual profit
- p Price per output unit
- Q Annual output (quantity)

1.1 Philosophical and Evolutionary Aspects of Energy

"Energy is life". Energy in the form of light is seen as the origin of the genesis (Genesis 1: 2–3). According to Greek mythology, history of human life starts with the stealing of fire by Prometheus—an act for which he was condemned to eternal pain.

These citations may be sufficient to highlight the philosophical dimension of energy. According to the second theorem of thermodynamics (also known as the law of increasing entropy), all forms of life, i.e. the existence of complex structures, depend on the availability and utilization of employable energy.[1] The American economist and philosopher Georgescu-Roegen formulated this as follows, "Given

---

[1]Employable energy that is capable of performing work is also called exergy.

that even a simple cell is a highly ordered structure, how is it possible for such a structure to avoid being thrown into disorder instantly by the inexorable Entropy Law? The answer of modern science has a definite economic flavor: a living organism is a steady going concern which maintains its highly ordered structure by sucking low entropy from the environment so as to compensate for the entropic degradation to which it is continuously subject" (Georgescu-Roegen 1971, p. 191f). Thus, each living organism needs to acquire useful energy, which is associated with effort or cost. In spite of the abundant global availability of energy, in particular solar radiation, useful energy is always a scarce good.

A characteristic feature of biological evolution is the diversity of ways used by species to absorb energy. Individual species use a variety of food as energy source, and different methods of approaching these energy sources; moreover, they assimilate the energy contained in their food in manifold ways. The methods of acquiring, storing, and using energy belong to their distinguishing characteristics, which also determine their rank within the evolutionary hierarchy.

Securing a continuous energy supply—condition for the sustainable existence of species—requires the ability to shift to other energy sources (e.g. food) in case those used thus far are exhausted. In turn, such adaptations affect the existence and living conditions of other species. Therefore, biological evolution can be understood as a mutual development of energy systems used by species, which determine their population growth and living conditions. This co-evolution can occur fast or slowly; however, it is never stationary as long as life continues.

The suggested energy-related interpretation of evolutionary patterns in biology is also relevant for the evolution of social systems. In fact, historical development is characterized by phases of stability and phases of disruptive innovations:

- One of the conditions for the development of human civilization was the control of fire. Before, energy in form of biomass was used for the biological metabolism of human bodies. Now, the thermal use of biomass became possible. The thermal use of biomass by hominids may have begun around 800,000 years ago. The control of fire became a key distinction between the Homo erectus, the ancestor of the Homo sapiens, and other species. It was also causal for the first forms of cultural life with the family as its roots.
- A further milestone of human civilization was triggered by the Neolithic revolution with the emergence of agriculture and farming 10,000–20,000 years ago. It required technological know-how concerning the use of energy along with the division of labor for creating the first urban infrastructures. This important societal change also marks the beginning of scientific research.
- About 5000–6000 years ago, the use of other renewable energy sources (sailing boats, later on wind mills and water mills) created the conditions of advanced civilizations.
- With the first industrial revolution, muscular power of animals and humans (often slaves) was replaced by engines, with coal becoming the fuel of mechanization. Industrial development was concentrated in areas with easy access to coal: instead of transporting coal to the people, people were moved from rural

areas to industrial centers. The implications were significant socially, giving rise to so-called Manchester capitalism, trade unionism, as well as concerns for the environment. A piece of evidence is the artificial word 'smog', which combines 'smoke' from the burning of coal and 'fog'. Indeed, disastrous air pollution led to several thousands of premature deaths in London and other industrial centers.
- At the turn of the twentieth century, coal was partly replaced by crude oil as the leading energy source, foremost in the United States. The ample availability of this relatively cheap energy source made the realization of the American Dream (meaning material prosperity for all) possible—though associated with excess use and waste of energy.
- The service, information, and communication society (the outcome of the second industrial revolution) depends on electricity as its key energy source. Development of the necessary power systems started with large-scale thermal power plants, including nuclear. Currently, these capacities are being replaced by distributed power generation based on wind, solar, biomass, and cogeneration (also known as combined heat and power). This transition has just begun; at this time, a future steady state is not yet in sight. However, it is quite possible that the character of society may change again, due to a massive acceleration of innovation transforming its infrastructure.

This short overview indicates that stages in the development of energy systems have paralleled the evolution of societies. Therefore a comprehensive analysis of energy systems has to cover much more than its engineering and economic aspects. Contemporary critical writers decry the unsustainable development of present energy systems. Some claim that a transition to a sustainable, environmentally friendly energy system needs to go along with basic societal change modifying the way of life in modern industrial societies—not to mention that in developing countries. Others reject the economic approach to solving energy problems, maintaining that a transformation designed to achieve sustainability should not be driven by economics but rather by social and ethical ideas.

While most energy economists accept the importance of ethical responsibility and social justice within and between generations, they also point to historical experience suggesting that societal guidelines and governance can have rather disastrous results if individual preferences and welfare are neglected. Transforming an energy system is not feasible if political decisions and interventions lack the majoritarian support of the society. Consideration of people's preferences and constraints with regard to energy is key to energy economics. The remit of energy economics is to seek solutions that take into account the preferences of consumers, managers, and owners of companies as well as political leaders. Of course, individuals who are altruistic and take the welfare of others into account facilitate such solutions, yet a society consisting mostly of altruistic individuals is likely to be an idealistic assumption.

1.2 Why Energy Economics?

General economic theory provides a number of relevant insights for analyzing energy markets. Notably, energy sources belong to the category of scarce goods even if they are physically abundant. Like in other markets, prices coordinate individual decisions on the supply and the demand side. At first sight, the model of an ideal market seems to apply to many energy markets: They can be clearly defined, products traded on them are highly homogeneous at least from a physical point of view, and many prices are transparent. If the number of independent suppliers is large, the corresponding energy market fits the model of perfect atomistic competition. This means that individual suppliers can only choose the quantity of energy Q they would like to offer (acting as so-called price takers). Let them maximize their per-period profit, i.e. the difference between revenue $\bar{p} \cdot Q$ and total cost $C(Q)$,

$$\Pi(Q) = \bar{p} \cdot Q - C(Q). \tag{1.1}$$

The solution to this problem can be found by setting the derivative of the profit function (1.1) with respect to the produced quantity Q equal to zero,

$$\frac{d\Pi}{dQ} = \frac{d(p \cdot Q)}{dQ} - \frac{dC}{dQ} = \bar{p} - \frac{dC}{dQ} = 0 \quad \rightarrow \quad C' := \frac{dC}{dQ} = \bar{p}. \tag{1.2}$$

Under atomistic competition, producers cannot individually influence the sales price p, causing them to take it as a predetermined constant $p = \bar{p}$. Thus, as long as the sales price exceeds the extra cost of producing an additional unit C' (known as marginal cost), producers have an incentive to expand output. Otherwise, they will curtail production.

If each supplier decides according to the marginal cost rule, the resulting market price equals the marginal cost of the last unit needed to meet overall demand. The corresponding supplier is called marginal supplier, while those with marginal cost below the market price earn a producer surplus that allows them to recover at least part of their fixed cost of production.

On the demand side, marginal willingness to pay derives from marginal utility of consumption. Demand for a good is triggered as long as its marginal utility exceeds the marginal cost of consumption (the market price in this simple model). In the case of energy, this is a derived demand because utility does not emanate directly from the consumption of energy but rather from the services associated with it, such as lighting, heating, use of appliances, and transportation. Therefore, the contribution of energy to the production of these services (its marginal productivity to be precise) has to be taken into account to determine the marginal utility of energy.

This description is highly simplified. In actual fact, consumers are interested in more than just one good. The rule, "Marginal utility equal price" therefore has to be generalized to become, "The ratio of any two marginal utilities equals the ratio of their prices". Accordingly, the 'utility of energy' amounts to the marginal utility

1.2.1 Price Mechanism and Market Coordination

In a market economy, the function of prices is the decentralized coordination of supply and demand. No market participant needs to have knowledge of the situation of other market participants (regarding their individual cost and opportunity cost in particular). Knowledge of the market price is sufficient for coordination through markets. For market prices to play their intended role, they need to have an impact on demand and supply quantities. This is generally the case. On the supply side, a higher sales price causes aggregate supply to increase (see the positive slope of the supply function in Fig. 1.1). In the short term, this means that producers are running down stocks and increasing capacity utilization, while in the long term, this entails an increase in production capacity by incumbents and market entry by newcomers. On the demand side, a higher price leads to reduced consumption (see the negative slope of the demand function in Fig. 1.1). An increase in price of the good in question drives up opportunity cost since its purchase leaves less income to be spent on other goods and services. Short-term reactions in the case of energy include setting thermostat values at a lower level and traveling shorter distances, while intermediate and long-term reactions can be purchasing energy-efficient appliances, insulating buildings, and substituting expensive fuels (e.g. gasoline) with less expensive fuels (e.g. diesel).

In Fig. 1.1, the price of energy (relative to that of other goods and services) is depicted on the vertical axis, although it is the argument of both the demand and the supply function (this is an idiosyncrasy of economists). As long as the demand function (shown as the solid decreasing line) describes the current behavior of energy consumers, the equilibrium energy price is p_E^* and the traded volume, Q^*. Costumers willing to pay at least this price are served, while suppliers asking for a price equal or below p_E^* can sell. Thus supply and demand are balanced at the

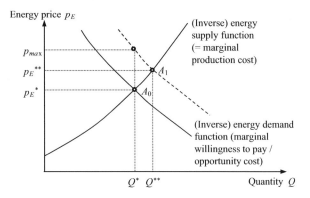

Fig. 1.1 Market price coordinating supply and demand

equilibrium, indicated by point A_0. For reaching this equilibrium, the only information that must be available to all agents is the market price. It permits each market participant to individually decide how much to demand and how much to supply, without taking into account the behavior of other market participants.

The coordinating function of a market also becomes evident when an exogenous change in market conditions occurs. For example, let an increase in income boost willingness to pay of consumers. This implies that they are prepared to pay a higher price of a given quantity of energy (depicted as the vertical shift of the demand curve to become the dashed line of Fig. 1.1). Alternatively, consumers can be said to demand a higher quantity at a given price, which amounts to an outward shift of the demand curve. Under either interpretation, the shift of the demand curve leads to a shift of the market equilibrium from A_0 to A_1, with a new, higher equilibrium price $p_E^{**} > p_E^{*}$ and a new, higher quantity transacted $Q^{**} > Q^{*}$.

However, supply may not be as flexible in the very short term as depicted. In the extreme, it does not respond to the higher sales price at first, implying that the supply curve runs vertical at point A_0. Accordingly, price will shoot up to the level p_{max}. The increased price signals to suppliers that it is profitable to expand production at the prevailing market price, causing prices to fall from p_{max} to p_E^{**} while the quantity transacted rises to Q^{**}.

Given perfect competition (no market power, no discrimination against any consumer or producer, no external effects, and transparency with respect to price), the equilibrium is Pareto-efficient. This means that no supplier and no consumer can reach a better position unless at least one market participant is made worse off. To see this, consider a price slightly higher than the initial equilibrium price p_E^{*}, with the solid demand curve obtaining. Of course, this would improve the situation of suppliers. However, consumers would suffer. Moreover, at p_E^{*} the minimum value of marginal willingness to pay of those served still suffices to cover the marginal cost of the extra unit of energy made available to them. This means there is no squandering of resources. Therefore, in a Pareto-optimal state the market allocation is efficient.

It would be desirable if this simple law of supply and demand offered conclusive answers to the strategic issues relating to energy, such as:

- How much scarce capital should be invested in the exploration, development, and distribution of new energy sources?
- What quantities of scarce production factors should be allocated to the extraction of already known energy deposits of inferior quality?
- What quantities of scarce factors of production should be made available for substituting fossil energy with renewable energies or the implementation of energy efficiency measures, respectively?
- How much should be invested in the abatement or management of environmental emissions?
- How much should be devoted to improving the safety of energy systems?

In many instances, the simple model of a competitive market may provide first hints towards answering these and similar questions. Yet deeper analysis shows that this model is not always appropriate for explaining and analyzing the complex reality of energy markets. Indeed, a simplistic model may in the extreme even result in misleading statements about a particular market characterized by crucial particularities.

1.2.2 Particularities of Energy Markets

If the idealized model of atomistic competition were a perfect representation of energy markets, there would be no reason for energy economics as a specific field of economics to exist. The role of energy economists would simply be the collection and evaluation of energy market data using standard economic concepts. However, energy economics is more than just the mere collection and statistical analysis of market data. Most markets for energy have particularities due to physical, geological, geographical, and technical properties of the energy source traded, making them deviate from the idealized economic model. The following list contains some of these characteristics:

- Without energy, no economic activity is possible. In economic language, energy is an essential factor of production, very much like labor (whereas a subsistence economy can do without physical and human capital). Disruptions of energy supply (e.g. the oil crisis of 1973/1974, electricity blackouts) can cause severe damages to the economy and society.
- Energy is necessary to satisfy basic human needs. Economic progress in many poor societies is hampered by an insufficient supply of energy, which in turn is often caused by a lack of ability to pay. Therefore, low incomes lead to unavailability of energy which in turn depresses productivity and hence incomes—the classical example of a poverty trap.
- Most energy infrastructure is characterized by long periods of planning, investment, and operation. As a consequence, its adjustment to economic and social change is slow. Since trends in energy demand cannot be easily predicted, relatively long spells of excess capacity and lack of capacity may occur.
- In many countries property rights of underground resources and hydropower are vested with the public rather than the private sector. Likewise, the construction of infrastructure (e.g. pipelines or transmission lines) often requires the right to use public grounds such as streets. Depending on the authority in charge (local, regional, or national government), energy markets are generally more dependent on political decisions (and with them public pressure) compared to other markets.
- Reserves of fossil energy reserves such as crude oil and natural gas are concentrated in a few countries, whose economy is dominated by the extraction industry. This facilitates a symbiosis between (often multinational) companies and domestic politicians which may be beset by corruption. In addition,

resource-abundant countries face a major challenge when their extraction industry starts to decline due to the depletion of resource deposits.
– A well-known and widely discussed issue is negative environmental impacts of the extraction, transformation, transmission, and use of energy. Indeed, the energy sector is the largest single source of emissions into air, water, and soil. In economic terms, these emissions represent negative externalities which are normally not reflected in the prices of energy sources, causing markets not to be Pareto-efficient.
– Another challenge of technical energy systems is the risk of large-scale accidents. This risk is not only relevant for nuclear power generation but also wherever large quantities of energy are locally concentrated, e.g. in a boiler or an oil tanker. Beginning in the nineteenth century, inspection authorities have been created whose mission is to protect people working in plants and living in surrounding areas. Yet, they suffer from an asymmetry of information in that plant managers know more about the level of safety achieved than the regulator (this is a core issue in the economic theory of regulation).
– Negative environmental externalities can be reduced by saving energy and improving energy efficiency, but demand for and supply of investment in energy efficiency is not developing as fast as intended due to a number of distortions. As a result, political interventions designed to speed up the process may be initiated.
– Physical depletion of fossil energy sources and the risk of climate change due to large scale emissions of greenhouse gases give rise to the issue of intergenerational justice. This type of justice requires that current decisions concerning energy systems should reflect the interests of both present and future generations in an efficient way.
– Many renewable energy technologies presently are not fully competitive but may become competitive in the future, when prices of exhaustible resources are bid up. Consumers may have an interest in their market entry being sped up, possibly justifying their subsidization by government in the aim of ensuring a sufficient future supply of energy. Since these new technologies may fail to become competitive, economic analysis designed to determine the conditions under which subsidies of this type are efficiency-enhancing and serving intergenerational justice is called for.
– Many energy markets are characterized by monopolies or oligopolies rather than perfect competition. In the transmission and distribution grid industries (natural gas, electricity, and district heat), the monopoly can even be said to be 'natural' since the establishment of competing infrastructures would be wasteful. The downside is a potential abuse of power by the single provider. In order to prevent this, governments generally regulate these industries.

In view of this long list, it is evident that many energy markets function and are governed by rules in ways that do not correspond to the model of a perfect market. They therefore need to be analyzed using more complex modeling approaches. While economists have developed a manifold of them, the analysis of monopolistic markets provides first guidance in many instances. The basic idea is that a

1.2 Why Energy Economics?

monopolistic supplier does not consider its sales price p as an exogenously given market price but rather influences it by its own actions. Indeed, being a monopolist means being confronted with the aggregate demand function and its negative slope. This implies that quantity sold Q (and hence production) and sales price p are negatively related. Therefore $dp/dQ < 0$, contrary to the case of atomistic competition where $dp/dQ = 0$ (see Eq. 1.2). Using the quantity produced as the decision variable, one obtains the first order condition for profit maximization,

$$\frac{d\Pi}{dQ} = \frac{d(p(Q) \cdot Q)}{dQ} - \frac{dC}{dQ} = p + Q\frac{dp}{dQ} - \frac{dC}{dQ} = 0. \quad (1.3)$$

Here, Π again denotes profit per period (e.g. a year), Q production, C total production cost, and p the sales price. Equation (1.3) can be solved to yield

$$\frac{dC}{dQ} = p + Q\frac{dp(Q)}{dQ} < p. \quad (1.4)$$

Under atomistic competition each supplier determines its production according to the "marginal cost = price" rule (see Eq. 1.2). By way of contrast, the monopolist has an incentive to observe the inequality "marginal cost < price" by holding back its production in order to enforce a higher price. By holding back production, the monopolist in fact deprives some consumers of the good or service, although they are willing to pay a price that covers the extra cost of serving them. Therefore, this outcome cannot be (Pareto-) efficient.

1.2.3 Energy Policy

In cases where self-interested behavior of market participants alone fails to reach a Pareto-optimal state due to particularities of energy markets, the term 'market failure' applies. Market failures are an argument for energy policy to intervene into markets in order to correct market failures. Ideally, a Pareto-optimal state can be achieved.

Public energy policy has been in existence for a long time. Prior to the first oil price shock in 1973, its basic aim was to secure the supply of energy by stimulating investment in coal mining, oil extraction, power plants, as well as transmission and distribution grids. It was completed by government control of the safety and reliability of technical installations and of market power—with the exception of electricity, gas, and district heat where monopolies were even sometimes encouraged. Since 1973, energy policy has extended its scope. Triggered by the oil price shocks, the issue became securing the supply of energy, also by diversifying primary energy sources and transportation routes. In addition, energy saving and energy efficiency entered the political agenda. In the 1980s, the new themes were societal skepticism regarding nuclear power generation and the development of renewable energy supplies. Since the 1990s, the energy policy of many

Fig. 1.2 Magical triangle of energy policy goals

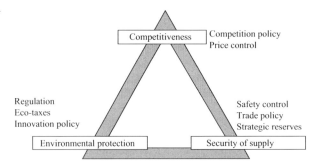

countries has been focusing on the liberalization of energy markets, abatement of greenhouse gas emissions, and sustainable development. Yet from the viewpoint of energy economics, the common theme of all these challenges and debates is the attempt to correct different types of market failure.

To structure the debate, the so-called magical triangle shown in Fig. 1.2 has proved helpful. According to it, energy policy has a triple mission: It should secure the supply of energy, contribute to economic competitiveness, and render the use of energy compatible with the environment. While these objectives are generally accepted in principle, their pursuit by policy-makers meets with complications. Indeed, objectives can be related to each other in three different ways.

– Complementarity: In this case, progress in the achievement of one objective contributes to the achievement of the other. An example is the positive impact of a more efficient energy use on the security of energy supply.
– Neutrality: Progress in the achievement of one objective has no impact on the achievement of the other.
– Antagonism: Progress in the achievement of one objective undermines achievement of the other, forcing a trade-off on policy-makers. Trade-offs are typical for many decisions in energy policy, calling for their multi-criteria evaluation. Ideally, an objective function should be defined as the weighted sum of multiple target indicators with their weights reflecting individual preferences.

If individuals in a society have significantly different preferences, social decision-making meets with great difficulty. First, individual preferences need to be consistent. Someone who ranks compatibility with the environment higher than security of supply and ranking it in turn higher than economic competitiveness, is expected to also rank compatibility with the environment higher than the economic competitiveness when the two are pitted against each other.

But even when individual preferences are consistent, democratic decision-making used for their aggregation may lead to inconsistent social preferences. This was shown by Nobel Prize laureate Kenneth Arrow (1951) and can be demonstrated simply for a society consisting of three individuals with three different preference orderings,

- Individual 1: environment $\succ$ competitiveness $\succ$ supply security;
- Individual 2: competitiveness $\succ$ supply security $\succ$ environment;
- Individual 3: supply security $\succ$ environment $\succ$ competitiveness.

Here, the sign '$\succ$' symbolizes "strictly preferred to". Assuming democratic majority voting on pairwise alternatives, the outcome is

- environment *versus* competitiveness   2:1
- competitiveness *versus* supply security   2:1

An implication of these voting results is that compatibility with the environment is strictly preferred to supply security. However, a vote directly pitting supply security against the environment leads to the opposite preference ordering.

- supply security *versus* environment   2:1

This failure to achieve a consistent social preference ordering through simple majority voting has become known as the Arrow paradox. It is likely to occur in societies whose individual members and interest groups representing them have heterogeneous preferences. In this case, decision-making with respect to energy policy may be blocked, with the political debate producing no more than formal compromises, an outcome that can be often observed in real life.

Governments may try to prevent the blockade by avoiding a vote on energy issues. However, there is also the alternative of so-called logrolling. In the example above, it is sufficient for one individual to modify his or her preference ordering to achieve consistency in the aggregate. This modification can be brought about by the promise to support the individual on another issue. Logrolling in parliament therefore permits to reach consistency of social preferences; yet it is viewed by suspicion by voters who fear that their delegates betray them in their own personal interest (they also may not attribute much importance to the other issue facilitating the logrolling).

The Arrow paradox provides an explanation of the conditions that may lead to unsuccessful attempts at correcting failures in energy markets. Additionally, there is another problem. Political interventions are usually not costless. They require the gathering of information, impose costly controls, and may not be executed in an optimal manner. Selfish interests of political decision-makers and governmental institutions need to be taken into consideration as well, causing acts of energy policy not always to be in the overall interest of society. Therefore, the results of political intervention in energy markets may even be less Pareto-efficient than the situation without intervention, an outcome known as policy failure as opposed to market failure.

1.3 History of Energy Economics

Energy economics is a comparatively young field of teaching and research. Interest in it was triggered by an influential study published by the Club of Rome in 1972. Written by Dennis Meadows, it was titled "The Limits to Growth" (Meadows et al. 1972). His work used approaches borrowed from system dynamics to predict the collapse of the world economy as a consequence of declining oil reserves and increasing emissions harmful to the environment. Shortly after this publication, the two oil price shocks of 1973 and 1979 appalled the world, seemingly confirming this pessimistic view.

In response, a few economists began to develop new models, emphasizing the impact of price on the behavior of market participants. According to these models, the relative price of oil would have to rise, stimulating substitution processes long before the world runs out of oil. Therefore, the increase in the oil price was to be seen as a step towards the solution of the energy problem. In fact, global oil consumption began to decline, as predicted by the economic models. Among the best known contributions of the time are the Hudson-Jorgensen model (Hudson and Jorgenson 1974, 1978) and the ETA-MACRO model (Manne 1978). These and other early models improved the understanding of energy markets as well as the quality of recommendations guiding energy policy.

With the drop of oil prices in early 1986, the attention shifted to environmental problems. From the economist's viewpoint it was obvious that the price mechanism should again help to solve them. Energy prices were to not only reflect cost as calculated by the energy industry but also the external costs associated with environmental damage caused by producing, transporting, and using energy. Energy economists put considerable effort into the conceptualization and quantification of externalities and their evaluation as external costs. Perhaps the most prominent study in this regard is the ExternE project sponsored by the European Union between the early 1990s and 2005. The fruit of these efforts was the introduction of ecological taxes followed by tradable emission rights, constituting an instance of successful energy policy consulting.

Since its beginning in the 1970s, energy economics has also revolved around the analysis of institutions and rules governing energy markets, with market power in grid industries becoming a crucial topic. These activities resulted in concepts of competition and deregulation of grid industries, which started to be implemented by Ronald Reagan in the United States and Margret Thatcher in the United Kingdom in the early 1980s. Another cornerstone was the European single electricity market directive (EU Directive 96/92/EC). With the implementation of this directive, European power markets changed faster than ever before in their history. A few years later, similar developments occurred in the European gas industry (EU Directive 98/30/EC).

At present, ongoing reforms of electricity markets are not the only source of change affecting the energy industry. Volatile prices of fossil fuels and ever more frequent government interventions in terms of market regulation, emission trading, renewable energy, and capacity markets challenge actors in energy markets again and again. Business concepts that have been successful in the past may turn out to be a recipe for future disaster. A high degree of adaptability, fast and smart decision-making, and vigorous action are required for energy companies to succeed in a market environment that is difficult to predict.

In future, energy economics will be able to keep its consultancy role for business and public policy only by shifting its attention from processes of substitution to dynamic and complex processes of innovation. It was rather successful with its proposition that substitutability is the key to the solution of many energy problems. It has also been quite strong in elucidating the conditions that facilitate efficient solutions, e.g. in climate policy and renewable energy development. Given the recent acceleration of market dynamics, however, an understanding of the interactions between innovations and adaptive markets is critical. During the past 40 years, energy economics has developed into something far more than a mere academic activity. It is about to become as relevant to public policy as monetary economics and public finance. May this book accompany its readers on this path.

References

Arrow, K. J. (1951). *Social choice and individual values*. New York: Wiley.
Georgescu-Roegen, N. (1971). *The entropy law and the economic process*. Cambridge, MA: Harvard University Press.
Hudson, E. A., & Jorgenson, D. W. (1974). U.S. energy policy and economic growth 1975–2000. *The Bell Journal of Economics, 5*, 461–514.
Hudson, E. A., & Jorgenson, D. W. (1978). Energy policy and U.S. economic growth. *American Economic Review, 68*(2), 118–123.
Manne, A. (1978). ETA-MACRO: A model of energy-economy interactions. In R. Pindyck (Ed.), *The production and pricing of energy resources, Advances in the economics of energy and resources* (Vol. 2). Greenwich, CT: JAI Press.
Meadows, D. H., et al. (1972). *The limits to growth*. New York: Universe Books.

Energy in Science and Engineering 2

Energy markets cannot be analyzed without discussing the relationship between energy and the natural sciences. Energy itself is a term with origins in physics. All types of energy conversion are based on physical, chemical, or biological processes. Professional statements regarding energy economics require an appropriate usage and correct interpretation of basic thermodynamic principles and properties.

The relationship between energy, the natural sciences, and engineering gives rise to several issues:

- What is the role of energy in physics, chemistry, and biology?
- How can different forms of energy be measured and how can they be converted?
- What information is contained in an economy's energy balance?
- What is the relationship between primary, final, and useful energy?
- How does the energy balance relate to an economy's national accounts?
- Why does a comprehensive measurement of a country's energy requirements call for input-output analysis?

The variables used in this chapter are:

E	Energy (in energy units)
F_j	Final demand for goods and services of sector j
CER	Cumulated energy requirement
P	Pressure
ϑ	Temperature
V	Volume
X_i	Gross production of sector i
X_{ij}	Energy supply from sector i to sector j
ω	Fuel efficiency factor

2.1 Energy and the Natural Sciences

This section presents an overview of energy-related terminology and the role of energy in several scientific disciplines. It further highlights the many ways in which energy can be defined.

2.1.1 Physics

From the standpoint of physics, energy is defined as the ability to accomplish work (mechanical energy). The unit of measurement is the joule (1 J = 1 kg m^2/s^2). One joule represents the work required to lift a body with a mass of 102 g × 1 m. This amount of work is needed to overcome the Earth's gravitational force, resulting from the acceleration g = 9.807 m/s^2 caused by the Earth (measured at the norm location in Paris, France). In physics, force is equal to mass (kg) times its acceleration (m/s^2), measured in Newton (N),

$$1 \text{N} = 1 \text{ kg m/s}^2. \tag{2.1}$$

Mechanical energy can exist as potential energy (e.g. water stored in a mountain reservoir) or as kinetic energy (e.g. a rotating turbine). The work performed per unit of time is called power and is measured in watts (W) or kilowatts (kW),

$$1 \text{ kW} = 1000 \frac{\text{J}}{\text{s}} = 1000 \cdot \frac{\text{kg m}^2}{\text{s}^3}. \tag{2.2}$$

A kilowatt hour (kWh) is the energy quantity released by a device working with a power of one kilowatt (kW) operating for one hour (h). This energy can be converted into joules (J) or megajoules (MJ) as follows,

$$1 \text{ kWh} = 3600 \text{ kWs} = 3.6 \cdot 10^6 \text{J} = 3.6 \text{ MJ}. \tag{2.3}$$

A kilowatt year (kWa) is equal to 365 · 24 = 8760 kWh or 31.54 · 10^9 J, respectively.

For thermal energy, the pertinent unit of measurement is the calorie (cal). A calorie equals the energy required to heat water with a mass of 1 g from 14.5 to 15.5 °C. In comparison, the melting heat of (frozen) water is 80 cal/g, while the boiling heat is 539 cal/g.

The relationship between mechanical and thermal energy was discovered by the Scottish physicist James Joule. It is governed by the principle of energy conservation. He discovered that mechanical energy can be completely converted into heat (but not *vice versa*) which was one of the first principles of energy conservation. The conversion factor, the so-called heat equivalent of mechanical energy, is

$$1 \text{ cal} = 4.187 \text{ kJ or } 1 \text{ kJ} = 0.2366 \text{ cal}. \qquad (2.4)$$

In the twentieth century, more principles of energy conservation were discovered, such as the principle of equivalence between energy and mass (as expressed in the formula of Albert Einstein $E = mc^2$) and the quantum law of radiant energy (radiation law of Max Planck $e = h\nu$ with Planck's constant h and the frequency of radiation ν).

The physical knowledge of energy can be summarized by the two laws of thermodynamics. The first law of thermodynamics states that in closed systems, the total amount of energy is constant. The following forms of energy can be distinguished.

- Mechanical energy: energy capable of performing work, also called exergy, among others orderly kinetic energy;
- Chemical energy: bond energy of molecules (Coulomb force);
- Electrical energy: energy of electromagnetic fields;
- Thermal energy: kinetic energy of atoms and molecules;
- Radiant energy: energy through radiation (if energy in form of photons impacts matter, the energy is absorbed or reflected; the absorbed energy can be further transformed into internal heat or transformed in chemical processes, e.g. photosynthesis);
- Nuclear energy: energy of mass (so-called mass defect).

According to the first law of thermodynamics and contrary to common language, energy can neither be created nor consumed but only transformed. For example, there are processes such as those for transforming the chemical energy stored in fossil fuels into kinetic or thermal energy. What is consumed therefore is the energy source. The share of the stored energy that can be transformed into work (rather than dissipated heat) is called exergy, while the share that cannot be transformed into work is called anergy.

The second law of thermodynamics states that the energy capable of performing work gradually decreases in a closed system (law of the increase of entropy). Rather than being based on macroscopic deterministic relationships, the second law of thermodynamics is derived from probabilistic information (so-called statistical mechanics) about microscopic details. More precisely, the second law of thermodynamics reflects the high degree of freedom in thermodynamic systems with its many atoms or molecules. However, it is applicable only to closed systems (Nicolis and Prigogine 1977). Thermodynamically, the globe is an open system in which entropy can decrease, for example through the storage of solar radiation in fossil energy sources.

2.1.2 Chemistry

The chemical view of energy is connected to the physical principles of energy conversion. However, its focus is more on the outcome of specific energy conversion processes. A particularly important chemical transformation process is combustion (oxidation). The result of this (so-called exothermic) process is molecules with lower bond energy (known as Coulomb force) compared to the bond energy of the original molecules. Examples of these transformation processes are the combustion of carbon (C atom) and hydrogen (H atom),

$$\begin{aligned} 1 \text{ kg C} + 2.7 \text{ kg O}_2 &\to 3.7 \text{ kg CO}_2 + 32.8 \cdot 10^6 \text{J} \\ 1 \text{ kg H}_2 + 7.9 \text{ kg O}_2 &\to 8.9 \text{ kg H}_2\text{O} + 142 \cdot 10^6 \text{J} \end{aligned} \quad (2.5)$$

While hydrogen reacts with oxygen and burns producing water vapor, the combustion of carbon-based fuels with oxygen leads to the formation of carbon dioxide (CO_2) in a (stoichiometric) ratio of 3.7 kg CO_2 per kg carbon. In these combustion processes, energy (measured in joule J) is released.

Vice versa, many chemical processes only take place if energy is added (so-called endothermic processes). This includes the opposite reactions of combustion processes, e.g. when producing hydrogen. Electrolysis of hydrogen requires energy in the form of electricity. Regarding the steam reforming of natural gas (methane CH_4) to hydrogen, the following chemical reaction takes place,

$$1 \text{ kg CH}_4 + 2.2 \text{ kg H}_2\text{O} + 15.8 \cdot 10^6 \text{J} \to 2.7 \text{ kg CO}_2 + 0.5 \text{ kg H}_2. \quad (2.6)$$

Therefore, the production of 1 kg H_2 through steam reforming calls for an energy input of $31.6 \cdot 10^6$ J and releases 5.4 kg CO_2.

2.1.3 Biology

From a biological perspective, energy transformation is closely linked to photosynthesis and cell respiration. In photosynthesis, solar radiation (energy in the form of photons) is used to break up carbon dioxide and water molecules (CO_2 and H_2O), as well as to transform them into hydrocarbon compounds (e.g. carbohydrates) with higher bond energy through the release of oxygen. In this process, chlorophyll acts as the catalyst.

In the case of cell respiration, chemical energy of organic hydrocarbon compounds is transformed in a combustion process involving oxygen. Energy flows in the living human body serve as a quantitative example. The metabolic rate of a human body at rest is approximately 80 watt (W), 20 W of which is accounted for by human brain. At normal everyday physical activity, the total metabolic rate is 100–120 W. Because this average is in use during 24 h per day, a daily energy intake of 2.4–2.9 kWh (or 2000–2500 kcal, respectively) is necessary. In addition, humans can perform physical labor with 100 W for a few hours. In

Table 2.1 Metabolic rate for continuous physical labor, humans vs. work animals

	Metabolic rate for physical labor
Human body in rest	0 W
Physical labor of a human	ca. 100 W
Physical labor of a mule	ca. 250 W
Physical labor of a bullock	ca. 400 W
Physical labor of a horse	ca. 600 W

Source: Erdmann and Zweifel (2008, p. 19)

Table 2.2 Conversion table (based on IEA data)

	MJ	kcal	kWh	toe	bbl	tce
1 MJ	1	238.8	0.2778	23.88 E^{-06}	175 E^{-06}	34.14 E^{-06}
1 kcal	0.0042	1	0.00116	0.1 E^{-06}	0.73 E^{-06}	0.143 E^{-06}
1 kWh	3.6	860	1	86 E^{-06}	630 E^{-06}	123 E^{-06}
1 toe	41,880	10 E^{+06}	11,630	1	7.33	1.430
1 bbl	5713	1.36 E^{+6}	1587	0.1364	1	0.195
1 tce	29,290	6.995 E^{+6}	8136	0.6995	5.127	1

this case, the required energy intake increases by at least 0.5 kWh for every hour of physical labor.

According to Table 2.1, mules, bullocks, and horses have a higher capacity for physical labor than humans. This is why they have been very valuable to mankind for many millennia. Before the industrial revolution, an estimated 30% of agriculturally usable surfaces in Central Europe were used for supplying energy to pack and draught animals.

The figures cited can be used to calculate the biological energy needed for maintaining a world population of about 7.4 bn humans. The required annual quantity of energy amounts to some $0.74 \cdot 10^{12}$ kWh per year or 910 mn tons of crude oil equivalent (toe, see Table 2.2). For comparison, current oil consumption is about 35 bn bbl or 3.63 bn toe annually, i.e. the fourfold of the energy needed for nutrition (see IEA 2016). This energy is provided through food in the form of high-grade biomass, which is obtained from about 5 bn toe of biomass per year harvested worldwide through farming and fishing.

2.2 Engineering and Energy

Being available in several forms, energy can be measured in different units. In energy engineering, focus is on the development, construction, and operation of equipment and devices designed to transform energy. The need to measure their performance has resulted in statistical concepts and information that are indispensable for energy economics.

2.2.1 Energy Units

What is considered as an energy source from an engineering standpoint depends on the technical knowledge about how to make use of its energy content, as well as on the (economic and social) willingness to make use of it. For instance, uranium oxide (U_3O_8) has only become an energy source with the invention of the controlled fission of uranium isotopes ^{235}U.

Accordingly, there is a multitude of energy sources. In order to compare them, it is necessary to convert their specific energy contents into a common energy unit. While the joule (J) is the base unit for energy of the International System of Units (SI for *Système International d'Unités* in French) and the appropriate unit in physics, several industry-specific energy units are in use. Some of the more common are:

- Tons of coal equivalent (1 tce = 29.3 GJ);
- Tons of oil equivalent (1 toe = 41.87 GJ);
- Barrels of crude oil (1 bbl = 159 l crude oil): 1 bbl is equivalent to 5.7 GJ (approximation: 1 bbl = 50/365 toe);
- Standard cubic meter of natural gas (at a temperature of 0 °C and a pressure of 1.013 bar, 1 m³ natural gas = 36.43 MJ);
- British Thermal Unit (BTU): 1 BTU represents the energy required to heat 1 lb of water by 1°F (1 BTU = 1055 J). For larger energy quantities there are the British therm (thm), with 1 thm = 10^5 BTU = $105.5 \cdot 10^6$ J = 29.31 kWh and the quad unit (1 quadrillion BTU) with 1 quad = 10^{15} BTU.

Instead of decimal powers, the following symbols are often used:
exa (E) 10^{18}
peta (P) 10^{15} femo (f) 10^{-15}
tera (T) 10^{12} pico (p) 10^{-12}
giga (G) 10^9 nano (n) 10^{-9}
mega (M) 10^6 micro (μ) 10^{-6}
kilo (k) 10^3 milli (m) 10^{-3}

Table 2.2 shows some basic conversion factors between these units. Its first three rows and columns represent energy units that are based on definitions in physics. The units in the last three rows and columns are derived from fossil energy sources that occur in nature. Because of the different properties of geological deposits, reference is made to tons of oil equivalent (toe) instead of tons of oil, and tons of coal equivalents (tce) instead of tons of coal.

The conversion factors exhibited in Table 2.2 are based on lower heating values (H_i). The lower heating value is the quantity of energy that is released during a complete combustion, net of the energy needed for the condensation of the steam contained in the exhaust gas (so-called condensate enthalpy), assuming an exhaust gas temperature of 25 °C. By way of contrast, the upper heating value (H_s) includes the energy contained in the condensate enthalpy. The difference between these two values depends on the water content in the exhaust gas and ranges between 5 and 30%, depending on the energy source. The usable energy of a combustion process is

2.2 Engineering and Energy

Table 2.3 Energy conversion processes (examples)

Output / Input	Mechanical energy	Thermal energy	Chemical energy	Electricity	Radiation
Mechanical energy	–	Frictional heat	–	Hydropower turbine	–
Thermal energy	Heat engine	–	Thermo-chemistry	Electrical generator	–
Chemical energy	Combustion engine	Boiler	–	Fuel cell	Gas lamp
Electricity	Electric engine	Induction heater	Electrolysis	–	Electric bulb
Radiation	Laser	Microwave oven	Solar chemistry	Photovoltaic	–
Nuclear energy	–	Nuclear reactor	–	–	Radioactivity

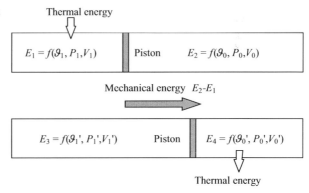

Fig. 2.1 Principle of a steam engine

generally indicated by the lower heating value, which is used in most energy statistics. Exceptions are the energy statistics of the United States and those of the natural gas sector, where upper heating values are traditionally used.

2.2.2 Energy Conversion

There are many technical processes for the conversion of energy, some of which are listed in Table 2.3. In order to perform work, energy needs to be available in so-called transient form. For example, a temperature differential is necessary to convert thermal into mechanical energy. A wide variety of energy in transient form occurs in nature, such as rivers, wind, and geothermal heat. Fossil as well as nuclear energy sources, in contrast, are only capable of performing work after one or more conversion processes. In the course of these conversion processes, part of the energy content turns into heat rather than work.

The thermodynamics of energy conversion can be explained using the example of a steam engine (see Fig. 2.1). Water or another medium is heated in the left chamber through the combustion of a fossil fuel. There, the increase in temperature causes pressure to increase (assuming that the volume in the chamber remains constant). This follows from the equation of state (here simplified for an ideal gas),

$$\frac{P\,V}{\vartheta} = \text{constant} \tag{2.7}$$

with pressure P (measured in Pascal), volume V (measured in cubic meter), and temperature ϑ (measured in Kelvin, where 1 K $= -273\,°C$). The piston moves to the right until pressure in the two chambers is equalized. This movement amounts to a release of mechanical energy (top of Fig. 2.1). In modern heat engines, the equalization of pressure drives a turbine, which is subject to a smaller loss of exergy caused by friction than a piston.

The potential to convert the energy in the left chamber into mechanical energy is exhausted as soon as pressure and counter-pressure are equalized by the movement of the piston. Equivalently, the temperature in the heated chamber adjusts to the temperature on the other side. An excess of energy $E_4 > E_2$ (in the guise of heat) is created in the process of the decompression on the other side of the piston (the turbine, respectively). This excess thermal energy needs to be dissipated to permit continuous operation of the heat engine. In large thermal power plants, cooling towers are used for this purpose.

Evidently, the usable mechanical energy converted by such a heat engine is substantially lower than the amount of energy contained in the fuel. An inverse measure of technical conversion losses is the efficiency factor,

$$\omega = \frac{\text{useful energy output}}{\text{energy input}}. \tag{2.8}$$

Maximum mechanic efficiency of an ideal steam engine with an input temperature ϑ_1 and a discharge temperature ϑ_0 (measured in Kelvin) is given by the so-called Carnot efficiency,

$$\omega_{\max} = \frac{\vartheta_1 - \vartheta_0}{\vartheta_1} = 1 - \frac{\vartheta_0}{\vartheta_1} \text{ (Kelvin equation)}. \tag{2.9}$$

In reality, efficiencies are below their theoretical maximum values because of friction, heat loss to the environment, plastic deformation, and other thermodynamic irreversibilities. For example, a combined cycle gas turbine (CCGT) with an input temperature of $\vartheta_1 = 1230°C$ and a discharge temperature of $\vartheta_0 = 20°C$ has a theoretical fuel efficiency of $\omega = 80\%$. Currently, actual fuel efficiency is about 60%.

The traditional goal of energy engineering has been to attain the highest possible efficiency in the provision of energy. Of course, the thermodynamic laws and constraints cannot be transcended.

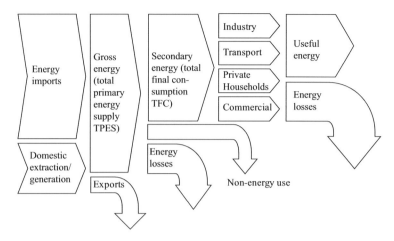

Fig. 2.2 Energy flow chart

2.3 Energy Balance

To obtain a quantitative overview of a country's energy economy, one makes use of the information made available by statistical offices, business associations, energy companies, and research institutions. A particularly important data source is the energy balance, which provides a comprehensive overview of a country's flows of energy.[1] The energy balance documents the overall supply and use of the different energy sources during a given period of observation.

Energy flow charts are often used to illustrate an energy balance. A simplified example of an energy-importing country is shown in Fig. 2.2. The widths of the arrows reflect the country's energy structure. The terms used as well as their interpretation are explained below.

2.3.1 Gross Energy (Primary Energy)

The available gross energy of a country consists of domestic energy sources plus energy imports minus exports. Sometimes, the expression 'total primary energy supply' (TPES) is used, although this is not entirely correct. Primary energy consists of those energy sources that have not undergone any transformation process, e.g. crude oil or coal. In contrast, energy sources that have undergone at least one transformation process are called secondary energy. Due to growing

---

[1]In the context of accounting and economics, the term 'balance' is used for stock quantities. Energy balances however represent aggregated flows per period, typically a year. Their equivalent in accounting is the income statement.

imports of secondary energies such as gasoline or electricity, the expression 'total primary energy supply' is becoming increasingly inaccurate.

After subtraction of conversion and transportation losses as well as non-energetic uses from gross energy, one obtains total final energy consumption (TFC). Total final energy consumption amounts to the energy delivered to end users for energy purposes. In industrialized countries, it traditionally equals commercial energy sold by energy companies. However, end users might also have access to non-commercial energy, e.g. from self-collected firewood or solar collectors. Because of the difficulties of measurement, most data regarding non-commercial energy are estimates.

Table 2.4 shows the basic structure of an energy balance, using the European Union as an example. The table consists of three matrices. The upper section contains domestic gross energy supply by origin and energy source. Nuclear fuels are traditionally classified as a domestic energy source even though most of them are imported. The reason for this international convention is that nuclear fuels are usually stored within the country over a period of several years. From a supply policy perspective, nuclear fuels can therefore be considered equivalent to a domestic energy source.

The middle section of the energy balance shows how the available domestic supply of gross energy is transformed into secondary energy. The columns again report the primary energy sources, whereas the rows list the transformation technologies. Negative entries reflect energy inputs, positive ones, outputs after transformation. Therefore, horizontal summation results in energy loss attributable to the corresponding transformation technology (see the last column). The third row explicitly reports statistical differences originating from inconsistencies in the data sources. Furthermore, the two rows towards the bottom in the middle section exhibit the energy industry's own use of energy and its losses (e.g. due to transportation), respectively.

The row entitled 'total final consumption' (TFC) results from the vertical summation of the two upper sections of the energy balance. Comparing this row with the Total Primary Energy Supply (TPES), one can deduce the energy 'lost' in transformation and transportation processes. In the case of the European Union (see Table 2.4), about 70% of primary energy is available to final consumers.

However, statements of this type must be interpreted with great care. While assessing final energy provided by nuclear, hydro, wind, or solar power plants is rather straightforward, statistically specifying their primary energy supply is challenging. There are three main approaches to deduce primary energy supply from final energy.

- The substitution principle: One derives primary energy supply from final energy assuming that it was transformed in a typical conventional thermal plant. Often, the average fuel efficiency of installed thermal capacities (for electricity usually around 35–40%) is used to derive a primary energy supply.
- The efficiency principle: Here, one uses the actual efficiency of the respective transformation technology to derive the primary energy supply from the final

2.3 Energy Balance

Table 2.4 Energy balance of the European Union 2011

(mn toe)	Coal	Crude oil	Oil prod.	Gas	Nuclear	Hydro	Wind, PV, etc.	Biomass	Electricity	Heat	Total
Production	167.4	84.2	–	140.1	236.4	26.4	27.7	121.9	–	0.8	804.9
Imports	143.9	585	310.9	353.6	–	–	–	11.4	27.2	–	1432
Exports	–26.0	–52.7	–295.7	–83.8	–	–	–	–4.7	–27.1	–	–490
Stock changes	0.2	5.5	2.3	–8.5	–	–	–	–0.1	–	–	–0.6
TPES	285.6	622.0	–74.9	401.5	236.4	26.4	27.7	128.4	–	0.8	1654

(mn toe)	Coal	Crude oil	Oil prod.	Gas	Nuclear	Hydro	Wind, PV, etc.	Biomass	Electricity	Heat	Total
TPES	285.6	622.0	–74.9	401.5	236.4	26.4	27.7	128.4	–	0.8	1654
Transfers	–	15.5	–12.8	–	–	–	–	–	–	–	2.7
Statistical diff.	–1.1	1.4	–3.0	0.5	–	–	–	0.1	0.1	0.3	–1.7
Power plants	–146.5	–	–9.5	–65.3	–233.4	–26.4	–24.9	–19.8	221.3	–0.2	–304.6
CHP plants	–66.6	–	–10.5	–60.5	–3.0	–	–	–23.8	58.2	43.3	–62.9
Heat plants	–4.6	–	–0.8	–8.2	–	–	–0.1	–5.5	–0.1	14.8	–4.5
Oil refineries	–	–650.0	644.7	–	–	–	–	–	–	–	–5.3
Coal transform.	–19.3	–	–1.5	–	–	–	–	–	–	–	–20.9
Other transform.	–0.2	15.2	–15.6	–0.4	–	–	–	–0.2	–24.2	–0.4	–1.5
Own use	–5.4	–	–35.7	–14.4	–	–	–	–0.2	–17.3	–5.7	–85.6
Losses	–0.9	–	–	–3.5	–	–	–	–	–	–4.1	–25.9
TFC	40.2	4.6	480.5	249.6	–	–	2.7	79.1	238.0	48.8	1143.5

(mn toe)	Coal	Crude oil	Oil prod.	Gas	Nuclear	Hydro	Wind, PV, etc.	Biomass	Electricity	Heat	Total
TFC	40.2	4.6	480.5	249.6	–	–	2.7	79.1	238.0	48.8	1143.5
Industry	26.3	2.1	29.4	82.8	–	–	–	24.5	88.8	15.3	269.1
Transport	–	–	293.8	2.9	–	–	–	13.9	5.8	–	316.4
Residential	9.6	–	37.3	101.5	–	–	2.0	35.9	69.1	20.3	275.7
Commercial	1.7	–	17.5	41.7	–	–	0.5	1.9	69.2	8.2	140.7
Agriculture	1.1	–	14.1	3.5	–	–	0.1	1.6	4.2	0.3	24.9
Non-specified	0.1	–	1.9	3.3	–	–	0.2	1.3	1.0	4.7	12.5
Non-energy use	1.3	2.5	86.5	13.9	–	–	–	–	–	–	104.2

TPES Total primary energy supply, *TFC* Total final consumption, *PV* Photovoltaic, *CHP* Combined heat and power. Source: International Energy Agency IEA

energy (e.g. up to 36% for nuclear power, approximately 80% for hydro pump storage, 10–25% for photovoltaic systems, and up to 55% for wind turbines).
- The fictive efficiency factor principle: According to this principle, electricity from renewables and from imported power is treated as a primary energy source. Thus, an efficiency factor of 100% is implicitly assumed. As a consequence, the share of renewable energies in total primary energy supply (TPES) is underestimated.

The three approaches lead to very different estimates of total primary energy supply, limiting the comparability of energy balances between countries or covering different time periods. For detailed analysis, it is absolutely necessary to check the approach used.

2.3.2 Final Energy Consumption

The lower part of the energy balance (see Table 2.4) indicates total final energy consumption (TFC) by consumer group, e.g. industry, transportation, commercial, and residential consumers. Also, non-energy uses are singled out in the bottom row. Note that this classification differs from that used in national accounts and other sources of macroeconomic data (see Table 2.8). An example is fuel consumption for road transportation, which should be allocated to business (passenger and freight traffic) and private households, respectively for national accounting. Energy balances fail to make this distinction because filling stations do not differentiate between their customers.

2.3.3 Data Sources

There is an abundance of publicly available energy statistics (particularly on the internet). A recognized data source for primary energy supply by individual countries and world regions is the annual BP Statistical Review of World Energy, published by the British Petroleum group. In addition, the International Energy Agency (IEA), the American Department of Energy (DOE) and the statistical office of the European Union (Eurostat) publish statistical material regarding the international energy economy, e.g. the development of energy prices. Information about the consumption of non-commercial energy can be found in the annual World Development Report of the World Bank.

The purpose of energy balances is to obtain information on the structure and the development of technical energy systems. As an example, Table 2.5 shows figures on global primary energy supply, which have been calculated according to the substitution principle. In the 1950s, coal was still the most important energy source. Currently, crude oil dominates the global energy system, but its share is declining in favor of coal. The shares of natural gas, hydropower, and nuclear energy are mostly

2.3 Energy Balance

Table 2.5 Global commercial primary energy supply

	1950		1975		2000		2013	
	(mn toe)	(%)	(mn toe)	(%)	(mn toe)	(%)	(mn toe)	(%)
Mineral oil	500	27	2290	44	3519	39	4185	33
Coal	1120	61	1640	18	2157	24	3827	30
Natural gas	180	10	930	32	2217	25	3020	24
Hydropower	30	2	300	6	617	7	859	7
Nuclear power	–	–	20	0	585	6	563	4
Renewables[a]	–	–	–	–	–	–	279	2
Total	1830	100	5180	5180	9015	100	12,730	100

[a]Without noncommercial energy. Sources: Darmstadter et al. (1971, p. 10) and BP (2014)

stable. While non-commercial sources such as firewood and dung are still important in developing countries, they are not included in Table 2.5.

2.3.4 Useful Energy (Net Energy) and Energy Services

From both the engineering and the economic perspective, final energy is an intermediary good. It is used by energy-converting devices, machines, and facilities to perform useful function. The main purpose of final energy is the utility it creates, such as

- heat (e.g. space heating, hot water, high and low-temperature process heat);
- work (e.g. transportation, information and communication, cooling);
- light (e.g. lighting, laser technology);
- chemically bound energy (e.g. electrolysis, reduction processes in batteries).

For obtaining utility from final energy, end users operate boilers, motors, lighting systems, air conditioners, furnaces, etc., generally on their own account. Just like in any other conversion process, operation of these devices goes along with losses, particularly in the form of unused heat. The statistical recording of these losses is difficult because there is no stringent definition of useful energy (also called net energy). An example is the measurement of heat provided by a central heating system. Should this heat be measured at the exit of the burner or at the radiator? While the heat distribution losses are included in the first case, they are excluded in the second.

The term 'energy service' takes the concept of useful energy even further. The idea is that it is not the warm radiator or hot water that is ultimately demanded but rather a pleasantly heated room or a well-formed piece of steel. These examples show that not only the technology matters (e.g. thermal insulation standard, optimized design of engine performance), but also the behavior of the final energy user. An example is a short and intense instead of a long and moderate airing of a room which might ultimately lead to the same level of utility for the consumer but with lower energy consumption.

Traditional energy balances do not include useful energy and energy services because the appropriate figures cannot be observed on market. However, according to estimates, significant conversion losses occur at final energy users. From a macroeconomic point of view, the share of primary energy in useful energy and energy services is estimated to lie between 10 and 20%. If it were possible to further minimize the conversion losses along the entire value chain linking primary energy sources to energy services, total energy expenditure would significantly decrease with an unchanged level of energy services. Additionally, energy-related environmental damages and greenhouse gas emissions would also be mitigated.

2.4 Cumulated Energy Requirement

The cumulated energy requirement (CER) of goods and services is defined as the sum of the total primary energy amount required for the production (CER_P), the use (CER_U), and the disposal (CER_D) over the entire lifetime of the product (so-called life-cycle assessment):

$$CER = CER_P + CER_U + CER_D. \tag{2.10}$$

The cumulated energy requirement is used as an indicator for the assessment of measures to reduce the energy consumption of buildings, vehicles, and appliances. Reductions in energy consumption during the use of an appliance could e.g. be cancelled by an increase in the process of its production. Countervailing developments of this type need to be considered when assessing energy-saving measures.

Other instances are solar and wind power plants. While their operation requires almost no energy, their construction does. The energy payback time is defined as the operating time of a plant needed to recover the energy amount for their construction and disposal. The harvesting factor, or 'energy returned on energy invested', respectively, indicates how often a plant recovers the CER during its lifetime.

The CER concept is also helpful for an in-depth assessment of a country's technical energy flows. While its energy balance documents immediate energy flows within its confines, it does not account for the energy used in the production of imported goods (so-called 'gray energy'; see Spreng 1988). Countries with high energy prices tend to outsource the production of energy-intensive goods, resulting in a decrease in their primary energy demand but without an effect on its global amount. It is the calculation of the CER that makes such facts transparent.

In general, there are two different methods to calculate the CER, process chain analysis and energy input-output analysis. Process chain analysis is a detailed assessment of energy inputs at each stage, from production to disposal of a good (see Frischknecht et al. 1994). This method is relatively simple to apply if the necessary data is available. Table 2.6 shows an example using the results of the

2.5 Energy Input-Output Analysis

Table 2.6 Cumulated energy requirement (CER) in 2012

	CER (non-renewable) (kWh prim./kWh final)	CO_2 equivalent (g/kWh)
Heating oil extra light	1.13	311
Natural gas H	1.14	247
Liquid gas (ethane, butane)	1.13	272
Hard coal	1.08	439
Lignite	1.21	452
Power mix (Germany)	2.22	607

Source: GEMIS Version 4.8 (GEMIS 2014)

GEMIS model developed by IWU Darmstadt (Fritsche et al. 1999). According to this model, the supply of 1 kWh of heating oil requires 1.13 kWh of primary energy, while the supply of 1 kWh of electricity requires about 2.22 kWh of primary energy (in the case of Germany). The third column of Table 2.6 indicates the greenhouse gas emissions (in CO_2 equivalents).

However, it is impossible to take all of the economic interdependencies in the production of a good into account in this way. At some point, process chain analysis must stop, resulting in errors which can be avoided using the method of energy input-output analysis.

2.5 Energy Input-Output Analysis

Input-output analysis is based on the division of the national economy into economic sectors. The goods and services that are exchanged between these sectors are summarized in input-output tables. The sectors are defined by homogeneous product groups (so-called functional differentiation), in contrast to national accounts, where they are defined institutionally.[2]

Table 2.7 contains a greatly simplified example of an input-output table with five sectors, two of which are energy sectors. Here, transactions are valued at production cost net of value-added taxes and excise duties such as taxes on mineral oil or tobacco. Imports are valued at cif-prices (including cost, insurance, and freight), exports, at fob-prices (free on board). Trading margins are registered as an output of the service sector.

The rows of an input-output table show the value of a sector's deliveries to economic sectors (so-called first quadrant or intermediate consumption matrix) and to final consumers.[3] For example, companies producing oil, gas, and coal had sales of 0.09 monetary units (MU) to other companies in the same sector and of 0.07 MU

---

[2]In an institutional differentiation of sectors, companies are consolidated into sectors following their main focus of economic activity.

[3]Final consumption consists of private consumption, public consumption and investment, exports, and stock changes.

to electricity generators. However, the largest demand came from final consumers with 5.72 MU, bringing the total of deliveries (so-called gross output) to 13.10 MU.

The columns show the cost of production factors of each sector consisting of purchases from economic sectors (again shown in the first quadrant or intermediate consumption matrix) and primary inputs.[4] Companies producing oil, gas, and coal bought 0.07 MU of it from other companies in the same sector but only 0.01 MU from electricity generators. Of course, imports loom large with 8.16 MU, while wages and salaries paid for the purchase of labor amount to a mere 0.83 MU. In total, inputs amount to 13.10 MU.

Note that for every sector, the sum of its row entries (sales revenues) is equal by definition to the sum of its column entries (expenditures and profits), reflecting equality of the two sides of a company's income statement.

Input-output tables are published by statistical offices in regular or irregular intervals, usually with a delay of several years. For the European Union, Eurostat is in charge, for the United States, the Bureau of Economic Analysis of the Department of Commerce (BEA).

The cells printed in bold of Table 2.7 relate to the economy's energy sector. If they are in energy rather than monetary units, the table becomes an energy input-output table (see the example shown in Table 2.8). Its source is the energy balance, transposed and structured to conform to the division of the economy in sectors. Average prices of the energy supplied to the other sectors and for final consumption can be calculated by dividing the sales revenues of the monetary input-output table by the corresponding energy flows of the energy input-output table.

Input-output tables can be used as a basis for input-output models. The most important variant is associated with the Russian economist and Nobel laureate Wassily Leontief (1970). With N sectors, total output of each sector X_i (the gross output of sector $i = 1,\ldots, N$ in monetary units) can be expressed by the following core equation of the Leontief input-output model,

$$X_i = \sum_{j=1}^{N} X_{ij} + F_i, (i = 1\ldots,N), \qquad (2.11)$$

where X_{ij} represents deliveries from sector i to sector j and F_i final demand for goods or services in sector i.

The linear Leontief input-output model is based on the assumption that relationships between the sector inputs X_{ij} and outputs X_i are constant, at least in the short term. These constant relationships are expressed by input coefficients,

---

[4]Primary inputs consist of imports, cost of capital (depreciation, interests, and profits), cost for labor (wages and salaries, including surcharges for social security), and indirect taxes (excluding subsidies).

2.5 Energy Input-Output Analysis

Table 2.7 Sample input-output table of a country (in monetary units)

	Oil, gas, coal	Electricity	Agriculture	Industry	Services	Final demand F_i	Output X_i
Oil, gas, coal	**0.09**	**0.07**	**0.18**	**2.86**	**4.18**	**5.72**	**13.10**
Electricity	**0.01**	**0.28**	**0.09**	**1.18**	**2.22**	**3.67**	**7.45**
Agriculture	0.00	0.00	0.90	11.54	1.33	3.31	17.08
Industry, constr.	0.01	0.61	3.82	45.08	26.02	143.42	218.96
Services	0.06	0.82	1.98	20.01	38.48	159.62	220.97
Imports	**8.16**	**1.24**	1.29	62.15	15.18		88.02
Depreciations	0.98	1.26	2.98	11.23	17.26		33.71
Interest, profits	0.26	0.62	3.07	9.49	32.92		46.40
Wages, salaries	0.83	1.25	3.51	44.89	72.72		123.20
Indirect taxes/subsidies	2.70	1.30	-0.74	10.53	10.66		24.50
Input X_j	13.10	7.45	17.08	218.96	220.97	315.74	793.30

Table 2.8 Sample energy input-output table of a country (in energy units)

	Oil, gas	Electricity	Agriculture	Industry	Services	Final consumption F_i	Output X_i
Oil, gas	8.2	4.7	11.6	157.3	149.6	206.2	537.6
Electricity	0.6	20.6	3.1	56.4	46.2	130.4	257.3
Imports	571.1	56.1					627.2

$$a_{ij} := \frac{X_{ij}}{X_j} = \text{const.}, (i,j = 1, \ldots, N). \tag{2.12}$$

Thus, the ratio of inputs to outputs in production is predetermined and fixed by the prevailing technology. In this case, the production function is of fixed proportions or Leontief type. The input coefficients a_{ij} represent the average production technology characterizing sector j during the period of observation. Substitution processes between inputs driven e.g. by changing input prices or new technologies, are not taken into consideration in Eq. (2.12). Possibilities to relax this very restrictive assumption are discussed at the end of this section.

Using the input coefficients a_{ij}, gross production X_i of sector i is given by

$$X_i = \sum_{J=1}^{N} a_{ij} \cdot X_j + F_i, (i = 1, \ldots, N). \tag{2.13}$$

In this way, the inter-sectoral production relationships can be represented by a system of linear equations. In matrix form, one has

$$\begin{pmatrix} X_1 \\ X_2 \\ \ldots \\ X_N \end{pmatrix} = \begin{pmatrix} a_{11} & a_{12} & \ldots & a_{1N} \\ a_{21} & a_{22} & \ldots & a_{2N} \\ \ldots & \ldots & \ldots & \ldots \\ a_{N1} & a_{N2} & \ldots & a_{NN} \end{pmatrix} \cdot \begin{pmatrix} X_1 \\ X_2 \\ \ldots \\ X_N \end{pmatrix} + \begin{pmatrix} F_1 \\ F_2 \\ \ldots \\ F_N \end{pmatrix} \tag{2.14}$$

This equation system can be solved for the gross production values X_i knowing that total input equals total output for each sector and that the corresponding matrix below is always invertible. The solution is given by another linear equation system of equations,

$$\begin{pmatrix} X_1 \\ X_2 \\ \ldots \\ X_N \end{pmatrix} = \begin{pmatrix} 1-a_{11} & -a_{12} & \ldots & -a_{1N} \\ -a_{21} & 1-a_{22} & \ldots & -a_{2N} \\ \ldots & \ldots & \ldots & \ldots \\ -a_{N1} & -a_{N2} & \ldots & 1-a_{NN} \end{pmatrix}^{-1} \cdot \begin{pmatrix} F_1 \\ F_2 \\ \ldots \\ F_N \end{pmatrix} \tag{2.15}$$

or in elementary form,

$$X_i = \sum_{j=1}^{N} f_{ij} \cdot F_j, (i = 1, \ldots, N). \tag{2.16}$$

The coefficients f_{ij} (elements of the inverted matrix in Eq. (2.15)) are called Leontief multipliers. They indicate by how many monetary units (MU) gross production of sector i needs to expand if final demand of sector j increases by one MU.

The Leontief multipliers pertaining to the input-output Table 2.7 are given in Table 2.9. Note that the values on the diagonal all exceed 1. For instance, if power

2.5 Energy Input-Output Analysis

Table 2.9 Leontief multipliers corresponding to the input-output Table 2.7

	Oil, gas	Electricity	Agriculture	Industry	Services
Oil, gas, coal	1.007	0.015	0.019	0.021	0.026
Electricity	0.001	1.041	0.010	0.009	0.014
Agriculture	0.000	0.008	1.075	0.074	0.018
Industry, constr.	0.002	0.133	0.332	1.304	0.190
Services	0.006	0.155	0.189	0.156	1.236
Total	1.016	1.352	1.625	1.564	1.484

generators are to produce one extra MU worth of electricity, they trigger an extra demand of 1.041 MU worth of electricity in their own sector because they have to e.g. employ more workers who in turn use more electricity. Moreover, they call on additional inputs provided by the service sector, which adds another 0.155 MU worth of power. The sum of column entries indicates that if the country's demand for electricity increases by one MU, national production of electricity must increase by the equivalent of 1.352 MU.

Using the input-output table, the energy requirements of products and services can be estimated. First, direct energy coefficients e_{kj} are calculated from the energy input-output table for all M energy sectors,

$$e_{kj} = \frac{\text{energy supply from sector } k \text{ to sector } j}{\text{gross produktion of sector } j}, (k=1,\ldots,M; j=1,\ldots,N). \tag{2.17}$$

Summation of e_{kj} over the M energy sectors yields e_j, which indicates how much energy sector j (in energy units) uses directly per MU of its gross production,

$$e_j = \sum_{k=1}^{M} e_{kj}, (j=1,\ldots,N). \tag{2.18}$$

In addition to these direct energy supplies to sector j, there are indirect ones from the non-energy sectors. Total (direct and indirect) supplies $\hat{e}_{kj}$ from sector k to sector j can be determined with the help of Leontief multipliers,

$$\hat{e}_{kj} = \sum_{i=1}^{N} e_{ki} \cdot f_{ij}, (k=1\ldots,M; j=1\ldots,N). \tag{2.19}$$

The total value of direct and indirect energy requirements of sector j per MU of gross production can be obtained by summing $\hat{e}_{kj}$ over all M energy sectors,

$$\widehat{e}_j = \sum_{k=1}^{M} \widehat{e}_{kj}, (j = 1\ldots,N). \tag{2.20}$$

Up to this point, the energy requirements of non-energy imports (known as gray energy) and the energy contained in the depreciation of capital have been neglected. Both can be estimated using data from input-output tables. In order to estimate the gray energy, consider the row 'imports' (in MU) of Table 2.7. To deduce the energy requirements for these imported goods, the cumulated energy requirement (CER) needs to be calculated from the input-output tables of the corresponding exporting countries. In practice, these estimates are limited to the most important countries of origin.

The energy content of used-up capital can be derived from the row 'depreciation' of Table 2.7. Here, the assumption is made that the energy directly and indirectly required for the production of capital goods needs to be accounted for only when they are depreciated. The correct approach would be an estimation using input-output tables of past years.

Despite the elegance of the input-output model, the assumption of fixed proportions in production according to Eq. (2.12) presents a serious shortcoming. It can be neglected when calculating the CER for a particular year. However, for other energy economic purposes, a dynamic input-output table may be necessary. In this case, the sectoral consistency condition must absolutely be satisfied which states that the sum of sectoral inputs (in MU) is equal to the sum of sectoral outputs (in MU). Generally, there are two different ways to satisfy this condition:

- The input coefficients can be adjusted over time according to specific changes in sectoral production processes. For example, nuclear power plants may be substituted by gas-fired ones. For determining the macroeconomic consequences of this substitution, one has to first define the cost structure of the two types of power plant as two column vectors in the input-output table. From this, the changed cost structure of the electricity sector can be simulated, using exogenously given shares of nuclear and gas-fired plants in electricity production.
- Input coefficients can also be made flexible using economic models, with changes in the relative prices of inputs serving as an explanatory variable. These prices depend on the sectoral development of wages and productivities as well as changes in indirect taxes and import prices. The first empirical study adopting this approach was the Hudson-Jorgenson model for the United States (Hudson and Jorgenson 1974). Later studies are referred to as computable general equilibrium (CGE) models (see Shoven and Whalley 1992).

References

BP. (2014). *BP statistical review of world energy*. Retrieved from www.bp.com/statisticalreview/
Darmstadter, J., Teitelbaum, P., & Polach, J. (1971). *Energy in the world economy. Resources for the future*. Baltimore: Johns Hopkins University Press.

References

Erdmann, G., & Zweifel, P. (2008). *Energieökonomik - Theorie und Anwendungen (Energy economics – theory and applications)* (2nd ed.). Berlin: Springer.

Frischknecht, P., Hofstetter, P., & Knoepfel, I. (1994). *Ökoinventare für Energiesysteme (Ecological inventories for energy sytems)*. Zürich: Swiss Federal Institute of Technology.

Fritsche, U., et al. (1999). *Gesamt-Emissions-Modell integrierter Systeme (Modeling total emissions of integrated systems)* Version 3.08. Darmstadt: Öko-Institut.

GEMIS. (2014). *Global emissions model for integrated systems*. Darmstadt. Retrieved from www.iinas.org/gemis-de.html

Hudson, E. A., & Jorgenson, D. W. (1974). U.S. energy policy and economic growth 1975–2000. *The Bell Journal of Economics, 5*, 461–514.

IEA. (2016). *World energy outlook 2016*. Paris: International Energy Agency.

Leontief, W. (1970). Environmental repercussions and the economic structure. An input/output-approach. *The Review of Economics and Statistics, 52*, 262–271.

Nicolis, G., & Prigogine, I. (1977). *Self organization in non-equilibrium systems*. New York: Wiley.

Shoven, J. B., & Whalley, J. (1992). *Applying general equilibrium*. New York: Cambridge University Press.

Spreng, D. (1988). *Net energy analysis and the energy requirements of energy systems*. New York: Praeger.

Investment and Profitability Calculation 3

Capital budgeting and profitability accounting are necessary for assessing the economic viability of energy investments. Although the methodology for energy investments does not differ fundamentally from other applications, there are unique problems associated with it due to some particularities of investment in energy technologies. Long planning, construction, and operation periods make the result of an investment decision strongly dependent on the discounting of future cash flows.

These facts motivate consideration of the following issues:

- What is the meaning of (net) present value of a flow of revenues (expenditures, respectively)?
- Why is the interest rate especially important in investment projects relating to energy and what determines this rate of interest?
- How can one account for future inflation (deflation, respectively)?
- Would it be preferable to abstain from discounting altogether, in the interest of sustainability?
- What insights can be gleaned from recent developments in the theory of finance?

The variables used in this chapter are:

av	Individual risk aversion
Cap	Rated capacity of power plants and other energy technologies
C_{var}	Total variable cost (incl. fuel cost)
c_{var}	Variable cost per output unit
E_t	Annual energy production
Inv	Investment expenditure (incl. financing cost)
i	Interest rate, discount rate
ic	User cost of capital per output unit
ν	Capacity factor
NPV	Net present value
Π	Total profit
p	Price per output unit

© Springer International Publishing AG 2017
P. Zweifel et al., *Energy Economics*, Springer Texts in Business and Economics,
DOI 10.1007/978-3-662-53022-1_3

p_E	Price of energy
p_F	Price of a (energy) future
Q	Total output (quantity)
q_{market}	Market expectations regarding return on investment
q_s	Savers' time preference
PVF	Present value factor
ROI	Return on investment
σ_E	Standard deviation (volatility)
T	Assumed lifetime of the investment
w	Probability

3.1 Basics

Financial appraisal techniques require a forecast of future flows of costs and revenues over the lifetime of the investment. In this regard, only those costs and revenues that are directly linked to the planned investments are to be considered. For example, in the decision process of retrofitting a power plant, the initial construction cost of the plant is irrelevant; only the additional costs and revenues caused by the upgrade should be taken into account. Likewise, in a short-term production decision ("Should the existing power plant increase its rate of production?"), only the associated additional costs affect its outcome. The most important cost components are:

- Additional costs for fuel and emission rights, depending, among other things, on output-related fuel efficiency;
- Accelerated degradation of the installation due to thermal stress resulting from temperature change in boilers and pipes;
- Fuel losses during start-up and shut-off periods.

The sum of these costs divided by the additional production is the marginal unit cost that describes the economic impact on the plant operator if production is to increase or decrease by one unit. The investment outlay and other expenditures that are not affected by the production decision, such as personnel and administration, are irrelevant for the evaluation of short-term production decisions.

For the evaluation of a long-term investment decision, again only those economic variables that might be affected by it have to be considered. If a company plans for an incremental expansion of capacity, the cost of management should be excluded, for example. However, the additional expected sales revenues per period generated by the investment are relevant. They depend on:

- The capacity *Cap* to be installed (measured for example in tons of output per day or in megawatt of electricity);

3.1 Basics

- The capacity factor v, specifying the average expected percentage of annual full-load operation[1];
- The average expected price of energy sales p_E.

With power plant capacity denoted by *Cap* (measured in MW), annual output and corresponding annual sales revenues are calculated as follows,

$$Q = Cap \cdot v \cdot 8760 \tag{3.1}$$

$$p_E \cdot Q = p_E \cdot (Cap \cdot v \cdot 8760) \tag{3.2}$$

The financial counterpart of annual sales revenues are the expected future annual costs, which can be divided into a variable and a fixed cost component. Variable cost C_{var} includes the cost of intermediate inputs such as annual expenses for raw materials, fuels, emission rights, waste disposal, and to some extent also wages (given flexible employment contracts). When dividing expected variable cost by expected output Q, one obtains variable cost per unit output $c_{var} = C_{var}/Q$. The fixed cost amounts to the annualized investment outlay. The ratio, fixed cost/variable cost is an indicator of the capital intensity of an investment project. The contribution margin is defined as the difference between annual revenue and annual variable cost.

For investment decisions, investment outlay *Inv* including the cost of financing must be compared to the annual expected cash flows or contribution margins, respectively, during the project's lifetime. In a simplified analysis, one assumes the investment outlay to take place in period t_0, leading to a negative cash flow Inv_0 in this period. In the following years, the cash flows are given by $(p_{Et} - c_{var,t}) \cdot Q_t$. They should predominantly be positive in order to make the project economically viable. The time horizon is the end of the project's economic life T.

A time series of annual cash flows can only be meaningfully evaluated if their individual values are referenced to the period in which the investment is undertaken ($t = 0$). The resulting quantity is called Net Present Value (*NPV*). It is given by

$$NPV = -Inv_0 + \sum_{t=1}^{T} \frac{(p_{E,t} - c_{var,t}) \cdot Q_t}{(1+i)^t}. \tag{3.3}$$

The (real, inflation-adjusted) interest rate i discounts all future cash flows; it is therefore called discount rate. The term $(1+i)^{-t}$ is referred to as the discount factor.

Discounting reflects the fact that a cash flow that occurs later in time has a reduced value. If funds are received early, they can be re-invested to generate additional revenue. Assuming a common interest rate i for borrowing and lending, the re-invested funds increase by $(1+i)$ within 1 year.[2] Conversely, the present value

---

[1] A year has $24 \cdot 365 = 8760$ h (8784 h in a leap year). Thus a capacity factor of $v = 20\%$ equals $0.2 \cdot 8760 = 1752$ full load operation hours.

[2] The assumption that borrowing and lending occur at the same rate is equivalent to the assumption of perfect capital markets. Another important proposition is that all transactions are free of costs Sect. 3.2.

of one monetary unit received (or paid, respectively) 1 year from now amounts to $1/(1+i)$. At an interest rate of 5% e.g., this is 0.952 monetary units because $0.952 \cdot 1.05 = 1$. By analogy, funds received 2 years hence have a present value of $1/(1+i)^2$.

If annual cash flows remain constant over the entire life of the project, Eq. (3.3) can be rewritten to become

$$NPV = -Inv_0 + (p_E - c_{var}) \cdot Q \cdot \sum_{t=1}^{T} \frac{1}{(1+i)^t}. \quad (3.4)$$

The sum on the right-hand side is called present value factor PVF of an annuity,

$$PVF_{i,T} = \sum_{t=1}^{T} \frac{1}{(1+i)^t} = \frac{1}{i} - \frac{1}{i \cdot (1+i)^T}. \quad (3.5)$$

It defines the net present value of an annual cash flow consisting of one monetary unit paid T times, at a given discount rate i. Table 3.1 shows the PVF for different investment periods T and discount rates i. For example, at an interest rate of 8%, 1 EUR paid ten times has a present value of only 6.7101 EUR rather than 10 EUR because most of the payments come in with a delay. At an interest rate of 10%, the present value drops to 6.1446 EUR. The effect of discounting is even more marked for longer time horizons; 1 EUR paid 20 times is 'worth' only 8.5136 EUR today at 10%—with no inflation whatsoever.

The reciprocal of the PVF is the capital recovery factor CRF,

$$CRF_{i,T} = \frac{1}{PVF_{i,T}} = \frac{i \cdot (1+i)^T}{(1+i)^T - 1}. \quad (3.6)$$

It defines the constant annual amount necessary to repay a loan of one monetary unit within a time T and at a given discount rate i. Using the capital recovery factor, the cost of an initial investment outlay Inv_0 can be rewritten as a sequence of negative cash flows over T time periods. This yields so-called annual capital user cost,

$$ic = Inv_0 \frac{1}{PVF_{i,T}} = Inv_0 \frac{i \cdot (1+i)^T}{(1+i)^T - 1}. \quad (3.7)$$

According to Eq. (3.4) the NPV of an investment depends on several variables, in particular the discount rate i, the expected sales price p_E, and the lifetime T of the project. When setting $NPV = 0$, Eq. (3.3) or (3.4) can be solved with respect to each of these variables. This generates three different evaluation indicators:

– Solving with respect to the discount rate i yields the so-called internal rate of return IRR, an indicator of return on investment (ROI). IRR is calculated by

3.1 Basics

Table 3.1 Sample present value factors (*PVF*) of an annuity of 1 paid *T* times

Years *T*	Interest rate *i*							
	0.03	0.04	0.05	0.06	0.07	0.08	0.09	0.10
1	0.9709	0.9615	0.9524	0.9434	0.9346	0.9259	0.9174	0.9091
5	4.5797	4.4518	4.3295	4.2124	4.1002	3.9927	3.8897	3.7908
10	8.5302	8.1109	7.7217	7.3601	7.0236	6.7101	6.4177	6.1446
15	11.9379	11.1184	10.3797	9.7122	9.1079	8.5595	8.0607	7.6061
20	14.8775	13.5903	12.4622	11.4699	10.5940	9.8181	9.1285	8.5136
25	17.4131	15.6221	14.0939	12.7834	11.6536	10.6748	9.8226	9.0770
30	19.6004	17.2920	15.3725	13.7648	12.4090	11.2578	10.2737	9.4269
40	23.1148	19.7928	17.1591	15.0463	13.3317	11.9246	10.7574	9.7791
50	25.7298	21.4822	18.2559	15.7619	13.8007	12.2335	10.9617	9.9148

simulating Eq. (3.3) or (3.4) under varying interest rates until the net present value becomes zero. Figure 3.1 shows a fictitious example resulting in $IRR = 11.5\%$.

- By solving Eq. (3.4) for the energy price p_E, one obtains the break-even price required to recover investment outlay Inv_0 and unit variable cost c_{var}. It is often referred to as unit production cost or the levelized cost of energy,

$$p_E = \frac{Inv_0}{Q \cdot PVF_{i,T}} + c_{var}. \qquad (3.8)$$

Figure 3.2 shows how this break-even price depends on project life T and the discount rate i. The figure assumes costs that are typical of an investment in onshore wind power. As long as break-even price pE exceeds the wholesale price of power, the investment is not competitive. However, the government may mandate electrical grid operators to purchase e.g. wind power at a fixed feed-in tariff. In this case, wind power installations become virtually economic if their break-even prices are below the fixed feed-in tariff. Other support schemes such as market premiums[3] and investment subsidies may have similar effects on investment in wind power and other renewables.

- By solving Eq. (3.4) for T, one obtains the break-even payback time T^*. This is the time needed for recovery of a given investment outlay including compound interest through future revenues. For simplification, introduce $AN = (p_E - c_{var}) \cdot Q$ in Eq. (3.4), use Eq. (3.5), and solve for Inv_0 to obtain

$$Inv_0 = AN \left(\frac{1}{i} - \frac{1}{i(1+i)^T} \right) = \frac{AN}{i} - \frac{AN}{i(1+i)^T}. \qquad (3.9)$$

- By multiplying both sides by i/A, one obtains

$$\frac{i \cdot Inv_0}{AN} = 1 - \frac{1}{(1+i)^T} \quad \text{or} \quad 1 - \frac{i \cdot Inv_0}{AN} = \frac{1}{(1+i)^T}. \qquad (3.10)$$

---

[3]Market premiums are payments to wind power operators on top of the revenues they receive from selling to the market or directly to final customers.

3.1 Basics

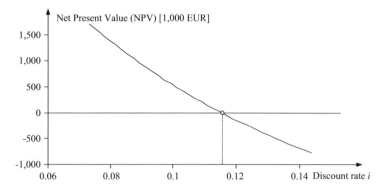

Fig. 3.1 Net present value as function of the interest rate. Assumptions: Investment outlay $Inv_0 = 5500$ EUR; variable cost $c_{var} = 200$ EUR/a; sales revenue 850 EUR/a; operation period $T = 20$ years

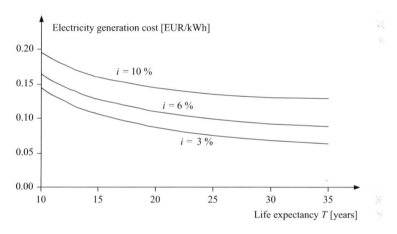

Fig. 3.2 Energy cost as a function of lifetime and interest rate. Assumptions: investment cost $Inv_0 = 2000$ EUR/kW; variable cost $c_{var} = 0.01$ EUR/kWh; capacity factor $\nu = 0.2$

Taking the logarithm and solving for T gives break-even payback time,

$$T^* = -\frac{1}{\ln(1+i)} \cdot \ln\left(1 - \frac{i \cdot Inv_0}{(p_E - c_{var}) \cdot Q}\right) \qquad (3.11)$$

Therefore, a project characterized by high initial investment expenditure Inv_0 needs to have a short payback time *ceteris paribus* to be economically viable—a condition not easily satisfied in the energy sector. Conversely, a high profit margin ($p_E - c_{var}$) and a large volume of expected future sales Q both make a project attractive, which is also true of a low rate of interest i.

3.2 Interest Rate and Price of Capital

Due to the long-term character of most investment in the energy sector, the result of a financial appraisal is greatly affected by a variation of the discount rate i. The choice of the discount rate must therefore be well-founded, calling for an understanding of the nature of interest rates and of the key variables influencing them.

According to economic theory, the interest rate amounts to the price for obtaining funds for a specified time; thus, short-term interest rates generally differ from long-term ones. In the following, a contract duration of 1 year is assumed. Since lenders have no access to their money during this time, they expect investors to provide an appropriate financial incentive in addition to a compensation for the risk that the creditor may default. As in any other market, price is determined by the intersection of supply and demand so that the market is cleared. Supply of capital is provided by savings, while demand originates with entrepreneurs in need of funds to finance their investments.

The supply of savings importantly depends on the (marginal) time preference of consumers q_s. They are willing to abstain from one unit of consumption at time t_0 if they can consume at least $(1+q_s)$ units in the next period t_1. Thus q_s is referred to as the (marginal) rate of substitution between present and future consumption. As long as the yield on savings outweighs this rate ($i > q_s$), individuals will normally[4] delay consumption, permitting them to offer funds on the capital market up to the point where $i = q_s$.

The demand for capital depends on the expected return on investment (*ROI*). It increases as long as *ROI* exceeds the rate of interest i investors have to pay for funds. Equilibrium is reached where *ROI* (which equals the internal rate of return of the last (marginal) investment project, denoted by *IRR*) is just enough to cover the cost of funds, thus where $i = IRR$.

Since both saving and investment are influenced by the market interest rate, the interest rate balances the two, causing supply of and demand for capital to match (see Fig. 3.3). Assuming a perfect, fully transparent capital market without transaction costs, equilibrium yields

$$q_s = q_i = i = ROI = IRR. \qquad (3.12)$$

The importance of the cost of capital for the macroeconomic assessment of an energy investment is illustrated by the following example. At decision time t_0, let the project call for investment outlay of 1 EUR; therefore, other economic sectors must reduce consumption or investment by the same amount. Let the project have a benefit of $G(t_1)$ EUR in the next period t_1, expressed in additional consumption

---

[4]This holds provided the substitution effect—the incentive to move consumption from today to tomorrow holding wealth constant—outweighs the wealth effect of interest and dividend payments, which may induce consumers to consume, i.e. to reduce saving.

3.3 Inflation-Adjusted Interest Rate

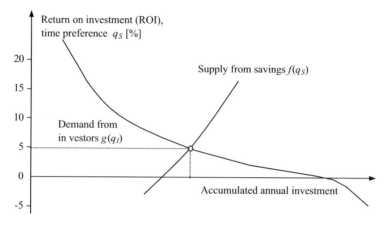

Fig. 3.3 Aggregated capital demand and supply

possibilities. Focusing on private consumption for simplicity, one can say that the project has a positive effect on the economy as long as its net present value (discounted using time preference q_s of savers) is greater than the loss in terms of current consumption caused by the drain on capital. This condition can be written as $G(t_1) > 1+q_s$.

On the other hand, realization of the project may 'squeeze out' investment elsewhere in the economy. This occurs if it yields a return above the *ROI* of competing projects, which is the case if $G(t_1) > 1+ROI$. In a perfect capital market, equality (3.12) shows that a sacrifice in terms of current consumption and current investment lead to the same conclusion: The opportunity cost of a project is independent of the way it is financed because its benefits (returns, respectively) as well as costs should be discounted using the market interest rate.

3.3 Inflation-Adjusted Interest Rate

For the evaluation of long-term investments, expected future inflation must be taken into account (past inflation is irrelevant for a decision concerning the future). If nothing else changes, inflation causes nominal costs and revenues to increase over time. Let its expected rate $\Delta p^e/p$ be the same for both unit variable cost c_{var} and price p_E. If in addition it is constant over the entire planning period, inflation can be introduced into net present value calculation in the following simple way,

$$p_{E,t} = p_E \cdot \left(1 + \frac{\Delta p^e}{p}\right)^t \quad \text{and} \quad c_{var,t} = c_{var} \cdot \left(1 + \frac{\Delta p^e}{p}\right)^t \quad (3.13)$$

with current energy prices p_E and current variable unit cost c_{var}. Inserting this into Eq. (3.3) results in

$$NPV = -Inv_0 + (p_E - c_{var}) \cdot Q \cdot \sum_{t=1}^{T} \frac{(1 + \Delta p^e/p)^t}{(1+i)^t}. \quad (3.14)$$

As long as the future expected rate of inflation is low (below 10%, say), this equation can be approximated by

$$NPV \approx -Inv_0 + (p_E - c_{var}) \cdot Q \cdot \sum_{t=1}^{T} \frac{1}{\left(1 + (i - \Delta p^e/p)\right)^t} \quad (3.15)$$

Accordingly, inflation effects can be accounted for by subtracting the expected inflation rate $\Delta p^e/p$ from the rate of discount rate. Accordingly, one defines an expected real rate of discount,

$$i^e := i - \frac{\Delta p^e}{p} \quad (3.16)$$

to be used in discounting inflation-adjusted cash flows and costs. Conversely, Eq. (3.16) states that the nominal market rate of interest rate i is the sum of the real rate i^e (which in turn equals time preference of savers who are interested in real rather just nominal consumption) and the expected rate of inflation $\Delta p^e/p$.

Inflation confers an advantage on owners of physical assets, which appreciate in value. Conversely, creditors suffer to an equivalent degree. Therefore, inflation gains and losses correspond to each other. Suppose that consumers, expecting an inflation rate of 3%, would like to see their real consumption possibilities increase by 5% within a year, equal to their rate of time preference. They then would ask for a nominal interest rate of 3+5 = 8%. Investors who expect that their net revenues will also rise in correspondence to the inflation rate would be willing to pay that rate.

Yet on closer inspection, this line of argument is short-sighted. Neither creditors nor investors are immune to erroneous predictions. The greater the uncertainty about future inflation rates, the greater the risk to lenders of capital. If they should underestimate the real rate of inflation, they may end up with a negative real rate of interest and hence reduced rather than enhanced consumption possibilities. Taking such risk into account, lenders may ask for a risk premium, resulting in a still higher nominal rate of interest. Alternatively, they may place their savings in tangible assets such as gold and other precious metals rather than the capital market. For this reason alone, economists widely view inflation as something that should be avoided. Moreover, they fear its tendency to accelerate once inflationary expectations are built into wage negotiations and pricing decisions, resulting in the so-called wage-price spiral.

3.4 Social Time Preference

When evaluating energy investments with an economic life of 40 years or more, high discount rates have a strongly negative effect on the viability of a project. This is because cash flows occurring late in time are reduced to just about zero in present value through discounting. Capital-intense investments in renewable energy or in energy efficiency are affected in particular because their evaluation depends on the expectation that the real price of conventional fuels rises over time. However, the Hotelling rule of Sect. 6.2.1 predicts that this rise is no faster than the real rate of interest. If the *ROI* currently applied by investors exceeds this rate (for instance because they are skeptical about the longer-term prospects of the economy, causing their planning horizon to be short), future cash flows contribute little to net present value.

Indeed, the discount rate can be interpreted as the market's 'shortsightedness'. Figure 3.4 illustrates this. An investor assuming an interest rate of 4% discounts 1 EUR of cash flow that comes in after 40 years according to the formula of compound interest, resulting in

$$\frac{1}{(1+i)^t} = \frac{1}{1.04^{40}} = 0.208. \tag{3.17}$$

Therefore, only 20% of this cash flow contributes to the project's *NPV*. If the investor applies an interest rate of 8%, this contribution is reduced to even less than 5%. Evidently, the higher the discount rate, the less likely is a positive *NPV* for a project with a long life such as 40 years, *ceteris paribus*. Short-term projects have a better chance. Thus, one can say that high rates of discount cause investors to become myopic.

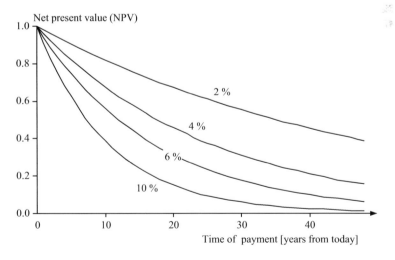

Fig. 3.4 Net present value of future financial flows at different interest rates

From a macroeconomic point of view, the question arises whether investments that have the benefit of sustainability should not be evaluated using a lower social rather than the market discount rate. In the scientific literature, lower values and even a zero value for the discount rate have been proposed (see Lind et al. 1982), partly on philosophical rather than strictly economic grounds:

- The human being is in a permanent conflict between the subconscious (considered to be irrational) and the conscious (associated with rationality). The irrational part seeks the fast, instant satisfaction of desires, while mid-term or even long-term projects require a higher tolerance of frustration. The interest rate is the economic equivalent of this behavioral fact but in the end reflects irrational myopia. Pigou (1932) called this effect 'defective telescopic faculty'; Harrod (1948) referred to it as 'pure time preference'.
- The choice of a social discount rate can be seen as the outcome of a negotiation between different social groups. In the case of long-term projects in the interest of sustainability, relevant stakeholders such as future generations are not represented at the negotiating table, causing the outcome to be distorted if present market conditions and in particular the market discount rate are used for the evaluation of these projects.
- In addition to their pure time preference reflected by market behavior, citizens of today may have diverging social rates of time preference. This is expressed on the political level; people may want the government to take responsibility for future generations but are not willing to include it in their individual decisions. They use a social discount rate when participating in political referendums on projects in the interest of society. Since voters differ with respect to this rate, it is the median voter (who turns a minority into a majority in a two-party system) who determines the social discount rate. This rate (implicit in the outcome of pertinent referenda) may be used for calculating the net present value of long-term projects.
- A similar argument can be derived from the distribution of wealth, which is heavily skewed in most societies. Wealthy individuals, disposing of substantial capital funds, influence the market interest rate more than poor ones. When deciding on projects in the interest of the society and of future generations, democratic decision rules require that poor individuals have the same weight as wealthy individuals.

Although those arguments seem reasonable at first glance, one should be careful to promote the use of social discount rates that are different from the market interest rate when it comes to evaluating energy investments of public interest. A low social discount rate would indeed support 'sustainability projects'. Yet projects of this type could be harmful to future generations because they need to be financed by government, private investors requiring a *ROI* in excess of the social rate of discount. To the extent that government debt increases, future generations are burdened with a debt that can be substantial in view of the high capital intensity of these projects. Indeed, future capital costs could outweigh the benefits of the project to them. An artificially low discount rate thus may run counter the good intentions of their promoters in the long run; the way to a more sustainable development cannot be cleared by manipulating the discount rate.

More generally, a basic principle of economic policy applies in this context. The Dutch Nobel prize laureate Tinbergen (1967) realized the analogy between a system of equations and the relationships linking a set of objectives to a set of policy instruments. The objectives can be viewed as dependent variables and the policy instruments, as arguments in a system of equations. A policy maker who wants to know how to reach his or her objectives needs to solve for the arguments; however, an equation system generally has a solution only if the number of functional relationships and hence arguments is at least as large as the number of dependent variables (for instance, a system of two unknowns can be solved only if there are at least two equations). This implies that by using only a single control variable such as the discount rate, policy makers cannot simultaneously attain the two goals of maximum inter-temporal efficiency (i.e. a high productivity of investment) and maximum inter-generational distributional justice.

Through some of its economic activities, the present generation puts the livelihood of future generations at stake. This can be counteracted by the introduction of fundamental rights of future generations to live in an unspoiled and livable environment on a par with the (constitutional) human rights of the current generation. These fundamental rights should not be discounted when deciding investment projects. However, long-term investment projects that do not affect them should be discounted using the market interest rate, with inflationary expectations taken into account as shown in Sect. 3.3.

3.5 Interest Rate and Risk

For most real-world investment, knowledge about future returns is limited. They are subject to a multitude of risks:

– Engineering and construction risks;
– Financial risks;
– Technical risks during operation;
– Customer risks (e.g. default of payments, declining demand);
– Supplier risks (e.g. supply interruptions);
– Price and exchange rate risks;
– Social risks (e.g. strikes);
– Political risks (market interventions).

Investors may try to quantify these risks by defining a set of possible scenarios, assigning to them subjective probabilities w_k describing the likelihood of occurrence,

$$0 \leq w_k \leq 1, \ k, k = 1...., N, \quad \text{with} \quad \sum_{k=1}^{N} w_k = 1. \tag{3.18}$$

In the limiting case, one of the scenarios has a probability of one while all other probabilities are zero. This is the case of certainty.

Applied to investment decisions, for each scenario k a rate of return on investment ROI_k is calculated. The expected rate of return is given by

$$\mathrm{E}(ROI) = \sum_{k=1}^{N} ROI_k \cdot w_k \qquad (3.19)$$

and the associated variance, by

$$\sigma^2 = \sum_{k=1}^{N} (ROI_k - \mathrm{E}(ROI))^2 \cdot w_k. \qquad (3.20)$$

In the case of certainty, variance σ^2 is zero. The risk of a project increases with σ^2 (or with raising standard deviation σ, respectively).

To the extent that market participants are risk-averse, they ask for a risk premium in addition to the rate of return pertinent to a corresponding risk-free investment.[5] Thus, investment decisions under risk take not only the expected rate of return $\mathrm{E}(ROI)$ of the project into account, but also its uncertainty, usually reflected by variance σ^2. According to the Bernoulli criterion, investors maximize a linear combination of expected profit and variance of profit

$$\mathrm{E}(ROI) - \frac{av}{2}\sigma^2 \to \max!. \qquad (3.21)$$

The term av denotes the individual's degree of risk aversion $av \geq 0$ (see also Sect. 11.3). Thus, Eq. (3.21) describes a trade-off between expected value and variance of returns promised by a project: Given $av > 0$, a project with higher expected profit is only preferable to a project with lower expected profit if it does not have the downside of a higher variance of profits.

3.5.1 Capital Asset Pricing Model (CAPM)

Up to this point, an investment project has been assessed in isolation. However, investors usually have a whole portfolio of project, providing them with the possibility of risk diversification (Markowitz 1952). This means that they evaluate a project not only in terms of its contribution to the overall expected return but also its contribution to the overall risk of their portfolio. In view of the trade-off discussed above, a single project may even lower the portfolio's expected rate of return provided it reduces the variance of the portfolio's return to a sufficient

---

[5]Risk-aversion exists if a possible loss has a higher influence on utility than a gain of equal size and equal probability of occurrence.

degree. This is possible if the project considered has a higher return than expected precisely when others perform worse than expected, and *vice versa*. Therefore, deviations from E(*ROI*) values of the project considered need to be negatively correlated with the *ROI* of the portfolio as a whole. Since a correlation coefficient is nothing but a normalized covariance, it is sufficient to calculate the covariance between the project's rate of return and the return of the entire portfolio held by the investor. For simplicity, investors are assumed to hold all assets traded on the capital market in proportion to their aggregate share, which is possible by buying stock of listed companies. Moreover, let the probabilities $w_{k,j}$ defined over the K scenarios of the project considered and the J scenarios of the market portfolio $q_{market,j}$ be the same. This is not unrealistic since the *ROI* values of individual investment projects and those pertaining to listed companies tend to move in parallel in response to the business cycle. With these simplifications, covariance is given by

$$COV = \sum_{k=1}^{K} \sum_{j=1}^{J} (ROI_k - E(ROI)) \cdot (q_{market,j} - E(q_{market})) \cdot w_{k,j}. \quad (3.22)$$

Thus, the deviations from expected values of *ROI* weighted by their probability of occurrence are summed up. Accordingly, COV can be positive (positive correlatedness, making some limited risk diversification possible; see below), negative (enabling marked risk diversification), or zero (enabling risk diversification especially for large portfolios). Note that calculating COV is confronted with at least three challenges. First, the relevant market portfolio needs to be defined. Frequently, the stock exchange of the investor's resident country has been used; however, especially big investors increasingly seek risk diversification across national capital markets. Second, the time window used for estimation makes a considerable difference. In particular, estimates of E(*ROI*) and COV depend strongly on how many years prior to the financial crisis of 2007–2009 are included in the sample. Third, COV values usually are employed for guidance 1 year ahead, sometimes even only a quarter into the future. Planning horizons this short do not match the long life of a typical energy investment.

With these caveats in mind, one can use the Capital Asset Pricing Model (CAPM) for determining the risk-adjusted rate of return required of an individual investment project ROI^* in case the investor's portfolio consists of very many components (Sharpe 1964),

$$ROI^* = i + \frac{COV}{\sigma_{market}^2} \cdot (E(q_{market}) - i) = i + \beta \cdot (E(q_{market}) - i). \quad (3.23)$$

Here, i denotes the risk-free interest rate and σ^2_{market} the variance of *ROI* values characterizing the capital market. The ratio

$$\beta = \frac{COV}{\sigma_{market}^2} \quad (3.24)$$

describes the relationship between the *ROI* of the project and the *ROI* pertinent to the capital market (in fact, it is nothing but the slope parameter of a linear regression linking ROI_k to ROI_{market}). Note that investors' risk aversion has no influence. Five cases can be distinguished.

- $\beta = 0$: The project's rate of return is uncorrelated with the reference market return. According to the CAPM, no risk premium is required for such an investment project, since the risk associated with the project is fully diversified away. Accordingly, returns can be discounted using the risk-free interest rate i. The yield of government bonds[6] is often used as an indicator of the 'risk-free' market interest rate.
- $\beta = 1$: The project's expected rate of return fluctuates in parallel with the reference market portfolio. With $\beta = 1$, the CAPM Eq. (3.23) implies E$(ROI) = \mathrm{E}(ROI)_{market}$: The project bears the same systematic risk as the general market portfolio and should therefore yield the same return.
- $0 < \beta < 1$: The *ROI* values of the project fluctuate less strongly than those of the market portfolio; the project contributes to risk diversification. Therefore, the appropriate value of the discount rate is below $\mathrm{E}(ROI)_{market}$. Until recently, power plant projects used to be of this type. Electricity demand is rather stable, largely independent of economic cycles; moreover, in a regulated monopolistic market, investors typically obtain the right to adjust rates in order to achieve a guaranteed *ROI* on their projects.
- $\beta > 1$: In the wake of liberalization, *t*his case has become more common in the energy sector, reflecting an increase in riskiness due to competition. Since a higher required *ROI** reflects a shortened panning horizon (see Sect. 3.4) the discount rate applied to energy investments varies with it. Therefore, under a regulated monopoly, the appropriate value of the discount rate is below E$(ROI)_{market}$, while for companies operating in a liberalized electricity market, it is in excess of $\mathrm{E}(ROI)_{market}$.
- $\beta < 0$: The *ROI* values of the project are negatively correlated with those of the capital market. One could say that the project in fact insures against the volatility of the capital market since its *ROI* is high when *ROI* values are low in general (and *vice versa*). An example could be a renewable energy project, whose carnings arc particularly high when conventional energy sources become scarce and expensive, thus putting pressure on the *ROI* of listed companies who have to buy electricity. According to Eq. (3.23) the discount rate can even be below than the risk-free interest rate i *in this case*.

---

[6]The yield of a bond is defined as its internal rate of return calculated by setting all discounted cash flows from that bond equal to its current market value.

3.5.2 New Asset Pricing Methods

In recent decades, the methods of risk-based evaluation of investment projects have been developed further. The point of departure is present value calculation, which however suffers from neglecting risks inherent in all components of future cash flows, such as sales prices, sales volumes, prices paid for energy inputs, and operating costs. Moreover, these components of cash flow cannot be assumed to be subject to the same risk. For example, if the energy company strikes a long-term sales contract with a reliable counterparty, the risk associated with future revenue is a minor one; at the very least, it can be assessed with some accuracy at the time of deciding about an investment.[7] However, future production costs may also be uncertain; for instance, a generator using gas as a fuel is exposed to the risk of price hikes. Present value calculation can be extended to take into account risks inherent in cash flow component by component (this is also known as Asset Pricing Method). Cash flow components assumed to be devoid of risk are evaluated according to the risk-free rate of return i.

Consider the sale of electricity in a future period T. Rather than selling on the (wholesale) market at the uncertain price prevailing at T, the generator can hedge the price risk by selling forward. This means striking a contract specifying delivery of Q_T units (MW) electricity in period T at the forward price p_F, which is usually comparatively low because the buyer acts as an insurer (see Sect. 12.2.5). The present value of the forward contract is

$$PV = p_F \, Q_T \frac{1}{(1+i)^{T-t}}, \qquad (3.25)$$

with i denoting the risk-free interest rate since it is now the counterparty who bears the price risk.

Alternatively, the generator can decide to bear the price risk, hoping that the spot price in period T will be higher than the current price. The first step is to replace the future spot price by its expected value, $E[p_{E,T}]$. However, the issue remaining is how to discount a risky future sales price to present value. As stated above, the forward sales price is usually relatively low. Therefore, the ratio p_F/p_E is substantially below one if buyers and sellers on the forward market deem the price risk to be important. Indeed, the forward price represents the best estimate of a risk-adjusted future spot price. Evidently, the ratio p_F/p_E takes the price risk into account. Hence, Eq. (3.25) can be rewritten as follows,

---

[7]More generally, there is so-called counterparty risk, meaning that a contractual partner fails to fulfill the contract. Sometimes counterparty risk can be transferred to a third party. For example, a company may sell power through an energy exchange. In this case, the exchange covers the counterparty risk, acting as a clearing house.

$$PV = \underbrace{\mathrm{E}(p_E) \cdot Q_t}_{SR_T} \cdot \frac{p_F}{p_E} \cdot \frac{1}{(1+i)^{T-t}}. \qquad (3.26)$$

The first two factors represent the expected sales revenue SR_T when selling to the spot market rather than concluding a forward contract. The ratio p_F/p_E takes the price risk into account, while the factor $1/(1+i)^{T-t}$ discounts to present value, using the risk-free rate because the price risk has been already corrected for.

The Asset Pricing Method assumes a market without transaction costs, permitting to switch freely between spot trades and forward contracts. In addition, cost of carry and convenience yield are neglected.[8] Their inclusion in the economic evaluation of investment projects is beyond the scope of this book, being the subject of ongoing research.

3.6 Real Option Valuation

Investment decisions are based on several assumptions that need to be scrutinized. Uncertainties characterizing them can be taken into account using the correction factors discussed in the preceding sections or sensitivity analysis. A particular problem is that the risk factors can change during a project's lifetime, a fact that has not been considered thus far. At the same time, investors may react with more or less flexibility to these changes. This flexibility needs to be integrated into the evaluation of an investment in ways to be expounded here.

According to Myers (1974), a project offering flexibility during its lifetime can be viewed as an option. This insight permits to apply financial option theory to the evaluation of physical investments, with the term 'real option' used to distinguish them from a financial option. The theory of real options has been developed starting in the mid-1990s (see Laughton 1998) and has found its way into project management since. Pioneers in adoption were energy companies with activities in mining and extraction (crude oil, coal, and natural gas in particular). These companies had gained a lot of experience in trading financial derivatives on commodity exchanges designed to hedge the risk of volatile sales prices on wholesale markets. While a detailed description of real option theory is beyond the scope of this book, some of its basics shall be discussed. For an introduction to the topic, the work of Dixit and Pindyck (1994) serves as the standard reference.

---

[8]Cost of carry refers to interest income forgone by receiving the sales revenue later (the cost of storage is of little relevance in the context of electricity). The convenience yield comprises all positive effects that are related to the physical possession of a good, in particular the option of selling it when its price is high.

3.6.1 Energy Investments as Real Options

To explain the theory of real options, terms used for both financial and real options need to be defined.

– Underlying: In a nutshell, most financial products are bets on some future outcome. The outcome the bet is placed upon is called underlying. For instance, in the case of an option (of the call type, see below) which entitles its owner to buy 1000 bbl of crude oil at the end of next year at a price of 80 USD/bbl, the underlying is 1000 bbl of crude oil possibly worth 80,000 USD.
– Derivatives: This term refers to all types of contracts that are not executed 'on the spot' (i.e. delivery now, payment with minimum delay). Derivatives include forward contracts (delivery delayed, payment now or possibly delayed somewhat) and options (delivery at the discretion of the buyer or seller, payment of an option premium now, remainder later).
– Call option: This option entitles its holder to the right, but not the obligation, to buy the underlying at a specified price (the so-called strike price) during a limited time specified in the contract (so-called time to maturity). The seller of the option (called option writer) is obliged to sell the underlying when the buyer exercises the option but keeps the underlying in case the option holder fails to exercise it. Option writers charge an option premium to compensate them for the risky position they take in the meantime.
– Put option: This is the opposite of a call option. It entitles the option holder to the right, but not the obligation, to sell an underlying at a specified price (strike price) during a limited time specified in the contract (time to maturity). The option writer is obliged to buy the underlying at the demand of the option holder but does not have to if the option holder fails to exercise it. Option writers also ask for an option premium to compensate them for the risky position the take in the meantime.

Besides applying classical strategies of risk mitigation (such as diversification), holders of a financial option can actually benefit from risk thanks to the flexibility offered by an option (see the discussion below). However, flexibility is not costless. Whether paying the option premium is justified depends on the value of flexibility to the option holder. Investments in projects which increase the ability to adapt flexibly to changes in market conditions are similar to financial options, except that they are 'real' in the sense of being written on tangible underlyings such as gas turbines. As will be shown in greater detail below, options are particularly valuable if

– the economic viability of the project depends on exogenous influences whose future development is highly uncertain;
– the company pursuing the project is able to react to these uncertainties in a flexible way;
– the project's *NPV* is not so high (or not so low) as to make it profitable (unprofitable) in just about any circumstance.

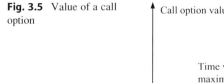

Fig. 3.5 Value of a call option

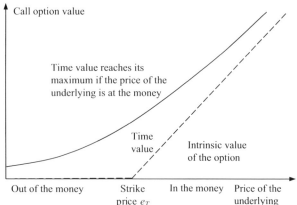

The first point is striking: The greater riskiness, the greater is the probability that during the project's lifetime new information becomes available on which the investor may react. Therefore, option values increase rather than decrease with volatility (using financial jargon again). While in the traditional view the value of an investment declines with risk, it increases with risk when its option value is considered.[9]

These factors are illustrated for the case of a call option in Fig. 3.5. The horizontal axis depicts the possible future prices of the underlying (of the barrel of crude in the example) e.g. during 3 years hence; therefore, the price of the underlying is not known at decision time. Focus is first on the kinky dashed line of Fig. 3.5. This component of the payoff function of an option is called its intrinsic value. Below a certain price of crude oil (the strike price), it will not be attractive for the investor to e.g. construct a platform for drilling in the sea because the *NPV* of future revenues does not cover the investment outlay. The project is 'out of the money'. However, as soon as the price of the underlying exceeds this strike price, the value of the project will increase proportionately. It will be 'in the money', causing the investor to exercise the option. Its intrinsic value increases in step with the price of the underlying, as indicated by the 45° slope of the payoff function.

The investor is assumed to hold expectations regarding the future price of the underlying. Let these expectations be reflected by a probability density function over the possible prices of the underlying (not depicted in Fig. 3.5), typically centered to the right of the strike price. Let this distribution first exhibit low uncertainty; it thus has little probability mass on both sides of the strike price. Due to the kink in the payoff function, the investor suffers no loss on the downside (by deferring construction) but does not stand to gain much either in case the option

---

[9]The positive relation between risk and the economic value of a project might convince investors to enter into especially risky projects. In the academic literature, this effect is seen as one of the reasons for the emergence of the new economy bubble at the beginning of this century and the banking crisis of 2008.

is in the money. In a second scenario, let the future price of the underlying possibly diverge by a great amount from the strike price, reflecting higher riskiness. This time, the distribution function is characterized by much more spread because extreme values are possible now. However, this means that while the probability of the option being out of the money is higher, it also has more probability mass to the right of the strike price. Therefore, the investor, while still not suffering a loss on the downside, stands to gain greatly from the call option (i.e. the opportunity to invest in the platform). This shows that volatility is in the interest of investors, especially if they are in fact diversified shareholders of many companies who lose little if any one of these companies ends up in bankruptcy. Note that the value of their shares can never be less than zero.

Turning to the second factor mentioned above, the intrinsic value of an option neglects the value of flexibility to the investor, who can either produce crude oil at a given price or decide against production depending on the market clearing price at any time of the option's lifetime. Again, consider two scenarios. In the first, let the probability density function reflecting beliefs be centered above the strike price, with limited spread. While this makes the investment somewhat attractive, very high values of the underlying are unlikely during the next 156 weeks (3 years) in the example given. Flexibility in the timing of the decision to invest is of little relevance in this case. Accordingly, the so-called time value of the option is close to zero, as reflected by the small vertical distance between the total payoff function and its dashed component (equal to the intrinsic value). Next, let the probability density function be centered below the strike price, again with little spread. This indicates that the investor is highly certain that the option will be out of the money for some time. Again, flexibility with respect to (not) exercising the option does not have much value. In sum, the time value of an option is small at the two extremes of the price line; conversely, it is highest when the probability distribution is centered at the strike price because it is there where the project has much probability of being in the money for a sufficient amount of time to make it economically viable. Being able to pick the time of deciding has great value in this case.

Finally, the importance of the third factor cited above can be illustrated as follows. First, let the probability distribution be centered at a value far above the strike price, with limited spread. This means that there is little (possibly even zero) probability mass at and below the strike price; the project is in the money in (almost) all circumstances. In addition, the time value of the option is close to zero, indicating that flexibility in timing of the decision is of little importance. Traditional economic project evaluation yields a clear conclusion in favor of the project in this case. Second, let the probability distribution be centered at a value far below the strike price, again with limited spread. Therefore, there is little probability mass at and above the strike price; the project is almost certainly out of the money. In this situation too, the option property of an investment project hardly matters. Conversely, the option property does matter when it is not clear whether the project is economically attractive or not.

3.6.2 Black-Scholes Model

The choice of methods available for assessing a risky investment presented so far is still not complete. Indeed, it comprises the following alternatives.

- Risk-adjusted interest rate: For the present value (*PV*) calculation of future cash flows, a risk-adjusted discount rate i is used. Since $\partial PV/\partial i < 0$, a project is more likely to be rejected when the discount rate is high (see Eq. (3.4)).
- Sensitivity analysis: A project's net present value (*NPV*) calculation is repeated, using different combinations of parameters (investment outlay, revenue and cost streams, useful life of the project, and values of i). In this way, one can identify the critical scenarios in which its *NPV* becomes negative.
- Monte Carlo simulation: First, the stochastic properties of the factors influencing the *NPV* of the project are analyzed, such as the distributions of and covariances between possible future prices, sales volumes, and costs. In each round of simulation, values of these parameters are drawn at random and the *NPV* calculated, resulting in a distribution of *NPV* values. Depending on the investor's risk preference, the project is accepted if the *NPV* is positive in more than e.g. 95% of simulations.
- Decision tree analysis: First, all possible outcomes of the project and the sequence of events leading to them need to be defined. Some so-called nodes of the tree are controlled by the investor (management, respectively), while some are controlled by Nature as it were. Next, the branches of these latter nodes are associated with their respective probabilities, permitting management to choose the action associated with the highest expected payoff at the nodes under its control. Also known as dynamic programming, this method yields optimal decision paths.
- Valuation of the project as a call option: The great insight of Black and Scholes (1973) was that a risk-free portfolio can be constructed by combining options. To see this, consider a so-called European option that can only be exercised at maturity, i.e. at the end of the contract period. Therefore, this type of option does not offer flexibility and thus can be depicted by the kinky dashed line of Fig. 3.5. If this line is matched with another one that slopes down to the right of the strike price, the resulting payoff function runs horizontal, indicating that such a portfolio is risk-free since it yields a payoff that is independent of possible future prices of the underlying. To achieve this, the investor would have to write a call option entailing the obligation to deliver the underlying in case the purchaser of the option exercises it, i.e. when the price of the underlying exceeds the strike price (recall that this would generate an option premium, which is abstracted from in Fig. 3.5). Alternatively, the investor could buy shares issued by a generating company with a similar project amounting to the value of the investment to hedge it, selling a call option as well as buying a put option on them. In this way, he or she incurs a loss on the call option if the project is 'in the money', which is offset by the value of the project in this case. In case the project does not perform and is 'out of the money', so is the call option on the shares; however, the put option has value in this case. Evidently, options on shares can also be used to form a risk-free portfolio (justifying the put-call parity mentioned

3.6 Real Option Valuation

below). However, a risk-free portfolio can be discounted applying a risk-free interest rate, which simplifies the valuation problem decisively.

The basic assumption of Black and Scholes is that the market price p of the underlying follows a so-called standardized Wiener process with drift μ and volatility σ, with dz denoting stochastic shocks drawn from a normal $N(0,1)$ distribution

$$\frac{dp_t}{p_t} = \mu \cdot dt + \sigma \cdot dz. \quad (3.27)$$

In this case, price changes between the present time t and a future date T are log-normal distributed[10] with mean

$$\ln p_t + \left(\mu - \frac{\sigma^2}{2}\right) \cdot (T-t) \quad (3.28)$$

and standard deviation

$$\sigma \cdot \sqrt{T-t}. \quad (3.29)$$

Finally, the right to any dividends is assumed to be retained by the owner of the share (the underlying). Then, the Black-Scholes formula for the valuation of a European call option is given by

$$CALL_t(T) = p_t \cdot N(d_1) - e_T \cdot e^{-i \cdot (T-t)} \cdot N(d_2) \quad (3.30)$$

$$d_1 = \frac{\ln\left(\frac{p_t}{e_T}\right) + \left(i + \frac{\sigma^2}{2}\right) \cdot (T-t)}{\sigma \cdot \sqrt{T-t}} \quad (3.31)$$

$$d_2 = d_1 - \sigma \cdot \sqrt{T-t} \quad (3.32)$$

p_t Present spot market price of the underlying
e_T Exercise price of the option at maturity T (strike price)
i Risk-free interest rate
σ Annualized volatility of p_t
T Time to maturity (in years)

The value of a put option can be calculated from the so-called put-call parity,

$$PUT_t(T) = CALL_t + e_T \cdot e^{-i \cdot (T-t)} - p_t. \quad (3.33)$$

---

[10] Log-normal distribution means that the logarithm of the random variable is normally distributed.

Table 3.2 Variables used for financial and real option valuation

	Option on a financial asset	Real option
Option right	Right to purchase or sell an underlying against paying the exercise price	Right to the cash flows of a project against paying the investment outlay
p_t	Current spot market price	Present value of cash flows (expected contribution margin) (+)
e_T	Exercise price (strike price of the underlying)	Investment outlay (−)
σ	Annualized volatility of the underlying	Riskiness of cash flows (+)
T	Time to maturity	Time by which the investment project ceases to generate cash flows (+)
i	Risk-free interest rate	Risk-free interest rate (+)

(+) and (−) indicate the direction of the influence on the option value

The put-call parity follows from the fact that options can be combined in a way as to result in a risk-free asset; note the crucial role of discounting the exercise price e_T to present value using the risk-free rate of interest i in Eq. (3.33). Evidently, the parameters of the Black-Scholes model, which refer to financial options, need to be translated into terms referring to investment projects. The corresponding equivalencies are shown in Table 3.2, along with the influence of the parameter on the option value. In particular, the exercise price becomes the investment outlay; the higher its value, the more the kink in the payoff function of Fig. 3.5 shifts to the right, indicating a reduction of probability mass over positive payoffs and hence a reduction in the value of the call option. Also, a high risk-free interest rate means that the purchaser of the option can reap substantial benefits from an investment in a risk-free asset up to maturity, which lowers the present value of payment for the option and therefore increases its value. This effect is the more important, the farther maturity T lies in the future (see Eq. 3.30). Finally note the crucial importance of the normality assumption of the Wiener process; $N(d_1)$ and $N(d_1)$ symbolize the probability of the price of the asset attaining a certain value (T-t) periods in future. However, returns of investment projects typically are characterized by an asymmetric distribution, with substantial probability mass to the left of the expected value (positive skewness). While a log-normal random variable does exhibit positive skewness, returns to investment have been found to have 'flat tails', i.e. a higher probability of extreme values occurring than indicated by log normality. Therefore, the Black-Scholes formula may lead investors to underestimate the riskiness of a project.

3.6.3 Application to Balancing Power Supply

Often, the dispatch of a power plant is flexible in so far as the rate of production per time unit (usually, a quarter of an hour) can be increased or decreased. This gives the plant operator the possibility to balance deviations from day-ahead schedules by increasing or decreasing production output, and thus save on purchases of balancing

3.6 Real Option Valuation

power from the grid operator (see also Sect. 13.1.3). Therefore, investment in a flexible power plant can be considered as the purchase of a real option which can be exercised to minimize cost caused by deviations from the schedules.

The underlying of the option is the avoided cost associated with the purchase of balancing power from the grid operator. Let this cost be log-normally distributed with a mean of 0.9 EUR ct/kWh and an annualized volatility of 40.5%, which determines the values of d_1 and d_2 as well as their associated probabilities given a log-normal distribution. For an estimated annual operating time of 5500 h/year, the expected annual contribution margin adds up to $5500 \cdot 0.009 = 50$ EUR/kW installed capacity. The calculation is carried out on the basis of a time to maturity of 10 years.

Table 3.3 shows the input values, the interim values, and the results of the Black-Scholes model for this example. Given the assumptions, the call option value of the capacity is 23 EUR/kW/year. Capitalizing this value yields the additional value the plant operator should be willing to pay for the possibility to avoid the purchase of balancing power.

Additional insights can be obtained by calculating the partial derivatives of the Black–Scholes formula with respect to the input variables. These derivatives quantify the sensitivity of the option value in response to marginal changes in these variables.

- Delta: Change of the option value due to a change of the price of the underlying or of the expected annual contribution margin p_t;
- Gamma: Change of Delta due to a change of the annual contribution margin p_t;
- Theta: Change of the option value due to a different time to maturity T;
- Vega: Change of the option value as a function of changing volatility of the expected contribution margin p_t;
- Rho: Change of the option value due to a change of the risk-free interest rate i.

Figure 3.6 shows the intrinsic value of the real option (represented by the kinked broken line) and the associated option value (the solid line) as a function of the expected annual contribution margin. The slope of the solid line corresponds to the Delta defined above. At 50 EUR/kW, the option value amounts to 23 EUR/kW installed capacity per year (see Table 3.3 again). The vertical dashed line at that

Table 3.3 Value of the real option 'power plant' according to the Black-Scholes formula

	Inputs		Output
Annualized contribution margin	p	50.00 EUR/(kW·a)	$d_1 = 0.592$
Annualized investment cost	e_T	58.75 EUR/(kW·a)	$d_2 = -0.688$
Volatility	σ	40.5%	$N(d_1) = 0.723$
Risk-free interest rate	i	1.0%	$N(d_2) = 0.246$
Project lifetime	T	120 months	$CALL = 23.09$ EUR/kW p.a.

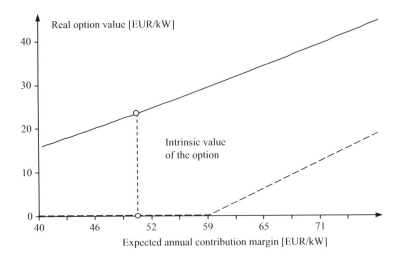

Fig. 3.6 Option value as a function of the expected contribution margin

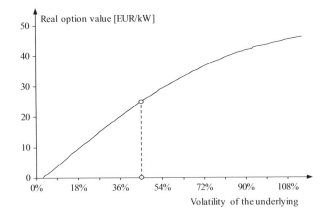

Fig. 3.7 Option value as a function of volatility (Vega)

point reflects the time value of the option due to the flexibility in production afforded by the investment in capacity. With the assumptions of Table 3.3, the real option has an intrinsic value of zero at 50 EUR/kW per year, while the total value of the option boils down to its time value.

Both the relationships between the present value of cash flows and the volatility of the underlying on the one hand and the option price on the other hand are monotonously increasing. If all the other parameters are known, the market price of a call option can be used to determine the inherent volatility, which is nothing but the amount of risk perceived by market participants (Fig. 3.7).

References

Black, F., & Scholes, M. (1973). The pricing of options and corporate liabilities. *Journal of Political Economy, 81*, 638–659.

Dixit, A. K., & Pindyck, R. S. (1994). *Investment under uncertainty*. Princeton: Princeton University Press.

Harrod, R. F. (1948). *Towards a dynamic theory*. London: MacMillan.

Laughton, D. (1998). The potential for use of modern asset pricing methods for upstream petroleum project evaluation. *The Energy Journal, 19*(1), 149–154.

Lind, R. C., et al. (1982). *Discounting for time and risk in energy policy*. Washington: Resources for the Future.

Markowitz, H. M. (1952). Portfolio selection. *Journal of Finance, 12*, 77–91.

Myers, S. (1974). Interactions of corporate financing and investment decisions – implications for capital budgeting. *Journal of Finance, 29*, 1–25.

Pigou, A. C. (1932). *The economics of welfare* (4th ed.). New York: Macmillan.

Sharpe, W. F. (1964). Capital asset prices: A theory of market equilibrium under conditions of risk. *Journal of Finance, 19*, 425–442.

Tinbergen, J. (1967). *Economic policy: Principles and design*. Amsterdam: North Holland.

Bottom-Up Analysis of Energy Demand

Traditionally, energy economics has dealt with energy supply rather than demand. In contrast, this book gives demand precedence over supply, in keeping with the rule that without a minimum demand, supply does not come forth. Energy demand is often discussed in relation to the question of how to achieve 'energy savings', a term devoid of meaning without some prior knowledge of the factors affecting energy demand. These factors importantly derive from the profit-seeking actions of business managers and utility-oriented actions of consumers.

Over the years, two fundamentally different analytical approaches to the demand for energy have emerged: macroeconomic modeling (often called the top-down approach) and microeconomic process analysis (the bottom-up approach). The latter, to be expounded below, is based on the premise that energy demand is determined by the existing stock of energy-using capital, the intensity of its use, and its energy efficiency.

This approach gives rise to a series of questions:

– Why is it important to distinguish between energy-using capital and the intensity of its use for analyzing energy demand?
– What are the factors determining the acquisition of a particular energy-using capital good?
– What are the factors determining the intensity of their use?

In addition, the issue of energy efficiency needs to be addressed:

– Why is energy 'wasted' if it is a costly factor of production?
– How can efficiency be improved?
– Is there market failure in the case of investment in energy efficiency?
– How can innovation boost energy efficiency?
– How is energy efficiency defined to begin with?

The variables used in this chapter are:

C	Total cost of ownership
c	Average cost
Cap	Stock of appliances (measured in units of installed capacity)
CCE	Cost of conserved energy
CDD	Cooling degree day
D	Variable affecting the stock of appliances
E	Annual energy requirement
HDD	Heating degree day
i	Interest rate
Inv	Investment expenditure
ν	Intensity of use
OC	Annual operating cost
p_E	Energy price
Q	Production volume
sh	Market share
$Temp$	Daily mean temperature
U, V	Utility indices
w	Probability
X	Stochastic variable

4.1 Process Analysis

In process analysis, aggregate energy demand is split up into energy sources on the one hand (electricity, heating oil, natural gas, gasoline, diesel, hydrogen, etc.), and types of energy consumers (branches of industry, households, small businesses, and the transport sector) on the other. Demand is further differentiated by types of use (low-temperature heat, high-temperature heat, work, lighting, and electrolysis).

The demand for each type of energy per unit of time depends on three factors:

- Energy-using capital stock (appliances, buildings, machinery, vehicles);
- Intensity of use of this capital stock (e.g. km driven per month);
- Energy efficiency (e.g. liters of gasoline per 100 km driven; miles per gallon, respectively in the United States).

Figure 4.1 exhibits the process-analytical model. Demand for energy $E(t)$ of a particular type in time period t is a function of the stock of energy-using capital $Cap(t)$ and the intensity $\nu(t)$ of its use at a given level of energy efficiency (which is not yet analyzed at this point in the interest of simplicity). Desired stock $Cap^*(t)$ generally deviates from the given stock $Cap(t-1)$. The gap between $Cap^*(t)$ and $Cap(t-1)$ is not immediately closed but at a rate α, $0 < \alpha < 1$. Partial adjustment makes economic sense for several reasons. Investors need to find out whether the changes in factors influencing $Cap^*(t)$ are really long-term or just transitory, they

4.1 Process Analysis

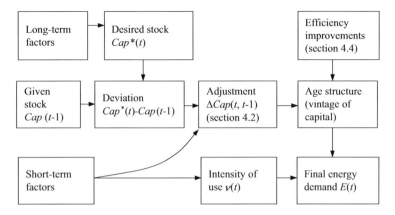

Fig. 4.1 Process analysis for modeling energy demand

may face financial constraints due to imperfect capital markets, and they may have to deal with delays in the construction and deliveries. Net investment $\Delta Cap(t)$ is therefore given by

$$\Delta Cap(t) = \alpha \left(Cap^*(t) - Cap(t-1)\right), 0 < \alpha < 1. \qquad (4.1)$$

Note that α need not to be constant. Rather, it is a decision variable whose value depends on the cost-benefit ratio of fast adjustment in comparison to the cost-benefit ratio of slow adjustment. For instance, when the user cost of capital is expected to rise (say due to a surge in interest rates), the opportunity cost of slow adjustment becomes high, causing $\alpha \to 1$.

In addition to the user cost of capital, investment entails costs of procurement. While these costs do not necessarily affect desired capital stock $Cap^*(t)$, they do affect energy efficiency and hence the demand for energy. Due to technological innovation, the conversion of final energy into useful energy usually becomes more efficient with the procurement of new energy-using capital stock.[1]

The demand for energy also depends on the age structure of the energy-using capital stock. In the Vintage Capital Growth model, $Cap(t)$ consists of vintages $Cap_i(t)$, with $i = 1,\ldots$ symbolizing additions to capital ('layers' as it were) in a past period i. In this way, $Cap_{i-1}(t-1)$ is carried forward to $Cap_i(t)$:

---

[1] Note that improvements in energy efficiency do not necessarily imply that energy-using capital stock should be replaced sooner. One also has to take into account the costs of commissioning and decommissioning an appliance or a vehicle (in terms of money or of energy consumed). A shortened useful life implies an increase in these costs, which can only be balanced by marked increases in the energy efficiency of new vintages.

$$Cap_i(t) = (1 - \delta_{i-1}) \cdot Cap_{i-1}(t-1), 0 < \delta_{i-1} < 1$$
$$Cap_1(t) = \Delta Cap(t-1) \qquad (4.2)$$
$$Cap(t) = \sum_i Cap_i(t)$$

The variable δ_{i-1} denotes the rate of depreciation pertaining to a particular vintage i. Since current capital stock is the sum over vintages of many periods, improvements in energy efficiency affect only a small part of its total, causing adjustments to exogenous shocks such as a hike in the price of energy to be sluggish.

In Fig. 4.1, two sets of factors affecting the demand for energy are distinguished.

- Long-term factors: These affect the stock of energy-using capital as well as improvements in energy efficiency. Capital stock is adjusted in response to demographic and sociological variables, such as household size and composition, commuting distances, and lifestyle. Investment in energy efficiency is driven by technological change, government policy (e.g. the setting of efficiency standards for vehicles and appliances), and deliberate choices by pioneering companies and households. However, the most important determinants of both energy-using capital stock and efficiency belong to the economic sphere. These are business sales, disposable income and wealth, the rate of interest as a component of capital user cost, and the price of energy relative to other goods and services (e.g. public transportation), along with expectations concerning their future development.
- Short-term factors: These affect the intensity with which the stock of capital is used. These factors not only include fluctuations in temperature, the business cycle, and calendar effects, but also fluctuations in income and energy prices that are not expected to be permanent.

4.2 Stock of Appliances, Buildings, Vehicles, and Machineries

For modeling the demand for energy applying process analysis, it is useful to distinguish final users of energy (households, commercial businesses, industry, transport) and to match them with uses of energy (heat, work, lighting) on the one hand and components of capital stock (appliances, buildings, machinery, and vehicles) on the other. The variables listed in Table 4.1 have proved to be statistically significant in surveys and econometric studies of energy demand.

Taking household demand for electricity as an example, it is obvious that stocks of electricity-consuming household appliances (such as ovens, washing machines, refrigerators, and dishwashers) must be among the determinants. These stocks are in turn the product of the number of households and the probability of these households owning the appliances cited. While the number of households and their composition are usually viewed as demographic variables, ownership

4.2 Stock of Appliances, Buildings, Vehicles, and Machineries

Table 4.1 Indicators of energy demand

Consumption	Indicators
Households	
Heat	Number of households, heated living space
Work	Number of washing machines, dish washers, and other appliances
Lighting	Living space
Commercial	
Heat	Floor space
Work	Air-conditioned space, types, and numbers of electric appliances
lighting	Floor space
Industry	
Heat	Steel production, output of other energy intensive industries (chemistry, cement, glass)
Work	Installed capacity of electric appliances
Electrolysis	Aluminum production
Lighting	Floor space
Transport	
Fuels (cars)	Types and numbers of passenger vehicles, passenger-kilometers, length and quality of the roads
Fuels (trucks)	Number of light and heavy duty vehicles, distances travelled, production of raw materials and finished goods
Electricity	Length of electrified railways, train frequency

probabilities are susceptible to economic influences. Ownership probability is defined as a dichotomous stochastic variable X_n,

$X_n = 1$ (household n owns the appliance or vehicle in question);
$X_n = 0$ (household n does not own the appliance ore vehicle).

Economic theory predicts that decision-makers purchase an appliance or vehicle when its net utility exceeds that of all other alternatives under consideration. While subjective, individual utility depends on several objectively measurable factors (often called 'drivers') D_j. In the case of a household, they include the comfort and time-saving afforded by the appliance or vehicle, household size, and composition (in particular double-income status), disposable income, and type and location of residence. On the negative side, one has the total cost of ownership C (which includes the cost of energy consumed),

$$C = Inv + \sum_{t=1}^{T} \frac{p_{E,t} \cdot E + OC}{(1+i)^t}. \quad (4.3)$$

with Inv denoting investment outlay, $p_{E,t}$ the price of energy in period t, E the amount of energy consumed (per period), OC operating cost such as maintenance, and i the rate of interest applied in discounting to present value. For simplicity, E,

OC, and i are assumed to be constant up to the planning horizon T. For simplicity again, utility V_n of household n (an index rather than a cardinal quantity) is related in a linear way to its determinants D_j,

$$V_n = \beta_0 + \sum_j \beta_j D_{j,n}. \tag{4.4}$$

Here, β_0 denotes a baseline utility level, while the β_j symbolize the importance of determinant D_j for decision-maker n (note that this importance is assumed to be identical across decision-makers). However, in any practical application the complete set of determinants is never observed. There are unmeasured influences on utility which are represented by a stochastic term ε_n. Individual utility U_n derived from owning the appliance in question is then given by

$$U_n = V_n + \varepsilon_n = \beta_0 + \sum_j \beta_j D_{j,n} + \varepsilon_n. \tag{4.5}$$

Evidently, utility is split into a systematic, deterministic component V_n and an unsystematic, stochastic component ε_n. This approach is known as the Random Utility Model (McFadden 1974). It predicts that the probability w of owning an appliance or a vehicle increases with the net utility afforded by it.

A probability is bounded by the [0, 1] interval. Therefore, estimating a linear regression of the observed values ($X_n = 1$: household owns the appliance or vehicle, $X_n = 0$: does not own it) on the determinants of utility leads to the problem of rendering predicted values outside this interval. A regression function with a codomain in the [0, 1] interval is called for. Sigmoid functions of the type shown in Fig. 4.2 meet this condition and are often employed in this context. The main choices are the standard logistic function used in the Logistic (also called Logit) regression model and the cumulative distribution function of the standard normal distribution used in the Probit regression model.

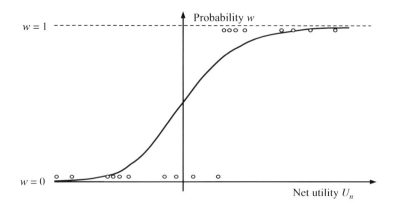

Fig. 4.2 Logistic function for modeling ownership probability

4.2 Stock of Appliances, Buildings, Vehicles, and Machineries

In the case of the Logistic regression (this choice is justified below), the probability w of owning an appliance or a vehicle is estimated using the logistic function of the individual utility U_n,

$$w = \text{logistic}(U_n) = \frac{e^{U_n}}{1+e^{U_n}} = \frac{1}{1+e^{-U_n}}. \qquad (4.6)$$

Equivalently, individual utility U_n can be expressed as a function of the probability w of owning an appliance or a vehicle using the inverse of the logistic function defined in Eq. (4.6), the so-called logit function,

$$U_n = \text{logit}(w) = \text{logistic}^{-1}(w) = \ln\left(\frac{w}{1-w}\right). \qquad (4.7)$$

Using household survey data, the unknown coefficients β_0, β_1, β_2, etc. can be estimated by maximizing the pertinent log-likelihood (see Greene 2011),

$$\ln L(\beta_0, \beta_1, \ldots | X, D_1, D_2, \ldots) = \sum_n X_n \cdot \ln w_n + (1 - X_n) \cdot \ln(1 - w_n) \qquad (4.8)$$

with $\quad w_n = \dfrac{1}{1+e^{-V_n}}.$

Provided the stochastic component ε_n follows the logistic distribution, this results in consistent, efficient, and asymptomatically normally-distributed estimates of the parameters β_j.[2]

For an assessment of the econometric evidence and public policy, one would like to know the importance of a particular influence D_j. This is usually measured as the marginal impact of D_j on ownership probability w (the household index n is omitted for simplicity). Partial differentiation of Eqs. (4.4) and (4.8) yields

$$\begin{aligned}\frac{\partial w}{\partial D_j} &= -\frac{1}{(1+e^{-V})^2} \cdot (-\beta_j) \cdot e^{-V} \\ &= \beta_j \cdot \frac{1}{1+e^{-V}} \cdot \frac{e^{-V}}{1+e^{-V}} = \beta_j \cdot w \cdot (1-w)\end{aligned} \qquad (4.9)$$

Clearly, the marginal effect of a determinant on the probability of ownership w depends on the initial value of w. This effect is most pronounced at $w = 0.5$ since $w(1-w)$ attains its maximum at $w = 0.5$. On the other hand, the predicted effect of D_j goes to zero when $w \to 0$ or $w \to 1$. A remaining problem is the fact that a determinant can be measured in different ways. For instance, disposable income can be expressed in thousands of EUR rather than EUR, and per month or per year. The solution is to denote the change in the parameter D_j in relative terms, resulting in a so-called semi-elasticity,

---

[2] Consistency means that the estimated β values approach the true parameters with increasing sample size; efficiency means that the variance of the estimates is minimal.

$$\eta^* = \frac{\partial w}{\partial D_j/D_J} = \frac{\partial w}{\partial D_j} D_j = \beta_j \cdot D_j \cdot w \cdot (1-w). \tag{4.10}$$

The induced change in w is still expressed in percentage points rather than a percentage. If one prefers to relate percentage changes in w to percentage changes in D_j, one can calculate a conventional elasticity by dividing Eq. (4.10) by w.

As indicated above, an alternative specification is the Probit model, which is in fact nothing but the cumulative distribution function Φ of a normal random variable,

$$w(X_n = 1) = \Phi(U_i) = \int_{-\infty}^{U_n} \frac{1}{\sqrt{2\pi}} \exp\left(\frac{-X^2}{2}\right) dX. \tag{4.11}$$

While the Probit model has the advantage of reflecting the normality assumption (which in turn is based on the Central Limit Theorem), the Logit model permits a much simpler interpretation of the market share of an appliance (or vehicle). Consider two competing heating systems, assuming that they are identical except for their expected operating costs c_1 and c_2, respectively. According to economic theory, their market shares sh_1 and sh_2 should be inversely related to their relative cost c_1/c_2, however without suggesting that one of the two systems will be driven from the market when its operating cost is but marginally higher than that of its competitor. A functional relationship with these properties is

$$\frac{sh_1}{sh_2} = \left(\frac{c_2}{c_1}\right)^g \quad \text{or} \quad \ln\left(\frac{sh_1}{1-sh_1}\right) = g \ln\left(\frac{c_2}{c_1}\right) \quad \text{with } g > 0 \tag{4.12}$$

In the unlikely case of parity in terms of cost ($c_1 = c_2$), Eq. (4.12) implies a market share of 50% for each. Since market shares reflect aggregate ownership probabilities, $\ln(sh_1/(1-sh_1))$ is analogous to $\ln(w_2/w_1) = \ln(w_1/(1-w_1))$ in Eq. (4.7) and thus to the Logit model. The parameter g indicates the extent to which small cost differentials between competing heating systems affect their market shares. It therefore shows the ease with which they can be substituted for each other. In the extreme case of $g \to \infty$, a small cost advantage is predicted to drive the market share of the cheaper system toward 100% (note that this is the optimal solution of a linear programming model, which is non-stochastic but fully deterministic).

The binary Logit model can be refined in numerous ways. In particular, it can be generalized to K choice alternatives (McFadden 1974). In Eq. (4.13) below, $w_k(n)$ symbolizes the probability of household n favoring alternative k over all others. Omitting the household index n again, the so-called multinomial Logit model reads

4.2 Stock of Appliances, Buildings, Vehicles, and Machineries

$$\begin{aligned}
w_k(n) = w_k &= w(X = k) = w(U_k = \max\{U_1, U_2, \ldots, U_K\}) \\
&= w(U_k > U_j \forall j \neq k) \\
&= w(V_k + \varepsilon_k - V_j - \varepsilon_j > 0 \forall j \neq k) \\
&= w(\varepsilon_j - \varepsilon_k < V_k - V_j \forall j \neq k) \\
&= \frac{\exp(V_k)}{\sum_{j=1}^{K} \exp(V_j)} \\
&= \frac{\exp(\beta_{0,k} + \beta_{1,k} \cdot D_1 + \beta_{2,k} \cdot D_2 + \ldots)}{\sum_{j=1}^{K} \exp(\beta_{0,j} + \beta_{1,j} \cdot D_1 + \beta_{2,j} \cdot D_2 + \ldots)}, \; k = 1, 2, \ldots, K.
\end{aligned} \quad (4.13)$$

Due to the fact that only differences between utilities play a role in this model, the parameters $\beta_{0,k}, \beta_{1,k}, \beta_{2,k},\ldots$ are not identified unless they are fixed in some category. Usually, one chooses the first alternative ($k = 1$) as the benchmark category by setting $\beta_{0,1} = \beta_{1,1} = \beta_{2,1} = \ldots = 0$.[3]

The multinomial logit model is based on the assumption that the available alternatives are independent of one another (the so-called independence of irrelevant alternatives or IIA assumption). This assumption often does not hold. For example, the IIA assumption in Fig. 4.3 would require the probability of owning a second car to be independent of whether or not there is already a car in the household. In reality, the alternatives 'no car', 'one car', and 'two cars' usually depend on each other.

The nested logit model permits to take dependencies of this type into account (see Greene 2011). For example, let the probability of owning two cars be related to the probability of already having one. This means that first the probability of owning one care needs to be determined. Then, the probability of purchasing a second one given this initial probability can be analyzed. This results in the following two equations,

$$\begin{aligned}
w(X = 1) &= \frac{\exp(V_1)}{\exp(V_0) + \exp(V_1)}; \\
w(X = 2) &= \frac{\exp(V_2)}{\exp(V_1) + \exp(V_2)} w(X = 1).
\end{aligned} \quad (4.14)$$

A logit model for car ownership was estimated by Brendemoen (1994), based on 1547 Norwegian households observed in the year 1985. While a bit dated, this sample is of interest because 23% of the households did not own a car at the time, justifying analysis of single-car ownership (which had a share of 60%). However, 15% of households owned two cars and 2%, three or more cars. Rather than applying the nested logit model in the guise of Fig. 4.3, the author directly estimates the probability of owning e.g. two cars (and not of none, one, and three or more cars).

---

[3] Provided the stochastic variable ε_k follows an extreme value distribution (also referred to as the Weibull or Gumbel distribution), the remaining β's can be estimated in a consistent way.

Fig. 4.3 Structure of a nested logit model (example)

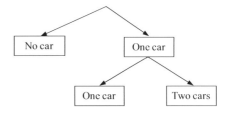

In addition, there are two extensions to the usual choice model as presented in Eq. (4.4). First, the utility function $V_n(\cdot)$ contains a term for the availability of one or more cars. Second, there is an explicit budget constraint stating that the sum of consumption expenditures of the household, including on operating j cars, is equal to the net income after deduction of the fixed cost of ownership jc, where c is the cost per car (whose average value in 1985 is known). Note that the impact of prices cannot be identified because they are approximately the same for all households across Norway. The utility function associated with having one rather than no car estimated in the author's preferred model C has the form (t ratios in parentheses),

$V_n = 3.58(7.40)$
$+0.12(0.86) \times$ Number of adults in household
$+0.22(2.07) \times$ Number of children in household
$-0.029(-5.56) \times$ Age of head of household
$-0.573(-3.03) \times$ Dummy for residence in Oslo, Bergen, and Trondheim
$-1.556(-4.76) \times$ Number of business cars available
$+0.267(2.18) \times$ Number of employed household members
$+15.35(9.17) \times \ln$(Household income net of fixed cost of ownership)

(4.15)

with a *pseudo-R^2* $= 0.44$ (this is the relative increase in the log likelihood).

While the number of adults in the household is not statistically significant, the number of children is, indicating an increased demand for transportation. Households with an older head, living in one of the country's major cities, and having access to business cars derive less utility from owning a car and are therefore less likely to own one. Conversely, probability of ownership increases with the number of employed persons in the household; it also increases with income (after deduction of the fixed cost of owning one car). The pertinent coefficient of 15.35 looks out of line; however, since net income is measured in logs, the partial derivative is $\partial V_n/\partial D_j = (\partial V_n/\partial D_j)(\partial D_j/\partial \ln D_j)$ rather than $\partial V_n/\partial D_j$ as indicated in Eq. (4.4). The estimated partial relationship thus amounts to $(\partial V_n/\partial D_j) \cdot D_j$. Therefore, the coefficient of 15.35 in Eq. (4.15) equals $\beta_j \cdot D_j$, implying $\beta_j = 0.109$ ($= 15.35/141$) since average income is $D_j = 141$ (measured in thousands of NOK). This value is comparable to the other ones shown in Eq. (4.15).

Of course, the estimated income elasticity is of crucial interest because incomes in Norway were expected to rise (and indeed did since). Brendemoen (1994) calculates the income elasticity of the probability of having one car (rather than none, two, three or more) as 0.12. This value results from deducting the income

4.2 Stock of Appliances, Buildings, Vehicles, and Machineries

Table 4.2 Income elasticities of probability of car ownership (Norway, 1985)

Elasticity	No car	1 car	2 cars	3 cars
Total sample	−0.94	0.12	0.82	1.17
Income quartile 1 (lowest)	−0.89	1.04	3.34	6.28
Income quartile 2	−1.12	0.09	1.51	3.04
Income quartile 3	−0.98	−0.14	0.88	1.98
Income quartile 4 (highest)	−0.78	−0.19	0.39	0.80

elasticities associated with having a number of cars unequal to one and therefore cannot be calculated from Eq. (4.15) using Eq. (4.10).

In addition, income elasticities depend on the level of income (see Table 4.2). Among households in the lowest quartile of the sample, a 10% increase in income is estimated to raise the probability of owning one car by 10.4%, that of owning two cars, by 33.4% (albeit from a very low initial value). In the top income quartile, the same relative increase in income would primarily reduce the probabilities of owning no car or just one car. Households in that quartile would respond by owning two and three cars, with ownership probabilities increasing by 3.9% and 8.0%, respectively. Of course, with car ownership close to 100% by now, analyzing the demand for cars with certain characteristics (e.g. categorized by fuel consumption) would be more important than just predicting car ownership *per se*.

An application of the multinomial logit model by Henkel (2013) goes in this direction. It seeks to identify the determinants of the market development of eight different heating systems: natural gas (baseline), fuel oil, wood pellets, heat pump, fuel oil & solar, natural gas & solar, wood pellets & solar, and heat pump & solar. The quantitative analysis is based on a survey carried out in 2009–2010 involving German households who recently had installed a new heating system; the survey also asked the reasons for their choice. In the Logit model, the independent variables are classified into decider-specific and alternative-specific ones.

- The alternative-specific variables are the net present value of the life-cycle cost of the alternatives (calculated by using an interest rate of 4.3%) and the annuity of the investment costs divided by the monthly household income (indicating the financing capacity of the household).
- The decider-specific variables are
  - *Eco-friendly*: environmental friendliness of the heating system is important;
  - *Space*: required space for heating system is important;
  - *SmallVillage*: place of residence has fewer than 5000 inhabitants;
  - *Maintenance*: maintenance of the heating system is important;
  - *PanelHeating*: existence of a panel heating system.

Decider-specific variables are equal for all heating systems while alternative-specific variables vary across heating systems. Given eight alternatives, every alternative-specific variable adds one parameter to be estimated to the model.

Table 4.3 Marginal effects of decider-specific variables on probability of ownership

In percent[a]	Fuel oil	Natural gas	Wood pellets	Heat pump	Fuel oil and solar	Nat. gas and solar	Wood pellets and solar	Heat pump and solar
Eco-friendly	−3.8	−4.9	0.9	*0.5*	2.2	4.2	0.5	0.5
SmallVillage	15.4	−16.4	0.9	−1.1	1.7	*−0.9*	*0.0*	0.4
Space	*0.1*	−6.6	−1.3	2.1	0.0	5.7	−0.4	0.5
Maintenance	6.2	2.6	−1.1	−4.5	1.4	−3.0	−0.8	−0.9
PanelHeating	−6.2	*−1.6*	1.1	1.9	−0.8	4.6	*0.3*	0.6

[a]Figures in italics are insignificant (significant at 10%, respectively); the others are significant at 5% or better

With every decider-specific variable, which relates to one of the eight systems, another seven are added (eight minus one for the base alternative).

The model as a whole and the majority of estimated parameters are statistically significant at the 1% level. The R^2 (McFadden) is 0.321, which represents an acceptable model fit. According to the Hausmann test (see Hensher et al. 2005), the IIA assumption cannot be rejected for seven of eight alternatives (except for 'natural gas & solar'). The marginal effects of the decider-specific variables are shown in Table 4.3. As all decider-specific variables are binary dummy variables, the marginal effect is the gain (or loss) in choice probability if households assume the variable to be important (unimportant, respectively). The rows in Table 4.3 sum up to zero: If the choice probability for one alternative increases, it must decrease for the others.

The interpretation of the marginal effects is as follows. If environmental friendliness *Eco-friendly* is regarded to be important, decision-makers have a lower probability of choosing conventional heating systems (by −4.9% in the case of natural gas, −3.8% in the case of fuel oil) but are more likely to choose a 'natural gas & solar' system. Living in a village with fewer than 5000 inhabitants reduces the probability of choosing a natural gas heating system by −16.4% while increasing that of adopting a fuel oil-based one (the benchmark category) by 15.4%. If a decision-maker considers *Maintenance* to be important, this reduces the probability of opting for a heat pump and wood pellets but increases the probability of choosing one of the conventional heating systems. Decision-makers who own a house with a panel heating system (*PanelHeating*) are less likely to prefer a conventional heating system but more likely to select one of the (unconventional) alternatives, in particular a heat pump. While all these findings are plausible, the results for the variable *Space* are surprising: If the space requirement of a heating system is considered to be important, the probability of buying one based on natural gas decreases (one would expect the opposite), mainly in favor of combined natural gas & solar. Violation of the IIA assumption for this alternative may be responsible for this implausible result.

4.3 Energy Efficiency

4.3.1 Definitions

In economic theory, the following hierarchy of terminology is employed. The highest-ranking criterion is (Pareto) optimality; it is achieved when demand preferences are served in the best possible way given the best use of productive resources available. Optimality requires the slopes of the representative consumer's indifference curve and the economy's transformation curve to be equal (in technical terms, the marginal rate of substitution in preference equals the marginal rate of transformation in production). Efficiency is next; it is achieved when the factors of production are employed in such a way that a point on the transformation curve is reached and the ratio of marginal productivities equals the ratio of factor prices. Productivity comes last; it is a one-dimensional concept meaning that the input of one factor of production (an energy source in the present context) generates the maximum possible output.

In energy economics, however, a different terminology prevails. Here, energy efficiency is understood as the productivity of the single input 'energy'. This entails the risk of losing sight of the fact that energy is not the only factor of production. A reduced use of energy comes at the price of increased inputs of capital in particular (e.g. for insulating buildings) and land (e.g. for solar panels or growing crops for use in energy generation). Energy could in principle be substituted by labor, too; yet in today's developed economies, the proposal to do away with gas-guzzling caterpillars in favor of ditch-diggers in construction would likely be met with resistance. One could argue that improvements in energy efficiency (as defined above) permit to reduce energy consumption without an increase in other inputs. Yet on closer inspection, it becomes evident that these improvements require an investment of physical as well as human capital (in the guise of skilled labor).

There exist a variety of approaches for the measurement of energy efficiency. The thermodynamic efficiency factor

$$\omega = \frac{\text{useful energy output}}{\text{energy input}} \quad (4.16)$$

is often employed, with both numerator and denominator expressed in units of energy (lower heating value).

However, this definition neglects the energetic quality of input and output. This is taken into account by the exergetic efficiency factor, which is based on the second Law of thermodynamics,

$$\omega = \frac{\text{useful energy output}}{\text{exergy input}}. \quad (4.17)$$

Exergy is defined as the quantity of energy that can be converted to work (rather than heat, which is viewed as being of inferior quality because it cannot be transformed into work without considerable losses, if at all).

When output variables other than energy or exergy are used, energy efficiency approaches the concept of productivity in the economic sense. Some of the corresponding indicators are

$$\frac{\text{heated living space}}{\text{energy input}}, \quad \frac{\text{passenger-kilometers}}{\text{energy input}}, \quad \frac{\text{steel production}}{\text{energy input}}.$$

Their inverses indicate the energy input required for producing a given quantity of energy services. As stated above, these indicators neglect the fact that a reduction of energy inputs (holding production constant) can ultimately be achieved only by the increased input of other factors of production. For example, a ton of steel can be produced with less energy if blast furnaces are better insulated. This however means an increase in the use of insulation materials, and therefore of capital in the form of building investment. If the reduction of energy inputs results from technological advances, an increase in expertise or of human capital (achieved through education of the workforce) is required.

Generally, provision of goods and services requires the input of factors of production whose scarcity is expressed by their price (neglecting external effects at this point). Energy is one such scarce factor of production, whose money value can be compared with the money value of outputs produced. Examples of such efficiency indicators are

$$\frac{\text{rental payments received}}{\text{energy input of the building}}, \quad \frac{\text{value added}}{\text{energy input}}.$$

The first of the two is still a one-dimensional concept, whereas the second can be said to measure efficiency in the economic sense because value added comprises the whole set of goods and services produced by an economy. Its inverse is often called 'energy intensity of a country's Gross Domestic Product GDP'.

The efficiency indicators cited not only serve to describe and forecast energy demand but also assume the status of norms because the supply and consumption of energy is intricately tied to problems of sustainability and environmental degradation. From a normative perspective, energy efficiency means conversion of energy with the lowest possible losses. This view is beyond dispute in the public debate, but only as long as the cost of preventing these losses is neglected. Energy efficiency is enhanced by better resource management or by replacing devices with unfavorable energy ratings. Both cases imply substitution processes: Better resource management calls for the substitution of energy by human capital and know-how, while the upgrading of devices entails the substitution of energy by capital.

These processes are often associated with the term 'energy savings'. However, energy savings differ from efficiency improvements in the following ways:

- Energy savings can be forced upon consumers to the extent that they are caused by technical failures or supply shocks resulting from political, social, and military tensions and conflicts. In an attempt to ensure a fair distribution of energy, governments often resort to rationing, e.g. by using fuel cards and rotating brownouts and blackouts in the case of electricity or natural gas. None of these measures affect energy efficiency.
- Energy savings may be consumers' response to a price hike, causing them to curtail their demand for energy, as well as for energy services and energy-intensive products. For example, let heating oil become more expensive relative to other goods. The expected response is a lowering of room temperature during the heating season, resulting in a decline in energy consumption.[4] Other substitution strategies include moving to a smaller residence, replacing a mid-sized passenger car by a compact one, and switching to public transport for commuting. These strategies are remotely related to energy efficiency in that e.g. at smaller residence may also require less heating oil per square meter of floor space.
- Energy savings are often hoped for as a consequence of 'changed values' or 'change in lifestyle', i.e. a change in consumer preferences. Some experts even make normative statements, urging households and businesses to adopt new standards of behavior in consideration of global warming and the exhaustion of fossil fuel resources. In fact, most consumers in advanced economies would suffer little loss in terms of their quality of life if they were to marginally reduce their consumption of energy. Yet, changes in lifestyle have not occurred on a noticeable scale to this day, supporting the economic view that preferences are not easily modified.

Engineers are able to point out a multitude of opportunities for increasing energy efficiency. However, decision-making in the economic sphere revolves around the provision of energy services at minimum cost. There is an interest in enhancing energy efficiency only to the extent that the corresponding investment pays off. The relevant parameters are the associated (extra) investment outlay ΔI, the attainable reduction in energy consumption energy ΔE [kWh/a], the expected price of energy p_E [EUR/kWh], and the present value factor $PVF_{i,T}$ (see Sect. 3.2) which depends on the investor's planning horizon T. When comparing alternatives for producing a given quantity of energy service, the investor will select the one promising the highest rate of return, given by the annuity AN,

$$AN = \frac{-\Delta I}{PVF_{i,T}} + p_E \ \Delta E > 0 \qquad (4.18)$$

---

[4]At an average outside temperature of 4 °C, lowering the room temperature from 21 °C to 20 °C leads to an energy saving of 4%.

which needs to be positive to begin with. The first term is the investment outlay distributed over the T years of the project, taking into account the rate of interest i that could be earned on the capital market. The second term shows the return in terms of avoided expenditure on energy.

Dividing the inequality by ΔE and solving for p_E shows that the price of energy places an upper bound on the annuitized investment outlay per unit energy conserved,

$$CCE = \frac{\Delta I}{\Delta E} \frac{1}{PVF_{i,T}} < p_E \; . \tag{4.19}$$

Thus, the so-called (marginal) cost of conserved energy (CCE) must not exceed the unit price of the energy whose consumption can be reduced. Note that the maximum-return solution is equivalent to a least-cost solution (calling for minimum capital user cost which is again an annuity).

However, minimum-cost planning often clashes with the attainment of maximum energy efficiency, the engineer's preferred solution. This is illustrated by Fig. 4.4, taking the insulation of a building as an example. A typical engineer would like to push insulation to the point where the investor does not lose money, implying that the project has a net present value (and hence annuity) of zero (indicated by point C). However, investors seek to maximize the net present value of the project, leading them to opt for a degree of insulation that minimizes their user cost of capital (recall that their capital has alternative uses, also outside the energy sector). The investor's optimum is marked as point B. Compared to the initial point A, there is an improvement of energy efficiency, which however still falls short of point C, which engineers consider economically viable.

Optimization of energy efficiency is not easy in actual practice. Reductions in energy consumption depend on users' individual behavior, which is unpredictable for the investor. In addition, devices often fail to reach their nameplate energy ratings. For instance, the newest generation of offshore wind turbines has been reported to have more downtime due to repair and maintenance than expected. Quite generally, the possibility of seemingly viable projects turning into loss-making ones cannot be ruled out.

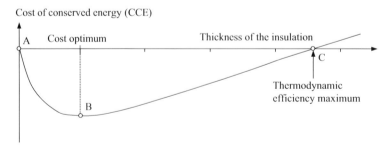

Fig. 4.4 Energy efficiency: engineering and economic definitions

4.3.2 Determining Energy Efficiency Potential

Often, more than just one opportunity for investment in energy efficiency presents itself. This situation calls for a ranking of projects according to their (marginal) cost of conserved energy (*CCE*), resulting in the staggered schedule labeled 'theoretical potential' of Fig. 4.5. In accordance with inequality (4.19), the *CCE* values are compared to the unit price p_E of avoided energy consumption. Note that p_E corresponds to the marginal return on investment. For the attainment of economic efficiency, marginal cost needs to equal marginal return. This condition is satisfied at point A of the figure.

A further complication is that efficiency-enhancing measures may influence each other. For example, installing turbines that are more efficient in converting hydro power into electricity often makes economic sense only if the voltage of power lines delivering the energy generated is increased as well. However, the efficiency gain thanks to higher voltage is limited by the capacity of the entire network. This bottleneck may prevent the new turbines from reaching their nameplate efficiency.

An iterative procedure is necessary in the presence of multiple projects. The initial step is to select the measure with the lowest *CCE* value, as before. Next, the marginal cost of all other measures needs to be calculated anew, adjusting their multipliers $\Delta I/\Delta E$ (see inequality (4.19) once again). Usually, this adjustment is upward, indicating that a given reduction in energy consumption now requires an increased investment. If the next-best investment still satisfies inequality (4.19), it can be added to the program—again with the consequence that the *CCE* values of the remaining projects have to be determined anew. Note that this procedure still revolves around theoretically given efficiency potentials.

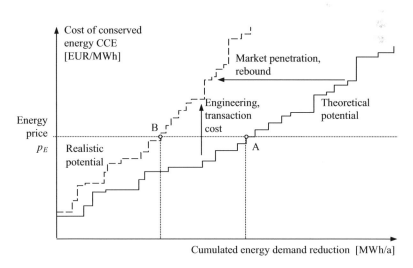

Fig. 4.5 Theoretical and achievable efficiency potentials

Yet theoretical potentials cannot be achieved in actual practice, as indicated by the distance between the dashed and solid schedules shown in Fig. 4.5. The gap between them has several causes:

- The implementation of efficiency-enhancing measures entails transaction costs, for example, for planning, engineering, and financing.
- According to the so-called rebound effect, energy efficiency measures have a much smaller impact on energy consumption than anticipated by simple calculations. A successfully implemented efficiency measure causes the cost of the associated energy service to decline, but this may stimulate the demand for this service. The increased efficiency of lighting provides a famous example. It lowers the cost of lighting but multiplies the use of electric light. A more indirect rebound effect is that the lowered cost of an energy service (e.g. space heating) enables consumers to purchase more other goods and services, which may have substantial energy requirements of their own.
- The so-called persistence effect refers to inertia on the part of investors and consumers, stating that efficiency-enhancing measures and investments are undertaken only when appliances, buildings, and vehicles need to be replaced.

There are economically viable prospects for the reduction of energy consumption (corresponding to point B of Fig. 4.5), as has been confirmed in many empirical studies. However, the effective amount of attainable reduction remains contested ground. Many observers attribute the gap between theoretical and effective potential to market failure, a topic taken up next.

4.3.3 Energy Efficiency: A Case of Market Failure?

Engineering specialists often claim that even cost-minimizing measures designed to improve energy efficiency are not undertaken. Since the markets involved (for appliances, buildings, and vehicles as well as engineering services) are reasonably competitive, there is no reason to suspect suppression of innovation by a monopolist. Economists have advanced the following explanations (see Sorrell 2004 in particular). On the whole, they suggest that much of what is seen as market failure by engineers, environmentalists, and politicians in fact reflect rational decisions by households and businesses.

- Perceived irrelevance of efficiency-enhancing measures: Research has shown that many energy consumers—large and small—have little knowledge of the options, technologies, and costs of efficiency-enhancing measures. Yet from an economic point of view, this ignorance can be rational. After all, information gathering entails costly effort (e.g. management time) with certainty, while returns are uncertain (they are zero if one finds inequality (4.19) not to be satisfied). Applying the economic decision rule, "marginal cost equal expected marginal return", risk-averse potential investors stop collecting information at

4.3 Energy Efficiency

an early stage. In addition, their perception that effort directed at improvements in energy efficiency do not pay off may make them put expected returns close to zero, preventing information gathering from the beginning. Expectations of slowly rising prices or taxation of energy are hardly sufficient to change this. It likely takes shock-like energy price hikes and supply crises for the decision rule cited above to be affected.

- Divergence of decision-making powers (investor/user problem): In many cases, the economic benefits of an efficiency-enhancing measure do not accrue to the investor. An important example is the case of rental housing. While owners pay for improved heat insulation and more efficient boilers, tenants benefit from the reduction in energy expenditure. It is easy to conclude that owners lack the economic incentive to implement these measures. However, this may not be fully true as soon as a change of occupancy is considered. Potential new tenants will likely consider the total cost of housing, which includes outlays on energy. This gives owners an incentive to invest in energy efficiency.
- Myopia of decision-makers (see Hausman and Joskow 1982): Potential investors demand so-called payback times of a few months (in the case of households) or a few years (in the case of companies) when it comes to energy efficiency. This means that the reduction in energy expenditure must be sufficient to 'pay back' the investment outlay over a short time period. In terms of inequality (4.19) above, investors either think that they have alternatives outside the energy sector yielding a high internal rate of return IRR or estimate the useful life T of the project to be short, either resulting in a low value of $AVF_{i,T}$. This behavior of course clashes with the requirements of the energy economy, which tends to revolve around big investments with long payback periods.

Table 4.4 presents an example of two electrical heating systems A and B that have identical properties except that B is more efficient but calls for a higher investment outlay. Its extra investment outlay ΔI amounts to 2830 EUR. In return, its energy consumption is lower by 4500 kWh/year than B's. According to $AVF_{0.1,10} = 6.145$, the investment outlay is to be distributed over 6.145 (rather than 10) years. Capital user cost thus amounts to 2830/6.145 = 460.5 EUR annually, or 0.102 EUR/kWh, respectively. This is the cost of conserved energy CCE. As it is below 0.15 EUR/kWh, the assumed electricity price, the energy-efficient alternative B would be profitable. To calculate the internal rate of return IRR of this project, one has to set $AN = 0$ in condition (4.18) and solve for $PVF_{i,T}$,

$$PVF_{i,T} = \frac{\Delta I}{p_E \, \Delta E} = \frac{2830}{675} = 4.192. \qquad (4.20)$$

Using trial-and-error over the interest rate i, it turns out that (4.20) holds for an interest rate $i = 20\%$ (assuming $T = 10$ years).

An internal rate of return of 20% is comparatively high; still, there are empirical studies showing that many projects designed to improve energy efficiency are not realized although their IRR exceeds that of other investments. This absence of

Table 4.4 Sample calculation of an investment into energy efficiency

	Conventional appliance A	Efficient appliance B	Difference A − B
Investment (EUR)	20,000	22,830	2830
Electricity requirement (kWh/a)	13,000	8500	−4500
Electricity price p_E (EUR/kWh)	0.15	0.15	0.15
Expenditure on electricity (EUR/a)	1950	1275	−675
Expected useful life (years)	10	10	10
Annuity value factor $PVF_{0.1;\ 10}$ with $i = 10\%$ and $T = 10$ years[a]			6.145
Cost of conserved energy CCE (EUR/kWh)[b]			0.102
Internal rate of return IRR			20%

[a]See Table 3.1; [b]See inequality (4.19)

so-called interest arbitrage normally is interpreted as a sign of irrationality. Yet there are reasons to doubt this interpretation:

- Companies are often subject to credit rationing, meaning that banks limit the amount of finance provided. Given limited financing, companies must set investment priorities. However, investments in energy efficiency are usually regarded as less important for economic survival than investments in new products or market development, causing them to be shelved despite high expected returns.
- Returns on investments in energy efficiency are often high as a result of public subsidies; yet governments may fail to honor their commitments. In fact, the public sector often is the laggard in terms of energy efficiency when it comes to its buildings and infrastructure.
- Companies outside the energy sector are not familiar with the peculiarities and uncertainties of energy markets. For them, investment in energy efficiency is fraught with increased risk, causing them to demand a higher expected rate of return (note that interest arbitrage in fact means equality of risk-adjusted rates of return).
- Investors may also suffer from an asymmetry of information. They have to rely on the advice of experts or product descriptions for estimating expected reductions in energy expenditure. Since this information is rarely impartial, they may deem such estimates to be overly optimistic.
- The useful life of an investment in energy efficiency often falls short of its expected value. For instance, a household may have to move in search of employment. Prospective buyers are usually not willing to honor the extra investment outlay in full, causing the investment in energy efficiency to not fully pay off.
- Regarding alleged myopia, decision-makers expect future technological change, which will cause a fall in the value of their investment. By deferring their decision, they retain the option of realizing the project later, benefitting from

4.3 Energy Efficiency

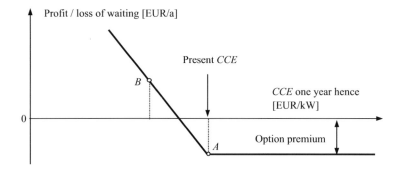

Fig. 4.6 Waiting as a real option

an increased *IRR*. Of course, this option comes at a price, which is equal to the opportunity cost of not investing, i.e. the forgone reduction of energy expenditure in the present context.

Figure 4.6 illustrates the optional nature of an unimplemented efficiency-enhancing measure. Its horizontal axis depicts the value of the asset (liability if negative) considered 1 year hence (the 'underlying' in the jargon of finance). In this case, this is a potential liability whose value amounts to the cost of conserved energy *CCE*. Should the *CCE* value be lower than at present (e.g. corresponding to point *B*), then the decision-maker is happy to have deferred his or her decision; the option is 'in the money'. At point *A*, the *CCE* value 1 year later is the same as at present. In this case, the investor already bears a cost in the guise of the forgone reduction of energy expenditure $p_E \cdot \Delta E$. Conversely, the *CCE* value may turn out to be higher 1 year later, e.g. because wages of construction workers have increased. In this case, the investor regrets having waited: the option is 'out of the money'. The price to be paid for the waiting is called the 'option premium'. It equals to $p_E \cdot \Delta E$, the forgone reduction of energy expenditure. Note that that $p_E \cdot \Delta E$ does not vary with *CCE*, making it a constant.

Yet how can one judge whether waiting pays or not? The answer to this question requires the determination of the option premium, which is the topic of real options theory (see e.g. Schwartz and Trigeorgis 2004 and Sect. 3.6).

4.3.4 Contracting

In markets characterized by asymmetry of information and interest arbitrage, there is scope for intermediaries. In the case of improvements in energy efficiency, the function of the intermediary is assumed by so-called contractors. They provide customers (owners or operators of property, swimming pools, hospitals, industrial plant, and exhibition parks, to name just a few) with specialized services. These services include the analysis, planning, installation, financing, management, servicing, and maintenance of efficiency-enhancing investments. In the case of a block heating power station, the services may comprise capacity planning, financing, the construction of the plant, and optimization of daily operations. At contract expiry, the facility is handed over to its final owner. Contractors benefit from the interest arbitrage explained above. They can derive a profit from the difference between the internal rate of return on investments in energy efficiency and the rate they have to pay on the capital market.

The commissioning of a specialist contractor can be attractive for customers who do not want to be exposed to the risks associated with energy supply while benefitting from the cost reductions afforded by improvements in energy efficiency. Yet contracting is not without its own costs and risks, which prevent it from reaching its full potential in actual practice. The following problems can be cited:

- A contracting project calls for an evaluation of the future energy requirements and an identification of the cost-minimizing portfolio of efficiency-enhancing measures. These activities can be quite costly.
- Improvements in efficiency imply that energy requirements fall over time. However, they may rise again because the customer boosts production in order to meet an increased demand for its goods and services. Therefore, the net present value of the project can only be determined through modeling.
- Conflicts over the terms and conditions of the contract may arise. For a banal example, is the contractor or the final owner, represented by the facility manager, responsible for the replacement of a defective light?
- Conflicts also may arise because of changes in laws and regulations during the life of the contract that were not foreseen at its conclusion. They typically cause delays, which tie up costly capital. Who is to bear the extra capital user cost?
- Contractors usually do not have rights to the property upon which the facility (e.g. a block heating plant) is built. They therefore lack collateral in the event that the customer becomes insolvent before contract expiry.[5]
- Contracting projects in the rental housing market have limited appeal to final owners as long as they cannot shift costs incurred to their tenants. However, there are still legal ambiguities to be resolved in this context.
- When a contract approaches expiry, contractors are tempted to act opportunistically, neglecting their servicing and maintenance obligations. The consequence is that promised improvements of energy efficiency (and hence rates of return on investment) are not achieved. Doubts about the reliability of service providers weaken potential customers' interest in the contracting business model.

Clearly, contracting projects must generate significant cost savings to be realized. In the past, they have been largely confined to the public sector. There,

---

[5]Because of their low risk of insolvency, public authorities are preferred customers in the contracting business.

authorities are caught between a lack of financing in view of budget deficits and pressure to improve maintenance of public properties while saving on energy-related operating cost. For them, contracting is an attractive solution. With increasing experience, rising prices of energy prices, and support by public authorities such as the European Commission, contracting may in future expand to the private sector.

References

Brendemoen, A. (1994). *Car ownership decisions in Norwegian households*. Discussion Papers SSB 116. Oslo: Statistics Norway.

Greene, W. C. (2011). *Econometric analysis* (7th ed.). New York: Prentice Hall.

Hausman, J. A., & Joskow, P. A. (1982). Evaluating the costs and benefits of appliance efficiency standards. *American Economic Review, 72*, 220–225.

Henkel, J. (2013). *Modeling the diffusion of innovative heating systems in Germany – decision criteria, influence of policy instruments and vintage path dependencies*. Dissertation. TU Berlin.

Hensher, D. A., Rose, J. M., et al. (2005). *Applied choice analysis*. Cambridge: Cambridge University Press.

McFadden, D. (1974). The measurement of urban travel demand. *Journal of Public Economics, 3*, 303–328.

Schwartz, E., & Trigeorgis, L. (Eds.). (2004). *Real options and investment under uncertainty*. Cambridge, MA: MIT Press.

Sorrell, S. (2004). Understanding barriers to energy efficiency. In S. Sorrell et al. (Eds.), *The economics of energy efficiency. Barriers to cost-effective investment* (pp. 25–93). Cheltenham: Edward Elgar.

Top-Down Analysis of Energy Demand 5

The practical use of bottom-up models for analyzing energy demand is faced with significant micro-data requirements. In order to keep such models manageable, the individual components of energy demand are usually linked to the same macroeconomic variables such as the Gross Domestic Product (GDP), per-capita income, and relative energy prices. This gives rise to the question, "Why not model energy demand directly as a function of these macro variables?". This macro approach is presented in this chapter, exploring the role of population growth, economic growth, and in particular changes in relative prices. However, this approach raises issues of its own:

- How does one differentiate between short-term and long-term adjustments of demand?
- Do rising and declining prices have the same effect on energy demand?
- How can the effects of technological change be isolated from the effects of changes in energy prices?
- Is the relationship between energy and other production inputs, in particular capital, substitutive or complementary?

Issues not discussed in this chapter include the possible instability of estimated relationships over time and reverse causality, i.e. the fact that GDP may not be exogenous but is in turn influenced by the price of energy (as evidenced by the recessions caused by the two oil price shocks of 1973/1974 and 1979/1980).

The variables used in this chapter are:

C	Total cost
c	Unit cost
ΔE	Change in demand for energy, $E_{t+1} - E_t$
E_t	Energy demand in period t
GDP	Gross Domestic Product
$\eta_{E,GDP}$	Income elasticity of energy demand
$\eta_{E,p}$	Price elasticity of energy demand

K	Capital stock
L	Labor
M	Input of materials
p	Price index
p_E	(Inflation-adjusted) energy price index
PCI	Per-capita income
POP	Population
Q	Real output (quantity)
sh	Cost share
σ	Elasticity of substitution

5.1 Population Growth

A first approach to top-down modeling is the following tautological relationship between population POP_t and the aggregate energy demand E_t,

$$E_t = POP_t \frac{E_t}{POP_t}. \tag{5.1}$$

Because

$$\frac{d\log E}{dE} = 1/E, \quad d\log E = \frac{dE}{E} \quad \text{holds, and hence} \tag{5.2}$$

$$\frac{\Delta E_t}{E_t} \approx \frac{\Delta POP_t}{POP_t} + \frac{\Delta(E_t/POP_t)}{(E_t/POP_t)}. \tag{5.3}$$

Therefore, the logarithmic differentiation of Eq. (5.1) yields the percentage change in energy demand as the sum of the percentage change in population and the per-capita energy demand, at least to a first approximation. The development of the demand for energy is thus tautologically given by the sum of population growth and change of per-capita energy consumption.

Table 5.1 shows the corresponding values and their percentage changes between 2000 and 2011. In 2011, the world population of nearly 7 bn people consumed 12.7 bn toe of commercial energy. However, while the per-capita energy consumption in China grew by no less than 7.5% p.a., it declined in several developed countries. Evidently there must be other factors at work beyond population growth that explain the demand for energy and its trend. Population growth alone is a misleading indicator.

However, population is of importance in a different context. Table 5.1 reveals substantial differences in per-capita energy consumption between countries. In the United States it is roughly twice as high as in Germany or Japan. With 0.17 toe per capita, the figure for Indonesia (as of 2011) is at the other end of the spectrum. The

Table 5.1 Population and per-capita primary energy supply

	Population 2011 (mn)	Change 2000–2011 (% p.a.)	Primary energy per capita 2011 (toe)	Change 2000–2011 (% p.a.)
Brazil	196.9	1.1	1.37	2.2
China	1344.1	0.6	2.03	7.5
France	65.3	0.6	3.87	−0.6
Germany	81.8	0.0	3.81	−0.6
India	243.8	1.4	3.07	3.1
Indonesia	1221.2	1.5	0.17	1.3
Italy	59.4	0.4	2.82	−0.6
Japan	127.8	0.1	3.61	−1.1
Nigeria	164.2	2.7	0.72	−0.2
Pakistan	176.2	1.9	0.48	0.7
Russia	143.0	−0.2	5.11	1.8
Turkey	73.1	1.3	1.54	2.2
United Kingdom	63.3	0.7	2.97	−2.2
United States	311.6	0.9	7.03	−1.2

Data source: World Bank (2014)

international disparities in energy consumption can be visualized by the so-called Lorenz curve. On the horizontal axis of Fig. 5.1, countries are ranked according to their shares of the world's population, with e.g. China accounting for the first 20%. The vertical axis exhibits the countries' respective shares of global energy consumption. If per-capita energy consumption were completely equal among countries, the Lorenz curve would be a diagonal running from point (0; 0) to point (1; 1). With increasing inequality, the Lorenz curve moves away from this straight line. According to the solid line, 60% of the world population accounted for only 17% of energy consumption in 2002.[1]

Yet the dashed Lorenz curve of Fig. 5.1 shows that income inequality between countries is even more marked than energy inequality, with 60% of the world population disposing of about 8% of world income only. This difference is an expression of the fact that energy has to be regarded as an essential good. Poor people devote a bigger share of their income to it than the rich. This observation suggests that the demand for energy increases less than proportionally with increasing income. Therefore, the so-called income elasticity of energy demand is smaller than one in the long run (see Sect. 5.2).

The World Energy Council (1993) stipulated 1.5 toe per capita as the benchmark to ensure economic and social development. This implies that global energy consumption would have to be about 40% higher than at present. The extent to

---

[1]This figure is not based on individual energy consumption but country-wide per-capita consumption. The Lorenz curve would look even more convex if referring to individual consumption values.

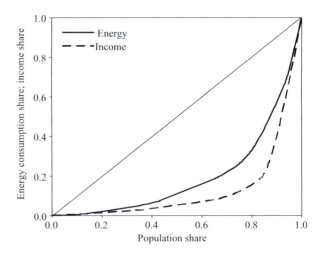

Fig. 5.1 Lorenz curves of the global energy consumption and income distribution. Data source: World Bank (2014)

which this postulate will be realized depends decisively on investment in energy technology, which in turn is driven by returns expected by investors and ability to pay of consumers.

5.2 Economic Growth

An increasing Gross Domestic Product (GDP) and the associated creation of value usually require an increased use of energy while at the same time leading to an improved capacity to pay for it. Similar to the tautology of Sect. 5.1, GDP can be inserted in the following way, with PCI_t denoting per-capita income,

$$E_t = POP_t \cdot \frac{GDP_t}{POP_t} \cdot \frac{E_t}{GDP_t} = POP_t \cdot PCI_t \cdot \frac{E_t}{GDP_t}. \tag{5.4}$$

After taking logarithms, the relative change in energy demand can be expressed as the sum of relative population growth, per-capita income growth, and the change in so-called energy intensity E_t/GDP_t,

$$\frac{\Delta E_t}{E_t} \approx \frac{\Delta POP_t}{POP_t} + \frac{\Delta PCI_t}{PCI_t} + \frac{\Delta(E_t/GDP_t)}{(E_t/GDP_t)}. \tag{5.5}$$

According to Table 5.2, energy intensity has decreased substantially between 2000 and 2011 in all countries sampled. Hence, consumption of energy has been increasing less than per-capita income, implying that the income elasticity of energy demand $\eta_{E,GDP}$ is smaller than one. It is defined as follows (see Eq. 5.2),

5.2 Economic Growth

Table 5.2 Development of population, per-capita income, and energy intensity

Development 2000–2011	Population (% p.a.)	Per-capita income (% p.a.)	Energy intensity (% p.a.)	Primary energy consumption (% p.a.)
Brazil	1.1	2.4	−0.2	3.4
China	0.6	9.7	−2.1	8.1
France	0.6	0.6	−1.2	0.0
Germany	0.0	1.2	−1.8	−0.7
India	1.4	5.9	−2.6	4.6
Indonesia	1.5	3.9	−2.5	2.8
Italy	0.4	0.0	−0.6	−0.2
Japan	0.1	0.6	−1.7	−1.1
Nigeria	2.7	5.7	−5.6	2.5
Pakistan	1.9	2.2	−1.4	2.6
Russia	−0.2	5.0	−3.1	1.5
Turkey	1.3	2.9	−0.7	3.6
United Kingdom	0.7	1.1	−3.2	−1.5
United States	0.9	0.7	−1.9	−0.3

Data source: EIA (2014)

$$\eta_{E,GDP} = \frac{\text{percent change of } E}{\text{percent change of } GDP} = \frac{\partial \ln E}{\partial \ln GDP} = \frac{\partial E}{\partial GDP} \frac{GDP}{E}. \quad (5.6)$$

Here, the partial derivative indicates the *ceteris paribus* condition: the other determinants of energy demand (among them, the relative price of energy in particular) are held constant (see Sect. 5.3).

In normal circumstances, the income elasticity of energy demand is positive. The following distinctions can be made.

- $0 < \eta_{E,GDP} < 1$: In this case energy intensity E/GDP declines with growing income.
- $\eta_{E,GDP} > 1$: In this case the opposite holds. This is typical of developing countries, many of which are characterized by a backlog of demand at the going price.[2] This backlog is usually created by an artificially low price of energy imposed by the government.
- In the case of $\eta_{E,GDP} = 1$, energy intensity is independent of income.

---

[2]This statement serves as a reminder that actual energy consumption is interpreted as the outcome of supply and demand, both of which depend (among other things) on the relative price of energy. However, when the government fixes price below its equilibrium value, the quantity demanded exceeds the quantity supplied, creating a backlog in demand.

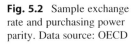

Fig. 5.2 Sample exchange rate and purchasing power parity. Data source: OECD

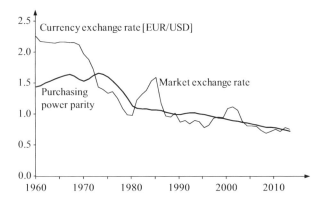

When GDP data of different years are to be compared, adjustment for inflation is necessary, as explained in Sect. 3.3. For international comparisons of energy intensity, one also has to convert GDP values expressed in national currency into a common currency (e.g. USD or EUR). In view of short-term exchange rate fluctuations, the average of a year (1995 in Table 5.2) or an average over several years (as is World Bank practice) may be the appropriate choice for depicting development over time.

Currency conversion can also be based on purchasing power parity (PPP), estimates of which are published by the OECD and the World Bank. This is a virtual exchange rate between two currencies, based on the notion that tradable goods have the same price everywhere. For example, if a hamburger costs 4 USD in the United States but 3 EUR in France (say), then 1 USD is apparently worth 0.75 EUR. When the hamburger is replaced by a basket of goods and services, one obtains the PPP. For most developing countries the application of PPP results in higher GDP values and hence lower estimates of energy intensity.[3] While exchange rates between industrialized countries tend to be closer to PPP values, there are deviations even in the EUR-USD exchange rate, as shown in Fig. 5.2.

5.3 The Price of Energy

The price of energy and its development over time (relative to the prices of other goods and services) are crucial determinants of the demand for energy. Considering the swath of energy prices, it is not easy to calculate a representative energy price index. Even for a given energy source, more than one price often exists. An

---

[3]The difficulty here is to establish the appropriate basket of goods and services. Goods and services have different weights between countries. In addition, price differences are justified by quality differentials, which must be filtered out. An alternative to taking a comprehensive basket of goods is to select one single good that is globally available. In the hamburger example, this results in the so-called Big Mac parity.

aggregated energy price index is constructed by weighting energy sources by their market shares. Since economic theory predicts that demand mainly depends on relative prices besides income or wealth, this index must be related to a macroeconomic price index (consumer price index, producer price index, or price index of the GDP). This ratio is often called the real price of energy. An increase over time signifies that energy prices grow faster than the average price of goods and services in general.

5.3.1 Short-Term and Long-Term Price Elasticities

Similar to the income elasticity, the energy own-price elasticity (often simply called price elasticity for short) is defined by using a change in the real price of energy p_E as the impulse,

$$\eta_{E,p_E} = \frac{\text{percent change of } E}{\text{percent change of } p_E} = \frac{\partial \ln E}{\partial \ln p_E} = \frac{\partial E}{\partial p_E} \frac{p_E}{E}. \tag{5.7}$$

Here as well, several cases need to be distinguished.

- $-1 < \eta_{E,p_E} < 0$: The demand for energy is inelastic (to price). If the price of energy goes up (relative to the rate of inflation), the quantity of energy demanded declines less than proportionally (e.g. price goes up 10% but quantity sold only 4%, leaving a bottom line of 6% to sellers). This implies that inelastic demand results in a strong market position for suppliers (often called a seller's market).
- $\eta_{E,p_E} < -1$: Demand for energy is elastic. If the (relative) price of energy increases, the quantity demanded declines more than proportionally (for instance a 10% price hike triggers a 12% fall in quantity sold, resulting in a bottom line of -2%). Elastic demand causes the market position of consumers to be strong (often called a buyer's market).

When energy markets become tight, the relative price of energy rises and the quantity traded decreases. This situation is shown in Fig. 5.3, where the supply curve shifts to the left. The original market equilibrium A is replaced by the one at point B, where the new supply function intersects with the short-term energy demand function. At first, a marked price hike combines with a limited decrease in quantity because immediate adjustment would be very costly for consumers. They often need to undertake an investment (e.g. by buying a car with higher fuel efficiency), a decision that is made only if the price change is viewed as permanent. Once undertaken, consumer adjustment gives rise to the long-term demand function (dotted line in Fig. 5.3), which is flatter (more price elastic) than its short-term counterpart and thus lies closer to the origin in the neighborhood of point B. This indicates reduced energy consumption at a given price, at least in the neighborhood of the initial equilibrium. Compared to B, the energy price drops slightly while the

Fig. 5.3 Short-term and long-term effects of a reduction in energy supply

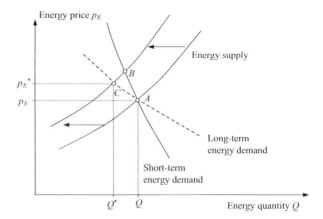

quantity traded continues to decrease until the new long-term equilibrium C is reached.

In normal circumstances, energy demand is a composite of demand for different energy sources E_i, $i = 1, \ldots, N$ with their relative prices p_i. This consideration gives rise to an extended definition of price elasticity,

$$\eta_{i,j} = \frac{\text{percent change of } E_i}{\text{percent change of } p_j} = \frac{\partial \ln E_i}{\partial \ln p_j} = \frac{\partial E_i}{\partial p_j} \frac{p_j}{E_i}. \quad (5.8)$$

For $i = j$ one obtains the own-price elasticity, for $i \neq j$ a so-called cross-price elasticity. While normally the own-price elasticity is negative, the cross-price elasticity can be of either sign. If the energy sources considered are substitutes, it is positive because a price increase $dp_j > 0$ leads to a response $dE_j < 0$, which triggers more demand for E_i, thus $dE_i > 0$. Yet E_i and E_j can also be complementary, in which case the cross-price elasticity is negative. A price increase $dp_j > 0$ again leads to a response $dE_j < 0$, which now causes a reduction $dE_i < 0$ in the complementary input E_i.

5.3.2 A Partial Energy Demand Model

A popular specification of a partial demand model reads[4]

$$E(t) = \alpha \cdot GDP(t)^\beta \cdot p_E(t)^\gamma. \quad (5.9)$$

---

[4]This approach can be understood as the result of the maximization of a so-called constant elasticity utility function, with energy and all other goods (at the price of 1) as its arguments, on the condition that the GDP is equivalent to income. See Varian (1992), Sect. 7.5.

5.3 The Price of Energy

Here, $E(t)$ symbolizes aggregate energy demand (in physical units), $GDP(t)$, the real (inflation-adjusted) Gross Domestic Product, and $p_E(t)$ the relative price of energy.

This formulation is partial rather than of the general-equilibrium type for three reasons:

- Consider a drop in the quantity of energy transacted. As the oil price shocks of 1973/1974 and 1979/1980 clearly demonstrated, this does not leave GDP unaffected. Therefore a reverse causality exists, running from $E(t)$ to $GDP(t)$.
- The observed consumption of energy is the outcome of an interaction between supply and demand. For example, if an increase in GDP causes the demand function to shift outward, the relative price of energy is predicted to go up. This time, causality runs from $GDP(t)$ to $p_E(t)$; superficially, it even seems to run from $E(t)$ to $p_E(t)$, indicating reverse causation.
- For all its importance, energy is just one factor of production both for households and firms. Therefore, a change in the relative price of energy has repercussions on the mix of factors of production. As a consequence, energy price developments may change inputs of other factors of production, which has an impact not only on the composition but also the size of GDP.

In keeping with the partial approach, economic theory indeed states that aggregate energy demand is determined by income and the relative price of energy. A mostly analogous formulation to Eq. (5.9) is

$$\frac{E(t)}{POP(t)} = \alpha \cdot \left(\frac{GDP(t)}{POP(t)}\right)^\beta \cdot p_E(t)^\gamma \qquad (5.10)$$

with POP denoting the resident population. While the parameter α is a constant determining the general level of demand, β represents the income elasticity, and γ the price elasticity, respectively. This can be shown either by taking logarithms or by partial differentiation. In the latter case, one obtains

$$\frac{\partial E(t)}{\partial GDP(t)} = \alpha \cdot \beta \cdot GDP(t)^{\beta-1} \cdot p_E(t)^\gamma = \beta \cdot \frac{E(t)}{GDP(t)}. \qquad (5.11)$$

Multiplication of both sides by $GDP(t)/E(t)$ yields β as the income elasticity $\eta_{E, GDP}$. Turning to the relative price of energy, one has

$$\frac{\partial E(t)}{\partial p_E(t)} = \alpha \cdot GDP(t)^\beta \cdot \gamma \cdot p_E(t)^{\gamma-1} = \gamma \cdot \frac{E(t)}{p_E(t)}. \qquad (5.12)$$

Multiplication by $p_E(t)/E(t)$ shows that $\gamma = \eta_{E,P_e}$.

As it stands, the partial model does not permit to distinguish between short-term and long-term elasticities. This distinction is important because current energy consumption is the result of a reaction not only to current income and price, but also to past incomes and prices through the inherited stock of energy-using capital. This also implies that current energy consumption is to some extent determined by past energy consumption. The stronger this link, the longer it takes for a change in income or price to exert its full impact.

Two variants of this modified demand model are discussed in the literature. The stock adjustment hypothesis posits that consumers orient themselves to a desired (planned) energy consumption $E_p(t)$, which is a function of the desired stock of energy-using capital. In addition, the hypothesis assumes that this stock and hence planned energy consumption is determined by current income and the current relative price of energy, resulting in

$$E_p(t) = \alpha \cdot GDP(t)^\beta \cdot p_E(t)^\gamma. \tag{5.13}$$

During any given period t, however, there is a discrepancy between desired and actual (inherited) stock because adjustment is partial in view of its cost. If adjustment is completed up to a portion $(1-\rho)$ of the gap while ρ still is to be undertaken, one has

$$E(t) = E_p(t)^{1-\rho} \cdot E(t-1)^\rho \quad \text{with } 0 < \rho < 1. \tag{5.14}$$

The parameter ρ reflects the speed of adjustment. In the case of $\rho = 0$, adaptation to new market conditions happens without any delay, while in the case $\rho = 1$ no adjustment occurs at all. Note that ρ is to some degree an economic decision variable reflecting the benefits and costs of fast versus slow adjustment. This adjustment of the stock of energy-using capital is not explicitly modeled, in contrast with Eq. (4.1).

By substituting Eq. (5.14) into (5.13), one obtains according to the stock adjustment hypothesis,

$$E(t) = \alpha^{1-\rho} \cdot GDP(t)^{\beta \cdot (1-\rho)} \cdot p_E(t)^{\gamma \cdot (1-\rho)} \cdot E(t-1)^\rho. \tag{5.15}$$

The second approach is called habit persistence hypothesis. It states that the energy consumption $E(t)$ of period t is a function of expected future income $GDP^e(t)$ and expected relative energy price $p_E^e(t)$ rather than their current values,

$$E(t) = \alpha \cdot GDP^e(t)^\beta \cdot p_E^e(t)^\gamma. \tag{5.16}$$

Of course, an auxiliary hypothesis concerning the formation of expectations is needed. A popular alternative has been adaptive expectations, meaning that expectations are formed as an extrapolation from previous and current observation. If again a geometric mean is postulated, the pertinent functions read

$$\begin{aligned} GDP^e(t) &= GDP^e(t-1)^\rho \cdot GDP(t)^{1-\rho}, \\ p_E^e(t) &= p_E^e(t-1)^\rho \cdot p_E(t)^{1-\rho}. \end{aligned} \tag{5.17}$$

5.3 The Price of Energy

Here, $0 < \rho < 1$ denotes the parameter of adjustment as before, which now refers to expectations rather than the stock of energy-using capital. By substituting these expressions into Eq. (5.15) and taking into account

$$E(t-1)^{\rho} = \alpha^{\rho} \cdot GDP^{e}(t-1)^{\beta \cdot \rho} \cdot p_{E}^{e}(t-1)^{\gamma \cdot \rho} \qquad (5.18)$$

by Eq. (5.16), Eq. (5.15) is obtained, with expected signs $\alpha, \beta > 0, \gamma < 0$, and $0 < \rho < 1$.

In both approaches, energy demand $E(t)$ of period t (the dependent variable) is thus a function of income $GDP(t)$, relative energy price $p_E(t)$, and energy demand of the previous period $E(t-1)$, the lagged dependent variable. In order to estimate the parameters, appropriate data must be collected and econometric methods applied. In the case of model (5.18) a testable linear specification results when taking logs and adding an error term $\varepsilon(t)$,

$$\begin{aligned}\ln E(t) = (1-\rho)\ln\alpha + \beta(1-\rho)\ln GDP(t) + \\ \gamma(1-\rho)\ln p_E(t) + \rho E(t-1) + \varepsilon(t).\end{aligned} \qquad (5.19)$$

The short-term income elasticity is $\beta(1-\rho) > 0$, the short-term price elasticity, $\gamma(1-\rho) < 0$. The long-term elasticities follow from considering the situation in which all impulses of a one-time income or price change have exerted their full effect, resulting in perfect adjustment (the unobserved energy-using stock of capital is constant). This means that energy demand is stationary,

$$E(t) = E(t-1). \qquad (5.20)$$

In a stationary situation the time index may be omitted, resulting in

$$E = \alpha^{1-\rho} \cdot GDP^{\beta \cdot (1-\rho)} \cdot p_E^{\gamma \cdot (1-\rho)} \cdot E^{\rho} = \alpha \cdot GDP^{\beta} \cdot p_E^{\gamma}. \qquad (5.21)$$

Therefore, β represents the long-term income elasticity and γ the long-term price elasticity. They can be obtained by dividing the estimated coefficients of Eq. (5.19) by the estimated ρ pertaining to the lagged dependent variable. The mean adjustment time (number of periods) following a one-time income or price change equals $1/(1-\rho)$. This follows from the fact that a discrepancy between desired and inherited energy consumption is reduced at the tune of $1-\rho$ per period. On average the discrepancy is thus eliminated in $1/(1-\rho)$ periods.

Yet this model is based on assumptions that prove to be restrictive:

- Rising and falling relative energy prices have a symmetric impact on energy demand, an assumption that is hardly plausible. So-called hysteresis is more likely, meaning that the consumption-reducing effect of a price hike continues even after price decreases again. After all, once equipment with higher energy efficiency is installed, it is not scrapped just because energy has become cheaper again. In order to model hysteresis, the price variable needs to be split in two,

$$p_E^+(t) = p_E^+(t-1) + \max(0, p_E(t) - p_E(t-1)) \quad \text{(the up component)},$$
$$p_E^-(t) = p_E^-(t-1) + \min(0, p_E(t) - p_E(t-1)) \quad \text{(the down component)}. \quad (5.22)$$

Taking the price $p_E(0)$ of the base period 0 and using Eq. (5.22) again and again, the first variable p^+ contains the sum of all price increases beyond $p_E(0)$, while the second variable p^- contains the sum of all price decreases. Evidently

$$p_E(t) = p_E^+(t) + p_E^-(t) \quad (5.23)$$

holds. The modified Eq. (5.18) then reads,

$$E(t) = \alpha^{1-\rho} \cdot GDP(t)^{\beta \cdot (1-\rho)} \cdot p_E^+(t)^{\gamma \cdot (1-\rho)} \cdot p_E^-(t)^{\delta \cdot (1-\rho)} \cdot E(t-1)^\rho \quad (5.24)$$

where γ symbolizes the long-term price elasticity in case of price increases and δ for the long-term price elasticity in case of price decreases. Unfortunately, the explanatory variables often turn out to be highly correlated (giving rise to the so-called multicollinearity problem), rendering precise estimation of the parameters difficult.

– In the demand model presented, the mean adjustment time $1/(1-\rho)$ is independent of whether adjustment is triggered by change in income or energy prices. This assumption can be relaxed as well. For simplicity, consider the extreme case where the demand for energy reacts immediately to a change in income, while it reacts with a lag to a change in relative price, as before. In this case, Eq. (5.16) is modified as follows,

$$E(t) = \alpha \cdot GDP(t)^\beta \cdot p_E^e(t)^\gamma \quad (5.25)$$

with $p_E^e(t)$ denoting the expected relative price of energy. In view of Eq. (5.17), this results in the specification

$$\frac{E(t)}{E(t-1)^\rho} = \alpha^{1-\rho} \frac{GDP(t)^\beta}{GDP(t-1)^{\beta \cdot \rho}} p_E(t)^{\gamma \cdot (1-\rho)}. \quad (5.26)$$

5.3 The Price of Energy

The parameter $\beta > 0$ represents the (short-term and long-term) elasticity, $\gamma (1-\rho) < 0$ the short-term and $\gamma < 0$, the long-term price elasticity. The mean adjustment time of energy demand to changes in price is once again $1/(1-\rho)$.

- A further assumption is that both short-term and long-term elasticities are constant. In particular, they do not depend on current values of income and price of energy. However, dropping this assumption calls for a much more complex modeling for demand (e.g. using the so-called translog specification, see Sect. 5.3.3).

Table 5.3 shows the results of a regression estimate of model (5.19) using annual data for the European Union and the United States covering the period from 1980 to 2013. The dependent variable is crude oil demand per capita. The explanatory variables are inflation-adjusted per-capita income and inflation-adjusted price of Brent crude. Demand for crude oil is fairly well explained: The coefficient of determination R^2 is between 0.88 and 0.91, indicating a high statistical fit. Though estimated income elasticities have the expected sign, they are statistically insignificant at the 1% level. However, the price elasticities and the lagged dependent variable are statistically significant at the 1% level.

Taking the results of Table 5.3 at face value, one is led to the following interpretation. In both the European Union and in the United States, the inflation-adjusted price of crude oil has a significant impact on demand. However, the long-term price elasticities are 0.220 or below in absolute value, which means that the demand for oil is inelastic. This view is confirmed by most econometric studies. Interestingly enough, consumers in the United States react with a shorter lag to oil price changes than Europeans.

Table 5.3 Income and price elasticities of crude oil demand

	EU-15	USA
Inflation-adjusted per-capita income (data source: World Bank)		
Short-term ($\beta (1-\rho)$)	0.022	0.008
Long-term (β)	0.146	0.037
Inflation-adjusted Brent price (data source: BP and World Bank)		
Short-term ($\gamma (1-\rho)$)	−0.034 (*)	−0.036 (*)
Long-term (γ)	−0.220 (*)	−0.163 (*)
Per-capita oil consumption (data source: BP and World Bank)		
Lagged dependent variable (ρ)	0.847 (*)	0.779 (*)
Adjustment lag (years)	6.5 (*)	4.5 (*)
Adjusted R^2	0.910	0.882
Standard error of estimate	0.0162	0.0147

Estimation period: 1980–2013; the significance of elasticities is denoted with * (1% level)

5.3.3 Substitution Between Energy and Capital

According to the process analysis discussed in Sect. 4.3, the relationship between energy demand and aggregate capital stock is substitutional rather than limitational (fixed proportions), meaning there is a choice between more and less energy-intensive modes of production and consumption. Substitution of energy is therefore possible through investment in capital goods. More generally, a given output quantity Q can be produced using more or less energy input E and commensurately modified quantities of other production factors. This is formally expressed by a production function,

$$Q = f(K, L, E, M) \tag{5.27}$$

which relates output Q to inputs of capital K, labor L, energy E, and materials M (non-energy raw materials). To be precise, Q denotes the maximum output achievable given the state of technology and input quantities, reflecting best practice.

Figure 5.4 depicts the production function by means of a so-called isoquant. An isoquant shows the quantities of production factors K and E (with inputs of labor L and materials M held constant in the present case) that are needed to produce a given quantity Q. The isoquant thus summarizes the efficient production frontier for a given quantity of output, depicting uses of an available technology ranging from energy-intensive to capital-intensive. Specifically, production process *II* is an energy-intensive variant that in turn uses little capital, whereas process *III* is capital-intensive but saves on energy. Production processes *I* and *IV* can be disregarded because of their excessive use of costly inputs; indeed, only technologies *II* and *III* are efficient.

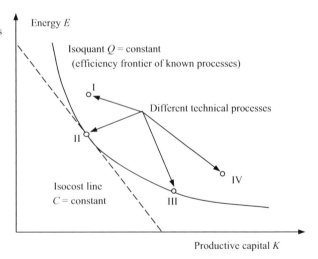

Fig. 5.4 Efficient and inefficient technical processes

5.3 The Price of Energy

In order to decide which production alternative is minimum cost, the prices of production factors have to be considered. For K this is capital user cost p_K, an annuity which reflects interest and depreciation (net of tax exemptions and subsidies); for L this is the wage rate (including non-wage labor costs) p_L; for E this is the average energy purchase price p_E; for M this is average unit cost p_M. When L and M as well as their unit prices are held constant, all factor combinations that are compatible with constant total production cost lie on a straight line (the so-called isocost line; see Fig. 5.4). Per definition all points on the isocost line are characterized by constant total production cost,

$$C = p_K K + p_E E + p_L L + p_M M. \tag{5.28}$$

To calculate the slope of this line and neglecting L and M (thus $dL = dM = 0$), this equation can be differentiated to become

$$\begin{aligned} dC &= 0 = p_K dK + p_E dE \quad \text{and therefore} \\ \frac{dE}{dK} &= -\frac{p_K}{p_E}. \end{aligned} \tag{5.29}$$

Thus the slope of the isocost line is $-p_K/p_E$. Consider a reduction in energy use, $dE < 0$. If the unit price of energy p_E is relatively high, the cost saving is substantial, permitting to use a lot more capital K while holding cost constant. Therefore, dE/dK takes on a low (absolute) value in this case. Conversely, if energy is cheap compared to the user cost of capital, $dE < 0$ generates a small cost saving which creates little room for an increased use of capital since this is relatively expensive. Accordingly, dE/dK takes on a high (absolute) value in this case.

Competitive pressure makes producers minimize cost. They therefore seek to attain the isocost line representing the lowest possible production cost. This is the one running closest to the origin in (K, E)-space, given the amount of output Q and hence the isoquant. Therefore, the isocost line needs to be tangent to the isoquant for cost minimization. This corresponds to the choice of technology *II* with its rather high energy intensity.

Note that the isocost line of Fig. 5.4 has a fairly steep slope, reflecting a situation where energy is cheap compared to the user cost of capital (as reflected by the annuity; see Sect. 3.1). If energy were to become more expensive relative to capital, the isocost line would exhibit a reduced slope, thus favoring a more capital-intensive mode of production. Therefore, a change in relative prices is predicted to affect the choice of production process within the technology available. This constitutes producers' short-run response, while the choice of technology (to be discussed in Sect. 5.4) amounts to their long-run adjustment.

For a given technology, the curvature of the isoquant representing it evidently is of great importance. The more pronounced the curvature, the smaller is the adjustment in the factor mix in response to a given change in relative factor prices. In the extreme case of a limitational technology, isoquants have an angular shape, which means that there cannot be any adjustment to a change in relative prices. Producers

Fig. 5.5 Isoquants with different elasticities of substitution

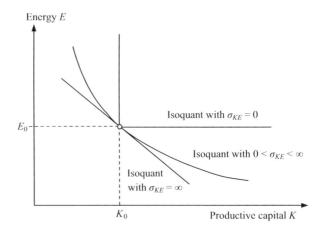

are stuck at the corner as it were (see Fig. 5.5). With reference to a pair of inputs, one defines the elasticity of substitution σ_{KE} as the parameter reflecting the degree of substitutability in production. It answers the question, "By how much (in percent) does the mix of inputs change when their relative price changes by 1%?". In terms of Fig. 5.4, one has

$$\sigma_{KE} = \frac{d(K/E)}{dR} \frac{R}{K/E} \quad \text{with the slope of the tangent given by}$$
$$R = -\frac{dK}{dE} = -\frac{\partial Q}{\partial E} \bigg/ \frac{\partial Q}{\partial K}. \tag{5.30}$$

Obviously, the slope of the (tangent to an) isoquant reflects relative marginal productivities. It is known as the marginal rate of (factor) substitution. Given choice of a minimum-cost production process, the marginal rate of substitution R is just equal to the (negative) relative price of the factors (the slope of the isocost line),

$$R = \frac{p_K}{p_E}. \tag{5.31}$$

Therefore, the elasticity of substitution can also be defined in terms of a change in relative factor prices,

$$\sigma_{KE} = \frac{d(E/K)}{d(p_K/p_E)} \frac{p_K/p_E}{E/K} = \frac{d\ln(E/K)}{d\ln(p_K/p_E)} = \sigma_{EK}. \tag{5.32}$$

The symmetry follows from $d\ln(K/E) = -d\ln(E/K)$ and $d\ln(p_K/p_E) = -d\ln(p_E/p_K)$. If capital and energy are substitutive factors of production, the elasticity of substitution must lie in the interval $0 < \sigma_{KE} < \infty$. A high value of σ_{KE} indicates that

5.3 The Price of Energy

substitution between these factors is easy. With an elasticity of substitution $\sigma_{KE} = 3$ e.g., a 10% increase in the relative price of energy results in a 30% reduction of the E/K ratio. If $\sigma_{KE} = 1.2$, the E/K ratio falls by 12% only. In the extreme case of $\sigma_{KE} = 0$, there is no substitution possibility between K and E but a fixed input relationship between them (this amounts to a fixed-proportions (limitational) production function, also called Leontief production function; see Sect. 2.5).

The situation becomes more complex when more than two production factors are considered. The partial elasticity of substitution defined above has to be replaced by the so-called Allen elasticity (see Allen 1938, Sect. 19.4). Any two factors of production may now be complementary rather than substitutive. For instance, labor has historically been substituted by capital and energy, making capital and energy complements in production. Since the elasticity of substitution is defined to be positive in the case of substitutability, the Allen elasticity is negative in the case of complementarities.

This raises the question of whether energy and capital are complements or substitutes in the context of the four-factor production function $Q = f(K, L, E, M)$. This is an empirical question which can only be answered by applying econometric methods. In doing so, one usually prefers not to focus on the isoquants but rather on (minimum) cost, which is a scalar measure. As shown by Fig. 5.4, the isocost line contains the same information as the isoquant in the neighborhood of the minimum cost combination of inputs. Indeed the problem, "Minimize production cost for a given output level" leads to the same solution as the so-called dual formulation, "Maximize output for a given cost budget". Thus, the dual to maximizing output given a cost constraint reads

$$C = C(Q, p_K, p_L, p_E, p_M) = Q \cdot c(p_K, p_L, p_E, p_M). \tag{5.33}$$

It states that minimum total cost C depends on the amount of output Q to be achieved and the (relative) prices of inputs. Since unit cost c is given by C/Q, one can also analyze unit cost c. Strictly speaking, this is possible only if scaling up by Q does not matter, i.e. if the cost function $C(Q, p_K, p_L, p_E, p_M)$ is homogenous of the first degree in Q. This is the case when a change of all production factors (e.g. doubling all of them) leads to an analogous change (doubling) of output, amounting to constant returns to scale.

This leaves the choice of functional form. Preferably, the functional form should not impose *a priori* restrictions on crucial parameters such as the elasticity of substitution. A popular solution is the so-called translog function (see Christensen et al. 1973; Berndt and Wood 1975). It results from a second-degree Taylor approximation to an arbitrary function, with the arguments and the dependent variable in logarithms. In the case of the average cost function, the translog form becomes

$$\ln c = \alpha_0 + \sum_{i=1}^{N} \alpha_i \ln p_i + \frac{1}{2} \sum_{i=1}^{N} \sum_{j=1}^{N} \beta_{ij} \ln p_i \ln p_j,$$
$$\sum_{i=1}^{N} \alpha_i = 1, \quad \sum_{i,j=1}^{N} \beta_{ij} = \sum_{i,j=1}^{N} \beta_{ji}, \quad \beta_{ij} = \beta_{ji}. \tag{5.34}$$

Here $\alpha_0 > 0$ is a constant and N is the number of production factors ($N = 4$ in the present context). The α_i are the first-order derivatives of the unit cost function with reference to the inputs. They sum up to one because of the assumed homogeneity of the first degree. The β_{ij} are the second-order derivatives. By Young's theorem, the order of differentiation does not matter for continuously differentiable functions, implying $\beta_{ij} = \beta_{ji}$.

Differentiating Eq. (5.34), one obtains

$$\frac{\partial \ln c}{\partial \ln p_i} = \frac{\partial c}{\partial p_i} \cdot \frac{p_i}{c} = \alpha_i + \frac{1}{2} \sum_{j=1}^{N} \beta_{ij} \cdot \ln p_j \tag{5.35}$$

Shephard's lemma states that the derivative of the minimum cost function with respect to factor price p_i yields the optimal input quantity x_i (see e.g. Varian 1992, Chap. 5). Therefore one obtains

$$\frac{x_i \cdot p_i}{c} =: sh_i = \alpha_i + \sum_{j=1}^{N} \beta_{ij} \ln p_j \tag{5.36}$$

with sh_i denoting the cost share of the i-th factor of production (see Diewert 1974). Thus, the shares of K, L, E, and M can be linearly related to the logarithm of their prices p_K, p_L, p_E, and p_M, making estimation of the β_{ij} by ordinary least-squares (OLS) possible.

Also, the Allen partial elasticities of substitution between capital and energy can be recovered from the cost shares and price elasticities as follows (see Allen 1938, Sects. 19.5 and 19.6),

$$\sigma_{KE} = \frac{\eta_{K,p_E} + sh_E \cdot \eta_{E,p_E}}{sh_E}. \tag{5.37}$$

This is intuitive: Energy and capital are substitutes if their cross-price elasticity $\eta_{K,pE}$ is positive, resulting in a positive value of σ_{KE} (the own-price elasticity $\eta_{K,pE}$ is always negative). Conversely, they are complements if their cross-price elasticity is strongly positive and the own-price elasticity of energy as well as its cost share sh_E are small in absolute value, resulting in a negative value of σ_{KE}.

Econometric estimation of substitution elasticities between energy and capital was motivated by the first oil price shock of 1973. Policy-makers wanted to know whether it was easy or difficult to substitute energy by other production factors, in particular capital. The first evidence exhibited in Table 5.4 was disappointing:

Table 5.4 Elasticities of substitution between capital, labor, and energy

Elasticity of substitution	Berndt and Wood	Griffin and Gregory	Hunt (1984)	Hunt (1986)
	United States		Great Britain	
	1975	1976	(neutral technological change)	(non-neutral techn. change)
σ_{KL}	1.01	0.06	1.58	0.37
σ_{KE}	−3.22	1.07	−1.64	2.68
σ_{LE}	0.64	0.87	0.84	0.08

Berndt and Wood (1975) found a complementary relation between energy and capital. Yet another estimate by Griffin and Gregory (1976) points to substitutability ($\sigma_{KE} = 1.07$). This triggered a lively discussion among economists (see e.g. Solow 1987). Later studies using more recent data and including technological change also show ambiguous results. However, the estimate presented in the last column of Table 5.4 confirms substitutability between energy and capital once it is assumed that producers have a choice of technology. This leads to the conclusion that companies have not exhausted the substitutional potential suggested by bottom-up process analysis to the same extent as the potential for automation, which amounts to replacing labor by both capital and energy.

In conclusion, the relationship between energy and capital cannot be determined with sufficient precision even to this day. Likely reasons are the limited validity of aggregate data, difficulty in distinguishing between the short term and long term (K and E may be complementary in the short run but substitutes in the long run), and the challenges posed by isolating the effects of technological change.

5.4 Technological Change

In economics, technological change is defined in the following way. Technological change enables a larger output Q to be produced with the same input quantities of capital K, labor L, energy E, and materials M. An equivalent way of expressing the same idea is to say that a given output quantity Q can be produced using smaller quantities of production factors. An improvement in quality is a possible outcome, too.

In Fig. 5.6, technological change is depicted by a shift of the isoquant towards (and not away from) the origin of (K, E)-space. In the figure on the left, technological change does not affect the input mix as long as relative factor prices do not change, thus indicating neutral technological change with respect to energy and capital. In the figure on the right, technological change is energy-saving because the transition exhibits a lower E/K ratio at a given factor price ratio. Clearly, changing relative factor prices can also influence the choice of production technology, in addition to technological change.

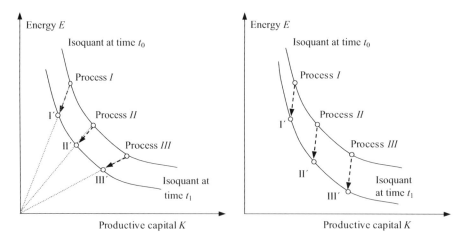

Fig. 5.6 Isoquants reflecting technological change

A mathematical formulation of factor-augmenting technological change is the following (see Stoneman 1983),

$$Q = f(K, L, E, M) = g[a_K(t)K, \ a_L(t)L, \ a_E(t)E, a_M(t)M] \quad (5.38)$$

where t denotes time and $a_K(t)$, $a_L(t)$, $a_E(t)$, and $a_M(t)$ are functions indicating factor-augmenting changes resulting in savings of capital, labor, energy, and materials. These functions may depend on investment in research and development, education and training of the labor force, improved management, institutional reforms, and much more. But if technological change is to be advantageous, these functions must obey

$$\frac{da_K}{dt} \geq 0; \ \frac{da_L}{dt} \geq 0; \ \frac{da_L}{dt} \geq 0, \ \frac{da_M}{dt} \geq 0. \quad (5.39)$$

Using these functions, the direction of technological change can be defined. For example, $da_L(t)/dt > 0$ while $da_K(t)/dt = da_E(t)/dt = da_M(t)/dt = 0$ indicates labor-saving technological change because only labor input is scaled up as it were (which implies less of it is actually used at unchanged relative factor prices). But if $da_L(t)/dt = da_K(t)/dt = da_E(t)/dt = da_M(t)/dt$, then all factors of production benefit from technological change to the same degree, a case which is often referred to as Hicks-neutral technological change. In the past, however, technological change has not been neutral but first and foremost labor-saving. Using the expression for sh_i derived from the translog unit cost function (5.36) and complementing it with $\gamma_i \cdot t$ to reflect technological change, one obtains (see Binswanger 1974; Hunt 1986)[5]

---

[5]In this formula, technological change is understood as autonomous. In fact, it may be linked to investment in capital and additions to the workforce. Thus, technological change is incorporated in

5.4 Technological Change

$$sh_i(t) = \alpha_i + \sum_j \beta_{ij}\ln p_j(t) + \gamma_i t. \qquad (5.40)$$

As before, $sh_i(t)$ stands for the cost share of production factor i and $p_j(t)$ for the respective price. As the shares of the factor costs have to add up to 1, one has

$$\sum_j \gamma_j = 0. \qquad (5.41)$$

Hicks-neutral technological change is equivalent to $\gamma_K = \gamma_L = \gamma_E = \gamma_M = 0$. However, using British industry data covering the years from 1960 to 1980, Hunt (1986) finds evidence suggesting $\gamma_L < \gamma_E < \gamma_K$. Therefore, in Great Britain at least, technological innovation has been above all labor-saving. It has also been energy-saving, though hardly capital-saving.

This finding gives rise to the question of which factors bring about such a bias to technological change. According to the induced bias hypothesis (see Stoneman 1983, Chap. 4), the direction of the technological change is conditioned by the market, meaning it depends on the development of relative prices. This was first formulated by Hicks (1932, 124f),

> A change in the relative prices of the factors of production is itself a spur to invention, and to innovation of a particular kind—directed to economizing the use of a factor which has become relatively expensive.

If the price of the production factor labor increases compared to the cost of other production factors, then labor-saving technological change will come about in due time. In addition to the movement along the isoquant as in Fig. 5.6, a change in the isoquant itself also takes place, which leads to a further substitution of labor even when relative factor prices no longer change.

It can be argued that the oil crises of the 1970s with their twin price shocks have guided innovation efforts towards improved energy efficiency. Interestingly, these efforts continued into the 1990s when relative oil prices were lower again, possibly because of the (expected) scarcity of energy resources and governments aiming at reducing greenhouse gas emissions and supporting energy-efficient investments. Apparently, the price hikes triggered an enduring technological change which has decoupled the demand for energy from economic growth. Quite possibly, this decoupling will be enhanced by the renewed increase in the relative price of oil between 1999 and 2014. Historic case studies show that problem awareness in the energy industry has influenced the direction technological change (see Weizsäcker 1988) as entrepreneurs hope to make a profit by developing energy-saving and environment-friendly technologies and products. These hoped-for innovation gains thus may play an important role in the future demand for energy.

---

the factors of production. This feature can be taken into account by the capital vintage model presented in Sect. 4.1.

References

Allen, R. G. D. (1938). *Mathematical analysis for economists*. London: MacMillan.
Berndt, E. R., & Wood, D. O. (1975). Technology, prices and the derived demand for energy. *Review of Economics and Statistics, 57*, 259–268.
Binswanger, H. P. (1974). A microeconomic approach to induced innovation. *Economic Journal, 84*, 940–958.
Christensen, L. R., Jorgenson, D. W., et al. (1973). Transcendental logarithmic production frontiers. *Review of Economics and Statistics, 55*, 28–45.
Diewert, W. E. (1974). An application of the Shephard duality theorem: A generalized Leontief production function. *Journal of Political Economy, 79*, 481–507.
EIA. (2014). *Miscellaneous data files*. Washington: Energy Information Administration. Retrieved from www.eia.gov/
Griffin, J. M., & Gregory, P. R. (1976). An intercountry translog model of energy substitution responses. *American Economic Review, 66*, 845–857.
Hicks, J. R. (1932). *The theory of wages*. London: MacMillan.
Hunt, L. C. (1984). Energy and capital: Substitutes or complements? Some results for the UK industrial sector. *Applied Economics, 16*, 783–789.
Hunt, L. C. (1986). Energy and capital: Substitutes or complements? *Applied Economics, 18*, 729–735.
Solow, J. L. (1987). The capital-energy complementary debate revisited. *American Economic Review, 77*, 605–614.
Stoneman, P. (1983). *The economic analysis of technological change*. Oxford: Oxford University Press.
Varian, H. L. (1992). *Microeconomic analysis* (3rd ed.). New York: Norton.
Weizsäcker, C. C. von (1988). Innovationen in der Energiewirtschaft (Innovations in the energy economy). *Zeitschrift für Energiewirtschaft, 3*, 141–146.
World Bank. (2014). *World development indicators*. Washington. Retrieved from http://data.worldbank.org/data-catalog/world-development-indicators

Energy Reserves and Sustainability   6

The finiteness of fossil energy sources gives rise to the question of whether sustainable economic development is possible at all since these resources will increasingly become scarce and even cease to be available. Resource economics—the theory of dealing with the efficient use of exhaustible resources—has been addressing this problem. Grounded in the pertinent economic models, this chapter revolves around the following issues:

- How are energy reserves measured and how large are they?
- What is the optimal extraction strategy for the owners of an exhaustible resource?
- What is the optimal rate of extraction from a welfare point of view?
- Does market failure occur, i.e. are there systematic deviations from the optimal extraction path?
- What are the consequences of the increasing physical scarcity of energy sources for the price of energy?
- How far can these prices rise?

However, the optimum from the point of resource economics, while resulting in an efficient use of exhaustible energy resources, need not be sustainable. The relationship between economic efficiency and (so-called weak) sustainability therefore needs to be clarified. This leads to additional questions:

- What are the conditions that make sustainable development possible in spite of continued use of non-renewable energy sources?
- For instance, does the global oil market satisfy these conditions?
- What interventions might be called for in order to satisfy the conditions for weak sustainability?

The variables used in this chapter are:

C	Consumption
c	Marginal unit cost
$Disc$	Discovery of energy reserves
δ	Depreciation rate
f	Rate of autonomous technological change
H	Hamiltonian function
η	Income elasticity of energy demand
i	Market interest rate
K	Reproducible capital (as distinguished from natural capital)
L	Lagrange function
λ	Opportunity cost of resource extraction (also called scarcity rent), a Lagrange multiplier
NPV	Net present value of cash flows
Π	Profit
Q	Production function
p	Price
R	Extraction of energy reserves
r	Social time preference
S	Stock of reserves
σ	Elasticity of substitution
T	Planning horizon
U	Utility function
W	Welfare (wealth), value of the objective function
ω	Opportunity cost of consumption, a Lagrange multiplier

6.1 Resources and Reserves

Whether a raw material constitutes a resource or not depends on available technological know-how and the capability of using it. For example, the uranium isotope U_{235} became an energy resource only after control over nuclear fission was achieved. Next, 'resources' have to be distinguished from 'reserves' (see Table 6.1).

Resources comprise all useful raw materials existing in the ground, including those whose deposits are only presumed to exist or are currently too costly to be extracted using available technologies. Reserves are those resources that exist with high probability and can be extracted at a cost below their market price. Accordingly, higher market prices can cause resources to become reserves. The same holds for increased efforts at exploring an assumed resource deposit and lowering the cost of a mining or extraction technology. Adding cumulated amounts extracted to the total stock of reserves and resources leads to an estimate of ultimately recoverable resources.

Table 6.1 Ultimately recoverable resources

Cumulated extraction	Remaining reserves		Resources that are not (yet) reserves	
Cumulated extraction	Physically proved, technically feasible and economically viable		Proved but technically not feasible and/or economically not viable	Not proved but possible according to geological evidence
	Certain	Probable		
		←—P—→		

Source: Erdmann and Zweifel (2008, p. 122)

Following the World Petroleum Council, reserves are classified according to the probability of economically viable extraction (see Campbell and Laherrere 1996):

- P (proved): probability of extraction >90%;
- 2P (proved + probable): probability of extraction >50%;
- 3P (proved + probable + possible): probability of extraction >10%.

The U.S. Securities and Exchange Commission as well as other financial regulators require that resource-extracting companies listed on the stock exchange use P-reserves when reporting their assets, whereas geologists as well as internal planners of resource companies use 2P-reserves as the relevant figure. As a consequence, published reserves can be higher merely due to reclassification of known deposits rather than new discoveries (resulting in so-called paper barrels). Indeed, experts such as the Texan investment banker Simmons claim that increases of oil reserves in recent years have been more due to such reclassifications than to the discovery of new deposits.

6.1.1 Resources

There is a multitude of publications concerning globally available energy resources. Estimates sometimes diverge substantially, as they are based on data provided by resource-extracting companies, governments, and independent experts.[1] According to Table 6.2, the oil resources amount to 470 bn toe or 3400 bn bbl, respectively.

Several models have been developed for determining the amount of an oil and gas resource that can be ultimately recovered. One of them is by geologist Hubbert (1956, 1962), stating that accumulated discoveries follow a logistic trajectory (see Fig. 6.1). Thus, when the industry is in its start-up phase, only few oil deposits are discovered. With more experience (and therefore decreasing marginal cost of exploration) the rate of discovery increases. However, when the bulk of existing

---

[1]Some experts doubt the credibility of data published by several OPEC countries, who have been stating constant reserves of crude oil for many years.

Table 6.2 Global fossil energy reserves and resources 2013

Energy source (bn toe)	Cumulated extraction up to 2013[a]	Reserves 2013[b]	Resources which are not yet reserves, 2013
Conventional oil	175	244	231
Unconventional oil[c]		69	392
Conventional gas	85	250	414
Unconventional gas		7	686
Coal	134	697	16,747
Uranium	18	21	228
Thorium			109

[a]BP (2014)
[b]BGR (2014)
[c]Hydrocarbons not capable of flowing

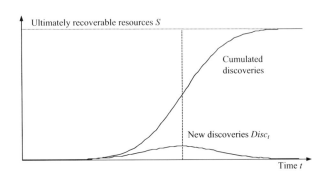

Fig. 6.1 Logistic path of cumulative global resource discoveries

deposits has been located, the rate of discovery falls again. Accordingly, cumulated discoveries increase more slowly, approaching the limit of ultimately recoverable resources.

If one assumes symmetry between the phases of increasing and decreasing rates of discovery $Disc_t$, cumulated discoveries up to time T follow the logistic equation

$$\int_0^T Disc_t \, dt = S \frac{1}{1 + \exp[-a(T - t_{max})]} \quad \text{with } a > 0 \quad (6.1)$$

Here, t_{max} denotes the year where the rate of discovery reaches its maximum and S, total reserves. It can be shown that t_{max} determines the time when one-half of the reserves have been discovered. Differentiation with respect to time yields

$$Disc_t = aS \frac{\exp[-a(t - t_{max})]}{(1 + \exp[-a(t - t_{max})])^2} \quad (6.2)$$

Econometric methods can be applied to derive Maximum Likelihood estimates of the unknown parameters a, t_{max}, and S from time series data on $Disc_t$ and t.

Therefore, the history of discovery rates permits to infer the unknown resource stock S—provided Eq. (6.1) holds.

From an economic point of view, however, this model is weak because it neglects exploration costs, technological change in exploration, resource prices as well as institutional conditions such as public versus private ownership of reserve deposits (Kaufmann and Cleveland 2001; Reynolds 2002). Moreover, the assumed symmetry between increasing and decreasing rates of discovery does not conform to reality.

6.1.2 Static Range of Fossil Energy Reserves

In spite of these qualifications, estimates of ultimate recoverable oil resources published in the literature seem to converge (see Fig. 6.2). This convergence may be the result of two opposing economic forces. On the one hand, reserves amount to an intermediate product since investment must be made in the exploration of deposits, in the purchasing of extraction rights, and in the enforcement of already acquired property rights. With decreasing global reserves, the price of oil is expected to increase, making it economically interesting to invest into the creation of additional reserves. Thus, changes in global reserves crucially depend on the expected value of exploration costs compared to expected oil prices. On the other hand, accumulated exploration leads to learning effects (see IEA 2000; Nakicenovic 2002), which are a major source of cost reductions. High oil prices and stepped-up exploration efforts have resulted in innovations (such as 3D seism in the 1990s and 4D seism and fracking since 2000) that serve to lower the cost of exploration. As stated by Adelman (1990), there is a permanent race between the decrease in the reserves remaining and the increase in technological knowledge.

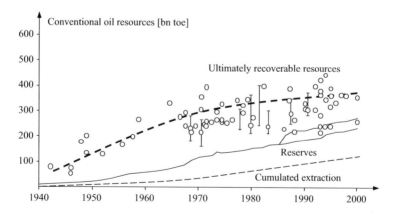

Fig. 6.2 Discovery of conventional oil resources over time. Source: Erdmann and Zweifel (2008, p. 125)

Reserves constitute an asset that is necessary for long-run production planning, securing deliveries, and market presence. Moreover, they help a resource-extracting company to attain a favorable credit rating. However, the returns on the investment needed for the acquisition of this asset have low net present values if extraction of a new resource deposit starts far in the future (see Sect. 3.1). From an economic point of view, exploration efforts should be exerted to the point where their marginal cost is still covered by the increase in the present value of expected returns on the oil found. As a consequence, an individual resource-extracting company is predicted to have reserves that are neither excessive nor insufficient. Whether reserves are excessive or insufficient depends, among other things, on the future expected price of oil. However, the price of oil not only determines the individually optimal amount but also the global amount of resources. Higher (expected) oil prices tend to increase the global amount of resources, at least in the long term.

A common indicator of remaining reserves is time to depletion (also called range). In its static variant, this is the ratio of remaining reserves over the current rate of extraction. In its dynamic version, the change over time in both quantities is accounted for. Figure 6.3 shows the static range for conventional crude oil and natural gas reserves. It is roughly constant during the past decades, in spite of increasing extraction rates of oil and gas. This constancy corresponds quite well to the optimality of investment in exploration discussed above. Moreover, the static range of natural gas consistently exceeds that of crude oil. This can be attributed to the fact that large gas discoveries often occur as a byproduct of oil field exploration (so-called associated gas).

However, the static range does not inform about how long the energy source will still be available. For one, reserves increase due to exploration and reclassification of reserves. The effective time to depletion can exceed the static range if the rate of annual extraction falls—and *vice versa*. Nonetheless, the static range is a helpful indicator of global reserves available. A decline in its value should be seen as indicating a need for increasing investment in exploration and efforts to substitute the resource by other (renewable) energy sources.

Fig. 6.3 Static range of conventional oil and natural gas reserves. Data source: BP (2014)

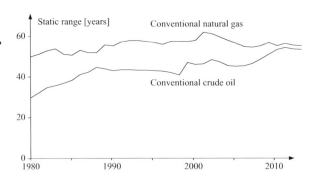

6.2 Profit-Maximizing Resource Extraction

In the same way that the transformation from resources to reserves is governed by economic considerations, the transformation of a reserve into money (i.e. extraction and sale) is an economic decision. It revolves around two alternatives:

- Leave the reserve in the ground and wait for a higher market price (which is to be expected due to increased scarcity);
- Extract the resource and invest the profit in securities or assets thereby earning the market interest rate.

6.2.1 Hotelling Price Trajectory

The Swedish economist Hotelling (1931) found a solution to the decision problem stated above, i.e. the profit-maximizing quantity of an exhaustible resource to be extracted during a given period. His model introduces several simplifying assumptions, notably competitive and efficient markets for resources, reserves, energy sources, and capital, profit-maximizing resource owners, perfect information regarding the amount of reserves, constant cost of mining and extraction, no inflation, no inventories after extraction, and an intertemporally stable demand function depending on the price of energy only. Given these assumptions, profit Π_t in period t is given by

$$\Pi_t = p_t R_t - c R_t. \tag{6.3}$$

Here, $R_t \geq 0$ is the quantity extracted and sold in period t, p_t the market price, and c the marginal cost of extraction, which is assumed to be constant and hence equal to unit cost for simplicity.

Postponing extraction is advantageous as long as (expected) profit in the following period Π_{t+1} exceeds profit achievable in the current period t, invested at the (real) rate of interest i,

$$\Pi_{t+1} = p_{t+1} R_{t+1} - c R_{t+1} > \Pi_t (1 + i). \tag{6.4}$$

In the opposite case, the firm extracts during the current period. If all extracting companies decide in this way, there will be an equilibrium market price p_t, determined by their decisions in the aggregate, which has to satisfy the equality condition,

$$\Pi_{t+1} = p_{t+1} R_{t+1} - c R_{t+1} = \Pi_t (1 + i). \tag{6.5}$$

Iterating this idea until the end of the planning horizon T—and assuming perfect foresight with respect to price—leads to the following decision problem of reserve-owners seeking to maximize the net present value NPV of their asset,

$$NPV = \sum_{t=0}^{T} \Pi_t \cdot (1+i)^{-t} = \sum_{t=0}^{T} (p_t R_t - cR_t)(1+i)^{-t} \to \max! \quad (6.6)$$

The decision variables of each company are the extraction rates R_t during the planning period $t = 1, \ldots, T$. However, their optimization is subject to the constraint that the sum of extractions must not exceed total stock in the ground S. On the other hand, it would not make sense for the reserve-owner to leave anything in the ground beyond the planning period T so that the constraint becomes

$$\sum_{t=0}^{T} R_t = S. \quad (6.7)$$

This constraint can be integrated into the objective function using a Lagrange multiplier $\lambda > 0$,

$$L = \sum_{t=0}^{T} (p_t R_t - cR_t)(1+i)^{-t} - \lambda \left(\sum_{t=0}^{T} R_t - S \right) \to \max! \quad (6.8)$$

This expression states that if accumulated extractions were to exceed the existing stock S, the value of the objective function L would be reduced because of $\lambda > 0$, causing the degree of goal attainment to fall. Therefore, one of the first-order optimality condition reads

$$\frac{\partial L}{\partial \lambda} = \sum_{t=0}^{T} R_t - S = 0. \quad (6.9)$$

It guarantees that the constraint (6.7) is always satisfied in the optimum. The second optimality condition concerns the rate of extraction R_t during period t. Since the other extraction rates $R_0, \ldots, R_{t-1}, R_{t+1}, \ldots; R_T$ are not affected by a decision in period t, one obtains

$$\frac{\partial L}{\partial R_t} = (p_t - c)(1+i)^{-t} - \lambda = 0. \quad (6.10)$$

Solving this optimality condition yields the so-called Hotelling price trajectory,

$$(p_t - c) = \lambda(1+i)^t \text{ or } p_t = c + \lambda(1+i)^t. \quad (6.11)$$

Equation (6.11) can be interpreted as follows.

– Marginal extraction cost c as lower limit on the price p: If the reserve were available in unlimited quantity, the constraint (6.7) would not be binding. From Eq. (6.8), one would obtain

6.2 Profit-Maximizing Resource Extraction

$$\frac{\partial L}{\partial S} = \lambda. \tag{6.12}$$

Therefore, the Lagrange multiplier reflects how much the objective function—the present value of profit in the present case—would increase if the constraint were to be reduced by one unit (or if the reserve initially were larger by one unit, respectively). However, if the reserve is unlimited, a further increase does not contribute to the value of the objective function, implying $\lambda = 0$. In this case, the market price of the reserve is equal to the marginal cost of extraction, in keeping with Eq. (6.11). Thus, one obtains the classical rule, "price equal marginal cost" that characterizes competitive markets without exhaustible resources.

- Surcharge on marginal cost, scarcity rent, user cost: The surcharge on the marginal cost of extraction depends on the value of the Lagrange multiplier λ. From the above interpretation of Eq. (6.12), one may infer that λ has a large value when the stock S is small and *vice versa*. Thus, the surcharge is high and increases fast when the reserve is small, causing λ to be large. Note that only the initial value of S is relevant for depletion along the Hotelling trajectory.
- Price increase over time: Even given a constant marginal cost of extraction, the market price of the reserve increases over time. This can be seen by writing Eq. (6.11) for period $t-1$,

$$p_{t-1} - c = \lambda(1+i)^{t-1}. \tag{6.13}$$

Dividing (6.11) by (6.13), one obtains

$$\frac{p_t - c}{p_{t-1} - c} = 1 + i \text{ or, after multiplying by } (p_{t-1} - c), \quad \frac{p_t - p_{t-1}}{p_{t-1}} = i. \tag{6.14}$$

Therefore, the (inflation-adjusted, real) price of the resource increases exponentially at a rate that equals the rate of interest on capital markets. This increase reflects the fact that the reserve becomes increasingly scarce as extraction continues, requiring its market price p_t to go up relative to the prices of other goods and services.

The difference $p_t - c$ is called scarcity rent (or user cost, respectively). It amounts to the economic value of the reserve in the ground. If a company were to acquire the property right of a deposit, it would have to pay a price according to this user cost, provided markets for property rights are efficient.[2] Indeed, the sum of so-called nonreproducible capital (i.e. the reserve in the ground) represents total fixed assets

---

[2] In many countries exhaustible resources are considered public property, which hampers trade in deposits and causes pertinent markets to deviate from economic efficiency.

of a resource-extracting company. In the optimum, both types of assets (reproducible, nonreproducible) achieve the same rate of return.

6.2.2 Role of Backstop Technologies

No price can increase without limit. Sooner or later, the price of a reserve will attain p_{subst}, at which some energy source becomes competitive as a substitute. Assuming that this alternative source can supply an amount sufficient to match demand at that price, the sales price of the reserve-extracting industry cannot exceed p_{subst} because its product would not be competitive anymore. This alternative energy source is the so-called backstop technology that will substitute the reserve, at the latest once it is exhausted (and possibly sooner).

This fact determines the optimum supply price in the current period, which can be shown as follows. If extracting companies are successful in maximizing net present value, the scarcity rent in the last period ($p_T - c$) must be equal to ($p_{subst} - c_{subst}$). Discounting back to period t, one obtains[3]

$$p_t - c = (p_T - c)(1+i)^{t-T} = (p_{subst} - c)(1+i)^{t-T}. \qquad (6.15)$$

More generally, the Hotelling price trajectory describes the stepwise transition from the least costly but scarce energy source to the next-best but more expensive substitute. This goes on until the most costly but unlimited backstop technology becomes competitive. In this process, the cheapest deposit is used up first, followed by a cascade of more costly deposits.

One last property of the Hotelling trajectory is noteworthy. Figure 6.4 shows how—depending on the rate of interest—optimal paths of the reserve extraction and the associated prices may look like given the assumptions made above. In this example, the initial stock of reserves is $S = 100$ and the price of the backstop technology, $p_{subst} = 80$. In all trajectories, the price of the backstop is reached, but the point in time depends on the rate of interest. At low interest rates, the optimal extraction period is long, the initial price of the reserve high, and the price increase over time relatively slow.

The reason is that at a low rate of interest, the opportunity cost of foregoing interest income by leaving the resource in the ground rather than selling it is low, causing the optimal extraction period to be long. Conversely, at a high rate of interest, this opportunity cost is substantial, calling for timely extraction. At extremely high rates of interest, it is optimal to deplete the deposit as quickly as possible. In that case, the owner of the extraction right does not take scarcity rent

---
[3]This is the typical approach for solving dynamic optimization problems: Calculation of the current optimal price is based on the optimal intertemporal price trajectory defined by the so-called transversality condition (6.14) which is a dynamic equation with at first unknown parameters. Based on the conditions for the final state, the optimal price given the parameter values can be determined, resulting from backward induction from future T to present t.

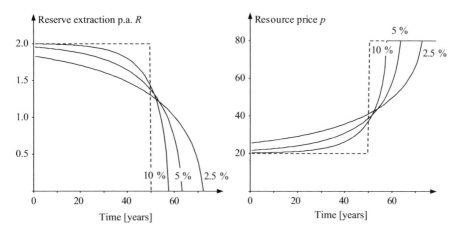

Fig. 6.4 Optimal extraction trajectories of an exhaustible resource

into account. This causes the remaining period of utilization to fall—by as much as two decades in the example of Fig. 6.4.

Another determinant of the optimal extraction period is the size of the cost advantage ($p_{subst} - c_{subst}$), also called differential rent. To illustrate, let T^* be the period in which ($p_{subst} - c_{subst}$) = ($p_T - c$) exceeds 5% of marginal extraction cost c. In view of Eq. (6.15), T^* must satisfy the following condition,

$$(p_T - c)(1 + i)^{-T^*} = 0.05 \cdot c \text{ or}$$
$$T^* = \frac{1}{\ln(1+i)} \cdot (\ln 20 - \ln c + \ln(p_T - c)). \quad (6.16)$$

According to Eq. (6.16), T^* does not depend on the stock of reserves S but on marginal extraction cost c, the cost advantage of the deposit, and the real interest rate i. The differential rent ($p_T - c$) is determined, among other things, by the (expected) backup cost c_{subst} [see Eq. (6.16) again]. If research and development leads to a drop in this cost, the differential rent decreases, causing the present rate of extraction R_t to increase and the price of the reserve to fall. Thus, lower backup costs are beneficial to the users of the resource and society in general.

However, the investment in backstop technology pays back only after T^*, when it becomes competitive. Private investors will hardly undertake investments into research and development if T^* is far off. Yet such investments generate a positive externality, which may provide a justification for their public (co-)financing (IEA 2000).

6.2.3 Role of Expectations and Expectation Errors

One of the assumptions underlying the Hotelling price trajectory [defined by Eqs. (6.14) and (6.15)] is perfect foresight. However, parameters such as the size of deposits, their quality, the future cost of extraction, and future market prices are highly uncertain. One may use average expectations held by market participants to render the Hotelling trajectory applicable to the case of uncertainty (provided market participants are risk-neutral).

However, expectations may turn out to be wrong. If a majority of market participants have to adjust their expectations, reserve quantities supplied and prices must adjust as well. Table 6.3 illustrates the case of two crude oil deposits with differing marginal cost of extraction. If the owner of the extraction right expects a price increase of 2 USD/bbl, the scarcity rent of the deposit increases by 6.7% for deposit A and 10% for deposit B, respectively. Assuming an interest rate of 8%, deposit A would be depleted, since its scarcity rent increases more slowly than the interest rate (0.067 < 0.08). Deposit B would be preserved for later use (0.10 > 0.08). This corresponds to the general rule that low-cost deposits are exploited first.

Now let the expected price increase be 5 USD/bbl, causing the owner of the extraction right to expect an increase of the scarcity rent of 16.6% and 25%, respectively. In this case, it becomes optimal to defer extraction for both deposits. As a consequence, current market supply is reduced and price tends to increase.

This example illustrates the phenomenon of self-fulfilling expectations. When the owners of extraction rights expect the price of their reserve to increase, they reduce the rate of extraction, thus reinforcing expectations. Since price expectations may change fast, for example due to revised estimates of reserves, resource markets are predicted to exhibit excessive price volatility. Indeed, the standard deviation of daily crude oil prices is high, amounting to some 30% according to Plourde and

Table 6.3 The role of expectations: a crude oil example

	Deposit A	Deposit B
Price in period t (USD/bbl)	50	50
Cost per barrel (USD)	20	30
	Expected price increase 2 USD/bbl	
Scarcity rent (USD/bbl)		
In period t	30	20
In period $t+1$	32	22
Growth rate of scarcity rent (%)	6.7	10.0
	Expected price increase 5 USD/bbl	
Scarcity rent (USD/bbl)		
In period t	30	20
In period $t+1$	35	25
Growth rate of scarcity rent (%)	16.6	25.0

Watkins (1998). This explains the need of both resource owners and their customers to apply appropriate strategies for hedging price risks.

6.3 Optimal Resource Extraction: Social Welfare View

The Hotelling price trajectory was derived from the profit-maximizing behavior of individual firms. This gives rise to the question of whether the outcome of individual decisions coincides with the interest of society. The model presented below (following Dasgupta and Heal 1979) rests on several assumptions, such as constant population, fixed homogenous reserve stock S, and constant social rate of time preference r (see Sect. 3.4).

Compared to the Hotelling formulation, the model is extended in two ways. First, the objective is not profit but utility derived from consumption of goods and services (the neoclassical definition of welfare). Second, the exhaustible reserve is not consumed directly but constitutes a factor of production that is used in the making of consumption goods. This second assumption is crucial because it opens up the possibility of substitution between exhaustible resources and reproducible capital, which can grow over time. In continuous time with an infinite time horizon, the objective function is the discounted sum of utilities W derived from consumption C_t ($t = 0, 1, 2,\ldots, \infty$),

$$W = \int_0^\infty U(C_t)\,e^{-rt} dt. \tag{6.17}$$

Using r to discount future utilities implies attributing reduced weight to the utility of future generations. This is a debatable assumption. However, without discounting, the infinite integral (6.17) would not converge toward a finite value.

There are two constraints that must be observed. First, the stock of the reserve S is finite, causing the sum of extractions $R_t \geq 0$ to be limited,

$$\int_0^\infty R_t\,dt \leq S. \tag{6.18}$$

Since it would not make economic sense to leave reserves in the ground at the end of an infinitely long planning horizon, this constraint becomes an equality. Moreover, (6.18) masks an equation of motion reflecting the effect of reserve extraction on the value of the remaining stock.[4] This becomes evident when the remaining stock S_t is differentiated with respect to time t,

---

[4]If the reserve is renewable as e.g. wood, a different formulation is appropriate: The decrease of reserve depends on extractions from and additions to the reserve through regeneration processes, which often are a function of the remaining stock.

$$R_t = -\frac{dS_t}{dt}. \tag{6.19}$$

The second constraint relates consumption C_t to output Q. Output is given by a production function with capital K_t and currently extracted reserves R_t as its arguments. If the production function is independent of time (thus neglecting technological change), consumption is given by

$$C_t = Q(K_t, R_t) - \frac{dK_t}{dt} - \delta K_t - cR_t \tag{6.20}$$

Net investment dK_t/dt, depreciation δK_t, and unit cost of extraction cR_t must be deducted from output $Q(K_t, R_t)$ to obtain the quantity available for consumption. In principle, the production function should also have labor as an argument (see Sect. 5.3), but in view of the assumed constancy of population and technology (implying constant labor productivity), neglecting labor does not modify the core findings while simplifying the analysis.

The objective function (6.17) cannot be analyzed using the methods of static optimization because the constraints, represented by the equations of motion, tie stock and flow variables together. This calls for dynamic optimization methods (see Dasgupta and Heal 1979; Chiang 1992). The point of departure is a generalized Lagrange function,

$$\begin{aligned} L = \int_0^\infty U(C_t) e^{-rt} dt + \lambda_t \left(R_t - \frac{dS_t}{dt} \right) + \\ \omega_t \left(Q(K_t, R_t) - C_t - \frac{dK_t}{dt} - \delta K_t - cR_t \right). \end{aligned} \tag{6.21}$$

The first term is the original objective function. The second term takes the constraint (6.19) into account, using the Lagrange multiplier λ_t. This multiplier indicates the extent to which the value of the objective function would diminish if in period t one unit of the reserve were to be extracted in excess of the optimal change in the stock dSt/dt. Therefore, λ_t reflects the opportunity cost of the reserve, which changes over time (in contradistinction to the Hotelling formulation, where it is constant). The third term introduces the constraint on consumption, using the Lagrange multiplier ω_t. This multiplier indicates the extent to which the value of the objective function would diminish if consumption in t were to grow in excess of optimal consumption. Therefore, ω_t denotes the opportunity cost of consumption, which also may vary over time.[5]

In the language of dynamic optimization theory, the Lagrange function has two state variables, K_t and S_t and two control variables, C_t and R_t. As the model has an infinite time horizon, no conditions concerning the final state need to be imposed.

---

[5]The term 'shadow price' is sometimes used instead of 'opportunity cost'.

6.3 Optimal Resource Extraction: Social Welfare View

For the derivation of first-order optimality conditions, the so-called Hamiltonian function is defined. One obtains two equivalent formulations,

$$H = U(C_t)e^{-rt} + \lambda_t \left(R_t - \frac{dS_t}{dt} \right) + \omega_t \left(Q(K_t, R_t) - C_t - \frac{dK_t}{dt} - \delta K_t - cR_t \right)$$
(values discounted to present value)
$$H_c = U(C_t) + \lambda_{c,t} \left(R_t - \frac{dS_t}{dt} \right) + \omega_{c,t} \left(Q(K_t, R_t) - C_t - \frac{dK_t}{dt} - \delta K_t - cR_t \right)$$
(current values)
with $\lambda_t = e^{-rt} \lambda_{c,t}$ and $\omega_t = e^{-rt} \omega_{c,t}$.

(6.22)

Whereas the first version refers to discounted utilities and Lagrange multipliers, the second version (to be expounded below) refers to utilities in current values.

For the Hamiltonian function in current values, the first-order optimality conditions read

$$\frac{\partial H_c}{\partial C_t} = \frac{\partial U}{\partial C_t} - \omega_{c,t} = 0, \text{ implying } \omega_{c,t} = \frac{\partial U}{\partial C_t}, \qquad (6.23)$$

$$\frac{\partial H_c}{\partial R_t} = -\lambda_{c,t} - \omega_{c,t} \left(\frac{\partial Q_t}{\partial R_t} - c \right) = 0, \text{ implying } \lambda_{c,t} = \omega_{c,t} \left(\frac{\partial Q}{\partial R_t} - c \right). \qquad (6.24)$$

The first condition thus states that the marginal value of consumption must always be equal to its opportunity cost. The second optimality condition shows that additional extraction R_t of the resource has two effects that must balance in the optimum. The first effect is a reduction in the reserve remaining which is valued using the opportunity cost of the reserve $\lambda_{c,t}$. The other effect is the extra production (net of extraction cost), enabling consumption to grow, which is valued using the opportunity cost of consumption $\omega_{c,t}$.

The Hamiltonian function needs to be differentiated also with respect to the two state variables, reserve stock S_t and reproducible capital K_t. They are to be considered as indirect decision variables because they are linked to R_t and C_t through Eqs. (6.20) and (6.21), respectively. Moreover, they affect their pertinent Lagrange multipliers $\lambda_{c,t}$ and $\omega_{c,t}$. The respective optimality conditions read (for the mathematical derivation see Chiang 1992),

$$\frac{\partial H_c}{\partial S_t} = \frac{d\lambda_{c,t}}{dt} - r\lambda_{c,t} = 0, \text{ implying } \frac{d\lambda_{c,t}}{dt} = r\lambda_{c,t}, \qquad (6.25)$$

$$\frac{\partial H_c}{\partial K_t} = \frac{d\omega_{c,t}}{dt} - r\omega_{c,t} = 0, \text{ implying } \frac{d\omega_{c,t}}{dt} = r\omega_{c,t}. \qquad (6.26)$$

Note that the first condition takes into account that the rate of depletion dS/dt does not depend on the current stock S_t, while the second condition is based on the simplifying assumption that any extra investment and hence acceleration in the buildup of capital, $d/dt(dK/dt) = d^2K/dt^2$, offsets the rate of depreciation δ.

Now Eq. (6.25) implies the so-called Hotelling rule (dropping the t subscript for simplicity),

$$\frac{d\lambda_c}{dt} \cdot \frac{1}{\lambda_{c,t}} = r. \tag{6.27}$$

Therefore, the welfare optimum requires the opportunity cost of the reserve to increase with the rate of social time preference r. If r equals the market interest rate i (which holds if capital markets are perfect), the Hotelling rule coincides with the Hotelling price trajectory. In this case, individual decisions of resource-extracting firms are in accordance with the social welfare optimum.

6.3.1 The Optimal Consumption Path

From Eq. (6.26) in combination with the Hamiltonian function (6.24), the so-called Ramsey rule for the optimal consumption path can be derived. Substitution of (6.24) solved for $d\omega_c/dt$ into (6.26) yields (dropping the t subscript again for simplicity),

$$\frac{d\omega_c}{dt} = -\frac{\partial H_c}{\partial K} + r\omega_c = r\omega_c - \omega_c \frac{\partial Q}{\partial K} = \omega_c (r - Q_K) \text{ with } Q_K := \frac{\partial Q}{\partial K}. \tag{6.28}$$

However, Eq. (6.23) also yields an expression for the opportunity cost of consumption ω_c. Differentiating with respect to time and again simplifying notation gives

$$\frac{d\omega_c}{dt} = \frac{\partial^2 U}{\partial C^2} \cdot \frac{\partial C}{\partial t} \text{ or } \frac{d\omega_c}{dt} = U''(C) \cdot \frac{dC}{dt}, \text{ respectively.} \tag{6.29}$$

Equality of these two equations leads to

$$\omega_c(r - Q_K) = \frac{dC}{dt} U''(C). \tag{6.30}$$

Finally, ω_c can be replaced by the marginal utility of consumption in view of Eq. (6.24)

$$U'(C)(r - Q_K) = \frac{dC}{dt} U''(C). \tag{6.31}$$

Division by C leads to the following expression for the relative change of consumption,

$$\frac{dC}{dt}\frac{1}{C} = \frac{U'(C)(r - Q_K)}{U''(C)C} = \frac{1}{\frac{U''(C)C}{U'(C)}}(r - Q_K). \quad (6.32)$$

The quotient on the right-hand side can be rewritten because the relative change in the marginal utility of consumption $\partial U'(C)/U'(C)$ divided by the relative change of consumption $\partial C/C$ is the same as the elasticity of the marginal utility of consumption with respect to consumption itself (recall that an elasticity relates two relative changes to each other). Under the usual assumption of a decreasing marginal utility of consumption ($U''(C) < 0$), the pertinent elasticity η is defined in a way as to obtain a positive value,

$$\eta := -\frac{\partial[U'(C)]/U'(C)}{\partial C/C} = -\frac{\partial[U'(C)]}{\partial C} \cdot \frac{C}{U'(C)} = -\frac{U''(C)C}{U'(C)} > 0. \quad (6.33)$$

Substitution into Eq. (6.32) leads to the Ramsey rule for the optimal consumption path,

$$\frac{dC}{dt}\frac{1}{C} = \frac{Q_K - r}{\eta}. \quad (6.34)$$

This rule states that consumption must decrease over time unless the marginal productivity of capital Q_K is equal to or exceeds the social rate of time preference r. Given a production function $Q(\cdot)$ without technological change, the marginal product of reproducible capital must decrease when capital stock K grows. This is the law of diminishing marginal returns, which holds when one or more of the other inputs are held constant. In the present case, the other input is the non-renewable resource which is not only held constant but even tends to decline over time. Therefore $Q_K < r$ holds sooner or later, suggesting that consumption C must decrease in the long run. However, a long-run fall in consumption is not only due to the depletion of reserves but also to the discounting of future utilities with $r \geq 0$. In Sect. 6.4.2 below, it is shown that a different formulation of the objective function permits, under certain conditions, a non-declining level of consumption in the long run.

Another element of the Ramsey consumption rule concerns η, the elasticity of the marginal utility of consumption with respect to consumption. This parameter determines the optimal speed of adjustment. Consider a reduction of consumption: Given usual assumptions, this causes the marginal utility of consumption to increase. If the value of η is large, this marginal utility increases fast (the utility function is strongly convex from below), indicating a high loss of utility if consumption is to fall. According to Eq. (6.34), optimal adjustment should be slow in this case. Conversely, if η is small, the utility function is almost linear; therefore, a fall in consumption causes a small loss of utility, indicating that optimal adjustment can be fast.

6.3.2 The Optimal Depletion Path of the Reserve

The model permits to derive another Ramsey rule, this time prescribing the optimal path of reserve depletion. The point of departure is Eq. (6.24), which relates the opportunity cost of the reserve $\lambda_{c,t}$ to the marginal product of the resource Q_R, repeated here for convenience,

$$\frac{\partial H_c}{\partial R_t} = -\lambda_{c,t} - \omega_{c,t}\left(\frac{\partial Q_t}{\partial R_t} - c\right) = 0, \text{ implying } \lambda_{c,t} = \omega_{c,t}\left(\frac{\partial Q}{\partial R_t} - c\right). \quad (6.24)$$

Differentiating with respect to time yields, noting the constancy of unit extraction cost c and dropping the t subscript again,

$$\frac{d\lambda_c}{dt} = \frac{d\omega_c}{dt} Q_R + \omega_c \frac{dQ_R}{dt}. \quad (6.35)$$

Since $d(Q_R - c)/dt = dQ_R/dt$ and in view of Eq. (6.24), the relative change in the opportunity cost of the reserve is given by

$$\frac{d\lambda_c}{dt}\frac{1}{\lambda_c} = \frac{\frac{d\omega_c}{dt} Q_R + \omega_c \frac{dQ_R}{dt}}{\omega_c Q_R} = \frac{d\omega_c}{dt}\frac{1}{\omega_c} + \frac{dQ_R}{dt}\frac{1}{Q_R}. \quad (6.36)$$

In the optimum, the relative change in the opportunity cost of the reserve must therefore be equal to the sum of relative changes in two other parameters,

- The marginal utility of consumption;
- The marginal productivity of the reserve.

According to the Hotelling rule, the rate of change in λ_c needs to be equal to the social rate of time preference r for overall optimality, implying $(d\lambda/dt)/\lambda = r$. Moreover, Eq. (6.28) can be divided by the opportunity cost of consumption ω_c to obtain $d\omega_c/\omega_c = r - Q_K$. Substitution of these expressions into the left-hand and right-hand sides of Eq. (6.36) yields

$$r = r - Q_K + \frac{dQ_R}{dt}\frac{1}{Q_R}. \quad (6.37)$$

From this, the Ramsey rule for the optimal resource depletion path follows immediately,

$$Q_K = \frac{dQ_R/dt}{Q_R}. \quad (6.38)$$

Optimally, the marginal product of the exhaustible resource Q_R must therefore increase at a rate equal to the marginal product of capital Q_K. In the absence of technological change, the marginal product of a production factor can only be increased by using less of it (law of diminishing marginal returns). Thus, the increase of the marginal product of the resource over time implies a diminishing rate of extraction.

6.3.3 Causes and Implications of Market Failure

Given equality of the social rate of time preference and the market rate of interest, society's welfare is maximized if the Hotelling rule is satisfied. Therefore, it would be beneficial for this rule to govern resource markets. As shown in Sect. 6.2, this would also be the optimal solution for reserve-extracting firms, at least under idealistic assumptions such as perfect information and atomistic competition. Yet the reality of resource markets is usually far from satisfying these assumptions. Besides discrepancies between the rate of social time preference and the market rate of interest caused by capital market imperfections, variations in the cost and quality of reserve deposits, and the presence of external costs, there are three problems that are of particular relevance in the context of exhaustible energy sources.

1. Suboptimal extraction capacity: For the Hotelling rule to hold, the rate of extraction R_t needs to be sufficiently flexible. However, geological conditions, limited extraction capacities and bottlenecks in logistics can cause R_t to fall short of the value required by the Hotelling rule. To keep extraction (and with it, production) on the optimal trajectory, additional investment in resource extraction is needed as a rule, which however may create excess capacities given that R_t is to decline in the near future. Anticipating this, companies tend to underinvest in extraction relative to the level that would be necessary to satisfy the Hotelling rule.

   The decision concerning investment in extraction capacity is based on a calculation at the margin. If extraction capacity falls short of the value required by the Hotelling rule, society suffers economic losses. Yet, a capacity expansion according to this rule may also cause losses due to future underuse of this capacity. In the optimum, the two losses must be equal. As long as capacity is below its Hotelling value, extraction occurs at the rate compatible with maximum capacity utilization. This causes the price of the resource to be in excess of the Hotelling price path, with the discrepancy indicating the opportunity cost of the capacity bottleneck. However, this discrepancy decreases over time since depletion of the reserve drives the resource price up and the extraction rate down until the bottleneck no longer exists. The market price then catches up with the Hotelling price path, as shown on the left-hand side of Fig. 6.5 (note that the abscissa is not time but cumulated extraction). Thus, the deviation from the optimal trajectory is transitory rather than permanent in this case.

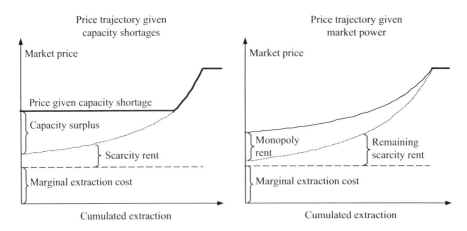

Fig. 6.5 Prices in the presence of capacity shortages and market power

2. Exercise of market power by cartels and monopolies: Market power also causes a deviation from the Hotelling price path. To the extent that owners of extraction rights succeed in imposing a price in excess of the competitive level, demand for the resource falls short of the volume predicated by the Hotelling path. This causes depletion to be slower than under competitive conditions. Therefore, the scarcity rent λ_c is lower than in the competitive case (see the right-hand side of Fig. 6.5), again noting that the abscissa shows cumulated extraction). However, due to the monopoly, the market price of the resource is higher than given competition.

On the one hand, one may hail the slowing of reserve depletion and the concomitant mitigation of environmental effects ("the monopolist is the environment's best friend"). On the other hand, society's welfare suffers (unambiguously in the absence of external costs) because of the higher resource price and the associated loss of consumer surplus. This time, violation of the Hotelling rule continues as long as prices are affected by monopoly power.

3. Market rate of interest higher than the social rate of time preference ($i > r$): A discrepancy of this type may be due to capital market imperfections. A high interest rate implies a high extraction rate, causing time to depletion to be shortened. The rate of interest may be high because financiers demand a surcharge for the risks associated with exploration, which they tend to overestimate due to information asymmetries. Another reason are poorly defined property rights. This may occur if several firms extract from the same deposit while reserves are geologically mobile, as is the case with conventional crude oil and natural gas fields. This creates an incentive for each company to extract as much of the resource as possible, to the detriment of its competitors (this is known as the common pool problem). An excessive rate of extraction is also to be expected if companies fear expropriation of their rights (through so-called nationalization). Finally, excess extraction can occur in situations where the

holders of the rights (who decide about the extraction rate) are distinct from the owners of the reserve (who claim the scarcity rent). In this case, the scarcity rent fails to provide an economic signal concerning the rate of extraction, which is necessary for the Hotelling price rule to work.

6.4 Sustainability

The sustainability concept originated in forestry, meaning that the use of timber corresponds to the maximum harvest that is compatible with a constant stock of trees. However, contrary to the timber industry, energy sources such as crude oil, natural gas, coal, and uranium are not renewable. The sustainability concept thus cannot be applied without modification to non-renewable energy sources since the stock of the reserves is constant only when extraction is abandoned altogether.

A definition of sustainability that is more suitable to non-renewable energy sources has been proposed by the Brundtland report. According to that report, any development is sustainable "(...) that meets the needs of the present without compromising the ability of future generations to meet their own needs" (WCED 1987, p. 43). Accordingly, a decreasing stock of non-renewable energy sources is admissible as long as the needs of future generations can be met with a reduced availability or even lack of non-renewable energy. This definition is called weak sustainability in distinction to strong sustainability, which calls for always keeping a minimum stock of reserves in favor of future generations.

6.4.1 Potential of Renewable Energy Sources

Weak sustainability is only conceivable if there is a sufficient potential of renewable energy sources globally, amounting to multiples of present global use of primary energy. In fact, the potential of renewable energy sources such as hydropower, solar radiation, wind, biomass, ocean energy, and geothermal energy is abundant. The energy of solar radiation hitting the outer atmosphere amounts to 0.14 W/cm^2 (the so-called solar constant). The insolated surface of the Earth is given by

$$6366^2 \pi \, (\text{km}^2) = 1\,273 \times 10^{15} (\text{cm}^2) \tag{6.39}$$

This corresponds to an energy inflow of 178,000 TWa, of which the continents receive 25,000 TWa. Some 6% of total radiation energy hits deserts and wastelands that have no alternate land use. If that solar energy could be transformed into usable energy with an energy efficiency of only 10%, the world would dispose of 37.5 TWa or 28 bn toe, respectively (the technical potential), which is a multiple of today's global energy consumption of about 12.7 bn toe (see Table 2.5).

Table 6.4 Worldwide potential of renewable energy sources

	Theoretical potential (EJ/a)	Technical potential (EJ/a)	Used potential 2013 (EJ)
Biomass (incl. non commercial energy)	2200	160–270	50.0
Hydropower	200	50–60	25.1
Geothermal energy	1500	810–1545	2.3
Wind energy	110,000	1250–2250	4.2
Ocean energy	1,000,000	3240–10,500	–
Solar radiation	3,900,000	62,000–280,000	0.8
Primary energy share			13.5%

EJ= 1 Exajoule = 10^{18} J = 2.39 bn toe
Sources: GEA (2012) and BP (2014)

Therefore, if used to its potential, solar radiation alone would be sufficient to fully eliminate the use of non-renewable energy sources worldwide (see Table 6.4). Additional potential energy sources come from wind, biomass, and possibly nuclear fusion. The technologies required for their use are known in principle. Non-renewable energy sources are thus entirely substitutable as long as there are no other, non-energetic constraints (such as scarcity of precious metals and rare earths as necessary inputs), and as long as harvest rates (see Sect. 2.4) in excess of 1 can be attained.

The limited use of renewable energies is mainly due to their still rather high cost, which in turn is caused by their low energy density (defined as energy flow per m^2 surface or m^3 volume). Therefore capacities for collecting renewable energy require relatively high volumes of material and capital. A second cause, related in particular to solar, wind, and tidal energy, is their discontinuous availability that usually implies low rates of capacity utilization and a backup system in the case of renewable electricity (see Sect. 12.2). Yet, there have been substantial preindustrial uses of renewable energy sources such as biomass and hydropower, benefiting from the fact that nature offers collectors for free in the guise of woody plants and rivers. Accordingly, harvesting these sources of energy is relatively cheap. Indeed, biomass and hydropower continue to constitute the most important renewable sources of the global energy system.

6.4.2 Hartwick Rule for Weak Sustainability

As shown in Sect. 6.3, the Hotelling rule implies a price signal that incentivizes the efficient extraction and use of non-renewable reserves. However, the corresponding Ramsey consumption trajectory [see Eq. (6.34)] does not ensure an increasing or at least non-declining level of consumption over time. Indeed, future generations could be confronted with a drop in their consumption possibilities, violating the criterion of weak sustainability (see Fig. 6.6).

6.4 Sustainability

Fig. 6.6 Ramsey and Hartwick consumption trajectories

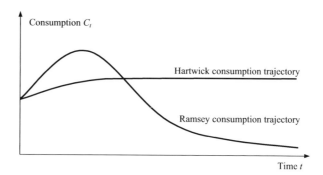

Going beyond neoclassical welfare optimization, economist Solow (1986) introduced the postulate that per-capita consumption must not decrease, in keeping with weak sustainability. Given a constant population, the Solow postulate reads

$$\frac{dC_t}{dt} \geq 0 \quad \text{for all} \quad t. \tag{6.40}$$

Loosely speaking, this guarantees that the welfare of future generations is at least as high as that of the present generation. Additional consumption by the present generation is admissible only if all future generations can attain at least the same or a higher level of consumption. This defines the so-called Hartwick consumption trajectory (Hartwick 1977, see Fig. 6.6). It is derived as follows.

In order to have a positive rate of consumption in spite of exhaustible energy sources such as crude oil and natural gas, it must be possible to substitute these sources completely with renewables at some future time. For achieving this, resource input R needs to be replaced by reproducible (also called manmade) capital K. An example of complete substitution are plants for hydrogen electrolysis that produce alternative fuels using wind power and photovoltaics. If complete substitution of this type can be attained, a positive amount of consumption should in principle be possible in all future periods.

Whether or not the current level of consumption (per capita) is sustainable in the future crucially depends on the answers to two questions:

- How easily can non-renewable reserves be substituted with reproducible capital?
- Is the current generation willing to finance the necessary growth of reproducible capital by partly renouncing to current consumption?

The first question refers to the elasticity of substitution σ_{RK} between the exhaustible resource R and reproducible capital K. As explained in Sect. 5.3.3, the elasticity of substitution indicates how much the cost-minimizing mix of factor inputs (in the present case R and K) adjusts to a change of relative factor prices (unit price of the resource p_R and cost of capital p_K) given that output is to be kept constant,

$$\sigma_{RK} = -\frac{d(R/K)/(R/K)}{d(p_K/p_R)/(p_K/p_R)} = -\frac{d\ln(R/K)}{d\ln(p_K/p_R)}. \quad (6.41)$$

Here, $\sigma_{RK} \geq 1$ indicates easy substitutability; if $\sigma_{RK} < 1$, the exhaustible resource and capital are not easily substitutable. In that case, the predicted increase of p_R (relative to p_K) requires a disproportionately high increase of capital in order to keep the level of production (and with it, consumption) constant, presumably rendering complete substitution impossible.

Assuming $\sigma_{RK} \geq 1$, thus substitutability between reserves R and capital K, the second question has still to be addressed. Here, the Hartwick rule states that weak sustainability ($dC/dt = 0$) is achievable provided the scarcity rent associated with the resource is entirely invested in reproducible capital. The scarcity rent is given by $(p_R - c) \cdot R$, i.e. the excess of the resource price over the unit extraction cost multiplied by the quantity of the resource used in production. Thus the Hartwick rule can be written

$$\begin{aligned}\frac{dK}{dt} &= (p_R - c) \cdot R \text{ and in its differentiated form,} \\ \frac{d^2 K}{dt^2} &= d\left(\frac{(p_R - c) \cdot R}{dt}\right).\end{aligned} \quad (6.42)$$

The proof that this rule ensures weak sustainability given $\sigma_{RK} \geq 1$ proceeds as follows. First, the production function $Q_t = Q(K_t, R_t)$ is differentiated with respect to time,

$$\frac{dQ}{dt} = Q_K \frac{dK}{dt} + Q_R \frac{dR}{dt} \text{ where } Q_K := \frac{dQ}{dK}, Q_R := \frac{dQ}{dR}. \quad (6.43)$$

Therefore, Q_K and Q_R denote the marginal productivities of capital and exhaustible resources, as before. An increase in the capital stock contributes to output depending on its marginal productivity Q_K, while an increase in resource input contributes to output depending on its marginal productivity Q_R.

Production can be used for consumption, gross investment (net investment dK/dt plus depreciation $\delta \cdot K$), and for recovery of the cost of extraction $c \cdot R$ [see Eq. (6.20)],

$$Q(K, R) = C + \frac{dK}{dt} + \delta K + cR. \quad (6.44)$$

Differentiation with respect to time leads to

$$\frac{dQ}{dt} = \frac{dC}{dt} + \frac{d\left(\frac{dK}{dt} + \delta K + cR\right)}{dt}. \quad (6.45)$$

6.4 Sustainability

At this point, the Hotelling price path is invoked. It states that the scarcity rent $(Q_R - c)$ per unit resource must grow in step with the real rate of interest, which in turn equals the marginal productivity of capital [see Eq. (6.25)]. Therefore, one has

$$Q_K = \frac{\frac{d(Q_R - c)}{dt}}{Q_R - c} = \frac{\frac{dQ_R}{dt}}{Q_R - c}. \tag{6.46}$$

The second equality sign takes into account that $dc/dt = 0$ since unit extraction cost is constant by assumption (for a relaxation of assumptions in several dimensions as well as a critical interpretation of the Hartwick rule, see Mitra et al. 2013). Substitution of Eq. (6.46) into Eq. (6.43) yields

$$\frac{dQ}{dt} = \frac{\frac{dQ_R}{dt}}{Q_R - c}\frac{dK}{dt} + Q_R\frac{dR}{dt}. \tag{6.47}$$

To show sufficiency for achieving a non-declining consumption path $dC/dt \geq 0$, the Hartwick rule is assumed to be satisfied.[6] This means that Eq. (6.42) can be used to replace dK/dt in Eq. (6.47), resulting in

$$\frac{dQ}{dt} = \frac{\frac{dQ_R}{dt}}{Q_R - c}(Q_R - c)R + Q_R\frac{dR}{dt} = R\frac{dQ_R}{dt} + Q_R\frac{dR}{dt}. \tag{6.48}$$

Provided the Hartwick rule holds, the change of aggregate production can thus be reduced to the sum of two terms:

- The change in the marginal productivity of the resource, weighted by the quantity of the resource;
- The change in resource use, weighted by its marginal productivity.

Equation (6.48) is the result of the differentiation of a product. Therefore, one has

$$\frac{dQ}{dt} = \frac{d(Q_R R)}{dt}. \tag{6.49}$$

Finally, solving eq. (6.45) for dC/dt using (6.49) and rearranging terms results in

---

[6] Withagen and Asheim (1998) have shown that the Hartwick rule is also a necessary condition for weak sustainability.

$$\frac{dC}{dt} = \frac{d(Q_R R)}{dt} - \frac{d\left(\frac{dK}{dt} + \delta K + cR\right)}{dt} = \frac{d(Q_R R - cR)}{dt} - \frac{d^2 K}{dt^2} - \frac{d\delta K}{dt} \quad (6.50)$$
$$= \frac{d(p_R - c)R}{dt} - \frac{d(p_R - c)R}{dt} - \frac{d\delta K}{dt} = 0$$

if the amount of capital depreciation δK is a constant. The last equality sign uses the differentiated form of the Hartwick rule (6.42). As a consequence, consumption remains constant over time ($dC/dt = 0$) as long as this rule is satisfied. If the present generation complies with it, future generations will be able to enjoy the same level of consumption as today's population.

However, the question remains whether this steady consumption level is strictly positive ($C > 0$) or not. Solow (1974) provided an answer using the Cobb-Douglas production function

$$Q = \alpha K^\beta R^\gamma \quad \text{with } \alpha, \beta, \gamma > 0. \quad (6.51)$$

According to Solow, maximum possible consumption in this case is given by[7]

$$C_{max} = (1-c)(S_0(\beta - \gamma))^{\frac{\gamma}{1-\gamma}} K_0^{\frac{\beta-\gamma}{1-\gamma}} \quad \text{with initial values } K_0 \text{ and } S_0. \quad (6.52)$$

Eq. (6.52) shows that a sustainable positive consumption level $C_{max} > 0$ requires two conditions to be simultaneously satisfied.

- $c < 1$: The marginal cost of extraction must not exceed the marginal productivity of the resource; otherwise, the reserve S_0 would lower output to begin with, causing the buildup of capital to be counter-productive (this is intuitive because the two factors of production are used in combination).
- $\beta > \gamma$: The elasticity of output with respect to the capital input must exceed the elasticity of output with respect to the resource input (which is intuitive, too).

The Cobb-Douglas production function is characterized by a unitary elasticity of substitution between the two inputs ($\sigma_{RK} = 1$). If $\sigma_{RK} > 1$, a higher level of consumption than the one determined by Eq. (6.52) can be sustained, whereas if $\sigma_{RK} < 1$, a positive level of consumption is impossible in the long run because production without any use of the exhaustible resource cannot be attained. Figure 6.7 illustrates the two cases. In the left-hand panel, a production function with an elasticity of substitution $\sigma_{RK} = 0.75$ is shown. No output is possible given $R = 0$ (at point A_0, for example). The right-hand panel shows a production function

---

[7]Given a constant rate of social time preference r, this (flat) consumption path is not optimal in the sense of the objective function (6.17) of Sect. 6.3. However, it can be shown that if r decreases over time according to $r_t = (1 + a \cdot t)^{-b}$ with $a, b > 0$, then the sustainable level of consumption according to Eq. (6.52) is also optimal.

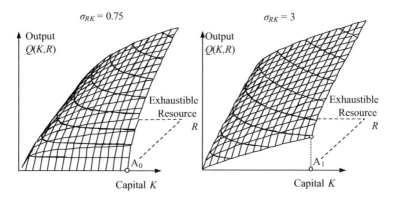

Fig. 6.7 Production function with alternative elasticities of substitution

with $\sigma_{RK} = 3$. Here, positive output ($Q > 0$) is feasible given $R = 0$ (at point A_1, for example).

Evidently, the elasticity of substitution is crucial for weak sustainability. Yet it is a local property of the production function and may change its value when inputs of capital K_t and reserves R_t vary in the course of time t. Indeed, the increasing scarcity of the exhaustible resource causes the two inputs to change over time. Weak sustainability requires that the average value of the substitution elasticity along its trajectory $\{\sigma_{RK,t}, t=t_0, t_1, \ldots \}$ is larger or equal to one, permitting the non-renewable resource to be completely substituted by reproducible capital.

The fact that the elasticity of substitution is a local property of the production function has important implications. This can best be explained using the example of wind power, which constitutes an option for replacing fossil fuels. With existing technologies, wind power can already today replace some fossil fuels.[8] However, the best sites for wind generation are the first to be occupied, leaving inferior sites for additional investment designed to substitute fossil fuels. Without technological change, future substitution may therefore become more difficult (σ_{RK} decreases). In this case, the expansion of wind power generation may bind a great deal of capital in the long run, leaving less production output for consumption. This may jeopardize the weak sustainability condition $dC/dt \geq 0$ even though substitutability between fossil fuels and wind power obtains at present.

6.4.3 Population Growth and Technological Change

Section 6.4.2 defines weak sustainability to mean non-decreasing per-capita consumption. Given a production function without technological change and an elasticity of substitution $\sigma_{RK} = 1$, this condition can only be satisfied if population does

---

[8]Substitution could be based on charging electric vehicles using wind power or on electrolysis which uses wind power to produce hydrogen (known as power-to-gas technology).

not grow. However, even with a growing population weak sustainability can be attained if—in addition to stocking up reproducible capital according to the Hartwick rule—factor productivities increase faster than population due to increased know-how and technological change.

Focusing on the latter, the simplest modeling approach is to view technological changes as exogenous and to incorporate it in the Cobb-Douglas production function (6.51) (see Stiglitz 1974),

$$Q_t = \alpha \cdot K_t^\beta \cdot R_t^\gamma \cdot e^{ft} \text{ with parameters } \alpha, \beta, \gamma, f > 0. \qquad (6.53)$$

If the rate of technological change f exceeds the rate of population growth, satisfaction of the Hartwick rule ensures weak sustainability, i.e. non-decreasing per-capita consumption.

The weakness of this approach is that it takes technological change as exogenous. In reality, it is endogenous, driven by (costly) investment in research and development. The many alternatives of modeling this endogeneity cannot be discussed here (see Stoneman 1983 for a survey). Suffice it to remark that 'knowledge' (the stock of know-how and human capital) could be introduced as a factor of production of its own. Its special feature is that it does not decrease but rather increases thanks to learning by doing, contrary to natural resources (through extraction) and reproducible capital (through depreciation). Moreover, its rate of increase depends positively on the amount of know-how already accumulated.

Following up on this idea, total capital stock can be viewed as consisting of reserves of exhaustible resources, reproducible capital, and human capital. In keeping with the Hartwick rule, the scarcity rent derived from resource extraction must entirely be invested in reproducible capital. However, growth in knowledge and know-how in excess of population growth permits to increase the rate of production and consumption per capita. Thereby future generations can attain a higher per-capita consumption level than present generations in spite of an increasing scarcity of exhaustible resources.

6.4.4 Is the Hartwick Rule Satisfied?

The Hartwick rule for weak sustainability demands that the scarcity rent from mining and extracting exhaustible resources be entirely invested as reproducible capital rather than used for consumption purposes. This requirement motivated the countries bordering on the North Sea to abstain from paying the revenues from their oil and gas fields into their social security schemes (i.e. for current consumption) but to rather devote them to investment.

Pearce and Atkinson (1998) checked the extent to which the Hartwick rule may be satisfied by resource-extracting countries. The authors define the total stock of capital as the sum of reserves of natural resources and reproducible capital. For this total stock not to decrease, aggregate savings must exceed net revenue from resource extraction $(pR - c) \cdot R$ plus depreciation of reproducible capital δK,

$$Savings \geq (p_R - c)R + \delta K. \qquad (6.54)$$

Countries with a high rate of savings[9] and little reserve extraction—among them Japan and many countries of Western Europe—turn out to be on the path of (weak) sustainability, at least during the observation period. Brazil, Indonesia, the United Kingdom, and the United States are borderline cases because their rate of savings (which is relatively low) combines with a good deal of reserve extraction. However, the African countries sampled fail to satisfy the Hartwick rule. Yet Proops et al. (1999) showed that this assessment changes drastically as soon as international trade in resources is accounted for. In particular, oil-exporting as well as oil-importing countries were found to live off their future generations. By way of contrast, Weitzman (1997) estimated the United States to be in accord with the rule; due to technological change, its future production and consumption possibilities increase much faster than they diminish due to resource extraction.

Political implementation of the Hartwick rule is an issue of its own. Norway is one of the first countries to follow it. Aware of the fact that the country's oil and gas reserves in the North Sea are limited, the Norwegian government began in 1990 to transfer its revenues from oil and gas sales to the Norwegian Government Pension Fund, which is not part of the public budget but is administered by the Norwegian Central Bank. The assets of the Fund, being invested on the international capital market, are exposed to the volatility of stock prices. Their use is decided by the Norwegian parliament, who has credited only the returns (adjusted for inflation) to the public purse until today, leaving the principal intact. With roughly 130 bn EUR at the end of 2004 and 600 bn EUR by the end of 2014, the Fund is one of the largest sovereign wealth funds worldwide. While its later use is not decided yet, the Hartwick rule suggests long-term investments in the development of alternative energy sources, infrastructure, education, and research. However, in view of fast growth of its assets, there is considerable political pressure to use it for consumption purposes as well.

The Norwegian Fund is designed not only to implement the Hartwick rule but also to insulate the public budget from the volatilities of oil and gas prices, and to protect the economy from the so-called Dutch disease. The Dutch disease is a scenario which can occur in small countries with an important resource extraction sector. The large-scale expansion of this sector generates important export revenues which usually are exchanged in domestic currency. This demand drives up the domestic currency, causing domestic goods to become expensive compared to foreign goods. As a consequence, the country's international competitiveness suffers, hampering its exports of other goods and services (e.g. by fisheries in the case of Norway).[10]

---

[9]Macroeconomic savings divided by the Gross Domestic Product.

[10]This phenomenon was first observed in The Netherlands at the beginning of an export boom at the beginning of the 1970s, hence its name 'Dutch disease'.

Indeed, large oil and gas deposits may turn out to be a curse rather than a blessing for many economies. Norway is one of the few energy-exporting countries to have clearly benefited up to now, motivating several oil-exporting countries to copy Norway by creating similar sovereign wealth funds.

Yet the accumulation of the scarcity rents derived from the extraction of oil and gas can pose another problem if it results in high amounts relative to global capital markets. According to the Hotelling price trajectory, scarcity rents grow over time, while according to the Hartwick rule, they need to be invested rather than consumed. However, do global capital markets offer sufficient investment opportunities? What happens to the (real) interest rate when the supply of capital continues to increase? What if the funds are invested in financial instruments only, in response to a lack of productive investment opportunities? Is the global financial system stable at all? Indeed, international capital markets may not be capable of accommodating the global inflow of scarcity rents which has surpassed 1000 bn USD annually, equivalent to 2% of the world's Gross Domestic Product. In addition, concentration of these funds in the hands of a few oil-exporting countries poses a particular risk to the countries hosting this foreign investment.

References

Adelman, M. A. (1990). Mineral depletion, with special reference to petroleum. *The Review of Economics and Statistics, 72*(1), 1–10.

BGR. (2014). *Reserven, Ressourcen und Verfügbarkeit von Energierohstoffen (Reserves, resources, and availability of energy Resources)*. Hannover: Bundesanstalt für Geowissenschaften und Rohstoffe. Retrieved from www.bgr.bund.de/DE/Themen/Energie/Downloads/Energiestudie_2014.pdf

BP. (2014). *BP statistical review of world energy*. Retrieved from www.bp.com/statisticalreview/

Campbell, C. J., & Laherrere, J. H. (1996). *The world's oil supply 1930–2050*. Geneva: Petroconsultants.

Chiang, A. C. (1992). *Elements of dynamic optimization* (pp. 210–211). New York: McGraw-Hill.

Dasgupta, P. S., & Heal, G. M. (1979). *Economic theory and exhaustible resources*. Cambridge: Cambridge University Press.

Erdmann, G., & Zweifel, P. (2008). *Energieökonomik - Theorie und Anwendungen (Energy economics – theory and applications)* (2nd ed.). Berlin: Springer.

GEA. (2012). *Global energy assessment – toward a sustainable future*. Cambridge University Press. Retrieved from www.iiasa.ac.at/web/home/research/Flagship-Projects/Global-Energy-Assessment/Home-GEA.en.html

Hartwick, J. M. (1977). International equity and the investing of rents from exhaustible resources. *American Economic Review, 67*(5), 972–974.

Hotelling, H. (1931). The economics of exhaustible resources. *Journal of Political Economy, 39*(2), 137.

Hubbert, M. K. (1956). Nuclear energy and fossil fuels. In American Petroleum Institute (Ed.), *Drilling and production practice*. New York: American Petroleum Institute.

Hubbert, M. K. (1962). *Energy resources. A report to the Committee on Natural Resources*. Washington, DC: Government Printing Office. Publication No. 1000-D.

IEA. (2000). *Experience curves for energy technology policy*. Paris: International Energy Agency.

Kaufmann, R. K., & Cleveland, C. J. (2001). Oil production in the lower 48 states: Economic, geological, and institutional determinants. *The Energy Journal, 33*(1), 27–49.

References

Mitra, T., et al. (2013). Characterizing the sustainability problem in an exhaustible resource model. *Journal of Economic Theory, 148*, 2164–2182.

Nakicenovic, N. (2002). Technological change and diffusion as a learning process. In A. Grubler, M. Nakicenovic, & W. Nordhaus (Eds.), *Technological change and the environment* (pp. 160–181). Washington, DC: Resources for the Future Press.

Pearce, D., & Atkinson, G. (1998). The concept of sustainable development: An evaluation ten years after Brundtland. *Swiss Journal of Economics and Statistics, 134*(3), 251–269.

Plourde, A., & Watkins, G. C. (1998). Crude oil prices between 1985 and 1994: How volatile in relation to other commodities? *Resource and Energy Economics, 20*, 245–262.

Proops, J., Atkinson, G., Scholtheim, B., & Simon, S. (1999). International trade and the sustainability footprint: A practical criterion for its assessment. *Ecological Economics, 28*(1), 75–98.

Reynolds, D. B. (2002). Using non-time-series to determine supply elasticity: How far do prices change the Hubbert curve? *OPEC Review, June*, 149–167.

Solow, R. M. (1974). Intergenerational equity and exhaustible resources. *Review of Economic Studies, 41* (*Symposium on the Economics of Exhaustible Resources*), 29–45.

Solow, R. M. (1986). On the intergenerational allocation of natural resources. *Scandinavian Journal of Economics, 88*, 141–149.

Stiglitz, J. E. (1974). Incentives and risk sharing in sharecropping. *Review of Economic Studies, 41* (*Symposium on the Economics of Exhaustible Resources*), 219–256.

Stoneman, P. (1983). *The economic analysis of technological change*. Oxford: Oxford University Press.

WCED. (1987). *From one earth to one world: An overview*. Oxford: World Commission on Environment and Development.

Weitzman, M. L. (1997). Sustainability and technical progress. *Scandinavian Journal of Economics, 99*(1), 1–13.

Withagen, C., & Asheim, G. (1998). Characterizing SUSTAINABILITY: The Converse Hartwick's rule. *Journal of Economic Dynamics and Control, 23*, 159–165.

External Costs

7

A great deal of man-made residue and emissions is connected with the energy economy—from extraction, transformation, and transportation on to the final use of energy. Concepts have been developed in environmental economics for solving the associated problems in an economically efficient way. They revolve around the terms externality, external cost, and avoidance cost (also called abatement cost). Provided damages and risks can be quantified and monetized, internalization strategies are available which shift external costs back to the consumers of energy in the guise of higher energy prices. Market participants are made to extend their avoidance effort to the point where the marginal abatement cost equals marginal damage cost avoided. This is the social optimum.

While these lines of thought look conceptually simple enough, there are several issues that need to be addressed:

- How can externalities be linked to specific emissions?
- How are they to be quantified and expressed in money as to become external costs?
- Frequently, marginal external cost avoided cannot be easily measured, as e.g. in the case of improved air quality. How is one to proceed for determining the optimum?
- An economic expression of the marginal benefit of avoidance is (marginal) willingness to pay of those affected by the externality. Are there ways to measure this?
- So-called market experiments have become popular for estimating willingness to pay. How can they be performed? What are their limitations?
- The so-called standard-price constitutes an alternative. In what circumstances is it to be recommended?

The variables used in this chapter are:
C_{ext} External cost
Em Emissions

Im   Immissions
L   Lagrange function
λ   Shadow price of emissions (Lagrange multiplier)
Π   Profit
p   Price of unit of output
p_e Price of an emission right
Q   Output (quantity)
tax   Tax rate on emissions
U   Utility function
W   Welfare function

7.1 The Coase Theorem

Before presenting the Coase theorem, several terms need to be defined first.

- Emissions: Impacts on the environment emanating from facilities, such as noise, tremor, odor, contamination, and radiation through air, water, and soil;
- Immissions: Concentration of emissions in the environment;
- Damages: Impacts of immissions on health, matter, environment and other aspects for the quality of life that are negatively valued by humans;
- External effects (also called externalities): Negative or positive impacts of an activity performed by an economic agent on other agents without compensation;
- External cost: Negative external effects valued in money.

For an exposition of basic principles, the analysis is first limited to two agents, for example a company operating a plant and the owner of a home in the plant's vicinity. Let emissions from the plant cause a loss of value to the property. The situation can be characterized by the profit function of the company $\Pi = \Pi(Em)$ and the external cost function $C_{ext} = C_{ext}(Em)$. Both are a function of emissions *Em*, which are assumed to vary in proportion with the amount of goods and services produced by the company. Accordingly, nothing is produced at the emissions level $Em = 0$, resulting in external cost $C_{ext} = 0$. In addition, marginal profit Π' is assumed to decrease with production and hence volume of emissions, such that profit reaches its maximum at Em_0, as shown in Fig. 7.1. Marginal external cost C_{ext}' is assumed to increase with *Em*.

If permitted to neglect external cost, the company chooses output and hence emissions in a way as to maximize its profit Π. Emissions therefore will amount to Em_0. Given external marginal cost as depicted in Fig. 7.1, the volume of production targeted by the company is not Pareto-optimal. If the plant were to decrease its production, the loss in terms of profit would be less than the benefit in terms of external cost avoided. The injured party (i.e. the homeowner) could offer to compensate the company for its profit foregone in return for a reduction in its emission and hence damage caused. Note however that generally the welfare-optimal emission level is not $Em = 0$, in contradistinction of what is usually suggested in the political debate.

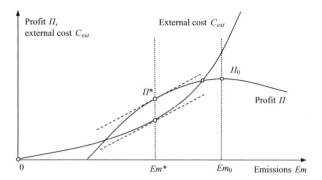

Fig. 7.1 Pareto-optimal output given negative external effects

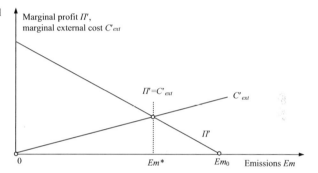

Fig. 7.2 Marginal profit and marginal external cost

This line of thought leads to the so-called Coase theorem (Coase 1960). It is based on the idea that rights to the environment can be allocated to the polluter or the damaged party in the guise of property rights. In the first case, the polluter has the right to cause an external effect. In the second case, the injured party has the right to live in an emission-free environment. Both parties (the company as the polluter and the homeowner as the injured party) could initiate negotiations. These negotiations would proceed depending on the initial allocation of the property right (see Fig. 7.2, which differs from Fig. 7.1 because the company's marginal profit is positive already at $Em = 0$; also note the transition from total to marginal quantities).

- The injured party owns the property right: The company cannot start production without the consent of the homeowner. Prior to negotiations, the point of departure is $Em = 0$. However, the parties should be able to agree on an emission level $Em > 0$ because the company could use part of the additional profit to compensate the homeowner for the negative externality suffered. The result of this negotiation would be an improvement for the company without deterioration for the homeowner. Negotiations would continue until marginal profit Π' coincides with external marginal cost C_{ext}' at Em^*.
- The polluter owns the property right: In this case, the point of departure is the level of emissions Em_0 that maximizes the company's profit. However, the

company should be willing to reduce its output and hence emissions if the injured party accepts to compensate it for the loss of profit incurred. As the injured party would otherwise suffer a much larger loss, it would benefit from such a solution. Once again negotiations would continue until marginal profit Π' equals external marginal cost C_{ext}' at Em^*.

In either case, the negotiation process thus results in a maximization of joint profit or utility, respectively. This optimum can be analytically determined using a welfare function W defined as follows,

$$W = \Pi(Em) - C_{ext}(Em). \tag{7.1}$$

This can be differentiated with respect to emissions Em to obtain

$$\frac{d\Pi}{dEm} - \frac{dC_{ext}}{dEm} = 0 \text{ or } \Pi' = C'_{ext}, \text{respectively.} \tag{7.2}$$

This is the condition, "marginal profit equals external marginal cost", which is satisfied at emission levels Em^* in Figs. 7.1 and 7.2, respectively. Since external marginal cost C'_{ext} increases with emissions, $Em^* < Em_0$ holds, indicating that the optimal amount of emissions is below the level that the company targets on its own (Pearce and Turner 1990, Chap. 4). At the same time, from an economic point of view it does not make sense in general to suppress production entirely because of external cost (therefore, $Em^* > 0$).

The Coase theorem states that given an unambiguous initial allocation of property rights, negotiations leading to a Pareto optimum can be initiated, without the initial allocation concerning the good in question ('unspoiled environment' in the present context) having an impact on the resulting quantity of emissions. In a frictionless market economy, property rights constitute tradable goods. The theorem therefore amounts to a generalization of the exchange model without production.

For the distribution of income and wealth, it obviously matters whether the property right is assigned to the polluter or to the injured party. Still, it would not make sense to prohibit the efficiency-enhancing exchanges of property rights predicted by the Coase theorem. Rather, if the original assignment is deemed unacceptable, an ex-post redistribution of income can be envisioned. Yet even then the application of the theorem is limited by a number of conditions that often fail to be satisfied.

– Negligible transaction costs: For the transition from Em_0 to Em^* to take place, the injured party must compensate the polluter not only for the profit foregone, but also for transaction costs (cost of negotiation, contracting, and monitoring—in short, costs of using the market). In reality, transaction costs are often too high to make negotiations over external damages worthwhile.

- Clearly identifiable cause-effect relationships: Frequently it is extremely difficult and costly to prove causality in the case of several polluters ("Who caused the damage?"). Liability law usually puts the burden of proof on the claimant, i.e. the injured party.
- Small number of parties: As a rule, there are too many emission sources and injured parties for bilateral negotiations to be feasible. This may even hold for the case where the injured parties form an interest group.
- No latency period in damages: Many damages caused by emissions become manifest with delay only. At the time of their emergence, the polluter may have exited from the market or lack the resources to compensate the external effect.
- No intergenerational damages: In many cases, the individuals who may suffer from current emissions are not yet born. Therefore, the injured parties are represented by non-legitimized agents only. This problem in particular characterizes so-called long-tail damages caused by greenhouse gases and nuclear radiation.

In sum, the Coase theorem shows that a market mechanism for property rights can lead to efficient levels of production and emission. However, in many circumstances important conditions for it to hold are not satisfied.

To the extent that some of the points mentioned above are relevant, the allocation of property rights and negotiations according to the Coase theorem may fail to result in a Pareto-optimal outcome. Market failure occurs, possibly calling for government intervention. For a Pareto-optimal outcome, government would have polluters reduce their emissions to Em^*. In view of the assumed proportionality between production and emissions, this amounts to a reduction of output produced.

The following sections are devoted to the question of how this can be achieved. However, note that government may fail in its endeavors as well.

7.2 Aggregate Emissions

Since an externality usually involves many polluters and injured parties, the analysis of the preceding section needs to be extended to the case of many companies and households. Let there be companies j that produce a single good, causing emissions Em_j. In addition, there are households i who buy the product but have to bear immissions Im_i whose impacts cannot always be expressed in money terms. Accordingly, the external cost function of the preceding section is replaced by the utility function $U_i(Im_i)$ of household i. This formulation supposes that a given household is affected by the immissions to an identifiable degree. In this way, immissions obtain the characteristics of a private good. This condition will be removed in a second step.

If company profits are combined with the utilities of the households to form a social welfare function, the optimal amounts of individual emissions Em_j and immissions Im_i can be determined from the following optimization problem (see Mas-Colell et al. 1995, Chap. 11D),

$$\max \sum_j \Pi_j(Em_j|p) + \sum_i U_i(Im_i|p) \qquad (7.3)$$

subject to
$$\Pi'_j(Em_j) \geq 0 \qquad \Pi''_j(Em_j) < 0$$
$$U'_i(Im_i) \leq 0 \qquad U''_i(Im_i) < 0$$
$$\sum_j Em_j = \sum_i Im_i.$$

As to the profit function Π_j of company j, it depends on the company's emissions Em_j and on the sales price p of its product. Similarly, utility U_i of household i depends on immissions Im_i as well as the sales price p of the product. In the mathematical formulation below, the simplifying assumption is made that variations of Em_j and Im_i do not affect p. As before, profits of the company increase with emissions but at a decreasing rate. Conversely, utility of households decreases with immissions, and at an increasing rate. This means that the marginal cost (in utility terms) of immissions is rising. This description is a simplification of the often intricate connection between aggregate emissions and the sum of immissions as perceived at the individual level.

The optimization problem incorporating the conditions contained in (7.3) can be solved using the Lagrange function,

$$\max_{Em_j, Im_i} L = \sum_j \Pi_j(Em_j) + \sum_i U_i(Im_i) - \lambda \left(\sum_j Em_j - \sum_i Im_i \right). \qquad (7.4)$$

This function may attain its maximum at a boundary, with e.g. $Em^*_j = 0$. The slope of the objective function would have to be zero or negative at that point, indicating that a zero or a negative value of Em is optimal. If however the maximum is in the interior of the solution space, it is characterized by the following first-order conditions,

$$\frac{\partial L}{\partial Em_j} = 0 \text{ and therefore } \Pi'_j\left[Em^*_j\right] = \lambda^*;$$
$$\frac{\partial L}{\partial Im_i} = 0 \text{ and therefore } U'_i\left[Im^*_i\right] = \lambda^*. \qquad (7.5)$$

The value of the Lagrange multiplier λ^* indicates how much a violation of the conditions stated in (7.3) would lower the value of the objective function (7.4). It therefore constitutes the shadow price of additional emissions (or immissions, respectively). Equation (7.5) states that in the optimum, this shadow price equals the marginal profit of company j, since this marginal profit is lost to the company in the case of a reduction of emissions. In this sense, λ^* also represents the marginal cost of the good 'emission reduction'. On the other hand, such a reduction spares

7.2 Aggregate Emissions

household i a utility loss which would be caused by additional immissions ($U'_i < 0$). Therefore, optimality conditions (7.5) state that in a social optimum, the marginal cost of the good 'emission reduction' coincides with its marginal utility. If a market for emission rights can be organized, λ^* indicates the corresponding market price.

This statement holds under the assumption that immissions have the character of a private good. If by contrast emissions have the properties of a pure public good, the optimization problem must be formulated in a different way. In this case, each household i is exposed to the total of emissions $\sum_j Em_j$ (or immissions, respectively). Therefore, only company-specific emissions Em_j remain as decision variables, causing the optimization problem to read

$$\max_{Em_j} \sum_j \Pi_j(Em_j) + \sum_i U_i\left(\sum_j Em_j\right) \quad (7.6)$$

The first-order optimality conditions are now given by

$$\Pi'_j\left(Em_j^*\right) = -\sum_i U'_i\left[\sum_j Em_j^*\right] \quad \text{for each company } j. \quad (7.7)$$

The right-hand side of Eq. (7.7) symbolizes the negative sum of individual marginal utilities and hence the marginal external cost of emissions in the aggregate. This must be evaluated at the sum of socially optimal emissions $\sum_j Em_j^*$. If an external effect exists, this expression is necessarily positive.

Since emissions cannot be attributed to households individually, the constraints in (7.3) are not relevant, causing $\lambda^* = 0$. Therefore, in this case there cannot be a market for emission rights with a positive price. Economic optimization at the level of the individual company then calls for

$$\Pi'_j\left[Em_j^*\right] = 0 \quad (7.8)$$

One therefore finds once again that in the absence of a market for emission rights, companies individually target a higher level of emissions than would be optimal from the social point of view.

Recall that in this derivation, the amount of total emissions $\sum_j Em_j$—and with it aggregate output $\sum_j Q_j$—has no influence on the product price. However, reductions in emissions go along with an increased scarcity of the final product, causing its equilibrium price to increase (to p^{**} in Fig. 7.3). The higher sales price shifts the marginal profit function upward, with the consequence that the aggregate Pareto-optimal output exceeds $\sum Q^*$, to attain $\sum Q^{**}$. A formal development of this modification is not performed here.

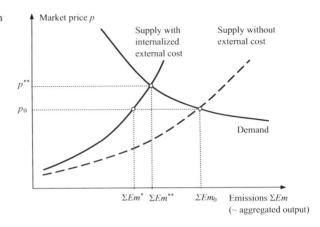

Fig. 7.3 Impact of emission reductions on the market outcome

7.3 Instruments of Environmental Policy

The analysis of the preceding section shows that it may be appropriate for the government to intervene in order to move the economy closer to the welfare maximum. Its interventions are of two types, so-called internalization approaches and standard-oriented approaches. The internalization approach calls for marginal external costs to be transformed into price signals which modify the behavior of market participants. However, agents remain free in their decision to respond to these price signals by reducing emissions or to pay for them. By way of contrast, when adopting the standard-oriented approach, the government determines emission levels—at the aggregate or the individual level—which are not to be exceeded in any circumstance.

7.3.1 Internalization Approaches

The main internalization approaches are the following.

– Voluntary agreement with sanctions: Polluters are asked to reduce their emissions on a voluntary basis; in case the agreement fails to be honored, the government threatens to apply other instruments. In the past, this instrument has proved effective in some instances. However, the actual imposition of the sanction is frequently deemed improbable, causing it to have little effect on behavior (i.e. polluters continue with business as usual). Sometimes, voluntary agreements are signed by industry associations, raising the issue of implementation because associations usually lack the authority to enforce such agreements (they cannot rein in their 'black sheep').
– Liability with mandatory insurance (Zweifel and Tyran 1994): If polluters are liable for environmental damages (see Sect. 7.3.2 below), they can still go

7.3 Instruments of Environmental Policy

bankrupt in order to escape payment of claims. This can be prevented by mandatory insurance coverage. Provided premiums are scaled according to probability and severity of environmental damages, insurance creates an incentive for the internalization of external cost.
- Pigouvian tax (see Pigou 1932; Baumol and Oates 1988): By taxing emissions, the government puts a price on them. Polluters can then decide whether and how much they want to reduce emissions, or whether they prefer to pay the tax. The government obtains tax revenue that varies with emissions (which may give rise to the perverse incentive of not fighting them 'too much').

Here, the Pigouvian tax is selected to illustrate the internalization concept and to point out some problems. Its optimal level can be derived from the optimality condition (7.7). Since the optimal rate tax_j^* must be equal to the marginal cost of emissions, one has from (7.7)

$$tax_j^* = -\sum_i U_i' \left[\sum_j Em_j^* \right] = \Pi_j' \left[Em_j^* \right]. \qquad (7.9)$$

If companies use the same production technology (implying that Π_j' has the same value for all), then the Pigouvian tax causes all companies to reduce their emissions to the same optimal value. In this special case, it therefore has the same effect as a norm limiting emissions. As soon as companies differ in their production technologies and hence are characterized by different marginal profit functions, the equivalence between the Pigouvian tax and a norm is lost.

For example, let all companies except one have the same production technology, with the exceptional one using a technology with lower marginal abatement cost. Since at a given rate of production and emissions, Π'_j is higher for this company j than its competitors, the uniform Pigouvian tax causes j to have a higher optimal level of emissions than all the others. For attaining the optimal level of aggregate emissions, its tax rate simply needs to be set higher compared to the case where all companies use the same technology. In contrast, a legal norm limiting emissions regardless of type of technology would force company j to scale back its emissions and output to a greater extent than its competitors, causing it to forego an excessive amount of profits. Therefore, as soon as technologies differ between companies, the Pigouvian tax dominates the emission norm in terms of efficiency.

On the other hand, informational requirements for an efficient implementation of a Pigouvian tax are high. According to Eq. (7.7), preliminary company-specific values Em_j need to be added up to calculate aggregate emissions. At that total, one has to determine the marginal utility loss of each individual affected. These values must again be plugged into Eq. (7.7), calling for a new set of values Em_j on the part of companies inferred from their marginal profit functions Π'_j. It may take several iterations to come up with optimal company-specific tax rates.

Failure of this procedure has important consequences. To illustrate, let the marginal profit function of a company be underestimated (Π'_a in Fig. 7.4; subscript

Fig. 7.4 Consequences of underestimated marginal profit

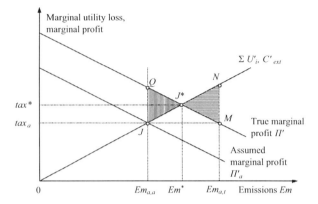

j is omitted for simplicity). Accordingly, the tax rate would be set too low at tax_a. This induces the company to target $Em_{a,t}$ rather than Em^*. Since marginal utility losses exceed marginal profit beyond Em^*, an efficiency loss equivalent to the area J^*MN results.

This problem becomes especially relevant whenever aggregate marginal utility losses (external marginal cost, respectively) cannot be estimated with precision. In sum, the internalization approaches have the advantage of taking differences in the marginal cost of abatement into account. However, they can themselves become a source of inefficiency as soon as they create wrong incentives for polluters.

7.3.2 Standard-Oriented Approaches

The most important standard-oriented approaches are the following.

– Environmental liability (Shavell 1984): Liability law serves to internalize external effects that occur in the guise of accidents. It is standard-oriented because lawmakers and courts determine the admissible amount of external effects beyond which the injurer must come up with compensation. However, enforcement of a claim against a polluter through the courts frequently is burdened with high transaction cost. Relieving the injured party from the burden of proof would mitigate this problem considerably but might trigger so many law suits that entrepreneurial activity would be stifled.
– Emission norms: Here, public authorities impose limits on emission levels (or rates, respectively), sanctioning violations. In actual practice, norms are the most frequently used instrument because they have a direct effect on emissions. In addition, they are deemed fair as they impose the same obligation on everyone. From an economic point of view, however, they cause efficiency losses as soon as polluters differ in terms of their (marginal) cost of abatement. In that situation, limits on aggregate emissions could be attained at lower cost. Finally, the threat of sanction must be credible. Yet imposing sanctions often goes along

7.3 Instruments of Environmental Policy

with high administrative expense and is subject to leakage effects, resulting in so-called administrative failure.
- Standard-price approach (Baumol and Oates 1988): Here, the regulatory authority determines the admissible level of aggregate emissions, setting the internalization tax at a level ensuring that this standard is not exceeded. In case the standard is exceeded, it increases the tax rate, otherwise, it lowers it. Conceivably, the tax rate can even go to zero provided the aggregate emission target continues to be met. The standard-price approach is attractive whenever (marginal) external costs cannot be quantified with any confidence. One example is the greenhouse gas problem (see Sect. 10.2).
- Tradable emission rights (Dales 1968): Again, the authority needs to determine the admissible amount of emissions. This quantity defines the amount of emission rights, which are allocated to polluters according to a predetermined formula. At the same time, polluters may cause emissions only to the extent that they dispose of the corresponding amount of certificates. Since emission rights are tradable, polluters can purchase extra certificates if necessary. Note that the price for emission rights is not determined by the authority anymore but by market forces. In this way, market participants receive a signal indicating how binding their constraint on emissions is at the time [see the Lagrange multiplier λ in Eq. (7.4)]. This instrument has been in actual use within the European Union since 2005 for industrial CO_2 emissions (see Sect. 10.3).

Among these alternatives, the emission norm is expounded here. In Fig. 7.4, the emission norm appears as $Em_{a,a}$. Ideally, it should satisfy efficiency condition (7.7). However, in this example, it has been set too low due to a wrong estimate of the marginal profit function (Π'_a rather than Π_j). While the true optimum is Em^*, the norm $Em_{a,a}$ forces the polluter to undertake excessive abatement efforts, causing an efficiency loss equivalent to the area JJ^*Q. Depending on the slopes of the marginal utility loss and marginal profit schedules, this efficiency loss may be greater or smaller than the one caused by a wrong internalization tax (J^*MN). If the schedule showing marginal utility loss runs less steep than the one showing marginal profit, the emissions norm is less efficient than the Pigouvian tax. In environmental economics, this case is considered to be the rule. Only if the marginal utility loss schedule runs steeply compared to the marginal profit schedule, indicating great additional damage if the optimal emission level is exceeded, does the emission norm dominate in terms of efficiency.

The ecological and economic advantages and disadvantages of these instruments have been debated extensively in the literature (see Baumol and Oates 1988). On the economic side, the efficiency criterion usually is center stage, calling for a given improvement of environmental quality to be achieved at minimum cost for society. However, other aspects need to be taken into account as well. In particular, the instruments of environmental policy differ in terms of distributional impact (for example, consider the formula determining the allocation of emission rights above). They also differ in their cost of implementation imposed on public authorities as well as polluters. Finally, they have different impacts on the introduction and diffusion of environmental innovation and hence economic development.

7.4 Measuring External Costs of Energy Use

As long as there are no markets for environmental goods, one must fall back on models to quantify (marginal) external costs (see also Sect. 10.3). This raises several methodological problems. Focusing on the bottom-up approach, one has to determine first the external effects that should be accounted for, if at all. From an anthropocentric point of view, all effects should be considered as damage if they are negatively valued by human beings, either by individuals or members of social groups and organizations. Note that this does not mean, "Man is at the center of the universe", but rather, "All value emanates from man". Thus, a biotope may qualify although it will never be seen by a human being and therefore cannot give rise to immediate utility, for it may nevertheless have so-called existence value to man.

In keeping with anthropocentrism in valuation, extensive lists of damage categories have been dressed up. One can distinguish five categories, with most empirical studies limiting themselves to the first two.

– Economic damages in the narrow sense: These comprise the destruction of physical assets causing losses of income and costs related to cleanup and repair.
– Losses of human life and health: These are measured by the number of exposed persons, resulting in an expected value of years of life lost. Alternatively, the duration of or expenditure for medical treatment is estimated.
– Losses of environment assets and environmental quality: Some of these losses may already be captured by category No. 1, potentially giving rise to double counting.
– Losses of quality of life: These comprise exposure to noise and vibration, but also fear of catastrophes, reduced autonomy and self-fulfillment.
– Loss of function: Economic, social and political institutions (e.g. civil protection, provision of medical care) are prevented from functioning normally.

Some authors also include the use of non-renewable energy resources as a damage category. However, this is open to debate. While it is true that this increases the future scarcity of the resource considered, there is no external effect as soon as its price reflects future scarcity (see Sect. 6.2). Similarly, including land consumption is debatable as well, because land is not really used up but (temporarily) withdrawn from other uses. Again, no external effect is usually involved since land use must be paid for in the guise of rent.

For each damage category distinguished, the relationship with energy-related activities needs to be determined. In many cases, this requires detailed scientific (particularly chemical and engineering) knowledge.

Usually, the first step is to measure the relevant emission at its source. Instances are emissions through the air (sulfur dioxide, nitrogen oxide, carbon monoxide,

7.4 Measuring External Costs of Energy Use

particulate matter, and dioxin), emissions of greenhouse gases (carbon dioxide and methane), water pollution (oil leakages), contamination of the soil (heavy metals), noise, odor and vibrations, as well as accident risks and the exposure to nuclear radiation.

Next, immissions are the consequence of emissions, causing pollution of air, water, and soil. They result from cumulated emissions and processes of transformation and decay. These natural mitigating processes sometimes can be enhanced by technical repair measures. Many of the connections between emissions and immissions are very complex, leaving questions open in spite of gains of knowledge achieved during the past decades.

Third, the relationships between immissions and damages are complex as well, with damages frequently depending on the level of pollution in a nonlinear way. Also, some damages occur only when several pollutants interact, posing great scientific challenges to the identification of dose-response functions. Duration of immissions plays a role as well. Some damages occur many years or even decades after the emissions causing them. Finally, emissions require the existence of receptors (human beings, animals, plants, buildings) in order to cause damage. Determining the location of an emission relative to these receptors may therefore be of importance, too.

Fourth, since profits are measured in money, damages need to be expressed in money terms as well in order to implement the optimum condition (7.7). For this monetization, one can use observations from market exchanges or try to measure willingness to pay for avoiding immissions. Several alternatives have been developed in economics.

- Estimation based on the cost of repair: One source of information is insurance payments for covered damages. At the aggregate level, one usually finds that the cost of repair increases progressively with the level or rate of emissions (increasing marginal damage cost).
- Estimation based on the cost of avoidance: If the cost of repair cannot be quantified, the cost of avoiding (partially) the damage may serve as a substitute. Since typically lower-cost measures are performed first, followed by the higher-cost ones, one can infer that marginal cost must increase with the quantity of emissions avoided. This means that the value of marginal cost can be established only after determining the admissible quantity of emissions (see the standard-price approach discussed in Sect. 7.3.2 above).
- In the case of the damage category 'human lives and health', the human capital approach is a popular alternative. Premature death or invalidity makes a person's knowledge and skills no longer available to society. For monetization, replacement cost or the present value of future labor income forgone has been used. Estimated values of a statistical life range from between 100,000 and 2 mn EUR. However, this approach singles out one dimension of human existence—gainful activity—thus rendering it questionable. Moreover, valuation is by society (through the labor market) rather than the individual person, reminiscent of a slave economy.

- Estimation based on market transactions (also known as hedonic price approach): The statistical value of a human life can be derived from observing individuals who (e.g. through their choice of a risky activity) are prepared to expose themselves to life and health risks in return for a financial advantage. Conversely, they may accept a financial disadvantage in return for a marginally lower risk. The statistical value of a human life can then be calculated as follows. If one percentage point more probability of survival is associated with x EUR, then the whole life should approximately be worth $100x$ EUR. Published values are in a range between 100,000 and 2 mn EUR. However, other types of damage can be monetized as well in this way, by measuring the effort required to avoid an emission. An example is the difference in the price of land between residential areas with good and mediocre air quality.
- Estimation based on surveys: Especially in the context of planned interventions and product innovations where actual behavior cannot be observed, economists increasingly rely on so-called market experiments. The objective is to measure (marginal) willingness to pay (WTP) for obtaining an advantage or avoiding a disadvantage. The conventional approach is Contingent Valuation (see e.g. Cummings et al. 1986; Hausman 1993). Here, all attributes of the hypothetical alternative to the status quo are held constant except price. While WTP can be elicited directly, the values obtained usually are overestimates. The reason is that respondents tend to excessively focus on price, neglect competing claims to their budget, and may be tempted to answer strategically. An extreme case is the value of human life; most respondents would deem this 'good' as non-tradable, causing refusal to state a money value. Otherwise, if stating a value at all, they typically would put it to infinity.

To avoid these problems, economists increasingly use so-called Conjoint Analysis. Respondents are confronted with a set of alternatives whose attributes take on different levels each time. In the Discrete Choice Experiment (DCE) variant of Conjoint Analysis, respondents merely have to indicate whether they prefer the status quo or the alternative in question. From their repeated choices, their indifference curve through the status quo point can be interpolated. Through the price of the product, their remaining disposable income becomes a product attribute, permitting to infer marginal WTP values from the slope of the indifference curve. Therefore, a WTP value can be estimated for each attribute and the alternative as a whole. Based on this more realistic approach, much lower values are usually estimated than with Contingent Valuation. For instance, Schneider and Zweifel (2004), using a DCE, obtain a marginal WTP value of the Swiss population of only 0.1 EUR ct/kWh for benefiting from improved financial security in case of a major nuclear accident (see also Sect. 11.3.3).

There are quite a few estimates of energy-related external cost. Due to different methods, model assumptions, and data, results differ substantially. One of the internationally important investigations was performed for the Commission of the European Union (ExternE; see Directorate General Research 2003). It uses the bottom-up-concept detailed above.

Table 7.1 External costs of power generation in Germany

	Coal power plant	Lignite power plant	Gas and steam turbine	Nuclear[a]	Photo-volt.	Wind power	Hydro power
	Marginal damage cost (EUR ct/kWh)						
Noise						0.005	
Health	0.73	0.99	0.34	0.17	0.45	0.072	0.051
Materials	0.0015	0.02	0.007	0.002	0.012	0.002	0.001
Agriculture				0.001		0.0007	0.0002
Sum	0.75	1.01	0.35	0.17	0.46	0.08	0.05
	Marginal abatement cost (standard price approach) (EUR ct/kWh)						
Eco systems	0.2	0.78	0.04	0.05	0.04	0.04	0.03
Greenhouse gas impacts	1.60	2.00	0.73	0.03	0.33	0.04	0.03

[a]Without a risk aversion factor (see Sect. 11.3); data source: ExternE (2003)

Table 7.1 exhibits estimated external marginal costs for several modern power generation technologies in Germany. They represent marginal avoidance costs, which should be pitted against marginal profit losses due to abatement for optimization. Since marginal abatement cost (excluding greenhouse gas effects which are singled out for separate analysis, see below) is lower than marginal damage cost throughout, more abatement effort is indicated for all energy sources. Marginal damage cost is lowest for hydropower, followed by wind power and nuclear. Therefore, the optimal internalization tax lies between 0.03 and 0.05 EUR ct/kWh for hydro power. It is typically higher in the case of nuclear power, with a range between 0.001 and a high 0.17 EUR ct/kWh, and attaining a maximum value in the case of lignite between 0.78 and 1.01 EUR ct/kWh.

The same study also contains estimates of the marginal external cost of transportation-related air emissions. For private passenger traffic in urban areas, it comes up with values between 0.08 and 1.03 EUR per 100 passenger-kilometers (pkm). For long-haul passenger trips, external costs depend on the mode of transportation. In the case of the railroad, they lie between 0.1 and 0.2 EUR per 100 pkm, in the case of the automobile, between 0.6 and 1.2 EUR per 100 pkm.

References

Baumol, W. J., & Oates, W. E. (1988). *The theory of environmental policy* (2nd ed.). Cambridge: Cambridge University Press.
Coase, R. (1960). The problem of social cost. *Journal of Law and Economics, 1*, 1–44.
Cummings, R. G., et al. (1986). *Valuing environmental goods: An assessment of the contingent valuation method*. Towata, NJ: Rowan & Allanheld.
Dales, J. (1968). Pollution, property & prices: An essay in policy-making and economics. New horizons in environmental economics. Toronto: Toronto University Press (reprinted by Edward Elgar Publishing 2002).

ExternE. (2003). *External costs. Research results on socio-environmental damages due to electricity and transport* (ExternE project). Luxemburg.

Hausman, J. A. (Ed.). (1993). *Contingent valuation. A critical assessment*. Amsterdam: North Holland.

Mas-Colell, A., Winston, M. D., & Green, J. R. (1995). *Microeconomic theory*. Oxford: Oxford University Press.

Pearce, D. W., & Turner, R. D. (1990). *Economics of natural resources and the environment*. Baltimore: Johns Hopkins University Press.

Pigou, A. C. (1932). *The economics of welfare* (4th ed.). New York: Macmillan.

Schneider, Y., & Zweifel, P. (2004). How much internalization of nuclear risk through liability insurance? *Journal of Risk and Uncertainty, 29*(3), 219–240.

Shavell, S. (1984). A model of the optimal use of liability and safety regulation. *Rand Journal of Economics, 15*(2), 271–280.

Zweifel, P., & Tyran, J. R. (1994). Environmental impairment liability as an instrument of environmental policy. *Ecological Economics, 11*(1), 43–56.

Markets for Liquid Fuels 8

This chapter focuses on markets for crude oil and oil products including gasoline, kerosene, diesel, heating oil, as well as biogenic fuels such as biodiesel, bioethanol, and synthetic fuels. Since the mid-twentieth century, crude oil has been the world's most important energy source. However, the future prospects of crude oil are more unclear than ever. A lot of issues have to be analyzed:

– What is the development of oil extraction?
– What technical and economic consequences are to be expected if conventional crude oil extraction falls short of the demand for liquid fuels?
– What about the so-called peak oil hypothesis from an economic perspective?
– At what oil prices would alternative fuels, such as unconventional oils, biogenic fuels, and liquefied coal become competitive?
– How can the structure of the oil industry be explained in economic terms?
– What is the role of governments in exporting and importing countries?
– What are the influences on the price of oil in the short, medium, and long term?
– What is the relationship between spot and future prices?
– To what extent are oil prices influenced by speculation?

The variables used in this chapter are:

c	Cost of carry (annualized cost of storage and insurance)
cy	Convenience yield (advantage of holding the physical asset rather than a future contract)
dz	Normally distributed stochastic variable
GDP	Gross Domestic Product
i	Risk-free interest rate
p	Spot market price (indexed if it refers to a particular traded product)
$p_F(T)$	Price of a future with delivery date T
σ	Standard deviation
Stock	Stock of inventory
T	Maturity (delivery date) in futures contracts

t   Trading date
Vola Annualized volatility

8.1 Types of Liquid Fuels and Their Properties

Under normal atmospheric pressure, liquid energy sources are in a liquid physical state. This makes their storage, transferal, and transportation easy, i.e. low-cost. Furthermore, liquid energy sources have high energy density. For example, a 50 l gasoline tank has an energy content of about $32.4 \cdot 50 = 1620$ MJ or 450 kWh, respectively (see Table 8.7). Assuming that the filling of such a gasoline tank takes two minutes, the filling capacity of a gasoline pump amounts to 13.5 MW (= $30\cdot450$ kWh/h). A single gas station with eight gasoline pumps therefore has the potential to sell the same amount of energy (i.e. 108 MW) as 54 wind turbines with a capacity of 2 MW each. These advantages are the reason for the dominance of oil products in the transportation sector and their overall leading position in global energy markets since the mid-twentieth century.

However, reserves of crude oil are limited and likely to be exhausted in a not-too-distant future (see Sect. 8.1.3). Additionally, there is the environmental burden caused by the emission of greenhouse gases associated with the combustion of crude oil products. The content of the 50 l gasoline tank in the example above leads to the release of 117 kg CO_2 into the atmosphere. On a global scale, about 40% of energy-related CO_2 emissions derive from the combustion of crude oil. While these two issues represent important challenges in the foreseeable future, there is no general consensus about how to deal with them. For instance, it remains unclear whether renewable liquid fuels or renewable electricity will be able to substitute fossil liquid fuels to a sufficient degree.

8.1.1 Properties of Crude Oil

There are many data sources regarding crude oil, albeit in differing units of measurement. Therefore, the data need to be converted to a common energy unit. While there are conversion tables, they often fail to achieve comparability because crude oil is a natural product and thus a heterogeneous good. In particular, energy content differs between production sites, depending on the so-called crude oil density of the liquid. Thus, the conversion factors presented in Table 8.1 are based on a crude oil density of 0.858 kg/l or 7.33 bbl/ton, respectively.

For the oil industry, two crucial dimensions of quality are the density of hydrocarbon compounds and the viscosity of crude measured in API grades defined by the American Petroleum Institute (see Fig. 8.1). The economic value of crude increases with higher API grades. Therefore, condensates and light varieties fetch a higher price than heavy oil and tar sands. Crude oil varieties with values below 25° API count as unconventional oils. Below a level of 10° API, hydrocarbon

8.1 Types of Liquid Fuels and Their Properties

Table 8.1 Standardized conversion factors for crude oil

	Metric ton	Cubic meter	Hectoliter	Barrel	U.S. gallon
Metric ton	1	1.165	11.65	7.33	307.9
Cubic meter[a]	0.858	1	10	6.29	264.2
Hectoliter	0.0858	0.1	1	0.629	26.42
Barrel	0.1364	0.159	1.59	1	42
U.S. gallon	0.00325	0.0038	0.038	0.0238	1

[a]Global average; data source: BP (2014)

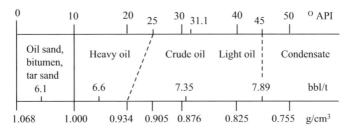

Fig. 8.1 Properties of crude oil varieties. Sources: American Petroleum Institute; Erdmann and Zweifel (2008, p. 173)

compounds are not capable of flowing and hence transportation by pipeline. Another important characteristic of crude oils is their sulfur content. Low-sulfur oil is called sweet crude, whereas sulfur-rich oil is called sour crude.

American West Texas Intermediate (WTI) and European Brent are high-quality crudes serving as a benchmark, with around 42° API and sulfur contents below 0.3%. Other crudes such as Dubai Crude with 31° API and 2% sulfur content constitute the benchmark for oil from the Persian Gulf. Usually sulfur-rich oil is traded at a price discount compared to WTI and Brent (see Table 8.2). However, since these benchmark crudes are physically available at different locations, transportation bottlenecks and perturbations of local markets have resulted in price differences in excess of 25 USD/bbl in favor of WTI in recent years.

8.1.2 Reserves and Extraction of Conventional Oil

Known and economically recoverable reserves of conventional crude oil are unevenly distributed over the globe. According to Table 8.3, more one-half of them are concentrated in the Middle East (most of it around the Persian Gulf) and in Central Asia. This region of the world plus Russia is known as the 'energy ellipse' which accounts for nearly 40% of global supply in terms of conventional crude oil.

By way of contrast, the global share of crude oil extraction in OECD countries is far higher than their global share of reserves. Therefore, OECD countries will have less control over the supply of oil in future, while countries in the energy ellipse and

Table 8.2 Quality levels and prices of crude oil

	API°	Sulfur content (%)	Price spread from WTI in 2004 (USD/bbl.)
Saharan Blend (Algeria)	44	0.1	−2.70
Bonny Light (Nigeria)	36	0.1	−2.60
Tia Juana Light (Venezuela)	31	1.2	−2.50
Isthmus (Mexico)	33	1.3	−2.60
Arabian Light (Saudi Arabia)	33	1.8	−5.50
Kuwait Blend	31	2.5	−4.70
Arabian Medium (Saudi Arabia)	29	2.9	−6.50
Arabian Heavy	27	2.8	−7.20

Source: Erdmann and Zweifel (2008, p. 173); WTI: Western Texas Intermediate

Table 8.3 Reserves and extraction rates of crude oil, 2013

	Crude oil reserves end of 2013		Crude oil extraction 2013[a]	
	bn bbl	Share (%)	mn bbl/d	Share (%)
Saudi Arabia	266	15.8	11.5	13.3
Iran	157	9.3	3.6	4.1
Iraq	150	8.9	3.1	3.6
Kuwait	102	6.0	3.1	3.6
United Arab Emirates	98	5.8	3.6	4.2
Russia	87	5.2	1.1	1.2
United States	44	2.6	10.0	11.5
Kazakhstan	30	1.8	1.8	2.1
Azerbaijan	7	0.4	0.9	1.0
Middle East	808	47.9	28.4	32.7
Energy ellipse	932	55.2	32.1	37.0
OPEC	1214	71.9	36.8	42.5
OECD	248	14.7	20.5	23.7
World	1688	100.0	86.8	100.0

[a] Includes shale oil, oil sands, and the liquid content of natural gas where it is recovered separately; source: BP (2014)

OPEC (Organization of Oil Exporting Countries) countries can be expected to exert a growing influence on the global market for conventional oil. However, as expounded in Sect. 8.1.4 below, technological change has been increasing the supply of unconventional oil.

The effect if this geographic concentration is exacerbated by widely varying costs of extraction. While they are below 40 USD/bbl in the Persian Gulf on average, they can be as much as twice as high in other regions of the world (see Fig. 8.2). However, this cost advantage may be undermined by technological change. An example is the cost reduction in offshore production during the

8.1 Types of Liquid Fuels and Their Properties

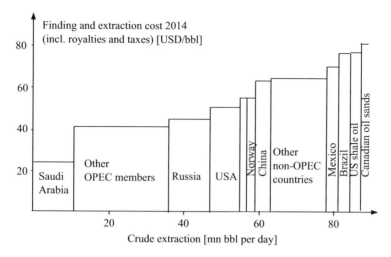

Fig. 8.2 Marginal cost of crude oil production (source: Oil Industry Trends)

1980s. In the early 1980s, retrieving oil from the North Sea cost 17 USD/bbl, causing production to become competitive only after the second oil price shock of 1979 when the sales price jumped from 10 to 30 USD/bbl. Yet, ten years later offshore production cost was down to 8 USD/bbl. This cost reduction occurred despite the fact that compared to other industries, the oil industry invests a small share of its earnings in research and development.

8.1.3 Peak Oil Hypothesis

Motorization in the United States led to a phenomenal increase in oil consumption during the 1950s. It was during this decade that geologists began to address the question of how long it would take for crude oil reserves in the United States to be depleted. At that time, the U.S. share in global production exceeded 50%. In 1956, geologist Hubbert (1956, 1962) predicted that oil production in the United States would peak by 1970 and decline from then on (in the so-called lower 48 states, thus excluding production in Alaska and offshore drilling in the Gulf of Mexico).

His forecast proved true (see Fig. 8.3). It was based on a logistic function, which in the present context implies that the accumulation of production will approach an upper limit which equals total reserves (see Fig. 4.2). More specifically, according to the standard logistic function, rates of production begin to decline once one-half of total reserves have been retrieved (this is also known as the depletion midpoint). By fitting observed production rates to the logistic function, Hubbert was able to determine the two parameters determining the logistic function, which in turn permits to predict the depletion midpoint and hence the year when the rate of production will attain its maximum.

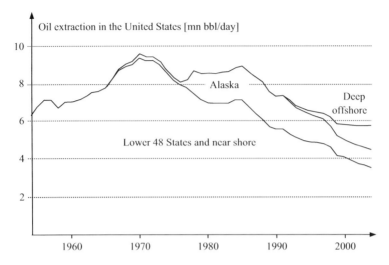

Fig. 8.3 Crude oil extraction in the United States (source: EIA, CGES)

Note that the use of the logistic function can be justified with a change in marginal cost: At the start of exploitation, few oil fields are known and experience in exploration is lacking, causing the cost of locating an additional field to be high. With cumulated exploitation and production, the marginal cost of discovering and developing an oil field decreases, facilitating a high rate of production. Beyond some point however, marginal cost begins to increase again because easily accessible fields are depleted. This puts downward pressure on the rate of discovery and ultimately, the rate of production—unless the sales price of oil goes up in real terms, as e.g. during 1970s with its two oil price shocks (Kaufmann and Cleveland 2001; Reynolds 2002). Moreover, pressure in developed oil deposits declines with cumulated production. In order to compensate for this, water, steam, or carbon dioxide is pressed into the deposit, a process known as enhanced oil recovery. Of course, enhanced oil recovery is associated with an increase in the marginal cost of production; thus, it slows the decline in production rates but does not reverse the trend.

In the meantime, the peak oil hypothesis has been applied to global oil production on the grounds that global reserves are limited as well. In keeping with the Hotelling price path (see Sect. 6.2.2), lower-cost reserves are exploited first, followed by higher-cost alternatives such as Alaska in the case of the United States. Indeed, Fig. 8.3 exhibits rising, then falling rates of production. Yet, the figure also points to an intriguing constancy. In 1956, Hubbert predicted peak oil for 1970, i.e. 14 years away. In 1970, oil production in Alaska began to take off—and peaked again about 15 years later. Shortly after the year 2000, some experts saw the rate of global production peak 8 to 22 years into the future (averaging 15 years), while some others did not predict a peak at all.

Table 8.4 Expert views on the production maximum of crude oil

	Publication year	Year of maximum oil extraction	Maximum oil extraction (mn bbl/day)
Sir John Browne, BP	2000	–	90
IEA (Paris)	2000	2020	115
Colin Campbell, ASPO	2002	2010	87
Richard Nehring, NRG & Associates	2003	–	<90
Pete Stark, IHS energy	2003	–	92
EIA (Washington)	2003	2025	119

Source: ASPO Conference Berlin (May 2004)

The prediction of 8 years has already proved wrong since between 2002 and 2010, global production of crude increased in 8 out of 11 years at rates up to 5%, while the maximum decrease was -1.7%. Overall, it continued to increase up to 2013 (U.S. Energy Information Administration). Cumulated global oil production exceeded 1200 bn bbl in 2002; this is equivalent to 330 years of peak production in the United States (3400 mn bbl/a = 365·9.5 mn bbl/day as of 1970; see Fig. 8.3). Therefore, up to present economic incentives have been causing resources to be transformed into reserves at a pace that has kept up with growth in production and consumption. In hindsight, Hubbert's success in predicting the 1970 peak in U.S. oil production, being based on the assumption of a predetermined amount of reserves, seems to be a coincidence rather than the result of in depth analysis (Kaufmann and Cleveland 2001).

Table 8.4 shows estimates of the expected dates and the quantities of maximum conventional crude oil extraction, all of them published before 2004. In spite of differences which might be related to the affiliation of the respective experts, the consensus at the time was that depletion midpoint will be reached by 2020 or 2025 at the latest.

Indeed, economists including Adelman (2002) and Lynch (2002) have argued that it has been possible to overcome resource scarcities through innovation up to now, suggesting that this might hold true in future as well. For example, Fig. 8.3 shows that the production decline in the United States predicted by Hubbert was substantially delayed thanks to advanced extraction technologies and the development of new oil fields (Alaska, deep offshore). At present, this view is confirmed by the growth of oil production in North America and other regions. Specifically, the 'cracking revolution' has again made the United States one of the largest oil producers worldwide and may even transform it into a net oil exporter before long. Globally, there are many inventions that have the potential to result in innovative technologies that will delay the peak in oil production (see Sect. 8.3.2, Fig. 8.10).

Sometimes the peak oil hypothesis is claimed to be supported by the fact that several private oil companies had to adjust their crude oil reserves downwards in recent years. But their reporting of reserves does not only depend on geological facts but also on institutions governing the market (see Sect. 6.1). Today, many oil fields are exploited under so-called production sharing agreements between public (governmental) and private partners. The private partner obtains a share of the reserves designed to ensure a rate of production and hence sales revenue that is sufficient to cover the cost of extraction plus a negotiated return on invested capital, while the public partner retains the rest. In case of rising oil prices, production sharing agreements typically permit governments to reduce the private share of reserves on the grounds that the same sales revenue can now be obtained from a lower rate of production (which is true in view of a short-term price elasticity of demand below one, as evidenced in Table 5.3. This causes the private partner to report less reserves, even though one would expect that rising oil prices lead to an increase in reserves.

8.1.4 Unconventional Oil

Unconventional crude oil includes heavy crude oil, oil sands, bitumen, tar sands, and shale oil. While estimates of reserves vary, the existence of huge deposits of heavy oil and tar sands is not in doubt. Deposits in the Orinoco basin in Venezuela and sands in Western Canada alone amount to 300 bn bbl of oil, a substantial addition to global reserves of conventional oil of roughly 1200 bn bbl (see Table 8.3).

Thanks to technological change, unconventional reserves can sooner or later be retrieved at a cost that makes them competitive against conventional alternatives. Oil sands even enjoy an advantage over conventional crude because their deposits are already known, obviating most expenses for exploration. However, extracting unconventional oil is far more complex and hence costly than extracting conventional crude. For this, there are two commonly used processes with the following properties:

- In the case of surface mining, oil sands are dredged and mixed with hot water. This mixture, also called slurry, is pumped through pipelines to treatment plants, where the bitumen is separated from the sand, mineral clay, salt, and water. After cleaning, the sand is recycled to fill the excavated mine, while the water is channeled to sedimentation tanks, to be used again eventually.
- In the in situ process, hot steam or CO_2 is injected into the oil layer in order to dilute the bitumen and make it flow. This mixture is extracted using conventional crude oil production technologies (i.e. steam-assisted gravity drainage, vapor extraction, and cyclic steam simulation). The in situ process also allows extraction of unconventional oil from deep deposits. A more recent technology is fracking, which was first applied to shale gas (see Sect. 9.1.2) but is now also used to retrieve shale oil.

As a rule, the production of unconventional oil is more expensive than the extraction of conventional crude oil. It also causes a greater environmental burden in terms of land use, energy input, and risks to drinking water. However, hikes in the price of crude oil have triggered large inflows of capital into research and development of extraction technologies as well as the development of unconventional deposits, preparing the ground for future growth of production.

8.1.5 Refineries and Oil Products

Profit margins are significantly higher in the extraction than in the refinery business, but refineries still represent the technological core of the oil value chain. In refineries, crude oil is processed into final energy sources such as gasoline, kerosene, diesel, and fuel oil. Their properties are listed in Table 8.5.

The refinery process can be divided into several sub-processes. Traditionally, the most important sub-process is distillation, where the chemical components of crude oil are separated in so-called fractions through heating and evaporation. Having different boiling temperatures (with water highest at 100 °C), they can be made to condensate at different levels in distillation towers. Particularly light fractions like methane, ethane, propane, and butane are collected at the top of the tower as so-called condensates or refinery gas. They are followed by gasoline and diesel in the medium levels, and residues in the lower levels of the tower.

Evidently, only products that are part of the raw material can be obtained through distillation. Yet refinery operators aim to maximize the output of light oil products which can be sold at higher prices. To increase their share, heavy fuel oil and distillation residues are further processed in conversion plants where their long and heavy hydrocarbon molecules are split into shorter and lighter molecular chains using so-called cracking.

There are three types of cracking processes: thermal, catalytic, and hydro cracking. In thermal cracking, the molecular bonds of large hydrocarbon molecules are broken up by heating the distillation residue up to a temperature of about 500 °C. Catalytic cracking uses a catalyst, e.g. synthetic aluminum silicate, for breaking up molecular bonds. The most flexible but also most costly conversion technology is hydro cracking. Here, hydrogen atoms are added at the ends of broken molecular chains in order to chemically stabilize them, making it possible to mainly produce gasoline and diesel. However, the process requires operation under high

Table 8.5 Properties of crude oil and oil products

	Density (g/cm^2)	Lower heating value (MJ/kg)	Remarks
Crude oil	0.85 (0.80–0.95)	39–43	Average 41.9
Heavy fuel oil	0.92–0.99		
Diesel/fuel oil	0.84 (0.82–0.86)	42.7	At 15–20 °C
Kerosene	0.74–0.84		
Gasoline	0.76 (0.71–0.78)	43.1	At 15–20 °C
Liquid petrol gas (LPG)	0.53	45.9	At 2–18 bar

Source: Erdmann and Zweifel (2008, p. 180)

Table 8.6 Product portfolio of modern oil refineries

	Without conversion (%)	Catalytic cracking (%)	Hydro cracking (%)
Refinery gas	1–3	21	7–18
Gasoline	13–22	47	28–55
Middle distillates	25–39	20	15–56
Heavy oil	38–60	7	–
Other products		5	

Source: Erdmann and Zweifel (2008, p. 181)

pressure (100–150 bar) and large quantities of hydrogen, often calling for the construction of a hydrogen-producing plant.

Table 8.6 shows a typical product portfolio of modern refineries. Without conversion, no more than 22% of output is gasoline, while up to 60% is lower-valued heavy oil. Catalytic cracking increases the gasoline share to 47%, hydro cracking, even to a maximum of 55%.

Refineries reach an average efficiency of about 82%. This is a high value since transportation to filling stations and other customers is deducted from output. Thus, the energy contained in all refined products sold to final consumers amounts to a 82% of total energy input from crude oil, natural gas, electricity, diesel, and gasoline.

An important managerial decision is where to locate a refinery. A distinction can be made between supply-oriented locations close to extraction sites and sea ports in importing countries and sales-oriented locations close to final consumers. Both types come with advantages and downsides. Sales-oriented locations facilitate cost-efficient, high-volume transportation of crude by pipeline and supertanker. This enables refineries to quickly adapt to changes in the structure of demand. Conversely, supply-oriented locations of refineries require more complex logistics because different products need to be transported over long distances. However, when sales prices are volatile and differ between destinations, supply-oriented locations make arbitrage possible. Oil companies simply redirect their deliveries (often already *en route* on the open sea) to the destination with the highest sales price (which usually offers the highest profit margin in view of low extra transportation cost). Therefore, supply-oriented locations of refineries may increase company profits while contributing to a convergence of prices of refined products.

8.1.6 Biogenic Liquid Fuels

Whereas in most uses of energy, oil products are in competition with other fossil fuels such as natural gas and coal, they continue to dominate in the transportation sector. Electric railways aside, this sector depends almost exclusively on oil. Yet considerable effort is being undertaken to introduce alternative fuels for transportation. The motivation is not only to enhance the security of energy supply by lessening the dominance of oil but also to reduce greenhouse gas emissions. Since

Table 8.7 Properties of liquid fuels

	Density (kg/l)	Lower heating value (MJ/kg)	Lower heating value (MJ/l)	Viscosity (mm^2/s)	Flame point (°C)
Gasoline	0.76	43.1	32.4	0.6	<-20
BtL, sun fuel	0.76	43.9	33.4	4	88
Methanol (CH$_3$OH)	0.80	19.7	15.8		11
Bioethanol (C$_2$H$_5$OH)	0.79	26.8	21.2	1.5	13
MTBE / ETBE	0.74	35.1	26.0		-21
Diesel	0.84	42.7	35.8	4–6	>55
Rapeseed oil	0.92	37.6	34.5	74	317
Biodiesel	0.88	37.1	32.6	7–8	120

Data source: FNR (2005). *MTBE* Methyl-tert-butylether; *ETBE* Ethyl-tert-butylether

these emissions are substantial in the conversion of gas to liquid (GtL) and coal to liquid (CtL), respectively, use of biomass as a liquid transportation fuel has been gaining attention. There are several options for biomass to liquid (BtL):

– Biodiesel (rapeseed oil methyl ester) is produced from oily plants (e.g. rape, soy, sun flower). Oil gained from conventional oil mills (e.g. rapeseed oil) contains viscous components (see Table 8.7) and therefore needs to be converted into fatty acid methyl ester (FAME) in order to become a diesel substitute. Furthermore, methanol is added to make up about 10% of the final product, which can be marketed as pure biodiesel or added to conventional diesel (so-called blending). In the European Union biodiesel production reached a volume of 9 mn tons by 2010 but has been declining since because biodiesel offers only limited environmental advantages over diesel. Its production cost varies between 0.55 and 0.70 EUR/l diesel equivalent. Assuming equal tax treatment of diesel and biodiesel, the renewable fuel would be competitive at prices of crude in excess of 100 USD/bbl only.[1]
– Bioethanol (alcohol) is produced by the fermentation of plants with high sugar content. In 2014, worldwide bioethanol production has reached 90 bn liter (of which the United States accounts for 57% and Brazil for 27%). Bioethanol is mostly sold as blend (as E10 in parts of the European Union, which is 90% gasoline and 10% bioethanol) because this obviates adjustments in refueling infrastructure and gasoline engines. Production cost of bioethanol ranges from

---

[1]These figures are based on an exchange rate of 1.30 USD/EUR and current cost structures of refineries. With these assumptions and a crude oil price of 60 USD/bbl, the wholesale price of gasoline is about 0.35 EUR/l and that of diesel, about 0.34 EUR/l. Note that one liter of biodiesel contains the energy equivalent of 0.9 l of conventional diesel (see Table 8.7).

0.20 USD/l in Brazil to 0.35 USD/l in the United States and on to 0.55 USD/l in the European Union. The energy equivalent of one liter of bioethanol corresponds to 0.65 liter of gasoline. This makes Brazilian bioethanol competitive at prices of crude oil of 50 USD/bbl while European ethanol becomes competitive at prices above 140 USD/bbl only.
– Biofuels of the second generation (also known as BtL, biomass to liquid) are produced using advanced technologies such as biomass gasification with a subsequent Fischer-Tropsch synthesis. Another innovation in the making is the utilization of enzymes for decomposing fibrous parts of plants designed to allow the energetic use of the entire plant mass. Unfortunately none of these technologies have been proven to be feasible outside the laboratory up to now.

With the exception of Brazilian ethanol, the supply of biofuels at present depends on political support such as (partial) exemptions from fuel tax and mandatory blending quotas for gasoline and diesel. Additionally, there are agricultural subsidies. The subsidization of biofuels has been justified by arguments derived from the theory of innovation. By creating a market niche for the corresponding technologies and cultivation practices, an industry can benefit from learning effects which might lead to cost reductions. The hope is that in future, increasing market shares can be obtained without political support (see IEA 2000; Nakicenovic 2002). The risk is that this support creates a pressure group that has a strong interest in its continuation. Experience shows that subsidies in particular are very difficult to terminate.

The production of biofuels is limited by the availability of arable land and yields. It can have a potentially negative impact on food security but also on biogas production (see Sect. 9.1.3). Table 8.8 shows the present range of yields for grains and oil plants in Central Europe. Using the example of biodiesel, 3.3 tons of rapeseed can be harvested per hectare given medium yields, resulting in 1.3 tons of rapeseed oil (given a yield of 0.4 tons rapeseed oil per ton rapeseed). Using the

Table 8.8 Yields of energy plants

(Tons/(ha a))	Very low	Low	Medium	Good	Very good
Grain					
Winter barley	5.22	5.69	5-6	6.70	7.51
Oat	3.93	4.32	4.57	4.85	5.33
Winter rye	3.86	4.66	5.24	5.88	6.73
Triticale (cross of wheat and rye)	4.77	5.18	5.60	6.21	6.83
Winter wheat	5.48	6.09	6.75	7.80	8.60
Grain maize	6.04	7.10	7.41	7.96	8.85
Oil plants					
Winter rapeseed	2.73	3.06	3.26	3.46	3.74
Sunflower		2.5		4.0	

Source: Erdmann and Zweifel (2008)

heating value of 37.6 MJ/kg in Table 8.7, the energy content of this harvest can be estimated at 49,000 GJ. About one-third of this energy is needed as an input into its transformation into biodiesel, leaving some 33,000 GJ per hectare for energy use. According to Table 8.7, this is the energy content of 1000 l biodiesel (32.6 MJ/l·1000 l ≈ 33,000 GJ) or 900 l diesel equivalent.

These yields could be increased in the future through the use of seeds that are especially developed for the production of energy plants. Some agricultural experts believe that a 50% increase of yield is achievable.

Some years ago, the European Union aimed to increase the share of renewable energies in the transportation sector to 10% by 2020 (directive 2009/28/EG). This would require an agricultural area of more than 15 mn ha, or about 10% of the arable area in the European Union. In the meantime however, EU strategy has changed in favor of electric vehicles.

8.2 Crude Oil Market

During the 150 years of its history, the oil industry has gone through clearly distinct phases, which were characterized by differing market structures. Transition between these phases caused major changes affecting the oil industry, market participants, and the governments of oil-producing and oil-importing countries. It is important to understand the reasons for the relative stability during these phases as well as the transitions between them. This calls for the application of economic theory, in particular industrial economics and game theory.

8.2.1 Vertically Integrated Monopoly

Oil production on an industrial scale began in 1859 in Pennsylvania (United States). With the development of distillation technology, kerosene produced from crude oil became the preferred energy source for lighting. Previously, oil lamps had been fueled with whale oil, almost causing the extinction of whales due to overfishing. Thus, the substitution of whale oil by crude oil can be cited as the timely solution to an urgent resource problem.

Thanks to its advanced refining technology as well as rude competitive practices, the Standard Oil Company founded by John D. Rockefeller was able to achieve a monopolistic position on the American refinery market within a decade. After 1880, the company became a dominant player also in the U.S. extraction, transportation, and distribution business. However, pursuant the Sherman Act of 1890 (also known as Antitrust Act), in 1911 the Standard Oil Company was split into 34 independent companies. Over time, some of these companies (Amoco, Chevron, Conoco, Exxon, Marathon, and Mobil) developed into the so-called oil majors that continue to operate on a worldwide scale to this very day.

The typical feature of oil majors is their vertical integration, meaning that they control the value chain from prospection, extraction, and transportation on to distribution to final consumers. What was the reason that the new oil industry evolved rather quickly into a vertically integrated monopoly (up to 1911)? The answer derives from an economic analysis of vertical integration, which emphasizes its efficiency advantages. Traditionally, economists have associated efficiency with arms-length market transactions, which are replaced by in-house command-and-control relationships in vertically integrated companies. Yet according to Grossman and Hart (1986), command and control tends to lose any initial efficiency advantage because the corrective of market competition is absent.[2] They argue that vertically integrated companies survive and may even dominate markets because they are able to force competitors out while preventing market entry by potential newcomers. Indeed, the oil industry's value chain has several characteristics that facilitate dominance by a vertically integrated company:

- Kerosene and other oil products are commodities with relatively homogenous properties. In this situation, the famous law of one price holds. Thus, a refinery operator who has lower cost of production than its competitors (e.g. thanks to better equipment) has a competitive advantage. If in addition the refinery stage exhibits economies of scale (i.e. marginal cost and with it, average cost declines with increasing volume of output), the company with the initial cost advantage can achieve an ever growing market share, leaving no chance to smaller competitors and newcomers.
- A company dominating one stage of the value chain may be able to extend its control to the next stage, e.g. by creating a network of sales outlets that closes the market to independent retailers (so-called vertical foreclosure, see Tirole 1988, p. 193). In the case of Standard Oil, vertical foreclosure was first achieved 'upstream', by making railway companies depend on its high volume of orders for transporting crude oil and finally buying them up. In this way, competing refineries were cut off from the supply of crude oil. In a second step, Standard Oil also performed 'downstream' foreclosure by so-called exclusive dealing, i.e. by creating a dense network of gas stations that agreed to purchase their supply from Standard Oil only.

However, vertical integration has also been viewed in a more favorable light, starting with the work of Nobel laureate Coase (1937) who was first to highlight the role of transaction costs. Transaction costs comprise the collection of information e.g. on the quality of the product or service to be traded, setting up contracts, and monitoring compliance with them. In the presence of low transaction costs, arms-length dealing through markets is efficient. Yet when transaction costs are substantial, performing transactions within a company rather than through markets may be more efficient. A famous example is putting together a team for producing a movie. The market solution would require every actor, every costume designer, and every

---

[2]The value-creating units of vertically integrated companies are nowadays often organized as profit centers in order to prevent this disadvantage.

grip to strike a contract with every other member of the team. The internal solution is for the director to be partner to all contracts, giving him a measure of command-and-control authority. Note that as long as vertically integrated companies remain in competition with each other, vertical integration is subject to the market test so may well be beneficial at both the microeconomic and the macroeconomic level. In the case of refining companies, there are at least two reasons for efficiency-driven vertical integration:

- According to Williamson (1971), investments in refineries are asset-specific (also known as factor-specific investments), meaning that they cannot be used for anything else but processing crude oil. In addition, refineries crucially depend on a continuous supply of crude oil, making them vulnerable to a 'hold-up' by oil extractors. Conversely, extracting companies would suffer from a 'hold-up' by refineries as soon as they rely on pipelines for low-cost transportation. In this situation, vertical integration can be an efficient alternative because it reduces the supply risks confronting refineries while stabilizing sales and earnings at the extracting stage. This makes investment in a vertically integrated industry attractive.
- Asymmetry of information between buyer and seller can be a problem calling for vertical integration. Usually, the seller knows more about the properties of the product than the buyer, who may have to undertake costly search for information. The buyer can avoid this cost by acquiring the seller, thus obtaining the right to inspect the product. During the early phase of the oil industry, asymmetric information was indeed a problem: The owner of an oil field had detailed knowledge about the quantity of oil in the ground, which the refinery operator lacked, being an outsider. However, a potential investor needed to have a reliable estimate of future supply in order to plan the refinery's capacity. The purchase of the oil field resolved this asymmetry of information.

If highly asset-specific investment combines with risk in market transactions along the value chain, a tendency towards vertical integration is to be expected. However, this tendency hurts the economy in case it leads to 'downstream' monopolization to the detriment of final consumers. For small countries, it may be sufficient to keep markets open to foreign competition, exposing domestic producers to the threat of market entry by newcomers from the world market. However, these newcomers may be multinationals who have at least as much market power as their domestic competitors, calling for intervention by competition policy (Zweifel and Zäch 2003). In large countries like the United States, the world market may be dominated by its own domestic producers, creating a situation that cannot be resolved without government regulation designed to prevent the abuse of market power. In the case of the Standard Oil Company, application of the Sherman Act of 1890 (known as the Antitrust Act) led to an extremely severe intervention, i.e. the forced unbundling of the monopolist. While vertical integration continues to characterize the oil industry, a vertically integrated monopoly is no more possible.

8.2.2 Global Oligopoly of Vertically Integrated Majors

With the shift from kerosene lamps to electric light, the market initially targeted by refineries vanished. Yet by historical coincidence, the combustion engine (with the gasoline engine patented in 1876 and the diesel engine, in 1892) created a new and much larger market for crude oil and its products. However, motor cars consume substantially more energy than kerosene lamps, causing people to worry already at that time whether there would be sufficient crude oil in the face of mass motorization.[3] With the discovery of large oil fields in Texas (in 1901) and in the Persian Gulf region (Iraq in 1904, Iran in 1908, and Saudi Arabia in 1921), these concerns vanished.

As a consequence of this shift of supply to the Persian Gulf, the successors of the former Standard Oil Company had to expand their sourcing of crude oil in order to hold on to their market position. Internationally, they were competing with European companies such as BP and Royal Dutch/Shell, who had started their oil business in the colonies of their home countries. This globalization had the added benefit of permitting to shift profits within the vertically integrated organization towards tax jurisdictions offering favorable terms. In this context, internal transfer prices (also known as posted prices) can be used to e.g. overcharge services provided by headquarters to an extracting division operating in the Persian Gulf. This leads to a reduction of profits recorded there, resulting in a lowered overall tax burden, provided the home country (which can be a tax haven like the Bahamas) offers a lenient taxation of profits.

By the 1920s, exploration of oil fields in the Persian Gulf exceeded growth in oil demand, leading to a fall in both the nominal and real price of crude (see Fig. 8.4). The U.S. Sherman Act of 1890 had created a new competitive environment which prevented the leading companies from individually controlling the market. In the aim of stopping the decline in oil prices, the three companies BP, Shell, and Exxon signed the Achnacarry Agreement in 1928, to be joined by Mobil, Gulf, Texaco, and Chevron later. This agreement froze the market shares of participating companies in all countries except the United States. A company who attracted additional customers was to share the extra demand with its competitors. Inevitably, the Achnacarry Agreement also froze market shares in the supply of crude. It constitutes a classic cartel designed to fix sales and production quotas. Also called the 'seven sisters' because it comprised the seven oil majors, it was able to control the international oil market until the 1970s. In particular, it thwarted attempts by the governments of concession countries to appropriate a greater share of profits by threatening to move production somewhere else. It also staved off nationalization, the most famous example being the creation of the National Iranian Oil Company in 1951 by Prime Minster Mosaddegh, who was ousted by a *coup d'état* led by British

---

[3]For example, representatives of the Detroit Board of Commerce voiced grave concerns about the future of crude oil supply at a 1906 Senate hearing in Washington DC.

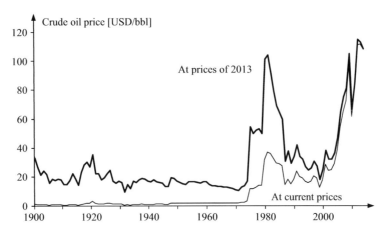

Fig. 8.4 Crude oil prices between 1900 and 2013 (data source: BP)

and U.S. intelligence agencies in 1953. From the viewpoint of the oil majors, their cartel was quite successful in keeping concession fees at a low level.

At that time, there was no antitrust legislation in most countries, with the exception of the United States. Indeed, for strategic reasons the U.S. government even encouraged domestic oil companies to expand worldwide. It saw no reason to intervene against the cartel because the Achnacarry Agreement explicitly exempted the United States, thus complying with U.S. antitrust legislation. Governments of the remaining consumer countries had no incentive to intervene either, likely because they viewed 'their' company as a conduit for transferring profits and hence tax revenue from producing countries. In fact, they benefited from a high import price, having started to tax gasoline in terms of a percentage levied on it.

Economists maintain that no cartel can live forever without an effective enforcement mechanism (often the government) because each of its members has an incentive to chisel. The temptation to sell more by secretly granting a price reduction is strong because the agreed sales price is usually way above marginal cost. Yet in the case of the 'seven sisters', the challenge came from another cartel, the Organization of Oil Exporting Countries (OPEC). This cartel became possible because governments of producer countries had achieved an increased degree of control over extraction (see Sect. 8.2.3).

In the wake of oil field nationalizations after the Second World War, the amount of crude available to oil majors fell short of their refinery capacities (see Fig. 8.5). As a consequence, these companies had to purchase crude oil on the international market to keep their refineries running. This made high prices of crude oil a mixed blessing for them: On the one hand, they reaped windfall profits on production from the fields remaining under their control; on the other hand, they incurred increased costs for purchasing the extra crude. In addition, the companies found it increasingly difficult to obtain new concessions in countries with nationalized oil fields.

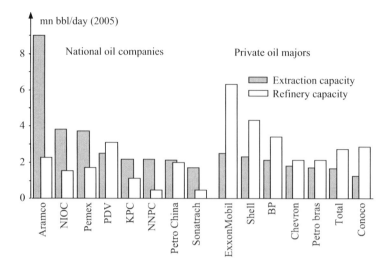

Fig. 8.5 Extraction and refinery capacities of oil companies. Data source: www.energyintel.com

Table 8.9 Mega mergers between oil majors

Partners	Company	Year of merger
BP + Amoco	BP, London (UK)	1998
Exxon + Mobil	ExxonMobil, Irving (U.S.)	1999
Total + Fina + Elf	Total, Paris (France)	1999, 2000
Gulf + Chevron + Texaco	Chevron, San Francisco (U.S.)	1984, 2001
Conoco + Phillips	ConocoPhillips, Houston (U.S.)	2002

While there were alternatives such as domestic offshore oil and enhanced oil recovery (mainly shale oil at present), they continued to be more costly than production in Persian Gulf region. A further challenge was that some oil-producing countries began to process crude oil on their own. This led to global refining overcapacities and decreasing refinery margins (see Sect. 8.1.5).

As a reaction to these challenges, private oil companies went through a wave of mega mergers by the end of the 1990s (see Table 8.9). As their motivation, they stated cost reductions and synergy effects, especially through an integrated optimization of refineries, logistics, and stocks. However, these mergers allowed the oil majors also to better control production capacities and oil flows, serving to boost their refinery margins and hence profits.

8.2.3 The OPEC Cartel of Oil-Exporting Countries

In September 1960, five countries (Iran, Iraq, Kuwait, Saudi Arabia, and Venezuela) founded OPEC, the Organization of Petrol Exporting Countries. Its objective was to forge a joint monopoly that could set a sales price in excess of the

8.2 Crude Oil Market

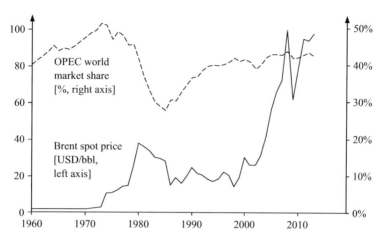

Fig. 8.6 Crude oil price and OPEC market share (data source: BP)

competitive market price. However, a high price entails a reduced quantity sold; therefore, a cartel must allocate production quotas to its members. Yet in view of high profit margins, each member has an incentive to chisel, i.e. to secretly sell additional amounts at a reduced price, thus undermining the cartel.

Over time, more countries joined OPEC: Qatar (1961), Indonesia[4] (1962), Libya (1962), the United Arab Emirates (1967), Algeria (1969), Nigeria (1971), Ecuador[5] (1973 and 2007), Gabon (1975) and Angola (2007). While these additions caused the market share of OPEC to increase during the 1960s (see Fig. 8.6), the member states were not able to capitalize on this development. This changed in 1970 when Libya and Algeria, two relatively small oil-producing countries, were able to negotiate higher concession fees with 'their' private oil companies. They were successful for two reasons. First, the increase amounted to only 0.40 USD/bbl; second, the companies operating in these countries were not oil majors but relatively small companies without alternative production sites. The success of these two small OPEC member states shed a negative light on larger OPEC countries as well as on OPEC as a whole, who had obviously failed to take advantage of the cartel's potential. However, OPEC soon had the opportunity to rectify this.

– The Yom Kippur War between Israel and its Arab neighbors in the fall of 1973 had a rallying effect on OPEC countries, who agreed to unilaterally increase the

---

[4]Indonesia left OPEC in 2009 because it became a net importer of oil.

[5]Ecuador left OPEC in 1992 due to restrictive production quotas and high membership fees but rejoined in 2007. Gabon left OPEC in 1992, also due to restrictive production quotas and high membership fees.

concession fee (in the guise of the so-called posted price[6]) by a factor of five, to 11.65 USD/bbl. This hike has become known as the first oil price shock. The oil majors were not able to shift their business elsewhere (North Sea, Alaska) in the short term. Therefore, OPEC did not lose market share until about 1977 (see Fig. 8.6).
- The second oil price shock occurred in 1979, as a consequence of the Iranian Revolution (also known as Islamic Revolution). With Saudi Arabia already having cut oil production by 25%, the political turmoil in Iran exacerbated the shortage, pushing the crude oil price from about 10 USD/bbl to over 30 USD/bbl. This time OPEC lost one-half of its market share because the oil companies were better prepared to shift their sourcing away from the Persian Gulf, to the North Sea in particular. In early 1986, Saudi Arabia (who had been stabilizing the cartel by accepting falls in its quota) decided to defend its market share by letting price drop to below 20 USD/bbl (see Fig. 8.6). This caused the OPEC cartel to break apart.

The two oil price shocks constitute the most important events of the twentieth century affecting the energy economy. They reflect the effectiveness of the OPEC cartel, who at least temporarily had acquired control over the global market for crude oil. Starting in 1982, OPEC countries had set extraction quotas that were compatible with a target price. Saudi Arabia, the OPEC country with the largest oil production by far, took on the role of the so-called swing producer by adjusting its production to achieve the desired price when other cartel members exceeded their quota. Between 1986 and 1999, however, Saudi Arabia was no longer willing to accept chiseling. In 1999 the quota system was reactivated in modified form. Semi-annual negotiated adjustments were replaced by an automatic adjustment if price (based on a basket of crudes sold by OPEC countries, the so-called OPEC basket) deviated from a defined range. This system has never come under pressure since 2004 because oil prices have been exceeding this range as OPEC countries lacked the capacities to meet the growing demand for oil in Asia, in particular China (see Fig. 8.6).

To conclude, OPEC has been able to influence and at times even control the global oil market. However, it has repeatedly experienced periods of weakness. As with all cartels, its members have an incentive to violate the cartel agreement by selling more than their quota (at the high price secured by the cartel), unless there is an effective sanctioning mechanism. This lack of cooperation can be explained by a game theoretic model, the so-called prisoner's dilemma (this term reflects the fact that two accomplices would have to be dismissed for lack of evidence if they cooperated; yet each one has an incentive to tell on the other, striking a deal with police).

Table 8.10 contains an illustrative example. For simplicity, OPEC is divided into two groups (Saudi Arabia and the rest of OPEC), each extracting 10 mn bbl/day. If

---

[6]The posted price is the sales price set by the government of the exporting country, who uses it for calculating the tax to be paid by oil companies. If this tax rate is high, e.g. 80%, the posted price in fact determines the cost of crude to companies.

Table 8.10 Payoff matrix for OPEC members in mn USD/day (example)

Strategy of Saudi Arabia (SA)	Strategy of the other OPEC countries (others)	
	Cooperative	Non-cooperative
Cooperative	SA: 600, others: 600	SA: 300, others: 750
Non-cooperative	SA: 750, others: 300	SA: 400, others: 400

both parties cooperate, the cartel can achieve a price of 60 USD/bbl; if they fail to cooperate, the competitive price of 40 USD/bbl obtains. However, there is another possibility: One party cooperates by sticking to its quota, while the other party chisels by selling in excess of its quota at a lowered price. Assume that each party is able to take over 50% of the other party's demand if it lowers the price by 10 USD/bbl to 50 USD/bbl. Then, its revenue equals 750 mn ($= 50 \cdot 15$) USD/day, whereas the cooperating party has revenues of only 300 mn ($= 60 \cdot 5$) USD/day.

The so-called payoff matrix shows the revenues accruing to Saudi Arabia and the rest of OPEC for the four combinations of strategies (see Table 8.10). Evidently, with 1200 mn ($= 60 \cdot 10 + 60 \cdot 10$) USD/day, cooperation maximizes the joint payoff, while failure to cooperate minimizes it (800 mn $= 40 \cdot 10 + 40 \cdot 10$). However, non-cooperation is profitable if the other party continues to cooperate, i.e. to stick to its quota. Therefore, each member of the cartel has an incentive to chisel, undermining the stability of the cartel.

This example suggests that cartels are likely to be inherently unstable.[7] In the case of OPEC, cooperativeness is further challenged by the asymmetry characterizing its members. Countries with a small but wealthy population (e.g. Kuwait, Saudi Arabia, and the United Arab Emirates) are pitted against countries with a large and relatively poor population (e.g. Algeria, Iran, and Iraq). The governments of the second group typically rely on budgeted revenues from oil sales. This implies that they seek to sell more rather than less when the sales price drops (keeping 'price × quantity' constant), which results in a supply function with negative rather than positive slope. This puts high demands on cartel management by the first group, in particular Saudi Arabia (Griffin and Steele 1986, p. 141).

The two oil shocks had a major impact on the economies of oil-importing countries (see Hickman et al. 1987). On the initiative of Henry Kissinger, the U.S. Secretary of State at the time, the industrial countries of the western world established the Paris-based International Energy Agency (IEA) in 1974. One of its missions has been the creation of stocks sufficient to cover oil demand for 90 days, to be released in case of emergency following a joint decision by all IEA member governments.

Several governments have built up additional stocks of oil that are not part of the IEA crisis mechanism. One example is the U.S. Strategic Petroleum Reserve whose use can be decided upon independently of other governments. From an economic perspective, state-controlled oil stocks amount to compulsory national insurance

---

[7]Based on an evolutionary approach, Axelrod (1984) examines the conditions that make cooperation rather than non-cooperation the stable equilibrium outcome. One such condition is that participants expect a high (infinite) number of iterations of the game.

against oil shocks. However, insurance coverage is known to induce so-called moral hazard. In the present context, it undermines preventive effort by private companies and consumers designed to deal with supply shortages. In fact, the amount of oil stocked by the private sector has significantly decreased with the introduction of state-owned stocks. Another problem is that governments may use oil stocks for other purposes than securing supply. In particular, some have released stocks in the past in order to reduce the price of oil products in an attempt to curry favor with voters at election time.

8.2.4 State-Owned Oil Companies

Nationalizations of private oil companies have a long history: Azerbaijan (1924), Mexico (1938), Romania (1948), Iran (1951-1953), Indonesia (1960), Algeria (1970), Libya (1971), Iraq (1972), Iran (1973), Venezuela (1975-1990), Canada (1975), Kuwait (1975), Saudi Arabia (1980), Venezuela (2004), Russia (2004), and Bolivia (2006) are just the most important cases.[8] However, only two of the eight largest oil companies were state-owned in 1972. By 2000, the situation was reversed, with only two of the eight major companies being privately owned (ExxonMobil and Shell). The four so-called super majors (ExxonMobil, Shell, BP, and Total) account for no more than about 11% of global crude oil extraction. A new form of state control over crude oil markets thus originates in oil-consuming countries, whose state-owned companies have been more successful than the private oil majors in the acquisition of foreign oil concessions.

In most countries, oil deposits, as well as deposits of other raw materials, are owned by the public sector, most often by central government. This also applies to offshore fields within the 200-mile economic zone. The transfer of extraction rights to private companies is based on extraction licenses or so-called concessions. In principle, governments are free to decide whom to award these licenses except that they have to respect international agreements, for example OECD norms regarding foreign direct investment or non-discrimination norms of the European Union.

Whether the extraction of raw materials, notably crude oil, should be allocated to the private or the public sector has been hotly disputed since the nineteenth century. Yet there is an economic argument in favor of oil extraction by public companies, derived from so-called principal-agent theory. This theory revolves around a principal who hires a specialized agent whose effort it cannot observe, a situation which creates leeway for the agent to pursue its own interest. To a government acting as the principal, effort deployed and cost incurred by a private company (the agent) are indeed largely unobservable. Thus governments are exposed to the risk of opportunistic behavior on the part of e.g. private oil companies, a risk that cannot be entirely eliminated even by contracts of the most sophisticated type. Therefore it

---

[8]The British company BP and the French company CFP were previously state-owned but are now in private ownership.

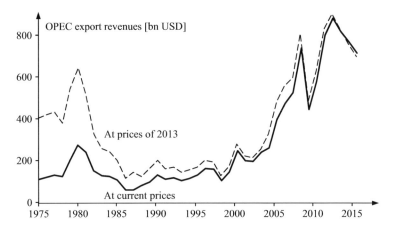

Fig. 8.7 OPEC revenues from oil exports (data source: EIA 2014)

may be preferable for governments to directly control oil production through their own national oil company (whose effort is assumed to be open to inspection).

Rosa (1993) has elaborated this argument further. His starting point is that "(...) the rationale for nationalization is to be found in the basic business of politics, the transfer motive" (Rosa 1993, p. 320). In order to appropriate the maximum amount of money from the oil industry, governments can tax extraction profits or nationalize the oil extraction business.[9] Either way, they obtain most of the scarcity rent associated with an exhaustible resource (see Sect. 6.2.1). Their rational choice depends on the cost-benefit ratio of these two alternatives. Since these cost-benefit ratios vary over time, the optimal choice may also vary, which would explain the long historic waves of privatization and nationalization. In keeping with this line of thought, the propensity to nationalize oil extraction is predicted to increase if

- scarcity rents increase, since this favors opportunistic behavior by private companies. According to Fig. 8.7, the revenues from oil exports (which reflect profits to a considerable extent because costs were far more stable) correspond closely with the two waves of nationalization in the 1970s and after 2000;
- foreign oil companies act more aggressively to reduce their tax burden, causing income from profit taxation to fall;
- the degree of corruptibility of public officials increases, since this also tends to decrease income from profit taxation;
- the interest differential between private and public loans increases (given that it is positive) because interest payments by private oil companies lower their

---

[9]Another way to transfer income and wealth to select groups is to regulate the sales prices of private or public companies. In the present context, this alternative becomes important only once a public company is in charge of providing oil products to consumers.

profits and hence tax payments while interest payments to former owners of nationalized resources become comparatively smaller;
- tax collection becomes more costly due to an increase in tax evasion and fraud.

Conversely, privatization becomes attractive if the government revenue generated by a national oil company falls short of the tax on profit attainable given that the company is privatized. Usually, this situation is the result of a high productivity gap between private and national oil companies. However, such a gap may in turn be caused by the fact that public companies pursue other goals than profit maximization (which goes along with high productivity). National oil companies may be used by government as a vehicle to reduce unemployment (through overstaffing) or to sell oil products to domestic consumers at below-market prices. Both measures correspond to the main business of government – transferring income and wealth to preferred voter groups (Hartley and Medlock 2008).

However, productivity gaps between private and public companies can be traced to other reasons, in particular a lack of innovativeness in state-owned firms. During periods of rapid innovation in the oil industry, the involvement of national oil companies in the extraction business tends to be harmful to the oil-producing country, motivating rational governments to privatize.[10] Conversely, during periods of slow innovative change, governments are predicted to prefer state ownership.

8.3 Oil Price Formation

With the creation of national oil companies in the 1970s, the private oil majors ceased to be vertically integrated, with the inevitable consequence of a substantial expansion of international trade in oil. There are two types of traders on wholesale oil markets (see Fig. 8.5):

- Companies with a long position (net suppliers) who dispose of more crude oil than they can refine and therefore have an excess of crude oil. Typical examples are national oil companies, who lack not only refining capacities but also access to consumer markets since most filling station networks continue to be controlled by the oil majors.
- Companies with a short position (net demanders) who depend on crude oil purchases for utilizing their refining capacities and supplying their filling station networks. Typically, these are the oil majors, having lost many of their oil fields and extraction rights.

---

[10]Without privatization, national oil companies can become dependent on the know-how of foreign private companies.

This structure encourages the development of wholesale oil markets. One has to distinguish between spot markets (for physical delivery), forward markets (ultimately for physical delivery), and markets for financial derivatives. On spot markets, conclusion of the contract, delivery, and payment occur more or less simultaneously. In the case of the oil industry, settlement is somewhat delayed for logistical reasons but usually does not take more than 15 days. On forward markets, delivery and payment are due several months or even years after conclusion of the contract. Volumes and prices are fixed ahead of delivery, permitting the party less able to bear risk to shift the risk (of a price change in particular) to the party who is better able to bear it, e.g. because its activities are more diversified (see Sect. 12.2.5 for an analogous discussion of forward electricity markets). On derivative markets, contracts relating to physical quantities rather than physical quantities themselves are traded, such as futures and options; accordingly, settlement is financial rather than physical. Derivative markets enable traders from outside the oil business, for example financial institutions, to participate.

Another distinction is between contracts concluded on an energy exchange or outside an exchange (so-called over-the-counter contracts, OTC for short). The reason for using energy exchanges instead of OTC markets is counterparty risk. Each party to a contract is exposed to the risk that the counterparty defaults, for instance due to insolvency. While this risk increases with time until settlement, it is eliminated if the energy exchange becomes the counterparty to the contract. The exchange is better able to bear this risk because it administers a huge number of contracts, causing the likelihood of multiple defaults to be very small. Still, exchanges acting as clearing houses protect themselves against financial risk by asking their members to provide collateral and to adjust it to market developments (so-called marking to market). This is the 'price of the counterparty insurance' and may amount to substantial transaction costs for traders. Another reason for using an energy exchange is anonymous trading; sellers and buyers do not need to know their counterparty.

The most important crude oil exchanges are the New York Mercantile Exchange (NYMEX) and the International Commodity Exchange (ICE) in London (formerly International Petroleum Exchange). Each defines a so-called benchmark crude for describing product quality. For the U.S. market this is West Texas Intermediate (WTI) traded at Cushing; for Europe it is North Sea Brent. More recently, Dubai Crude has been established as the benchmark crude for the Persian Gulf (see Sect. 8.1.1).

8.3.1 Oil Spot Markets and the Efficient Market Hypothesis

An important task of energy economists is to understand price developments on crude oil spot markets. According to the theory of efficient markets, the current spot price is the best possible forecast for the price of the following day (a so-called naïve forecast). The reason is that price incorporates all information available to market participants without any delay, causing daily spot prices p_t to follow a random walk. As there are no negative prices on the oil market, the logarithmic version of random Brownian motion is the appropriate model,

$$\ln p_t = \ln p_{t-1} + Vola \cdot dz \text{ or}$$
$$\Delta \ln p_t = \ln p_t - \ln p_{t-1} = \ln\left(\frac{p_t}{p_{t-1}}\right) = Vola \cdot dz. \tag{8.1}$$

The stochastic variable $dz \sim N(0, dt)$ is normally distributed, having expected value zero and variance dt, with dt denoting the time interval between quotations (e.g. a day if daily closing prices are to be analyzed). $Vola$ symbolizes annualized volatility. It is calculated by multiplying the standard deviation σ of the logarithmic difference $\Delta\ln p_t$ (the so-called price return) by the square root of the 252 trading days per year (261 weekdays minus 9 public holidays),

$$Vola = \frac{1}{T-1} \cdot \sqrt{\sum_{t=1}^{T}(\ln p_t - \ln \bar{p})^2} \cdot \sqrt{252} = \sigma \cdot \sqrt{252}. \tag{8.2}$$

The original time series (ln p_t, $t = 1, 2,\ldots$) with the property (8.1) has a stochastic trend. If the differentiated time series of price return $\Delta\ln p_t$ is stationary and statistically white noise, ln p_t is said to be integrated of order one.

According to Fig. 8.8, the daily relative changes in the price of benchmark crudes can be approximated closely using the random walk model (8.1). For 420 days in 2005 and 2006, observed average volatility of WTI spot prices was equal to $0.020 \cdot 252^{0.5} = 32\%$. Kurtosis (reflecting the 'thickness of the tails') is 3.454, exceeding the value of 3 characterizing the normal distribution. This means that large relative day-to-day changes in price are more frequent than would be expected under a normal distribution [and hence the model (8.1)]. However, with 3.788 the Jarque-Bera test statistic (which amounts to a χ^2 with two degrees of

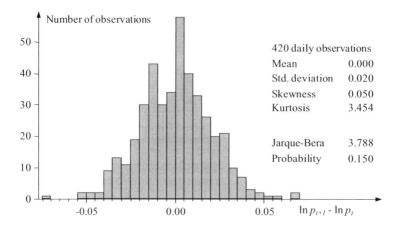

Fig. 8.8 Histogram of $\Delta\ln p_t$ for 420 days, 2005–2006

freedom) indicates that the summed squared deviations from a normal distribution are too small to be statistically significant. More detailed analysis shows that *Vola* was not constant over time, contrary to the model (8.1), suggesting that the parameter estimates presented may not be robust to changes in the observation period. Yet, overall the hypothesis of efficient markets need not be rejected in the case of benchmark crudes.

8.3.2 Long-Term Oil Price Forecasts and Scenarios

Naïve short-term price forecasts of the type presented in the preceding section are not satisfactory for an economic assessment of investments in the energy industry and for energy policy, which need to be based on long-term predictions. Accordingly, industry analysts (e.g. Prognoseforum in Germany), financial institutions (e.g. research divisions of commercial banks), research institutes (e.g. the Center for Global Energy Studies CGES), as well as public authorities (e.g. the International Energy Agency and the U.S. Department of Energy) regularly publish long-term oil price forecasts and scenarios.

Most commonly, they perform a so-called fundamental analysis, trying to predict future price developments by observing shifts in the supply of and demand for oil. Some factors influencing supply were mentioned in Sects. 6.2 and 8.2; at this point, a more comprehensive list of supply-side factors is presented.

- According to economic theory, the marginal cost of the last oil field needed to meet demand constitutes the lower bound of the price of crude oil. Over time, oil fields are exhausted, calling for the development of new fields which usually have higher marginal cost, however. Thus the marginal cost of crude oil tends to increase over time. In 2003, the Swiss Investment Bank CSFB estimated the break-even cost of crude oil extraction at 17.60 USD/bbl. Eleven years later, it was much higher (see Fig. 8.2). This partly explains the increase in the price of crude oil that has occurred since 2003. On the other hand, technological change can lead to a fall in marginal cost. This was particularly relevant in the 1980s and 1990s, contributing to a period of low oil prices (in real terms) between 1986 and 1999.
- Capacity utilization is another fundamental factor influencing price developments. When capacity utilization is low, an increase in the demand for oil can be met at little extra cost. In a market diagram, the supply schedule runs almost horizontal. When capacity utilization is high, extra demand can only be met by working overtime, working faster, and hiring more labor, all of which drives up marginal cost (in keeping with the adage, 'haste makes waste'). The supply schedule has a steep slope, indicating that any increase in demand boosts price. On the longer run, capacity is adjusted, usually by bringing in new machinery that incorporates technological change and hence serves to lower marginal cost. The supply schedule shifts out, causing price to fall (provided

demand does not continue to increase). The result is a cyclical development of the price of crude.
- Exploration and development of new oil fields may reinforce this cyclical pattern. The condition is that the new fields operate at the same or lower marginal cost as the existing ones, thus causing the supply schedule to shift out. Then, the cycle can be described as follows. At low capacity utilization and low demand, investment in new fields is unattractive (existing ones may even be abandoned). In this situation, a surge in demand causes the price of crude to rise. This triggers exploration effort, and with a lag of three to five years (Reynolds 2002), new discoveries result in an outward supply shift, which in turn exerts pressure on price.
- Available extraction capacities are not only influenced by economic considerations but also by wars, political boycotts, strikes, and expectations of such events. Political risks therefore have an impact on crude oil prices.
- Many analysts differentiate between capacity utilization in OPEC countries and in non-OPEC countries. In particular, large spare capacities in non-OPEC countries limit the potential of the OPEC cartel to increase oil prices. Conversely, spare capacities in OPEC countries can be irrelevant if cartel discipline of OPEC members is strong.
- More generally, the effectiveness of OPEC matters. It can vary greatly because the OPEC cartel is inherently unstable (see Sect. 8.2.3). Sometimes it can achieve a price markup over marginal cost, sometimes it cannot. Thus, analyzing the decision processes within OPEC, particularly during the bi-annual meetings of OPEC energy ministers, is part of fundamental analysis.
- In the case of an exhaustible resource, self-fulfilling expectations may induce volatility in price (see Sect. 6.2.3). If market participants expect increasing prices for crude oil, their production decisions differ from a situation in which they expect decreasing prices. Important sources for such expectations are scientific studies and their rendition in the media, in particular business newspapers. Arguably the first oil price shock caused by the oil boycott of OPEC in 1973 was amplified by the influential study by Meadows et al. (1972) on the limits to growth. Also, the oil price increase after 2000 coincided with a public debate about peak oil. In both cases, crude oil was believed to be in short supply before long, providing a seemingly sound justification for its price to increase.
- Prices of benchmark crudes are quoted at point of delivery. For WTI, this is Cushing, Oklahoma, for Brent it is the ports of Amsterdam, Rotterdam, and Antwerp. In the latter case, cargo rates directly influence price; rates in turn depend on availability of tanker capacity, fuel cost, and risk along major shipping routes (geopolitical for the Strait of Hormuz, piracy for the Strait of Malacca).

The most important demand-side factor for crude oil prices is growth of the global economy (see also Sect. 5.2). In order to empirically test this link, annual data on global economic growth rates published by the International Monetary Fund (IMF) can be used. A least-squares regression based on 24 observations covering the years 1990 to 2013 relates the relative changes in Brent spot prices p_{Brent} (data source: BP) and global GDP growth rates. The regression result reads

$$\frac{\Delta p_{Brent}}{p_{Brent}} = -33 + 12.5 \cdot \frac{\Delta GDP}{GDP} \cdot (-2.97)(4.20) \qquad (8.3)$$

The t-statistics in parentheses indicate statistical significance of the parameters, the coefficient of determination $R^2 = 0.42$ satisfactory statistical fit, and the Durbin-Watson statistic $DW = 1.87$, absence of serial correlation of residuals.

According to this estimation, global economic growth of 1% per year is associated with an increase in the Brent spot price increase of 12.5%, *ceteris paribus*. The *ceteris paribus* clause is important because market prices are determined by demand and supply, whereas Eq. (8.3) focuses on a demand-side influence only (for other influences, see below). Also, note that in the absence of growth ($\Delta GDP/GDP = 0$), the equation predicts price to fall by 33%, likely due to the supply-side influences discussed above. Finally, $\Delta GDP/GDP$ should be viewed as endogenous, reflecting the fact that an increase in the price of oil hampers growth in most of the world economy, while a decrease fosters it. Reassuringly however, an estimate linking relative changes in WTI spot prices to global GDP growth from 1990 to 2005 yields comparable results, albeit with a more marked declining trend (Erdmann and Zweifel 2008, p. 202).

There are other factors on the demand side that may influence the price of crude oil:

– Quality requirements concerning oil products affect the structure of demand. Stricter environmental norms have served to increase demand for high-quality (sweet or low-sulfur, respectively) crudes relative to demand for low-quality (sour or high-sulfur) ones (see Sect. 8.1.1).
– For several oil-consuming countries, demand for internationally traded oil is a net quantity because they have domestic supplies. For instance, the development of fracking has been reducing demand for imported oil by the United States (the country is even predicted to become a net exporter before long). This puts pressure on the price of internationally traded crude.

Evidently, there is a multitude of factors influencing crude oil prices. Quite possibly, their relative importance is not constant over time, making fundamental analysis difficult. This also means that price forecasts derived from fundamental analysis are unlikely to be accurate. This consideration suggests scenario modeling as a more modest approach. Scenario modeling yields only conditional predictions reflecting varying assumptions concerning the future development of factors determining the price of oil.

Most of the published oil price scenarios are based on the concept of adaptive expectations[11]. Market participants are assumed to base their predictions on a linear combination of past prices and the currently observed price. By changing the

---

[11] One of the exceptions is Erdmann (1995). His study is based on a non-linear stochastic simulation model that successfully forecast the end of low crude oil prices in the 1990s.

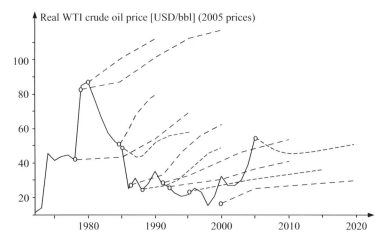

Fig. 8.9 Crude oil price forecasts published by the U.S. Department of Energy

relative weights entering this linear combination, analysts can generate price scenarios which amount to an extrapolation of trends estimated in different ways (see also Sect. 5.3.2). As an example, Fig. 8.9 exhibits oil price forecasts published by the U.S. Department of Energy (DOE). Forecasts are dashed lines showing future price paths predicted at the date of publication; actual price developments are represented by solid lines. As long as the existing price trend remains unchanged, these forecasts are relatively accurate. Yet whenever there is a change in trend, scenarios based on adaptive expectations can be seriously misleading.

Changes in trend (also called structural breaks or regime shifts) occur only sporadically. They are attributed to factors that slowly reach or exceed a certain threshold value, when they suddenly become important. Non-linear systems theory has been the tool of choice for analyzing such regime shifts. An example of a 'slow' variable is the change in the relative cost of production of different technologies. Evidently, the condition for a regime shift is met if the cost of production using an alternative technology falls below the cost of the conventional alternative. However, this does not lead to massive investment in the new technology right away. In the case of fracking, factors causing delay were concerns about a future drop in the sales price of crude, environmental risks, and government intervention protecting incumbent players and technologies. Yet with a continuing or even increasing cost advantage of the new extraction technology, the regime shift cannot be halted.

The upper panel of Fig. 8.10 shows the succession of technologies in U.S. oil extraction since 1900. The first oil price shock of 1973 fostered investment in technology suitable for offshore extraction, the second of 1979/80, in technologies suitable for the retrieval of unconventional crudes, notably fracking. As argued above, the introduction of a new extraction technology causes a surge in supply which puts pressure on price for a few years. The lower panel of Fig. 8.10 displays

8.3 Oil Price Formation

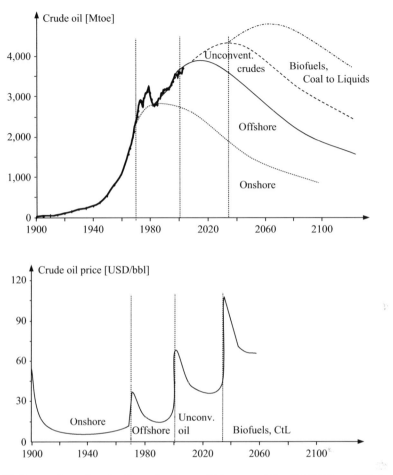

Fig. 8.10 Perspectives of crude oil supply. Source: Erdmann and Zweifel (2008, p. 207)

the cascade-like development of price in a stylized way. It reflects the expectation that by 2035, biofuels and coal liquefaction may well cease a spike in oil price initially triggered by the exhaustion of unconventional sources of oil.

Figure 8.10 can also be related to the peak oil hypothesis which predicts that the sum of onshore and offshore oil extraction will reach its maximum soon (see Sect. 8.1.3). However, recurring price spikes have made the introduction of new extraction technologies profitable in the past, causing the maximum to shift forward. If crude oil supply should again fall short of demand in future, this shift is likely to be repeated, with biofuels, coal liquefaction (Coal to Liquids, CtL), and even more advanced technologies based on hydrogen electrolysis (Power-to-Liquids, PtL) taking over the role of shale oil.

8.3.3 Prices of Crude Oil Futures

Once liquid spot markets for benchmark crudes are established, markets for derivatives can develop. The most important derivatives are oil futures traded on energy exchanges. Futures are standardized contracts (1000 bbl of a benchmark crude) to be settled at standard delivery times (middle of the month) at a price agreed upon in advance. While settlement in terms of physical quantities is possible, financial settlement is more common. In this case, the difference between the spot price observed on the exercise day (the price of the so-called underlying) and the price of the future is paid. If the spot price exceeds the price agreed upon in the future, the buyer of the contract receives the price difference from the exchange while the seller has to pay this difference to the exchange. If the spot price is below the future price, the buyer of the contract has to make up for the difference while the seller receives it.

The standard example is the operator of a refinery with excess capacity. One alternative is to buy crude oil on the spot market and to keep it in storage for use months later. This strategy comes with the so-called cost of carry which comprises cost of storage and insurance as well as forgone interest on the capital tied up. Alternatively, the operator can buy a future contract with the appropriate maturity T. As long the two alternatives differ in terms of cost, there is scope for arbitrage which can be used by the refinery operator to reduce its cost of sourcing. Conversely, if no scope for arbitrage exists at trading date t, the market is in equilibrium, which implies the following relationship between spot price p_t and future price $p_{F,t}(T)$ (Kaldor 1939; Hull 1999),

$$p_{F,t}(T) = p_t \cdot e^{(i+c)(T-t)}. \qquad (8.4)$$

Thus, the price of the forward contract must equal the spot price accrued for interest i and cost of carry c during $(T\text{-}t)$ time periods. Provided c is constant, Eq. (8.4) represents a cointegration equation of degree one, which means that the two time series, $(p_{F,t}, t = 1,...)$ and $(p_t, t = 1,...)$, cannot permanently diverge.[12] From Eq. (8.4), one therefore has

$$\lim_{t \to T} p_{F,t}(T) = p_t \qquad (8.5)$$

$$p_{F,t_0}(T) > p_{F,t_1}(T) > p_t \text{ for } t_1 > t \qquad (8.6)$$

The no-arbitrage conditions predict four things. In view of Eq. (8.4), (i) the future price should increase over time as long as the spot price increases *ceteris paribus*; (ii) according to Eq. (8.5), the price of a forward contract with given maturity T should approach the spot price as time t goes on; (iii) the forward price should always exceed the spot price in view of inequality (8.6); and (iv) this excess

---

[12] If arbitrage exists, arbitrageurs can perform risk-free trades. Their role can therefore be compared to that of the error correction term in cointegration models.

8.3 Oil Price Formation

should decrease over time since the difference $(T-t)$ goes to zero, again in view of inequality (8.6).

Figure 8.11 displays so-called forward curves for contracts with a given maturity. The data confirm prediction (i) in that the forward curves shift up in response to increases in the spot price. They also confirm prediction (ii) until 2002 in that forward prices indeed approach spot prices as time goes on, causing t to approach T. The forward curves are said to be in contango during this period. However, more recently a tendency towards convergence cannot be observed anymore; the forward curves are said to be in backwardation. As to prediction (iii), it is not vindicated because the majority of forward curves runs consistently below the spot price. Moreover, given that they are above the spot price, the excess often fails to decrease as time goes on, contrary to prediction (iv).

During periods of backwardation, futures with late maturity are cheaper than those with early maturity, indicating that the cost of holding a physical stock decreases rather than increases with time to maturity $(T-t)$. The solution has been to complement Eq. (8.4) with a so-called convenience yield cy which may dominate the cost of carry c,

$$p_{F,t}(T) = p_t \cdot e^{(i+c-cy)(T-t)}. \qquad (8.7)$$

The convenience yield could be due to the flexibility in use afforded by a stock of crude prior during time to maturity. While cy is constant in Eq. (8.7), Fig. 8.11 suggests it varies over time. Thus, this modification of the no-arbitrage condition (8.4) remains unsatisfactory as long as the convenience yield is not related to its determinants.

This challenge is taken up by the theory of normal backwardation (Hicks 1939, pp. 135–140), which explains the shape of the forward curve by a demand for

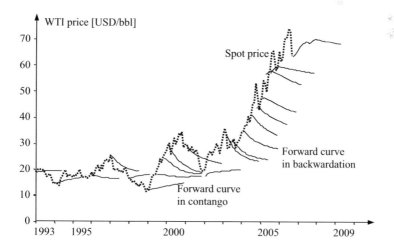

Fig. 8.11 Oil forward curves between 1993 and 2006. Data source: Centre for Global energy Studies (CGES)

hedging price risks which may differ between sellers and buyers and vary over time. In contango, buyers who seek to hedge their short positions dominate, while in backwardation, they are the sellers who want to hedge their long positions. The theory of backwardation is further explained in Sect. 12.2.5, where it is applied to the markets for electricity.

Another approach to explaining the development of price on the market for oil futures starts from the observation that the daily volume of derivatives traded (the so-called paper market) is 30–40 times bigger than the worldwide annual consumption of oil (the so-called wet market). This gives rise to the suspicion that in addition to fundamental market conditions, financial speculation might play a role.

For an analysis of speculative effects on price, backwardation and contango situations need to be considered separately. In the case of backwardation, speculators are predicted to purchase contracts with maturities far in the future (because they are cheap, see Fig. 8.11 again) while selling contracts with short-term maturities. As time goes on, contracts with long-term maturities become higher-valued contracts with short-term maturities. This strategy is profitable provided spot market prices do not fall (which would make a spot purchase an even better alternative). By way of contrast, in the case of contango arbitrage between short-term and long-term futures does not yield profits. The reason is that in contango it would be attractive to purchase contracts with short-term maturities before they become more expensive (see Fig. 8.11). However, as time goes on, these contracts cannot turn into higher-valued contracts with long-term maturity. The consequence of this behavior is that in backwardation, speculators buy up a lot of futures in the paper market, which serves to reduce quantities available on the wet market and hence to drive up spot prices. Conversely, in contango speculators stay away from the paper market, thus leaving supply to the wet market, which in turn causes spot prices to remain stable or even fall.

Indeed, between 2002 and 2006 (a period of backwardation), an inflow of financial capital into the derivative oil market amounting to at least 100 bn USD was reported by *The Washington Post*. This inflow may well have contributed to the increase in the spot price of crude from 30 to more than 60 USD/bbl in 2006. Likewise, the sudden outflow of financial capital in the autumn of 2008 may explain the drop to 40 USD/bbl in that same year.[13]

8.3.4 Wholesale Prices of Oil Products

As a first approximation, the wholesale price of an oil product is the sum of the crude oil price (i.e. the purchase price paid by refineries) and the cost plus margin of

---

[13] Oil prices need not to fall if speculative capital is withdrawn from oil markets. Rather, traders with an interest in holding physical quantities of oil may step in to replenish their stocks. It therefore may take some time for an oil price bubble to burst.

the refinery. In the literature, the spread margin is distinguished from the cash margin when quantifying refinery margins. The spread margin refers to the difference between the sales price of the oil product and the purchase price of the crude; it is transparent because it can be calculated from publicly accessible price data. The cash margin results from the difference between the revenue from selling the product and the cost of production. Its calculation requires knowledge of refineries' cost of operation which is not available to outsiders.

In view of the range of refinery products and their prices, the calculation of the spread is also complicated, calling for simplifying assumptions. The following formula is often used for estimating the so-called crack spread of refineries,

$$Crack\, Spread = \left(2 \cdot p_{gasoline} + p_{fuel\ oil}\right)/3 - p_{crude}. \tag{8.8}$$

In keeping with U.S. market conditions, the price of gasoline is weighted double relative to the price of heating oil (which includes diesel). Since prices need to be per unit energy for aggregation, the price of gasoline $p_{gasoline}$, heating oil $p_{heatingoil}$, and crude oil $p_{crudeoil}$ are converted to a common reference unit using their heating values (e.g. barrels of crude oil equivalent; see Table 8.1).

Figure 8.12 shows the crack spreads of U.S. and European refineries since 1993. Before 2000, the global refinery industry was characterized by large overcapacities (see Fig. 8.5). Once these overcapacities disappeared, the crack spread increased sharply. It is unlikely to return to its former levels since the refinery industry is heavily concentrated in most countries, facilitating collusion. In addition, barriers to entry are high for newcomers.

While crude oil prices and refinery margins do not display a seasonal pattern, there is one for refinery products, at least in the U.S. market. Summer is the driving

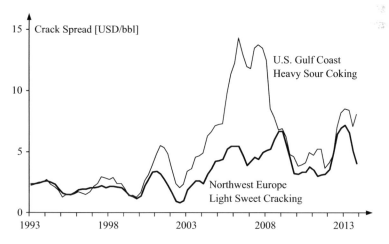

Fig. 8.12 Refinery margins (data source: BP 2014)

season, during which gasoline prices are high relative to heating oil prices.[14] Winter is the heating season, during which heating oil is expensive compared to gasoline. This pattern is confirmed by an ordinary least-squares regression based on weekly observations in the United States covering the years 2001 to 2014. The dependent variable is the ratio of prices for gasoline and heating oil; the explanatory variables are a seasonal term (represented by the cosine function), the available stocks of gasoline and heating oil, respectively, and a time trend that increases by one unit per week. The estimation result reads

$$\frac{p_{Gasoline,t}}{p_{Diesel,t}} = \underset{(31.6)}{1.300} + \underset{(22.2)}{0.059} \cdot \underset{(-26.0)}{\cos\left(\frac{t-10}{8.3}\right)} + \underset{(8.1)}{0.00099 \cdot Stock_{Diesel,t}} \quad (8.9)$$

$$\underset{(-7.6)}{-0.0017 \cdot Stock_{Gasoline,t}} \underset{(-20.5)}{-0.0099 \cdot \frac{t}{52}}$$

The t-statistics below the estimated parameters indicate that all coefficients are statistically significant, while the coefficient of determination $R^2 = 0.62$ indicates good statistical fit. However, the Durbin-Watson statistic $DW = 0.08$ points to a high degree of positive serial correlation between residuals. Therefore, when the predicted value of the price ratio exceeds the observed one for a given week, it is likely to be too high again in the following week. This lack of independence over time causes the standard errors of the coefficients to be underestimated and hence their t-statistics to be overestimated. It often reflects a neglect of additional explanatory variables, which in turn may result in biased parameter estimates.

With these reservations in mind, it can be concluded from the constant that gasoline would be 30% more expensive than heating oil, were it not for the other influences. One of them is seasonality, reflected by the highly significant coefficient of the cosine function. Another are stocks: Large stocks of heating oil depress its price and hence make gasoline more expensive relative to heating oil, while large stocks of gasoline serve to make gasoline cheaper relative to heating oil. Note that these stocks likely are endogenous in that they are held in view of expected sales prices (which in turn depend on current ones, as argued in Sect. 8.3.3). Finally, the time trend indicates that the price of gasoline declines over time relative to the price of heating oil. *Ceteris paribus*, the decrease is from 1.300 to 1.299 one year later ($-0.001 = -0.0099 \cdot 52/52$), reflecting the steady replacement of ordinary gasoline by premium qualities with higher heating values during the observation period.

Figure 8.13 shows the actual gasoline/heating oil price ratio (solid line) and the predicted values of the regression equation (dotted line) on the U.S. wholesale

---

[14]While in Europe diesel vehicles have a large market share, they do not play a substantial role in the United States.

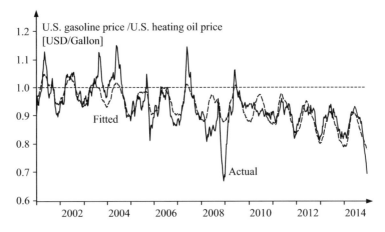

Fig. 8.13 Gasoline prices relative to heating oil prices in the United States. Data source: EIA (2014)

market. Clearly, the model (8.9) tracks the true values quite well, except for a few outliers. An estimate based on weekly data from 2001 and 2006 and more advanced econometric methods implies that the price ratio was even 2.4 in favor of gasoline save for other influences while stocks had a bigger impact (Erdmann and Zweifel 2008, p. 212). Yet, the predicted values exhibit the same pattern as in Fig. 8.13. In particular, they miss the spikes of 2003 and 2004.

References

Adelman, M. A. (2002). World oil production and prices 1947–2000. *Quarterly Review of Economics and Finance, 42*, 169–191.

Axelrod, R. (1984). *The evolution of cooperation.* New York: Basic Books.

BP. (2014). *BP statistical review of world energy.* Retrieved from www.bp.com/statisticalreview/

Coase, R. (1937). The nature of the firm. *Economica, 4*, 386–405.

EIA. (2014). *Miscellaneous data files.* Washington: Energy Information Administration. Retrieved from www.eia.gov/

Erdmann, G. (1995). *Energieökonomik - Theorie und Anwendungen (Energy economics – theory and applications)* (2nd ed.). Stuttgart: Teubner.

Erdmann, G., & Zweifel, P. (2008). *Energieökonomik - Theorie und Anwendungen (Energy economics – theory and applications)* (2nd ed.). Berlin: Springer.

FNR. (2005). *Biodiesel-Biokraftstoff in der Land wirtschaft (Biodiesel-biofuel in agriculture).* Fachagentur Nachwachsende Rohstoffe: Gülzow-Prüzen.

Griffin, J. M., & Steele, H. B. (1986). *Energy economics and policy* (2nd ed.). New York: Academic Press.

Grossmann, S. J., & Hart, O. D. (1986). The costs and benefits of vertical ownership: A theory of vertical integration. *Journal of Political Economy, 94*, 69–719.

Hartley, P., & Medlock, K. B. (2008). A model of the operation and development of a national oil company. *Energy Economics, 30*(5), 2459–2485.

Hickman, B. G., Huntington, H. G., & Sweeney, J. L. (1987). *Macroeconomic impacts of energy shocks.* Amsterdam: North Holland.

Hicks, J. R. (1939). *Value and capital*. Oxford: Oxford University Press.
Hubbert, M. K. (1956). Nuclear energy and fossil fuels. In American Petroleum Institute (Ed.), *Drilling and production practice*. New York: American Petroleum Institute.
Hubbert, M. K. (1962). *Energy resources. A report to the Committee on Natural Resources*. Washington, DC: Government Printing Office. Publication No. 1000-D.
Hull, J. C. (1999). *Options, futures, and other derivative securities* (4th ed.). Englewood Cliffs, NJ: Prentice-Hall.
IEA. (2000). *Experience curves for energy technology policy*. Paris: International Energy Agency.
Kaldor, N. (1939, October). Speculation and economic stability. *Review of Economic Studies, 7*, 1–27.
Kaufmann, R. K., & Cleveland, C. J. (2001). Oil production in the lower 48 states: Economic, geological, and institutional determinants. *The Energy Journal, 33*(1), 27–49.
Lynch, M. (2002). Forecasting oil supply: Theory and practice. *Quarterly Review of Economics and Finance, 42*, 373–389.
Meadows, D. H., et al. (1972). *The limits to growth*. New York: Universe Books.
Nakicenovic, N. (2002b). Technological change and diffusion as a learning process. In A. Grubler, N. Nakicenovic, & W. Nordhaus (Eds.), *Technological change and environment* (pp. 160–181). Washington, DC: Resources for the future Press.
Reynolds, D. B. (2002). Using non-time-series to determine supply elasticity: How far do prices change the Hubbert curve? *OPEC Review, June*, 149–167.
Rosa, J. (1993). Nationalization, privatization, and the allocation of financial property rights. *Public Choice, 75*, 317–337.
Tirole, J. (1988). *The theory of industrial organization*. Cambridge, MA: The MIT Press.
Williamson, O. E. (1971, May). The vertical integration of production. Market failure considerations. *American Economic Review, 61*, 112–123.
Zweifel, P., & Zäch, R. (2003). Vertical restraints: The case of multinationals. *Antitrust Bulletin, 48*(1), 271–298.

Markets for Gaseous Fuels

9

This chapter discusses markets for natural gas, biogas, and hydrogen. While the markets for biogas and hydrogen are still in their infancy, natural gas ranks third globally among primary energy sources (after crude oil and hard coal). One of its advantages are technologies with high fuel efficiencies which release relatively little carbon dioxide (CO_2). Another advantage is the fact that existing infrastructure can be used for distributing gas from new, unconventional reserves. On the other hand, its transportation calls for a capital-intensive and geographically inflexible network of pipelines which cannot be used for other purposes and is therefore factor-specific. This raises several questions concerning the properties of natural gas markets:

– Are pipeline investments economically viable without long-term contracts?
– Can market liquidity for gas be achieved without abolishing long-term contracts?
– How can supply be secured in the absence of long-term contracts?
– Is vertical integration along the value chain economically beneficial or not?
– Can liquid natural gas (LNG) play the role of a game changer, making consuming countries less dependent on suppliers with monopoly power and political clout?

In many regions of the world, the highly seasonal demand for space heating determines the sales of natural gas. As gas customers usually lack storage capacities, deliveries by suppliers must track demand closely. This raises further questions that will be discussed in this chapter:

– How can volatile demand be met?
– What role could gas storage capacities play?
– Regarding the potential for substitution between natural gas and heating oil, what are the implications for retail gas pricing?

The variables used in this chapter are:

a	Maximum willingness to pay
c	Average cost
Cap	Capacity
c_{prod}	Unit cost of extraction
$c_{transit}$	Unit cost of transit
d	Pipeline diameter
FLD	Full load days per year
FLH	Full load hours per year
ic	Capital user cost
K	Capital stock
LNG	Liquefied natural gas
l	Length of pipeline between two compressor stations
P	Pressure
Π	Profit of the importer (Π_{imp}) and the producer (Π_{prod})
p_{gas}	Wholesale price (based on the upper heating value)
p_{imp}	Average import price at the border
p_{hel}	Price of heating oil extra light (based on the lower heating value)
p_{retail}	Retail price paid by end users
Q	Quantity (in energy units)
$Temp$	Temperature
tr	Transit fee

9.1 Gaseous Fuels and Gas Infrastructures

Gaseous energy sources consist mostly of oxidizable substances, in particular methane (CH_4) and hydrogen (H_2). The energy content of a cubic meter depends not only on the chemical composition of the gas but also on pressure and temperature. This follows from the formula for an ideal gas,

$$\frac{PV}{\vartheta} = \text{constant} \tag{2.7}$$

with P symbolizing pressure, V volume, and ϑ temperature measured in degrees Kelvin (see Sect. 2.2.2).

For the purpose of standardization, the lower and upper heating values of a normal cubic meter Nm^3 of gases are measured at a pressure of 1.013 bar and a temperature of 0 °C, alternatively 15 °C. Whatever its chemical composition, 1 Nm^3 of gas always contains 44,614 gas molecules. International gas statistics use a variety of units. Therefore the conversion factors shown in Table 9.1 can be helpful. They are based on natural gas with a lower heating value of 10.4 kWh/Nm^3.

9.1 Gaseous Fuels and Gas Infrastructures

Table 9.1 Conversion factors for natural gas (at upper heating value H_s)

	Nm^3 natural gas	scf[a] of natural gas	kg LNG	MJ	mn BTU	Therm	kWh
Nm^3 natural gas	1	35.3	0.73	37.5	0.035	0.355	10.4
scf[a] natural gas	0.0283	1	0.0207	1.06	0.001	0.01	0.294
kg LNG	1.37	48.36	1	51.3	0.049	0.486	14.2
MJ	0.027	0.94	0.019	1	0.001	0.0095	0.2778
mn BTU	28.2	996	20.6	1055	1	10	293
Therm	2.82	99.6	2.06	105.5	0.1	1	29.3
kWh	0.096	3.40	0.07	3.6	0.0034	0.0341	1

[a] *scf* Standard cubic feet, measured at a pressure of 1.013 bar and a temperature of 60 F; one scf is equal to 0.0283 Nm^3 (normal cubic meter)

9.1.1 Properties of Gaseous Fuels

Table 9.2 presents an overview of the most important chemical components of gaseous energy sources, including inert gases devoid of a thermal contribution, such as oxygen and nitrogen.[1] Evidently, types of natural gas differ widely both in terms of density and heating values. Those containing a great deal of propane and butane are particularly valuable *ceteris paribus* because these components combine high density and high heating values, which serve to keep the cost of transportation, distribution, and storage low.

The following commercial products can be distinguished.

- Natural gas: This type of gas has a high share of low-density methane. In Northwestern Europe, one distinguishes between low-energy natural gas (L gas, with an upper heating value between 8.4 and 11.6 kWh/m^3, or 30.2 and 41.8 MJ/m^3, respectively) and high-energy natural gas (H gas, with an upper heating value between 10.2 and 13.1 kWh/m^3, or 36.7 and 47.2 MJ/m^3, respectively). Some types contain amounts of hydrogen sulfide (so-called sour gas) which may cause damage to the infrastructure. Since gas is invisible and odorless by nature, it is mixed with tetrahydrothiophene before distribution for detecting leakages, giving it an unpleasant odor.
- Liquid gas (also known as refinery gas): This type consists mainly of propane and butane, which are byproducts of oil refinery processes (see Sect. 8.1.5). Contrary to other components, propane and butane are heavier than air, which is an advantage for some uses. While gaseous at normal temperature and pressure, they can be liquefied using moderate pressure and sold in pressure bottles.

---

[1] The combustion properties of gases are reflected by their Wobbe number. Gases with the same Wobbe numbers are considered substitutable. Low-energy (L) gas has a Wobbe number of 12.4, high-energy (H) gas, of 15.0.

Table 9.2 Properties of gaseous fuels

		Density $(kg/m^3)^a$	Upper heating value H_s (MJ/m^3)	Lower heating value H_i (MJ/m^3)
Methane	CH_4	0.7175	39.819	35.883
Ethane	C_2H_6	1.3550	70.293	64.345
Propane	C_3H_8	2.0110	101.242	93.215
Butane	C_4H_{10}	2.7080	134.061	123.810
Hydrogen	H_2	0.08988	12.745	10.783
Carbon monoxide	CO	1.25050	12.633	12.633
Nitrogen	N_2	1.2504		
Oxygen	O_2	1.4290		
Carbon dioxide	CO_2	1.9770		
Air		1.2930		
Natural gas H		0.79	~41	~37
Natural gas L		0.83	~35	~32
Biogas		1.12	~27	~24

^{a}At a temperature of 0 °C and a pressure of 1.013 bar

– Town gas (also called cooking gas) is a byproduct of coke plants. It consists mostly of hydrogen (H_2) and carbon monoxide (CO). This gas is lighter than air and toxic due to its CO content.

Conditioning plants are used to modify gases by adding inert or liquid gas in order to attain certain quality standards. This can also be necessary for ensuring interoperability of different pipeline systems, a precondition for physical gas trade.

Compared to other hydrocarbons, storage of gaseous energy fuels is costly due to their comparatively low energy density (see Table 9.3). Even at a pressure of 200 bar, the volumetric energy content of natural gas is only 156 kg/m^3, i.e. some 20% of gasoline (see compressed natural gas CNG). Higher storage densities are achieved if the natural gas is cooled down to become liquid (LNG). However, hydrogen is even worse: At a pressure of 700 bar, a hydrogen tank contains 56 kg/m^3, i.e. only 7% of the energy contained by a gasoline tank of comparable size.

9.1.2 Reserves and Extraction of Natural Gas

According to Table 9.4, the static range of conventional natural gas reserves amounts to 67 (=185.7/2.763) years worldwide. While this value exceeds that of crude oil, this is an advantage that will be offset by expected growth of gas demand. Like conventional crude oil, conventional gas reserves are concentrated in the 'energy ellipse' extending from Siberia to the Middle East.

9.1 Gaseous Fuels and Gas Infrastructures

Table 9.3 Storage properties of hydrocarbons

	Temperature (°C)	Pressure (bar)	Density (kg/m^3)	Lower heating value (kWh/l)
Gasoline	20	1	750	9.0
Diesel	20	1	840	9.9
Methanol	20	1	794	4.4
Ethanol	20	1	793	5.9
Natural gas	20	1	0.80	–
Compressed natural gas (CNG)	20	200	156	1.9
Liquid natural gas (LNG)	−162	1	473	6.2
Hydrogen (H$_2$)	20	1	0.91	0.003
Compressed hydrogen (CH$_2$)	20	200	16	0.55
Compressed hydrogen (CH$_2$)	20	700	56	1.85
Liquid hydrogen (LH$_2$)	−252	1	71	2.4

Table 9.4 Reserves and extraction of conventional natural gas

	Natural gas reserves 2013		Natural gas extraction 2013	
	(tn m^3)	Share (%)	(bn m^3)	Share (%)
Iran	33.8	18.2	167	4.9
Russia	31.3	16.8	605	17.9
Qatar	24.7	13.3	158	4.7
Energy ellipse	132.5	71.4	1325	39.3
United States	9.3	5.0	688	20.6
Norway	2.0	1.1	109	3.2
The Netherlands	0.9	0.5	69	2.0
Great Britain	0.2	0.1	37	1.1
World	185.7	100.0	2763	100.0

Data source: BP (2014)

In addition to conventional reserves, several unconventional sources of natural gas exist, among them shale gas, coal bed methane, and methane hydrates. Currently, the most relevant unconventional gas resource is shale gas. Shale is a fine-grained sedimentary rock that can readily be split into thin pieces along its laminations. Methane trapped in shale formations is recovered using advanced extraction technologies known as fracking. According to 2014 estimates of the German Federal Office of Geo Science and Resources (BGR 2014), global shale gas resources amount to 210 tn m^3 of methane. Coal bed methane is extracted by drilling wells into the coal seam and pumping water from the well. The concomitant decrease in pressure allows methane to escape from the coal and to flow up the well to the surface. Finally, methane hydrates are a solid energy source found in ocean depths of more than 500 m, assumed to originate from the decomposition of microorganisms. At atmospheric pressure, methane hydrates melt, releasing up to 160 m^3 methane gas per m^3 hydrate.

Table 9.4 also reports rates of extraction of usable natural gas[2] according to geographical region. At present, the United States account for more than 20% of global gas extraction, making it the largest gas producer worldwide, whereas its estimated share of conventional reserves amounts to a mere 5%. Conversely, the countries of the 'energy ellipse' have a market share of less than 40% but control more than 71% of reserves. However, shares in extraction have changed substantially since 2000. From that year, the U.S. share grew by 40% while that of the European Union fell by 37%, a consequence of its resistance to fracking. Since natural gas might be associated with crude oil deposits and be exploited together with them, some oil majors are also trading on gas markets. However, due to missing pipeline infrastructures, not all of this so-called associated gas can be used commercially at present.

Similar to crude oil extraction, state concessions are needed in most countries (except in the United States) to exploit gas fields. In market-oriented economies, these concessions are allocated mainly to private companies through auctions. In most 'energy ellipse' countries, companies cannot purchase concessions unless majority-controlled by the government of the state where the deposit is located. This is an obstacle for companies who seek to vertically integrate the upstream parts of the value chain (so-called backward integration; see Sect. 9.2).

9.1.3 Biogas and Renewable Natural Gas

Biogas derives from the fermentation of biomass, whose output is a vapor-saturated mix of methane (40–75%) and carbon dioxide (25–50%) with some ammonia and hydrogen sulfide. Due to its high CO_2 share, it has a lower energy content than natural gas (see Table 9.2). Biogas escapes continually and unchecked from landfills, sewage plants, and liquid manure. If captured and used in combustion, it serves to mitigate the greenhouse gas problem since unburned methane has a greenhouse effect which exceeds that of CO_2 by a factor of about 21.

However, the typical sources of biogas are limited. Thus, renewable raw materials from agriculture, in particular maize, are used in combination with liquid manure and food waste as feedstock.[3] One hectare of farmland can provide 4.5 tons of maize per year. With an output of 180 m^3 gas per ton of maize and a methane content of 55%, the biogas return per hectare (ha) is about 450 m^3. McKendry (2002) estimates the energy harvest at 2 GJ, or a mere 554 kWh per ha and year, respectively. Evidently, producing energy from agricultural products claims a great deal of agricultural land that could be used for food production. In regions with

---

[2]The data exclude natural gas which is flared or reinjected into gas deposits.
[3]Nearly all biomass can be fermented, with the exception of lignin.

9.1 Gaseous Fuels and Gas Infrastructures

excess supply of food like the European Union, this is no cause for concern at present. Indeed, the European Union is about to cut back its set-aside program in agriculture, which creates scope for subsidizing this type of fuel (currently at the rate of 45 EUR per ha and year). However, producing biogas from renewable biomass is quite costly. While it can be obtained from landfills, sewage plants, and liquid manure at a cost of 0.03–0.05 EUR/kWh, it costs between 0.06 and 0.08 EUR/kWh if obtained from maize (at a price of 30 EUR/tons). The latter range is beyond that of natural gas, which is between 0.03 and 0.05 EUR/kWh.

This comparison still neglects the fact that biogas production units are located in rural areas close to maize fields since transporting maize more than 20 km is usually uneconomic. This means that input quantities are limited, resulting in plant output capacities below 250 m^3/h, too small for economies of scale. In the absence of a gas transport infrastructure, biogas must be burned on the production site, notably as a fuel for combined heat and power stations. Yet the electrical efficiency of these stations is usually below 40%. Moreover, the energy needed for fertilizing and harvesting the maize fields has to be taken into account.

Alternatively, biogas may be upgraded to attain the chemical and physical properties of natural gas, enabling it to be fed into local distribution grids (at a pressure of 5–8 bar) or into long-distance gas pipelines. This makes biogas a (mostly) renewable substitute of natural gas which can be sold on all types of gas markets in principle. To distinguish it from natural gas, it is labeled 'bio methane' or 'bio natural gas', respectively. Of course, quality upgrading, compression, and gas grid access result in additional costs. Currently bio methane exceeds the European natural gas wholesale price by a factor of three to four. A discrepancy of this amount is unlikely to vanish anytime soon because there is no prospect of a higher price of natural gas or a lower unit cost of biogas, respectively.

Yet for farmers, biogas or bio methane constitutes an attractive option if amply subsidized. One the one hand, they can generate additional revenue from selling the fuel or from renting the farm land to biogas producers. On the other hand, they can count on higher sales prices for food, which becomes scarcer. In fact, farmers have the option of offering their production on both the market for food and energy markets, wherever the profit margin is higher. To the extent that the cost of production is similar, they will supply the market that offers the higher price. The economic conclusion is that with an important biogas production, food prices will follow the price of natural gas or the biogas price guaranteed by the government through its subsidy, respectively. This causes the two prices to become cointegrated (see Sect. 8.3.2).

9.1.4 Hydrogen

In terms of energy systems, hydrogen (H$_2$) is a secondary fuel that does not exist on the globe as an accessible energy source, despite the fact that it is assumed to be the most common element in the universe. This is the consequence of its low density (see Table 9.2) and extreme dissipation. Most of the hydrogen on Earth exists as a chemically fixed component of molecules, for example water (H_2O) or methane (CH_4).

Hydrogen can be produced from practically any primary energy source. At present, hydrogen is mostly produced using natural gas through a two-step process with an overall fuel efficiency between 65 and 75%,

Steam reforming $CH_4 + H_2O \rightarrow CO + 3\,H_2$ (endothermic process)
Shift reaction $CO + H_2O \rightarrow CO_2 + H_2$ (exothermic process)

Another relevant technology is the electrolytic separation of water (H_2O) to become hydrogen (H_2) and oxygen (O). This process requires electricity as an energy input and attains energy efficiencies between 70 and 80%. However, since electricity is much more expensive than natural gas, electrolysis is usually too costly for applications at market scale. To the extent that it can accommodate the intermittent nature of wind and photovoltaic energy, it does offer a way to render renewable electricity storable. Thus, so-called 'renewable hydrogen' is widely seen as a key element of future carbon-free energy systems. It could be used in transportation (through fuel cells) or to produce electricity (through fuel cells or gas turbines), on demand. Yet these options will only become economically viable if inexpensive renewable electricity is available. Failing this, engagement by the private sector continues to be limited, with investment projects predominantly financed by government research and development programs.

At present, the global hydrogen production amounts to 500 to 600 bn m^3 or 120 mn tons per year, respectively. It is used in the following ways,

– Ammoniac synthesis (60–70% share);
– Refineries (hydro cracking, 15–25% share);
– Methanol synthesis (8% share).

Hydrogen is mostly used by chemical companies, who also produce it. Therefore, there is no liquid market providing reliable price information. Wholesale prices of around 10 EUR per kg of compressed hydrogen (at 350 bar), are reported in the literature, which represents an energy content of about 120 MJ or 33 kWh, respectively (see Table 9.2).

9.2 Natural Gas Economy

Historically, the natural gas industry is older than the oil industry because the first natural gas deposit was used as early as 1825 in the New York City area. However, until the 1950s exploration efforts were limited since natural gas was found alongside crude oil (so-called associated natural gas). Another source was town gas, a byproduct of coke plants which triggered investment in urban gas grids. These local grids created the opportunity for the building of long-distance pipelines connecting them to large-scale natural gas deposits.

In Europe, this process began later than in the United States, around 1970. The starting shot was the development of the huge Groningen gas field in the Netherlands, located quite closely to already existent local gas markets. Within a short period of time, additional high-pressure pipeline connections to gas fields in Western Siberia (Russia), the North Sea (Norway and the United Kingdom), and North Africa (Algeria, Tunisia) were built, along with LNG terminals on the shores of the Mediterranean Sea and the Atlantic Ocean. As a result, within 30 years quite a comprehensive infrastructure was established as the physical backbone of European gas markets.

9.2.1 Transport by Pipeline

High-pressure pipelines are used to transport natural gas over long distances. At a pressure of up to 80 bar, and with a diameter of 1200 mm, they cover up to 6000 km. Investment outlay varies between 0.5 and 1.5 mn EUR/km, depending on local conditions.

A single 80 bar pipeline is able to transport up to 3 mn m^3/h (or 26 bn m^3/a, respectively) of natural gas at a speed of up to 40 km/h. As an approximation, the throughput rate Q depends on pressures P_1 at the beginning of a pipeline section and P_2 at the end of it. With length of section l and pipeline diameter d, throughput is proportional to

$$Q \sim \sqrt{\frac{P_1^2 - P_2^2}{l/d^2}}. \tag{9.1}$$

Therefore, given a required pressure P_2 at the point of delivery, throughput is the greater the higher initial pressure P_1, the shorter the distance to be covered l, and the bigger the diameter of the pipeline d. Compressor stations designed to compensate pressure losses (0.1 bar per 10 km) and to keep the gas flowing are placed at intervals ranging between 80 and 400 km.[4] They contain turbines that usually take their energy from the pipeline, consuming about 10% of the gas over a distance of 5000 km. This requirement declines with the diameter and the quality of the tube.

At least during the early stages of gas infrastructure development, the transport capacity of a high-pressure pipeline tends to exceed both the market potential and the financial capacity of a single gas company. However, pipelines exhibit economies of scale (see Knieps 2002): When capacity is doubled, cost of construction increases by two-third only.

The solution could be for several companies to build and operate a pipeline in co-ownership despite the fact that they are competitors in the markets where the pipeline originates and/or where it ends (so-called pipe-in-pipe competition). Yet

---

[4]The pressure in a pipeline declines primarily due to frictional losses. In addition, it needs to be managed if elevation changes.

companies may sooner or later extend their cooperation beyond the operation of the pipeline to form a cartel fixing prices in the purchasing and/or sales markets. This risk can be avoided through ownership unbundling, requiring the owners of the pipeline to be independent of other companies along the value chain. However, experience shows that companies that are prevented from freely using an asset costing several bn of EUR are unwilling to make the investment.

Once a long-distance pipeline has been built, the capital expenditure is mostly sunk, i.e. it is lost unless the pipeline can be put to profitable use. A pipeline thus constitutes a factor-specific asset in that it can only be used for long-distance gas transport between the beginning and the end of the line and nothing else. Therefore, its owner must make sure there are customers at both ends who are willing to pay for transporting the gas.

In general terms, investors are in a strong strategic position *vis-à-vis* customers and governments before the start of the project but in a weak one after its completion because they cannot easily defeat opportunistic behavior on the part of their contractual partners. This situation is known in the economic literature as the 'holdup problem'. It can be solved by vertical integration, which however is in conflict with the requirement of unbundling cited above.

Absent vertical integration, investment and pricing behavior of two market participants with monopoly power in the pertinent market along the gas value chain needs to be analyzed. The usual approach is to formulate a two-stage game theoretical model. In its first stage, a monopolistic producer of natural gas decides about the optimal capital stock K reflecting the capacity of a planned pipeline. In the second stage, the producer and a gas importer, who has a monopoly over distribution to final customers, have to agree on the import price $p_{imp}(K)$ which is the producer's sales price. The outcome of this negotiation depends on pipeline capacity, which is also denoted by K for simplicity.

Since the producer rationally anticipates the import price when deciding about investment resulting in capital stock K, the model is solved in reverse order (so-called backward induction). Therefore, the outcome of the negotiation concerning the import price is determined first, assuming that both players seek to maximize profit independently of each other, resulting in a so-called Nash equilibrium (an equilibrium pertaining to a non-cooperative game).

On the part of the importer, it has to take into account that a higher retail price p_{retail} reduces the volume Q of gas sales. For simplicity, a linear demand function is posited,

$$Q = a - p_{retail}. \tag{9.2}$$

Here, a denotes marginal willingness to pay for the first unit of natural gas, which is the maximum price consumers are willing to pay (to see this, set $Q = 0$ and solve for p_{retail}).

Neglecting other costs the importer may incur (for distribution in particular), its profit Π_{imp} is related to the sales price p_{retail} and the import price p_{imp} paid as follows,

9.2 Natural Gas Economy

$$\Pi_{imp}(p_{retail}) = (p_{retail} - p_{imp}) \cdot Q = (p_{retail} - p_{imp}) \cdot (a - p_{retail}). \quad (9.3)$$

Since p_{retail} is the variable controlled by the importer, the profit function (9.3) needs to be differentiated with respect to p_{retail} for obtaining the first-order optimality condition. Also, given the optimal sales price, the optimal quantity sold and imported $Q = Q_{imp}$ is determined as well. Setting the derivative of (9.3) with respect to p_{retail} equal to zero, one has (* indicating optimal value for the importer),

$$p^*_{retail} = \frac{a + p_{imp}}{2}, \quad Q^*_{imp}(p_{imp}) = \frac{a - p_{imp}}{2}. \quad (9.4)$$

This equation points to an interesting fact. The importing company cannot pass on an eventual increase in the import price fully to its customers. In the case of a linear demand function, the degree of pass-through is 50%. The reason is that a higher degree of pass-through would cause sales to fall to an extent that results in a reduced profit. From Eq. (9.4), one can calculate the importer's maximum profit, which depends on the import price to be paid,

$$\Pi^*_{imp} = \left(\frac{a + p_{imp}}{2} - p_{imp}\right) \cdot Q^*_{imp} = \left(\frac{a - p_{imp}}{2}\right)^2. \quad (9.5)$$

Turning to the producer of the natural gas, assume that it seeks to maximize its profit, too, knowing the importer's demand function and hence optimal Q^*_{imp}. With $c(K)$ symbolizing unit cost of extracting and transporting gas (which depends on capacity) and in view of Eq. (9.4), the profit function is given by

$$\Pi_{prod} = (p_{imp} - c(K)) \cdot Q^*_{imp} = (p_{imp} - c(K)) \cdot \frac{a - p_{imp}}{2}. \quad (9.6)$$

Since the quantity $_{delivered}Q^*_{imp}$ is controlled by the importer, the decision variable left to the producer is the sales price p_{imp}. If $c(K)$ is independent of the produced quantity $Q = Q^*_{imp}$ and thus from price p_{imp}, the first-order optimality condition of the profit function calls for setting the derivative of (9.6) with respect to p_{imp} to zero. Doing this yields the optimal import price p^*_{imp} (* indicating now optimal value for the producer), and using this in Eq. (9.6), the optimal export quantity as well,

$$p^*_{imp} = \frac{a + c(K)}{2} > c(K), \quad Q^* = \frac{a - p^*_{imp}}{2} = \frac{a - c(K)}{4}. \quad (9.7)$$

The '>' sign is $_{justified}$ by the fact that gas production and gas trade is economically viable only if maximal willingness to pay a exceeds unit cost $c(K)$ such that $a \geq c(K)$. Neglecting the costs of capital, transport and distribution, maximum profit of producer and importer can be derived by inserting (9.7) into Eqs. (9.6) and (9.5), respectively,

$$\Pi^*_{prod} = \frac{1}{2} \cdot \left(\frac{a - c(K)}{2}\right)^2, \quad \Pi^*_{imp} = \frac{1}{4} \cdot \left(\frac{a - p_{imp}}{2}\right)^2. \tag{9.8}$$

Equations (9.4), (9.7), and (9.8) characterize a Nash equilibrium, defined as a situation where neither of the parties has an incentive to deviate from it (after all, both are optimizing on the premise that the other is optimizing as well, see Tirole 1988, Chap. 11).

An interesting conclusion can be drawn if the pipeline operator and the gas distributor are assumed to cooperate. This means that they maximize their joint profit, given by

$$\Pi_{coop} = (p_{retail} - c(K)) \cdot (a - p_{retail}). \tag{9.9}$$

In this case, the optimal retail price p_{retail} would be

$$p^{**}_{retail} = \frac{a + c(K)}{2} < \frac{a + p^*_{imp}(K)}{2} = p^*_{retail} \tag{9.10}$$

in view of Eq. (9.4) and the inequality in (9.7). Therefore, the retail price given cooperation is below the one in the non-cooperative situation. This means that a welfare loss results if two monopolistic companies along a value chain do not cooperate. The reason is so-called double marginalization: The monopolistic producer opts for a quantity of output where marginal revenue equals marginal cost rather than where sales price equals marginal cost. This leads to a sales price above marginal cost [see Eqs. (1.3) and (1.4) in Sect. 1.2.2]. However, this sales price constitutes the marginal cost of the monopolistic importer, who again imposes equality of marginal revenue and marginal cost. This accumulation of surcharges over marginal cost is called double marginalization. It can be avoided by cooperation (or vertical integration, see below) because now the two parties share an interest in keeping marginal cost as low as possible in order to maximize their joint profit. Therefore, retail price p_{retail} and hence market volume Q are higher given cooperation than given non-cooperation, benefitting consumers.

At the same time, joint profit given cooperation exceeds the sum of profits of two monopolists who fail to cooperate. Recalling Eq. (9.9) and using Eq. (9.10), one obtains

$$\Pi^*_{coop} = \left(\frac{a - c(K)}{2}\right)^2. \tag{9.11}$$

From Eqs. (9.8) and (9.7), one has by way of contrast

$$\Pi^*_{imp} + \Pi^*_{prod} = \frac{3}{4} \left(\frac{a - c(K)}{2}\right)^2. \tag{9.12}$$

9.2 Natural Gas Economy

Thus, the amazing conclusion is that both customers and companies benefit from cooperation since avoiding double marginalization is to the advantage of both. Note that the ultimate form of cooperation is vertical integration, i.e. a merger of the two companies, who become one. From the welfare point of view, this would be superior to a non-cooperative industry structure, *ceteris paribus*. However, one downside is so-called foreclosure, meaning that a newcomer in the distribution market (say) cannot compete against the incumbent monopolist because there is no natural gas available outside the vertically integrated value chain.

Now that the second stage has a solution, the first stage can be solved. Here, the pipeline operator decides the optimal capital stock K in view of the optimal quantities determined in the second stage of the game. The Nash equilibrium implies that the two companies agree on the optimal import price p^*_{imp} according to Eq. (9.7) once the pipeline is finished. Assume that the unit cost $c(K)$ of natural gas production and transportation (in the exporting country) declines with the amount invested, but at a decreasing rate,[5]

$$\frac{\partial c}{\partial K} < 0, \quad \frac{\partial^2 c}{\partial K^2} \geq 0. \tag{9.13}$$

Also, let ic denote capital user cost per unit, which itself may be a function of K [see Sect. 3.1, Eq. (3.7)]. Then, by Eq. (9.8) the owner of the pipeline determines optimal capital stock K by solving the following problem,

$$\max_{K \geq 0} \left(\frac{1}{2} \left(\frac{a - c(K)}{2} \right)^2 - K \cdot ic(K) \right). \tag{9.14}$$

However, the social optimum would call for the maximization of consumer surplus, given by the triangular area below the demand function (9.2) net of marginal cost $c(K)$. Also, fixed cost must be covered because otherwise the pipeline does not come into existence, resulting in the problem,

$$\max_{K \geq 0} \left(\left(\frac{a - c(K)}{2} \right)^2 - K \cdot ic(K) \right). \tag{9.15}$$

Obviously the two optimization problems have different solutions: Under the non-cooperative Nash equilibrium, the pipeline operator earns only 50% of the contribution margin that would be socially optimal. This weakened incentive translates into an investment in capacity that is too small. One could say that in the light of the two-stage theoretical model, failure to cooperate reduces the security of gas supply in the importing country (which among other things depends on the capacity of the transportation network).

---

[5] While implying that returns to scale are exhausted sooner or later, this assumption guarantees the existence of a single equilibrium.

Note that there are other approaches than vertical integration to solve the holdup problem. One alternative is for the gas producer and the distributor to establish a joint subsidiary that is responsible for investment in and operation of the pipeline. This subsidiary could even be open to competitors on both sides, although presumably on terms defined by its owners. Therefore, foreclosure would be mitigated but not eliminated. Other options are long-term contracts struck between the two companies in which a price prior to the undertaking of the investment in the pipeline is fixed (see Sect. 9.3.1).

A variant of the holdup problem is linked with gas pipelines that transit a third country. Once built, they cannot be rerouted. This lack of flexibility gives governments of transit countries scope for opportunistically appropriating part of the exporter's profit. This problem can also be formulated in terms of non-cooperative game theory (see Hirschhausen et al. 2005). The model considers an exporting and a (government-owned) transit company, who are both monopolists in their respective markets. The exporting company maximizes the product of quantity Q times the contribution margin per unit,

$$\max_{Q \geq 0} \left(p_{imp} - tr(Q) - c_{prod} \right) \cdot Q \tag{9.16}$$

where the contribution margin is equal to the sales price at the border of the importing country p_{imp} net of transit fee tr and unit production cost c_{prod} (assumed constant). Setting the derivative with respect to Q to zero yields the following first-order optimality condition,

$$p^*_{imp} = c_{prod} + tr - Q \cdot \left(\frac{\partial p_{imp}}{\partial Q} - \frac{\partial tr}{\partial Q} \right). \tag{9.17}$$

The transit company solves an analogous optimization problem,

$$\max_{tr \geq 0} \left(tr - c_{transit} \right) \cdot Q, \tag{9.18}$$

with $c_{transit}$ denoting constant unit transit cost. If the exporting company has no alternative than pumping the gas through this particular pipeline, the transit company could raise its fee to $tr \leq p_{imp} - c_{prod}$, leaving just a minimum profit to the exporter [see Eq. (9.16)]. Conversely, $tr \geq c_{transit}$ constitutes a lower bound, in which case the exporting company would reap maximum profit. Realistically, the transit tariff lies between these two extremes,

$$c_{transit} \leq tr \leq p_{imp} - c_{prod}. \tag{9.19}$$

The final result depends on the relative bargaining power of the exporter compared to the transit company. Let the exporter's bargaining power be formalized by a function $Q(tr)$, with $\partial Q / \partial tr = \kappa < 0$. Then, the first-order optimality condition for the transit company is given by

9.2 Natural Gas Economy

$$Q + (tr - c_{transit}) \cdot \kappa = 0 \quad \text{or} \quad tr = c_{transit} - \frac{Q}{\kappa} > c_{transit} \qquad (9.20)$$

where the bounds specified in (9.19) must be satisfied. Because of $\kappa < 0$, the optimal transit tariff increases with gas sales Q and declines with the bargaining power of the export company.

This model was complemented by Zweifel et al. (2009/10) in several ways. With the breakdown of the former Soviet Union in 1990, two transit countries, Ukraine and Belarus, became independent. The loss of control over the (now Ukrainian and Belarussian) pipelines caused the bargaining position of the Russian exporting monopolist Gazprom to be weakened. This means that cooperative game theory needs to be used for predicting whether Russia (who is part of all possible coalitions) teams up with Belarus, Ukraine, or both of them. Moreover, their relative bargaining power can be determined by calculating the so-called Shapley and Banshaf values (which reflect a player's contribution to the coalitions' total profit in slightly different ways). As could be expected, in 2004 Russia had the highest bargaining power, followed by Ukraine due to its relatively high transit capacity, and Belarus. With the opening of the North Transit pipeline (and even more so if the planned Yamal pipelines were to be built), the dominance of Russia is predicted to become even more marked in future, mainly to the detriment of Ukraine.

The conditional payoffs determined in the non-cooperative module lead to the prediction that the all-inclusive coalition will form because it generates maximum profit, while the cooperative module predicts that the lion's share of profit goes to Russia (who can use part of it to buy the participation of Belarus and Ukraine). However, all of these results are conditioned on an aggregate demand function characterizing Western Europe. With the advent of fracking and the possibility of liquefied natural gas being imported from the United States, this demand function may soon shift inward as far as Russian gas is concerned.

9.2.2 LNG Transport and Trade

An alternative to long-distance transport by pipeline is seaborne liquefied natural gas (LNG) trade. The LNG technology was developed for Japanese gas imports as this country cannot be supplied through pipelines still today. It has also been used for European gas imports from North Africa and the Middle East. The technology is complex and usually expensive compared to pipelines. A standard LNG chain has a capacity of 3.5 to 4.8 bn tons/a (4.8 · 6.6 bn m^3/a, respectively) and consists of the following elements (Cayrade 2004).

- Liquefaction plant in the export harbor: When cooled to ·163 °C, gas turns liquid, causing its volume to be reduced by a factor of 580. Investment outlay on a plant amounts to about 900 mn EUR. At 0.04 EUR per m^3 of natural gas, operating expenses need to be accounted for as well.

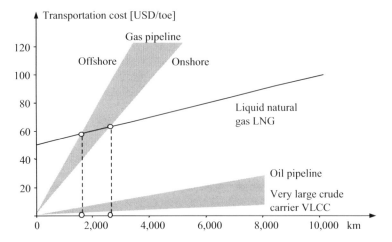

Fig. 9.1 Long-distance transportation costs of oil and gas. Source: Erdmann and Zweifel (2008, p. 233)

- Fleet of LNG vessels: Being special purpose, these vessels constitute factor-specific capital (see Sect. 9.1.2 for the consequences). LNG transport from Port Said in Egypt to Cartagena in Spain over a distance of 2700 km may serve as an example. It is performed by two vessels with a capacity of 135,000 tons each, requiring an investment of about 360 mn EUR. One trip takes 10.5 days, at a cost of about 0.014 EUR per m^3 of natural gas.
- Regasification plant including LNG storage: In Cartagena, three storage tanks with a capacity of 80,000 m^3 each are available. The investment outlay amounted to 320 mn EUR. The LNG is transformed into gas again at a cost of about 0.015 EUR per m^3 of natural gas.

An additional cost component of LNG derives from the fact that operation of the LNG chain requires about one-third of the energy contained in the gas that is delivered to the pipeline of the importing country. At a total unit cost of some 0.06 USD per m^3 of natural gas, LNG cannot compete with pipeline gas in many locations, depending on the length of the haul. According to Fig. 9.1, transporting natural gas through a pipeline is much more costly than transporting crude oil to begin with, especially when using a very large crude carrier. Moving gas from an offshore deposit in particular is so expensive that the LNG alternative becomes competitive beyond a distance of less than 2000 km; if the deposit is onshore, the critical distance increases to almost 3000 km.[6] However, this may change in future

---

[6]This comparison is flawed, however, as LNG vessels may have to travel longer distances around continents while pipelines can use the direct path. This difference does not obtain if deep oceans have to be crossed. Yet pipelines have not been competing against the LNG chain across deep oceans up to present.

because the unit cost of LNG is likely to fall thanks to improvement in the design of liquefaction and regasification plants.

In 2013, about 30% of natural gas was traded internationally. While this share has been increasing over many years, the share of international LNG trade has been growing even faster, from 27% in 2003 to more than 30% by 2013. The growing importance of LNG on global gas markets has several reasons:

- The LNG chain allows developing remote natural gas fields that cannot be connected by pipelines for geographical, geological, political, or economic reasons.
- Since gas fields close to consumers have the highest scarcity rents, they are developed prior to more remote gas fields (see Sect. 6.2.3). Yet when they are exhausted, more remote fields need to be developed for meeting demand, and according to Fig. 9.1 this improves the relative competitiveness of LNG.
- Compared to pipeline projects, the LNG chain is more flexible. While a pipeline is operational no sooner than the entire project is finished, capacities along the LNG chain can be used even if the chain is not yet complete. This serves to reduce the economic impact of project delays and operational disruptions compared to pipelines. This advantage becomes more important as the number of LNG installations is increasing globally, reflecting a so-called positive network externality.
- For both gas producers and consumers, LNG offers a chance for diversification, which mitigates the holdup problem associated with pipeline projects.

With international LNG trade, regional gas markets become more integrated. In its absence, gas prices on both sides of the Atlantic would develop quite independently from each other because there is no scope for arbitrage. While LNG export and import capacities cause natural gas prices to converge, convergence is not perfect due to the substantial cost of operating the LNG chain.

9.3 Gas Markets and Gas Price Formation

As in the case of the oil industry, wholesale gas markets are characterized by two types of companies:

- Gas producers such as state-owned Gazprom, Sonatrach, and Statoil as well as private companies such as BP, ChevronTexaco, ExxonMobil, Shell, and Total usually have supplies in excess of demand at the prevailing market price—they are long in gas.
- Gas importers and distribution companies such as E.ON, GdF, Wingas, ENI, and Tokyo Gas seek to meet a demand in excess of their own production at the prevailing market price—they are short in gas.

As long as the two types of companies are not vertically integrated, they need to trade gas in order to close their long and short positions, respectively. As shown below, there is a choice of design options for this wholesale trade.

9.3.1 Long-Term Take-or-Pay Contracts

Until recently, long-term take-or-pay contracts (ToP contracts) between producers and domestic importers of natural gas have dominated gas wholesale markets, particularly in Europe. These contracts used to have durations of 15 to 30 years. They make the importing company pay at least some 90% of the contracted gas even if its imports fall short of it because of reduced demand, e.g. due to a mild winter or an economic recession. The contracted price derives from a sliding-price formula that usually is based on the price of heating oil.[7] A typical long-term contract may use the so-called '6/3/3 rule', according to which the gas price depends on the six month average of the heating oil price, calculated with a lag of three months and applicable to deliveries over the following three months.

For a long time, the German Federal Office of Foreign Trade (*Bundesamt für Wirtschaft und Ausfuhrkontrolle* BAFA) has been publishing monthly gas border prices (solid line in Fig. 9.2). A simple ordinary least-squares (OLS) estimation explains the gas border price using a single independent variable, the monthly heating oil price along the Rhine river (in EUR/100 l; data source: German Federal Statistical Office),

$$p_t = \underset{(-14)}{-3.44} + \underset{(90)}{0.504} \cdot \sum_{k=3}^{9} \frac{p_{HEL, t-3-k}}{6} \qquad (9.21)$$

(t statistics in parentheses). The variable $p_{HEL,t-3-k}$ symbolizes the price of heating oil extra light, averaged over six months and lagged by three months, thus reflecting the popular sliding-price formula. For the 132 monthly observations from 2000 to 2010, this regression explains more than 98% of the variance of the gas border price (see the dotted line in Fig. 9.2).[8] However, an extrapolation of Eq. (9.21) beyond 2010 does not perform as well (see the light dotted line of Fig. 9.2). Simulated prices exceed actual ones by up to 10 EUR/MWh, indicating that the era of stable long-term ToP contracts has come to an end, at least in Continental Europe.

From an economic point of view, long-term contracts are an imperfect substitute of vertical integration; they are typically signed if vertical integration is prohibited.

---

[7]Some long-term contracts use other pricing factors, e.g., the wholesale prices of heavy oil or coal. Such arrangements are designed to keep gas competitive in power generation.

[8]As both time series are cointegrated of degree one, a cointegration equation should be estimated. The pertinent methodology is explained in Sect. 9.3.2: however, it does not affect estimation results in the present case.

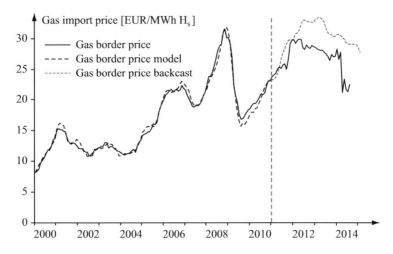

Fig. 9.2 German natural gas border prices (data source: BAFA (2014))

Note that they allocate risk in a particular way: The exporter bears the price risk, while the importer bears the quantity risk. Economic theory predicts that risk is allocated to the party who is better able to bear it. This gives rise to the question of why the exporter can manage the price risk better than the importer, while the importer can manage the volume risk better than the exporter.

- As to the importers, they usually make distributors accept a sliding-price formula as well. This is possible because gas distributors are mainly active in the market for space heating, where they compete with heating oil. A substantial markup on the price of heating oil would lead to a loss of sales.[9] In addition, many gas consumers are risk averse, causing them to value the assurance that the retail price of gas will always track that of heating oil, albeit with a lag according to Eq. (9.21) that may provoke public anger. Finally, gas importers can deal with the quantity risk by investing in gas storage facilities, which are necessary at any rate to balance seasonal fluctuations in demand.
- As to the gas exporters, they would run into problems if they had to bear both the price and the quantity risk because this would undermine the willingness of banks and financial institutions to provide the necessary loans for financing pipeline projects. Elimination of the quantity risk can be seen as contributing towards a minimum return on investment.

---

[9]Distributors charge a so-called gas netback price which contains a markup on their purchase price. This markup is stable as long as the prices of gas and heating oil move in parallel. Due to the advantages of natural gas in terms of cleanliness and comfort, a certain markup over heating oil can be enforced in retail markets.

Despite of their economic advantages, long-term contracts are viable only if both parties credibly commit to their obligations over an extended period of time. Concerning the export company, credibility importantly hinges on sufficient gas reserves. Concerning the import company, the determinants of its long-term credibility are less obvious, in particular if they lose their political protection and become exposed to competition. It is not surprising that the duration of long-term contracts has significantly shortened since 1997, when the liberalized European single gas market was created (see Neumann and Hirschhausen 2004).

The binding force of long-term contracts has been a topic in economics for some time. According to Crocker and Masten (1985, 1991), it should be effective to the extent that neither party has an interest in a premature termination of the contract unless this would be socially efficient. Thus, contractual penalties (inherent in ToP clauses) should be designed in a way that no party has an incentive to breach the contract if this would be socially inefficient.

Long-term contracts are viewed more critically by competition theory. The basic argument is that they lack transparency, reduce the liquidity of spot markets, and constitute a barrier to entry for new competitors. In addition, the price formula applied may not be flexible enough to accommodate new developments, e.g. the use of natural gas in combined cycle gas turbines (CCGT) for power generation in the present context. Finally, linking the price of gas to the one of heating oil not only creates an avoidable cluster risk but also prevents gas from becoming an instrument of risk diversification. These considerations have led the Commission of the European Union to adopt a negative attitude towards long-term contracts, even while recognizing their contribution to the security of energy supply (EU Directive 2003/55/EC).

9.3.2 Natural Gas Spot Trade

Another and more advanced market design is physical gas trade on spot and futures markets, first introduced in the United States (since 1978) and in Great Britain (since 1993). Liquid markets have evolved, generating transparent price signals. Finally, liberalization of European electricity markets around the year 2000 (see Sect. 12.2.2) created impetus to the development of liquid gas markets in Continental Europe as well.

However, physical gas trade is impossible unless traders can access the gas infrastructure (pipelines, LNG terminals), which is typically controlled by monopolistic companies. Third parties need to obtain access to this infrastructure for a market place to exist where gas can be exchanged between traders. Two types of gas exchanges have developed so far.

– Physical gas hubs: These are locations where pipelines, storage facilities, and liquefaction terminals meet like the spokes of a wheel, enabling the exchange of gas delivered though different pipelines. Pipelines that can be operated in both directions are particularly advantageous. An independent hub operator is called

9.3 Gas Markets and Gas Price Formation

for who provides non-discriminating access and processing of transactions, evens out short-term physical imbalances, and publishes market prices in timely manner. The first physical gas hub worldwide was the Henry Hub, located close to the gas fields of Louisiana and Texas in the southern United Sates. It is the most important to this day. Its liquidity derives from 14 gas pipelines which come together there, connecting large parts of the country. The Henry Hub gas price (quoted in USD per mn BTU) has become the benchmark for the entire U.S. wholesale gas market. It also provides the reference price for gas futures traded on the New York Mercantile Exchange NYMEX. In Continental Europe, the number one physical gas hub is located in Belgium, near Zeebrugge.

- Virtual gas hubs: Since there are few places in the world with a concentration of pipelines qualifying them for serving as a physical gas hub, parts of a high-pressure pipeline grid may constitute an alternative. The market place is defined by a number of entry and exit points, where traders can feed in and take out gas, to be delivered to final consumers. Since the pipelines may be owned by different companies, an independent hub operator is again necessary who coordinates entry and exit rights, processes transactions, and charges entry and exit fees which are used to finance the infrastructure. Trades must be executed in a timely manner as traders do not have the right to use the grid for storing their gas. The first virtual gas hubs were established in Great Britain (National Balancing Point NBP) and in the Netherlands (Title Transfer Facility TTF). In the meantime, there are also virtual gas hubs in Belgium (ZEE), France (Points d'Echange de Gaz, comprising Peg North, Peg South, and Peg TIGF), Germany (NetConnect Germany, Gaspool), and Italy (Punto di Scambio Virtuale).

The spot market price of an active and liquid gas hub[10] can become the reference price for gas contracts, serving to sever the link between long-term gas contracts and the heating oil price. This happened in Continental Europe around the year 2011 (see Fig. 9.2). However, the two prices are unlikely to diverge a great deal because heating oil and natural gas are close substitutes in the market for space heating. Moreover, fuel switching is facilitated by bivalent burners which can use either fuel. In fact a strong correlation between the two prices is observed on the U.S. gas market where price formulas based on heating oil are absent from long-term gas contracts. Yet divergences over extended periods of time do occur, which are due to the following factors:

- Gas prices are usually based on the upper heating value H_s rather than on the lower heating value H_i which is common on other energy markets. A cubic meter of natural gas with an upper heating value of 11.5 kWh/m^3 contains the same

---

[10]Liquidity can be measured using the so-called churn rate, defined as the ratio of traded volume to physically delivered volume.

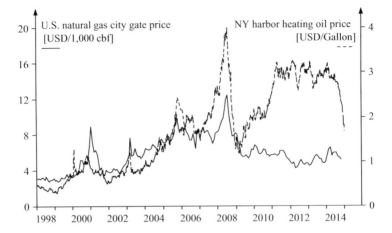

Fig. 9.3 Gas and heating oil prices on the U.S. spot market. Monthly price averages; data source: Energy Information Administration EIA

energy content as 1.05 kg (or 1.15 l, respectively) of heating oil.[11] However, even when this difference in measurement is accounted for, wholesale gas prices still differ from the energy-equivalent prices of heating oil due to a difference in the user value of the two fuels.

- Gas prices exhibit very strong seasonality, traditionally even more so than heating oil prices. In addition, they spike during extremely cold winter and hot summer days (see Fig. 9.3). The reason is the comparatively high storage cost of gas, which prevents the holding of stocks that buffer surges in demand.
- Volumes of storage that are high or low for the season as well as disruptions in the gas infrastructure (e.g. due to hurricanes) can also impact the spot price of natural gas.
- Finally, gas transportation cost may cause gas prices to differ between regional markets.

While the prices of wholesale gas and heating oil are expected to be related, these considerations serve to qualify this relationship. Indeed, until 2006 it used to be quite close in the United States but has fundamentally changed after 2009 at the latest (see Fig. 9.3). While the gas price still followed the 2008 hike in the price of heating oil, the two prices have become uncorrelated since 2009. Accordingly, a stable price relation is predicted until the end of 2006 or perhaps 2008 only.

In estimating this relationship, one is confronted with the following methodological problem. As is the case with most financial time series, the two fuel price series are not stationary, i.e. their means and variances are time-dependent.

---

[11]In U.S. units, one thousand cubic feet (cbf) of natural gas contain an energy equivalent of eight gallons of heating oil. Therefore, one would expect eight gallons of heating oil to fetch the same price as 1000 cbf of natural gas (which is not true, see Fig. 9.2.)

9.3 Gas Markets and Gas Price Formation

Table 9.5 Indicators for natural gas and heating oil spot market prices

	Natural gas price (p_{gas}) (U.S. city gate) (USD/1000 cbf)		Heating oil price p_{hel} (New York Harbor) (USD/Gallon)	
	$\ln(p_t)$	$\ln(p_t)-\ln(p_{t-1})$	$\ln(p_t)$	$\ln(p_t)-\ln(p_{t-1})$
Mean	1.724	0.002	0.327	0.008
Standard deviation	0.341	0.090	0.674	0.085
Skewness	−0.121	0.073	−0.435	0.041
Kurtosis	2.571	4.665	2.013	5.056
ADF test	−2.3	−13.5[a]	−1.8	−11.5[a]
PP test	−2.3	−13.5[a]	−1.7	−11.5[a]

202 monthly observations between 1998 and 2014
[a] Test statistics indicate stationarity at a significance level of 1%

Table 9.5 contains first indications suggesting that the (logarithm of) the two prices may not be stationary. In particular, the negative skewness points to an asymmetry in the distribution that may be due to a shifting mean or variance σ^2. Contrary to the normal distribution (whose skewness is zero because of symmetry), a log-normal distribution has positive skewness which depends on its variance. It is given by $(e^{\sigma^2}+2)(e^{\sigma^2}-1)^{1/2}$. With the values in Table 9.5, skewness given log-normality would amount to $(e^{0.3412}+2)(e^{0.3412}-1)^{1/2} = 1.096$ for the gas price and $(e^{0.6742}+2)(e^{0.6742}-1)^{1/2} = 2.711$ for the heating oil price. The observed values −0.121 and −0.435 are far away from these benchmarks, indicating that the logarithms of the two prices are not normally distributed, possibly due to a stochastic trend, i.e. non-stationarity.

First differences $\Delta \ln p_t = \ln p_t - \ln p_{t-1}$ usually do not contain a trend anymore. Also, amounting to percentage changes, they have a natural interpretation (see Sect. 5.1). Statistical tests for non-stationarity such as the Augmented Dickey-Fuller test (ADF test) or the Phillips-Perron test (PP test) are described e.g. in Engle and Granger (1987). According to the two bottom lines of Table 9.5, the hypothesis of non-stationarity can be rejected at a high level of significance for the percentage changes in both the U.S. city gate gas price and the New York harbor heating oil price. The two modified price series are therefore called integrated of order zero, while the original ones, integrated of order one.

If two time series are integrated of order one or higher, OLS regression is inappropriate as it may estimate a relationship where there is nothing but a common stochastic trend. While an OLS regression relating the percentage changes may solve this problem, its estimated parameters show only the short-term relation between the two prices but not a possible long-term relation. If such a long-term relation exists, the two time series are called cointegrated. This means that they tend to return to their long-term relation after some time; in the short term, however, they may develop independently of each other. The formal representation of this long-term relationship is the so-called cointegration equation, to be interpreted as the equilibrium relation between the two time series.

The error correction approach developed in the context of nonstationary time series analysis (see Engle and Granger 1987) has become the standard method to identify a possible cointegration equation. The first step is to find out whether two time series are cointegrated or not. Here the Johansen test can be used (Johansen 1991). Applied to the U.S. monthly fuel prices shown in Fig. 9.3, this test confirms cointegration for the period up to 2008 but not after, as revealed by Fig. 9.3. Next, the Johansen test also suggests the following cointegration equation for the common stochastic trend of the gas price p_{gas} and the heating oil price p_{hel}, estimated from 72 monthly data between 2001 and 2006 (t statistics in parentheses),

$$\ln\left(p_{gas,t}\right) = \underset{(83.0)}{-1.87} + \underset{(14.1)}{0.77} \cdot \ln\left(p_{hel,t}\right). \tag{9.22}$$

Thus, even in the absence of a contractual pricing formula, U.S. gas and heating oil prices are found to move together. Third, an error correction model is specified. It describes how prices return to the estimated equilibrium relation if disturbed by exogenous shocks (72 observations between 2001 and 2006; adjusted $R^2 = 0.59$),

$$\begin{aligned}
\Delta\ln\left(p_{gas,t}\right) &= \underset{(-6.9)}{-0.409} \cdot \left(\ln\left(p_{gas,t}\right) + 1.87 - 0.77 \cdot \ln\left(p_{hel,t}\right)\right) \\
&+ \underset{(1.4)}{0.110} \cdot \Delta\ln\left(p_{gas,t-1}\right) + \underset{(1.5)}{0.156} \cdot \Delta\ln\left(p_{hel,t-1}\right) \\
&- \underset{(-5.4)}{0.0025} \cdot \text{GASST-RESID}_t + \underset{(-.34)}{0.00027} \cdot \text{TEMP-RESID}_t - \underset{(-6.7)}{0.281} \cdot DMY.
\end{aligned} \tag{9.23}$$

Equation (9.23) can be interpreted as follows. Its first row explains what happens if the cointegration equation (9.22) is not satisfied at time t, resulting in a difference between the observed (logarithm of the) gas price and its value predicted by the regression using the heating oil price. The parameter -0.409 indicates the extent to which such a difference decreases per unit during period t. Accordingly, it takes on average $1/0.409 = 2.44$ months for a disequilibrium to be eliminated. For a comparison with European long-term gas import contracts with their price formula, one may interpret equation (9.21) as pertaining to a cointegration equation, neglecting the fact that it is in arithmetic rather than logarithmic values. However, any shock in month t would affect the moving average only with one-sixth of its value, and the moving average itself is lagged by three months. Therefore the estimated coefficient 0.504 shrinks to 0.084, indicating an adjustment period of $12 (= 1/0.084)$ months, to which three months have to be added. This exceeds the 2.44 months estimated above by far, indicating that adjustments to shocks are much more sluggish in European than U.S. imports of natural gas.

The second row of Eq. (9.23) shows the short-term relationship between relative changes in the gas price and the heating oil price. It is lagged by one month to render it predetermined in period t, thus making it unlikely that causality runs from the dependent variable $\Delta\ln(p_{Gas,t})$ to the explanatory variable rather than the other way round. According to the positive (but insignificant) sign of 0.110, the coefficient pertaining to $\Delta\ln(p_{Gas,t-1})$, gas price fluctuations may be somewhat self-reinforcing, implying high price volatility. This would motivate gas traders to hedge the price risk by signing long-term gas contracts, forwards, and futures.

The third row of Eq. (9.23) shows the impact of some shocks, represented by three exogenous variables.

- *GASST-RESID*: unusually high stocks of gas (in percent of the seasonal mean);
- *TEMP-RESID*: unusual temperatures during the heating season;
- *DMY*: dummy variable reflecting unusual events (hurricanes, spillovers from turbulences on financial markets).

As expected, unusually high stocks have a recognizable dampening effect on surges of the gas price. According to Table 9.5, the average value of $\Delta\ln(p_{Gas,t})$ is 0.008 or 0.8% per month. Compared to it, the coefficient of -0.0025 pertaining to *GASST-RESID* is anything but small, indicating that an extra percentage point in excess of the usual magnitude of gas stocks serves to slow the average price increase from 0.8 to 0.55 ($= 0.8 - 0.25$) percent per month ceteris paribus. Somewhat surprisingly, *TEMP-RESID* is statistically insignificant, while the occurrence of an unusual event swamps everything else by turning the 0.8% increase into a 27.3 ($= 28.1 - 0.8$) percent decrease in price.

In sum, the model (9.23) provides an interesting explanation of the U.S. wholesale gas market before the shale gas revolution. However, the new fracking technology led to a basic change, breaking up the stable relation between gas and heating oil prices. Between 2010 and 2014 wholesale gas prices are less than half the level predicted under the old regime. In addition, they were not affected by the collapse of heating oil prices at the end of 2014, suggesting that U.S. gas markets have become fully independent of the heating oil market despite the fact that the two fuels continue to be close substitutes. The likely reason is that at relatively low prices, gas has conquered new markets (in particular for power generation), where the relevant substitutive fuel is not heating oil but coal.

9.4 Third Party Access to the Gas Infrastructure

Third party access (TPA) describes a situation in which agents other than the owner of an asset are allowed to use the asset. In the case of natural gas, traders other than the owners of the gas infrastructure (in particular the grid) can use it for transport. Without TPA, the set of trading partners is limited to those companies who have their own transport capacities for their service area. Therefore a liquid natural gas market is possible only if the operators of the grid offer other parties effective, nondiscriminatory, and transparent TPA.

This access can be granted on a negotiated or a regulatory basis. In the first case, traders and grid operators need to sign contracts allowing the use of the grid and specifying the terms of its use. If more than a handful grid contracts are to be negotiated, they are quite unlikely to be nondiscriminatory in the sense that all traders benefit from the same access conditions. In the second case, contracts are still necessary but their rates and conditions are set by a public regulator, who denies the grid operator the right to reject third parties seeking to sign a contract. Conditions importantly specify the beginning and end of a gas transfer as well the quantity per time unit to be transported.

Regulated TPA comprises two very different variants.

- Contract path (also known as point-to-point system): Gas traders choose the entry and the exit points as well as the pipelines between the two points they want to use. The grid operator allocates this transport capacity provided it is available and charges the transportation fee, which may be a function of distance or a flat rate, depending on the type of regulation.
- Entry-exit system: Here, entry and exit capacities are booked and charged separately. This permits a trader who has booked entry capacities to sell gas during the reservation period to any party disposing of exit capacities for the same period. Conversely, traders who have booked exit capacities can contract with others who have entry capacities during the same period. The grid operator charges entry fees and exit fees but no distance-related transportation fees.

Entry-exit systems amount to virtual hubs or market areas, respectively. There must be an agent who controls the relevant part of the pipeline grid, maintains its pressure, registers applications for capacity by traders, and coordinates the gas flows through the grid. The condition is that these flows can be executed during each time interval given the capacities of the pipelines. The agent also identifies gas traders who have excess capacity and excess transportation demand relative to capacity and provides the necessary positive or negative balancing energy. While imbalances can often be offset at the aggregate level in this way, this is not always possible, exposing traders to the risk of failure to fulfil their contracts. Of course, traders are charged for their imbalances and may even be fined for them if they are sizable.

On the other hand, the separate booking of entry and exit capacities enhances trading opportunities: Traders who hold exit capacities but no entry capacities can purchase gas from traders who have entry capacities for the same time interval. Situations where the physical flow between an entry and an exit point turns out to exceed the capacity of the pipeline system can be avoided by limiting admissible gas flows at all entry and exit points to values that are compatible with capacity. This calls for specifying hydraulic load flow models and solving them for short (typically hourly) intervals. The objective is for the grid operator to offer firm rather than interruptible entry and exit capacities to the greatest extent possible.

Still, the risk of failure to fulfil contracts may persist. There are two ways to further lower it:

- The size of the market area may be reduced. This leads to fewer restrictions on the allocation of firm entry and exit capacities. On the other hand, smaller market areas diminish market liquidity, the number of market participants, and hence

9.4 Third Party Access to the Gas Infrastructure

trade benefits. Also, traders may enjoy more market power since they are less exposed to the pressure of competition from other market areas due to the transportation cost of border-crossing gas.
- Firm and interruptible capacities are offered alongside each other. This more common alternative enables the grid operator to avoid bottlenecks by blocking traders with (lower-priced) interruptible capacities from access at critical entry and exit points.

Bookings of entry and exit capacities may be honored on a first-come-first-served basis. This rule not only favors incumbents to the detriment of newcomers but also creates scope for traders to manipulate the wholesale gas market. An obvious strategy is the purchase of entry capacities designed to prevent competitors from delivering gas to the market area, resulting in so-called foreclosure. It is attractive if the achievable price markup exceeds the unit cost of these extra capacities. The regulator can counteract this strategy by imposing the 'use it or lose it' principle: Wholesale traders who hold firm entry or exit bookings but fail to order commensurate transportation services (before a defined closing date) lose their capacities to other customers. A more market-oriented approach is for the grid operator to create a secondary market for entry and exit rights that allows traders to buy and sell unused capacity rights. As always, abuse of market power may have to be reined in by public authorities.

Many grid-related aspects of the wholesale gas market are quite similar to those of the market for electricity, which are discussed in Chap. 13. However, European gas markets continue to be characterized by a few particularities. The gas year starts on October 1 at 6.00 a.m. and ends in the following year on October 1 at 5.59 a.m. Due to the importance of gas in the space heating market, the calendar year is not appropriate as it cuts into the heating season. Next, the smallest trading unit is a block of 1 MWh, i.e. 1 MW to be delivered during one hour. Day-ahead contracts with delivery within 24 h are typical of spot markets, while block contracts for months, quarters, and years are traded on futures markets.

Turning to the final users of natural gas, their demand exhibits a strong seasonal pattern because it importantly derives from their demand for space heating. However, gas consumers with other uses have a more balanced demand profile. Commonly used indicators are full load hours *FLH* or full load days *FLD*, respectively. For instance, annual gas sales can be expressed as the product of capacity (called maximum load) and degree of utilization (measured in hours per year). Division by the maximum load yields *FLH* (*FLD*, respectively if utilization is measured in days per year),

$$FLH = \frac{\text{Gas sales } [\text{m}^3/\text{a}]}{\text{max.load } [\text{m}^3] \text{ per h}} \text{ and } FLD = \frac{\text{Gas sales } [\text{m}^3/\text{a}]}{\text{max.load } [\text{m}^3] \text{ per day}}. \quad (9.24)$$

As shown in Table 9.6, average capacity utilization of the gas infrastructure is low, amounting to 3600 of 8760 h and 150 of 365 days (or 41%) per year, respectively. Moreover, there are substantial differences between consumer groups.

Table 9.6 Capacity utilization by final users of natural gas

	Full load hours (FLH) (h/a)	Full load days (FLD) (d/a)	Capacity utilization (%)
Private households	1500–2000	60–95	16–26
Real estate companies	1800–2700	75–110	20–30
Industrial customers	2500–5000	100–210	27–58
Market average	3600	150	41
Structured natural gas contracts with nearby wells	3000–4000	125–167	34–46
Block delivery	8000–8760	340–365	>93

Source: Erdmann and Zweifel (2008, p. 243)

While most of the demand by private households occurs during relatively few hours and days, resulting in a capacity utilization of no more than 26%, demand by industrial consumers is more regular, resulting in a capacity utilization of up to 58%.

In view of this high degree of volatility, predicting demand is important. One of the common explanatory variables is the heating degree day $HDD_t := \max(0, 15 - Temp_t)$, where $Temp_t$ is the average outside temperature of day t measured in degree Celsius (°C). It is positive on days with an average outside temperature below 15 °C and zero otherwise. Daily fluctuations in the demand for gas can be well explained by models using this variable. Yet even with reasonably accurate predictions, costly gas storage facilities are needed to optimize capacity utilization of the pipeline infrastructure.

An alternative is to provide financial incentives for using the gas infrastructure in a more regular way. For instance, costumers with a so-called structured gas contract reach a capacity utilization of up to 46% (see Table 9.6 again). These customers can be gas distributors or large-scale industrial users who agree to shift part of their demand out of peak periods if necessary. For a maximum relief effect, they should be located near a gas well, permitting them to obtain their regular supply without greatly burdening the transport infrastructure.

References

BAFA. (2014). *Aufkommen und Export von Erdgas sowie die Entwicklung der Grenzübergangspreise ab 1991* [Availability and exports of natural gas and development of border prices since 1991]. Eschborn: German Federal Office of Foreign Trade. Retrieved from www.bafa.de/bafa/de/energie/erdgas/index.html

BGR. (2014). *Reserven, Ressourcen und Verfügbarkeit von Energierohstoffen (Reserves, resources, and availability of energy Resources)*. Hannover: Bundesanstalt für Geowissenschaften und Rohstoffe. Retrieved from www.bgr.bund.de/DE/Themen/Energie/Downloads/Energiestudie_2014.pdf

BP. (2014). *BP statistical review of world energy*. Retrieved from www.bp.com/statisticalreview/

Cayrade, P. (2004). *Investments in gas pipelines and liquefied natural gas infrastructure. What is the impact on the security of supply?* Fondazione Eni Enrico Mattei. Nota di Lavoro 11.4.2004. Retrieved from www.feem.it/Feem/Pub/Publications/WPapers/default.htm

References

Crocker, K. J., & Masten, S. E. (1985). Efficient adaptation in long-term contracts: Take-or-pay provisions for natural gas. *American Economic Review, 75,* 1083–1093.

Crocker, K. J., & Masten, S. E. (1991). Pretia ex Machina? Prices and process in long-term contracts. *Journal of Law and Economics, 34,* 69–99.

Engle, R. F., & Granger, C. (1987). Co-integration and error correction: Representation, estimation, and testing. *Econometrica, 55,* 251–276.

Erdmann, G., & Zweifel, P. (2008). *Energieökonomik - Theorie und Anwendungen (Energy economics – theory and applications)* (2nd ed.). Berlin: Springer.

Hirschhausen, C., Meinhard, B., & Pavel, F. (2005). Transporting gas to Western Europe – a simulation analysis. *The Energy Journal, 26*(2), 49–68.

Johansen, S. (1991). Estimation and hypothesis testing of cointegration vectors in Gaussian vector autoregressive models. *Econometrica, 59,* 1551–1580.

Knieps, G. (2002). Wettbewerb auf den Ferntransportnetzen der deutschen Gaswirtschaft – Eine netzökonomische Analyse (Competition on the long-distance transportation networks of the German natural gas industry – an economic analysis). *Zeitschrift für Energiewirtschaft, 26,* 171–179.

McKendry, P. (2002). Energy production from biomass (Part 1): Overview of biomass. *Bioresource Technology, 83,* 37–46.

Neumann, A., & Hirschhausen, C. (2004). Less gas to Europe? An empirical assessment of long-term contracts for European energy supply. *Zeitschrift für Energiewirtschaft, 28,* 175–182.

Tirole, J. (1988). *The theory of industrial organization.* Cambridge, MA: The MIT Press.

Zweifel, P., Krey, B., & Schirillo, S. (2009/2010). Russian gas to Western Europe: A game-theoretic analysis. *The Journal of Energy Markets, 2*(4), 1–27.

Markets for Solid Fuels and CO$_2$ Emissions 10

Solid fuels are hard coal, lignite, and firewood. Their common properties are low energy densities resulting in high cost of transportation which in turn limits competition in solid fuel markets. Thanks to reduced costs of coal extraction, productivity increases in maritime transport, and reduced public subsidies, a global market for hard coal has nevertheless developed.

Due to coal's high carbon content, coal combustion is the major source of global CO$_2$ emissions, amounting to about three tons of CO$_2$ per ton of hard coal. In addition, coal mining is associated with emission of methane (so-called pit gas), another important greenhouse gas. Thus the economics of coal markets cannot be discussed without referring to international efforts designed to reduce global emissions of CO$_2$ and other greenhouse gases. In an attempt to achieve this aim, the European Union created a market for CO$_2$ emission allowances (EU Directive 2003/87/EC). Depending on the effectiveness of this system, CO$_2$ emissions may become sufficiently costly to increase the price of coal relative to that of other fuels, triggering its substitution by less harmful alternatives.

The issues addressed in this chapter are:

- What are the factors determining the development of the market for hard coal?
- What determines its price on the world market?
- Is the market for coal competitive?
- Is there a trend towards vertical integration as in the oil industry?
- What are the perspectives of solid biofuels and in particular wood as a substitute for coal?
- What determines the price of emission rights?
- How do these prices depend on the design of the market for emissions?

The variables used in this chapter are:

CDS Clean dark spread
DS Dark spread
Em Annual emissions [in tons of CO$_2$ equivalent]

M	Inventory of greenhouse gases in the atmosphere
p_{CO2}	Price of a CO_2 emission right
p_{coal}	Coal price
p_{el}	Wholesale price of electricity
ω	Fuel efficiency

10.1 Solid Fuels and Their Technologies

Solid fuels comprise types of coal, lignite, wood, and biomass fuels which differ widely in terms of their properties. Coal with a carbon content below 55% of dry matter belongs to the category of lignite, whereas fuels with a carbon content between 55% and 65% are categorized as hard coal. Table 10.1 presents some properties of economically relevant solid fuels. Their water content ranges between 6% in hard coal and up to 65% in soft lignite. On the whole, it varies inversely with the energy content measured using the lower heating value. Accordingly, anthracite has the highest heating value of up to 37.7 MJ/kg but still falls short of liquid and gaseous fuels (see Tables 8.7 and 9.2). The heating values of lignite, firewood, and other biomass fuels are lower, causing them to have comparatively high transportation cost per energy unit.

In return, biomass fuels have the advantage that their combustion is not associated with a net emission of greenhouse gases. The CO_2 emissions released from burning firewood are compensated by the growth of trees and other biofuels. Assuming a constant global stock of biomass, these fuels are therefore neutral with respect to CO_2 emissions (see Table 10.1 again). Conversely, the combustion of all types of hard coal is associated with very high CO_2 emissions, whether in terms of g CO_2/MJ or kg CO_2 per kg of matter. Properties not listed in Table 10.1 are ash content (varying from 4% to 10%) and sulfur content (0.3% to 1.1%). They may be of considerable relevance to the users of the fuel.

10.1.1 Biomass

Until the first half of the nineteenth century, firewood was the dominant fuel; yet with industrialization its supply could not keep up with demand. In its modern forms, biomass contributes but little to covering energy demand, for reasons that become evident from Fig. 10.1 which presents a classification of biomass fuels. Their potential depends on two parameters, the availability of land and its productivity. For instance, one ha of forest yields between 0.5 and 1.5 tons of dry matter per year but up to 15 tons if stocked with fast-growing trees (see short-rotation wood in Table 10.2). While residual timber from industry is economically quite attractive, its potential is largely exhausted since it cannot be burned untreated in countries with a restrictive greenhouse gas policy. Treated residual timber is more costly yet originally was charged with a disposal fee in some countries, causing it to

10.1 Solid Fuels and Their Technologies

Table 10.1 Properties of solid fuels

Solid fuel	Water (%)	Lower heating value (MJ/kg)	CO_2 emissions (g CO_2/MJ)	CO_2 emissions (kg CO_2/kg)
Anthracite	6	35.6–37.7	95–98	2.43–3.69
Lean coal	6	33.5–35.6	92–98	3.08–3.49
Fat coal	6	29.3–33.4	92–98	2.70–3.27
Coke	9	28	94.6	
Hard lignite	20–30	16.8–29.3	97	1.63–2.84
Soft lignite	45–65	7.5–12.6	104–113	0.78–1.42
Lignite briquettes	19	19	94.60	0
Firewood pellets	10	18	0	0
Dry wood	18	ca. 15	0	0
Straw, reed, crops	15	14.5	0	0
Forest wood	50	ca. 8	0	0
Maize		ca. 3.5		

Data sources: Umweltbundesamt (2005) and Fachagentur nachwachsende Rohstoffe (2005)

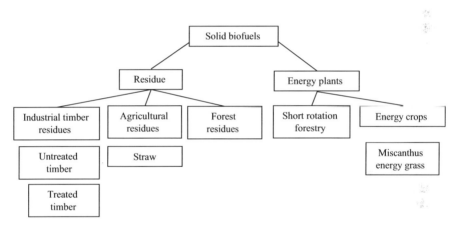

Fig. 10.1 Classification of solid biomass fuels

have a negative price. Meanwhile, it fetches a positive price, constituting one of the rare instances where a commodity changes from a negatively to a positively valued good.

An agricultural residue is straw, which however only yields up to six tons of dry matter per ha and year (see Table 10.2 again). Interestingly, it has an energy content of 17 MJ/kg, comparable to the other biomass fuels.

Turning to energy plants, Triticale is a novel cereal that can be used for nutrition or fuel production. Quite generally, biomass can be transformed into gaseous or liquid fuels by using biochemical processes (e.g. fermentation), chemical processes (e.g. esterification), or thermo-chemical processes (Fischer-Tropsch synthesis).

Table 10.2 Properties of solid energy biomass

	Dry matter (t/(ha a))	Lower heating value (MJ/kg)	Density (kg/m³)	Price 2006[a] (EUR/tons)
Fresh firewood	0.5–1.5	18		
Split logs			300–500	30–60
Firewood chips			200–300	40–70
Wood pellets			400–600	120–300
Short-rotation wood/triticale	5–15	18		
Crops	8–14	17		
Straw	4–6	17		

[a]Without transportation cost
Data source: Carmen e.V. (bioXchange.de); see also Table 8.8

These processes are characterized by substantial energy losses, partly because only the starch and oil components of the biomass are suitable for energetic use. Up to present, cellulose, lignin, and tannin can only be used when burning wood, whereas an efficient thermal use requires the biomass to be shred and dried. This serves to increase its density up to 600 kg/m³ (as in the case of wood pellets) and hence to lower its cost of transportation; however, these processes are themselves costly.

In sum, collection, transportation, and processing constitute the major cost components of solid biomass, which vary considerably depending on desired form of delivery (e.g. as piece goods or bulk goods) as well as topography. In addition, local and regional market conditions determine prices. Though firewood is typically cheaper than other fossil energy sources, it often loses this advantage due to higher outlays for burners, maintenance, and waste disposal.

10.1.2 Coal Reserves

The invention of the steam engine by James Watt in 1765 caused coal to dominate fossil energy markets for two reasons. On the one hand, it enabled the exploitation of underground coal mines because water could be pumped out in great quantities; on the other hand, growing coal extraction was necessary to run the steam engines. This mutual reinforcement of supply and demand is a typical feature of successful basic innovations to this day.

Although a non-renewable resource, coal has reserves that are still far from being exhausted. Their static range substantially exceeds 100 years (see Table 10.3). In view of this abundance, it is not surprising that a scarcity rent of coal is virtually nonexistent, in contradistinction with crude oil and natural gas (see the Hotelling model in Sect. 6.2.1). In addition, coal reserves are rather evenly distributed over the globe, with a large part located in industrial countries such as Australia, the United States, Canada, and China. For this reason, coal is called 'the energy source of the north'.

Table 10.3 Coal reserves and coal mining 2013

	Coal reserves 2013			Coal and lignite mining 2013	
	Hard coal (bn tce)	Lignite (bn tce)	Share (%)	(mn tce)	Share (%)
Russia	49.1	107.9	17.6	298	5.1
China	62.2	52.3	12.8	3680	47.4
Australia	37.1	39.3	8.6	478	6.9
India	56.1	4.5	6.8	605	5.9
European Union	4.9	51.2	4.5	543	3.9
South Africa	30.1	–	3.4	257	3.7
Indonesia	–	28.0	3.1	88	1.2
World	403.2	488.3	100	7896	100
OECD	155.5	229.3	43.2	2020	35.8

Source: BP (2014)

During the early coal era, mass transport of coal over long distances was quite expensive or even impossible, in spite of railways and inland waterways. Up to the nineteenth century it was cheaper to bring people to the coal than coal to the people. As a result, industrial clusters developed around coal fields, in particular iron, steel, manufacturing, and mechanical engineering industries. European examples are Central England, Northern France, the Meuse and Ruhr areas, and Upper Silesia. Today these regions are suffering from severe economic and social problems because electricity has replaced coal as the dominant energy source in production. Electricity can be transported to remote areas at low cost, thus lowering energy-related returns to agglomeration. Currently coal is used exclusively in electricity generation (as so-called steam coal) and steel production (as coke).

Nonetheless, global coal mining has kept expanding for many years for a number of reasons:

– Economic growth of emerging countries, in particular China and India, has been pushing demand for electricity and with it, coal;
– After several hikes in the prices of crude oil (see Sect. 8.3) and natural gas (see Sect. 9.3), coal has become a relatively inexpensive energy source;
– Many coal-producing countries have been reluctant to adopt greenhouse gas reduction strategies.

10.1.3 Surface and Underground Coal Mining

Two coal mining technologies can be distinguished, surface mining and underground mining (often simply called mining). The choice of mining technology is largely determined by the geology of the coal deposit. Surface mining (also known as opencast mining) requires the resettlement of households and companies who occupy a licensed mining area of many square kilometers—a socially sensitive, often conflict-laden, and time-consuming process. After closure of the mine, governments usually demand rehabilitation of the land, which is particularly costly in the case of surface mining. Yet surface mining can still be cheaper than underground mining if the coal beds are close to the surface, enabling the use of large-scale equipment and facilitating material flows comprising not only coal but also soil, rocks, and overburden removal.

Coal beds several hundred meters below the surface are exploited by underground mining through shafts and tunnels. Modern technology uses long wall mining, which involves the drilling of a section of 100–350 m length along the coal seam in one step using mechanical shearers. Self-advancing, hydraulically-powered supports temporarily hold the roof until the coal is extracted, after which the roof is allowed to collapse. While both surface and underground mining call for elaborate water management, the underground alternative additionally requires effort to prevent pit gas explosions that jeopardize miners' lives.[1] Another challenge confronting underground mining is surface subsidence affecting buildings, infrastructure, ground water, and local land use in its neighborhood.

The choice of technology has cost implications. Notably, labor productivity of surface mining ranges from 10,000 to 20,000 tons per worker and year, compared to 5000–8000 tons in underground mining—despite substantial increases in productivity. Since old mines have low marginal cost (see Sect. 1.2.1), surface mining tends to be more competitive than underground mining. This holds true in particular where infrastructure for transporting large volumes of coal to both domestic and international customers is in existence, creating scale economies.

10.1.4 International Coal Market

Steam coal accounts for about 70% of international trade in coal. It continues to be dominated by bilateral contracts (of the so-called over-the-counter or OTC type, respectively) between producers and wholesale customers. These contracts often have a duration of 10 years, with prices that are adjusted to the coal spot price annually in the fourth quarter. Since these prices need not be published, the world market for coal has been lacking transparency.

With the liberalization of electricity markets (see Sect. 12.2.2), the need for transparency has increased because generating companies seek to hedge their coal position on financial markets using regular price information. One such source are standardized surveys of traders, e.g. the weekly publication of the British *McCloskey Coal Information Services* (since 1991). Its quotations are in USD per metric ton of coal with a heating value of 6000 kcal/kg and a sulfur content of 1%. Another source is the British service provider *Tradition Financial Services* (*TFS*) who publishes a set of price indices, API#1 for the American market, API#2 for the

---

[1] Whereas extensive safety measures are used to protect miners in developed countries, developing and emerging countries regularly report major accidents in pits.

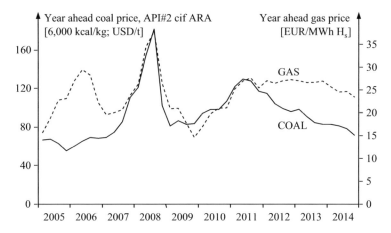

Fig. 10.2 Monthly coal and gas prices in Germany (data source: EEX). Note: 'cif. ARA' denotes inclusion of cost for insurance and freight for delivery to the ports of Amsterdam, Rotterdam, or Antwerp

European market, and API#4 for South Africa. Finally, energy exchanges such as the *European Energy Exchange* (*EEX*) also provide price data (see Fig. 10.2).

According to Fig. 10.2, coal prices spiked in 2008 and again in 2011, similar to those of natural gas and other fossil fuels. Starting in 2012, however, coal has become cheap compared to natural gas. Without attempting to explain these developments in detail, the following determinants can be cited.

- Decreasing coal exports from the United States: This country was home to major coal exporters until the end of the 1990s, who acted as swing producers. This stabilizing force has been absent since then.
- Development of Chinese coal exports: Caused by rapid economic growth, domestic demand for electricity and hence coal surged until 2012, reducing its availability for exports. This forced importing countries like Japan and Korea to obtain their supplies from more remote areas, causing freight rates to be bid up worldwide. Meanwhile, Chinese growth has slowed, making coal available again on the international market, with concomitant downward pressure on its price.
- The coal price in Europe also depends on the exchange rates of the Australian Dollar and the South African Rand. Australia and South Africa are home to major coal exporters, who quote their deliveries in their respective currencies.
- Finally, short-term price spikes may be caused by political and social unrest, military conflict, and outages of nuclear power.

10.2 The Greenhouse Gas Problem

More than 43% of energy-related CO_2 emissions originate from coal combustion, a share which is growing. In view of international attempts at mitigating the greenhouse gas problem in general and reducing CO_2 emissions in particular (see bottom lines of Table 10.4), the markets for coal cannot be discussed without addressing these issues.

The greenhouse gas (GHG) problem is the consequence of anthropogenic emissions of carbon dioxide (CO_2) and other greenhouse gases such as methane (CH_4) and nitrous oxide (N_2O, see Table 10.4) along with vapor into the atmosphere. According to climatologists, CO_2 allows short-wave solar light to pass the atmosphere while blocking the reflection of long-wave thermal radiation. Without this greenhouse effect, the mean temperature of the globe would be $-18\,°C$ rather than $+16\,°C$ at present. Since the beginning of industrialization around 1840, the CO_2 concentration in the atmosphere increased from 280 ppmv (parts per million by volume) to 390 ppmv as of 2011, according to the International Panel on Climate Change (IPCC). Over the same period, mean global temperature increased by $0.5\,°C$ (possibly even by $0.8\,°C$, depending on method of measurement), suggesting that global warming is caused by the increase in CO_2 concentration.

Annual CO_2 emissions keep increasing globally (see Fig. 10.3). While they have been slowly falling in Europe and remaining stable in North America since about 2007, they have been growing rapidly in the rest of the world, most notably in China in the wake of its economic growth. This has to do with the fact that the most important anthropogenic source of CO_2 emissions is the burning of fossil fuels.[2] The GHG effect of other emissions is expressed in CO_2 equivalents. According to Table 10.4, the CO_2 equivalent of methane (CH_4) is 25 and of nitrous oxide (N_2O), 298 if a time horizon of 100 years is adopted. It is important to note that CO_2 is no poison in the classic sense—it is even necessary for the growth of plants. Yet at the current annual rate of more than 35 bn tons of global CO_2 emissions (40 bn tons of CO_2 equivalents from all GHG emissions, respectively), the GHG concentration in the atmosphere will continue to increase. This is likely to lead to a considerable increase in average global temperatures, which is believed to have many negative long-term impacts. Among those cited are acidification of oceans, increased frequency of thunderstorms, changing distribution of precipitation, desertification, melting of glaciers, thawing of permafrost, a rising sea level, and changing habitats for plants and animals. However, some of the world's regions may also benefit from increased plant growth and reduced heating requirements due to warmer temperatures. Since most of these regions are in the rich North while those

---

[2] Global methane emissions are much smaller than CO_2 emissions, and their rate of decay in the atmosphere is higher as well. But one mole of methane has an impact on the climate that is 56 times (over a time horizon of 20 years) or 21 times (100 years) greater than that of one mole of CO_2.

10.2 The Greenhouse Gas Problem

Table 10.4 Indicators of the greenhouse gas problem

	Carbon dioxide CO_2	Methane CH_4	Nitrous oxide N_2O
Pre industrial concentration (ppmv)	280	0.7–0.8	0.23
Average atmospheric lifetime (years)	5–200	9–15	120
Global warming potential in 20 years	1	72	289
Global warming potential in 100 years	1	25	298
Contribution to the GHG problem (%)	77	14	8
Reduction target of the IPCC 1990 (%)	60–80	15–20	70–80

Source: International Panel on Climate Change IPCC (1990, 2014)

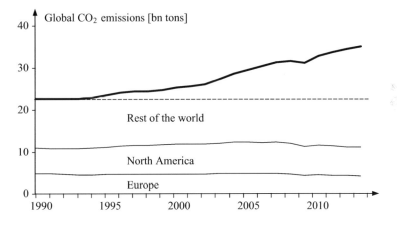

Fig. 10.3 Global CO_2 emissions (data source: BP 2014)

negatively affected are in the poor South, the GHG problem raises major equity concerns (Bretschger 2015, Chap. 4).

From the viewpoint of welfare economics, the reduction target should satisfy the following condition for Pareto optimality (see Sect. 7.2): The present value of expected damages avoided thanks to the last reduction project is to equal the present value of the expected cost of avoiding them. Note the qualification 'expected' on both sides of the equality; neither the amount of damage avoided nor the cost of meeting a reduction target are known with certainty. In particular, knowledge regarding future damage associated with present GHG emissions is not sufficient to implement the Pareto criterion. For example, Nordhaus and Boyer (2000) estimate the optimal CO_2 price (in the sense of a Pigouvian tax; see Sect. 7.3.1) to be around 10 USD per ton of CO_2. Therefore, this amount of tax would establish the equality of expected marginal benefit in the sense of damage avoided and expected marginal cost caused by reducing CO_2 emissions. By way of contrast, Böhringer and Rutherford (2000) conclude that even a rather modest reduction of GHG emissions would imply a cost of much more than 100 USD per ton of CO_2 equivalent. In view of divergences of this magnitude, there is no sound alternative for GHG reduction policy than to adopt the so-called standard-price approach (see Sect. 7.3.2).

The standard-price approach calls for a political decision with regard to a target value of emissions and putting a tax price on them that promises to reach this target. For example, let the long-term tolerable CO_2 concentration in the atmosphere be between 450 and 550 ppmv. The realized value is the result of annual CO_2 emissions and natural decay (Nordhaus 1994),

$$M_t = M_{t-1} - \frac{1}{\tau}\left(M_{t-1} - M_{pre}\right) + \beta \cdot Em_t. \qquad (10.1)$$

Here, M_t symbolizes the realized CO_2 inventory at time t, which is given by the previous inventory M_{t-1} minus the decay of inventory added to its pre-industrial level M_{pre} plus the share β of current emissions Em_t that adds to the stock of CO_2. The parameter τ reflects the average duration of CO_2 in the atmosphere ($\tau = 120$ years according to the International Panel on Climate Change IPCC); therefore $1/\tau = 0.0083$ is the estimated rate of decay per year. As to β, Nordhaus (1994) estimates an OLS regression to obtain $\beta = 0.64$. Therefore, 64% of CO_2 emissions end up in the atmosphere rather than being sequestered by oceans and notably trees.[3]

Once the tolerable concentration of CO_2 equivalents is fixed, GHG emission trajectories can be calculated using Eq. (10.1). These trajectories have the property that annual reductions need to be larger the later they begin (see Fig. 10.4). According to Stern (2006, p. 201), GHG emissions would have to reach their maximum before 2025 and then decline at rates between -3 and -4% per year if the tolerable GHG concentration is set at 550 ppmv CO_2 equivalents. Along this path, the GHG stock should not exceed 400 ppmv by 2015. In view of the 390 ppmv concentration of CO_2 in that year cited above, there is not much time left to act.

The trajectories shown in Fig. 10.4 derive from welfare economics very much like the models of optimal resource depletion discussed in Sect. 6.3. While the constraint here is not the stock of resources but the maximum tolerable GHG inventory, social time preference plays a role again. It governs the speed with which fuels causing GHG emissions need to be substituted by capital. Moreover, the pace and direction of expected factor-augmenting technological change is important (see Sect. 5.4).

---

[3]More sophisticated models also take the complex physical and chemical exchange between atmosphere, oceans, and land surfaces into account.

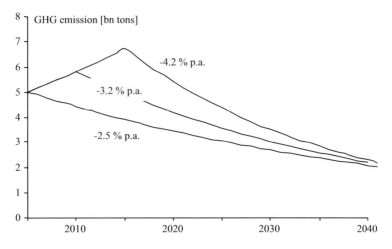

Fig. 10.4 GHG emission trajectories

Once the amount of tolerable emissions per year is determined, its distribution among claimants needs to be agreed upon, resulting in emission rights (also called emission allowances or permits). Several very different approaches exist:

- The grandfathering approach allocates permits according to emissions in a base period (e.g. the year 1990). It favors countries and industries with high emissions in the base year to the detriment of those with low emissions.
- The benchmark approach allocates allowances to industries such as power generation, production of steel and other base materials, transportation, and housing. Since the level of activity (measured e.g. by turnover) needs to be accounted for, rich countries stand to receive more emission allowances than poor countries.
- The egalitarian approach sets a uniform per-capita level of emissions. It therefore allocates permits predominantly to countries with large populations, typically poor ones.

10.3 Markets for Emission Rights

Any initial distribution of emission rights may be modified if rights are tradable. In keeping with the Coase theorem, this results in Pareto improvement (see Sect. 7.1). Emission trade would not only generate income for poorer countries through the sale of excess emission rights but also contribute to the overall efficiency of GHG abatement strategies. Figure 10.5 illustrates the argument. Let two companies cause certain amounts of emissions prior to the allocation of emission allowances. These amounts are determined by a marginal cost of abatement effort equal to zero, implying that neither company makes any effort. As soon as they begin to make

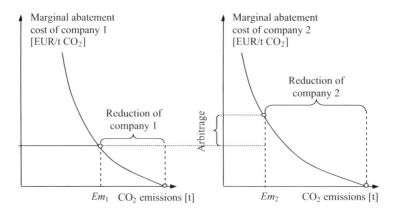

Fig. 10.5 Marginal emission abatement costs for two companies

effort designed to reduce emissions, they incur some cost of abatement. Let the marginal cost of these efforts increase when emissions are to be reduced. This assumption can be justified by noting that avoiding the first ton of e.g. CO_2 emissions usually does not cost much whereas avoiding another ton after a reduction by 100 tons becomes quite costly. Note that their marginal cost schedules usually differ. Let company 2 face more quickly increasing marginal cost than does company 1; for instance, it may have to pay higher wages to specialists who operate its abatement technology.

Now let the two companies obtain emission rights Em_1 and Em_2, respectively which are insufficient to cover emissions. Both companies therefore must reduce emissions, starting of course with the least costly measures (in terms of cost per ton of CO_2 avoided). In this way, they move up their respective marginal cost schedule until the remaining amount of emissions equals their respective permits Em_1 and Em_2. In the example shown in Fig. 10.5, this means that company 2 incurs much higher marginal cost for reaching its target than company 1. Its total abatement cost, given by the area below the marginal cost curve, is also higher.

For company 2, it would make economic sense to buy extra emission rights which would prevent it from moving up its marginal cost curve this far. It would be prepared to pay the marginal cost avoided for each permit. Company 1 in turn still benefits from its low marginal cost of abatement at Em_1. It would therefore have an incentive to reduce its emissions even further, enabling it to sell emission rights. It has an incentive to do so as long as the price for a permit paid by company 2 exceeds its marginal cost of abatement. Therefore, the difference in marginal cost at the respective values Em_1 and Em_2 creates scope for arbitrage trading which is profitable for both companies.

This arbitrage (characterizing a so-called cap-and-trade program) implies that company 1 reduces emissions beyond its allocation of rights Em_1, in return receiving revenue from selling them to company 2. On the other hand, company 2 purchases emission rights as long they are cheaper than its marginal abatement cost. In the optimum, arbitrage is eliminated through trade, resulting in equality of marginal abatement cost for both companies.[4]

In a dynamic perspective, the cap-and-trade program may motivate companies to intensify their emission abatement efforts. If successful, these efforts cause a downward shift of the marginal cost curves shown in Fig. 10.5. This has two consequences, which may occur in combination. The given amount of emission rights (and hence the emission target) can be attained at a lower cost; or at a given cost, the amount of emission rights can be reduced, reflecting a more ambitious target in terms of GHG concentration in the atmosphere.

Note that the introduction of a cap-and-trade program is not possible without the intervention of governments, who must determine the legal entities obliged to take part in it. In addition they need to verify emission reports and impose sanctions on those failing to comply. In the case of the emission trade system created by the European Union (EU-ETS; EU Commission 2003), a trading period extends over several years, presently from 2013 to 2020 and later on, from 2021 to 2030. Within a trading period, a shortfall of emission rights can be compensated by emission rights pertaining to the following year, whereas an excess of rights can be used not only during the following year but also during the entire next trading period. This raises the issue of the optimal length of a trading period: If the period is too long, the immediate incentive for reducing CO_2 emissions may be weak; if it is too short, the system does not incentivize investments that need time to be realized. Finally, governments must decide how the emission rights are to be distributed (see Sect. 10.2).

10.3.1 Prices for CO_2 Emission Rights

The European CO_2 emission trading system (EU-ETS) started in 2005. In its first year, it generated a volume of trade in excess of 320 mn tons of CO_2 emission rights along with financial transactions worth 8.2 bn EUR (Capoor and Ambrosi 2006, p. 13). Traders were not only operators of coal-fired power stations and steel works but also investment bankers.

As shown in Fig. 10.6, CO_2 prices shot up to almost 30 EUR/tons in 2005 but plunged to just about zero by 2007 (see below for an explanation). The jump back to prices above 25 EUR/tons in 2008 can be attributed to an increase in the fine for missing the target (or for failure to purchase a sufficient amount of emission rights, respectively) from 40 to 100 EUR/tons pursuant the European Directive 2003/87/EC (EU Commission 2003). In 2011 prices dropped again, likely because aviation

---

[4]Speculative trade may dominate markets for emission rights, depending on the expectations of market participants. If an increase in the price of certificates is expected, speculators go long (i.e. purchase rights in excess of marginal abatement cost) and *vice versa*. If their expectations turn out to be right, speculators make a profit, otherwise they suffer a loss.

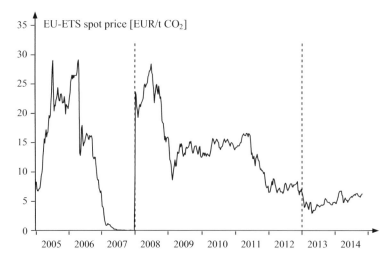

Fig. 10.6 Prices of CO_2 emission rights (data source: EEX)

was to be brought into EU-ETS in 2012, with 85% of the rights given away free of charge, however.

Since then, CO_2 prices have been consistently below 10 EUR/tons. According to the argument expounded above, this level should correspond to the marginal abatement cost of the last project that is required to meet the current European CO_2 emission target (derived from the GHG reduction target of 20% between 1990 and 2020). Such projects could be investments in energy-efficient production facilities but also in power plants that use natural gas or renewables instead of coal. At 10 EUR/tons CO_2, the wholesale price of hard coal would increase by 41%, from 0.8 to 1.13 EUR ct/kWh (see Table 10.5). By way of contrast, natural gas would become only 9% more expensive, from a higher base value of 2.2 EUR ct/kWh, however. At the resulting price of 2.4 EUR ct/kWh, natural gas is still too expensive to induce fuel switching.

This situation is likely to persist because on European markets, the price of coal has been low compared to that of natural gas for several years and may remain so even in the face of a more ambitious GHG policy (see Fig. 10.2). In addition, CO_2 prices during the first 10 years of EU-ETS have been rather volatile, causing risk-averse investors to shy away from projects designed to lower marginal abatement costs. Nevertheless, the European Union expects to achieve its GHG targets for 2020 (in spite of a substantial increase in German CO_2 emissions due to the country's '*Energiewende*') even in the absence of major growth in pertinent investment (EEA 2015). In fact, there are several options for reducing CO_2 emissions without investing in abatement technology. One is to move (parts of) the production from the European Union to regions without a CO_2 cap-and-trade system; another, to scale back electricity generation by coal-fired plants and to purchase power from outside the European Union (see Sect. 12.2).

10.3 Markets for Emission Rights

Table 10.5 Energy wholesale prices in Germany given a CO_2 price of 10 EUR/tons

	Carbon content		Assumed wholesale energy price	Price markup (10 EUR/tons CO_2)
	(kg CO_2 per GJ)	(kg CO_2 per kWh)	(EUR ct/kWh)	(%)
Lignite	108	0.39	0.6	65
Hard coal	93	0.33	0.8	41
Heavy heating oil	78	0.28	1.2	23
Fuel oil	74	0.27	1.9	14
Natural gas	55	0.20	2.2	9

Data source: Umweltbundesamt (2005)

If participants in the market for CO_2 permits expect these alternatives to abatement to ensure that the EU-ETS is long at the end of the trading period, they abstain from purchasing emission rights while their price is high. This thought suggests that the CO_2 price is not anchored in the marginal cost of CO_2 abatement but rather depends on the market situation expected at the end of the trading period. A short market means that some companies cannot come up with enough emission rights and must pay the penalty of 100 EUR/tons (European Directive 2003/87/EC, EU Commission 2003). Therefore, they are willing to pay as much as the sum of the forward price plus this penalty for emission rights because they are obliged to make up for the shortfall of permits during the following trading period. Conversely, there is no reason to pay more than the forward price if the market is long since excess permits can be used later.

This argument provides an explanation of the price drop in April 2006 (see Fig. 10.6): Until that date, most market participants had assumed the market to be short at the end of the first trading period 2005–2007. Yet in April 2006, the European Commission reported that in 2005 available emission rights had exceeded emissions by about 60,000 tons. As these rights could be used until the end of 2007, there was no doubt that the market would be long at the end of the first trading period, causing CO_2 prices to be low until its end. Developments during the second trading period 2008–2012 can be explained in a similar way. Before September 2008 most market participants had expected a short market by the end of 2012 but revised their in view of the financial crisis and the ensuing recession in Europe. They (correctly) predicted a drop in the demand for electricity and hence in the demand for coal. Since the market would almost certainly be long at the end of the trading period, there was no reason to hoard emission rights; accordingly, the CO_2 price plunged from almost 30 EUR/tons to a minimum of 5 EUR/tons.

Many observers argue that the EU-ETS has failed because it cannot ensure CO_2 prices that are high enough to force coal-fueled power generation out of market. However, the EU-ETS was not invented to guarantee a certain CO_2 price but to reach ambitious emission reduction targets at the lowest possible economic cost. Since these targets have been met so far, the system has been rather successful—even more successful than originally thought. This is reflected in low CO_2 prices.

As long as the basic cap-and-trade principle of the EU-ETS is not abandoned, politicians can bring about a substantial increase in CO_2 prices by making market participants believe that the ETS market will be short at the end of the next trading period, e.g. by introducing more ambitious emission reduction targets. However, if market participants believe the market to be short at the end of the trading period, CO_2 prices will be close to the penalty of 100 EUR/tons or even exceed it, resulting in disadvantages for the international competitiveness of European industry.

10.3.2 Clean Dark Spread

In quite general terms, an excess of the sales price over marginal cost indicates an incentive to increase to increase production (see Sect. 1.2.2). It also approximates the profit margin since marginal cost usually is not much above average cost. In the case of coal-fired electricity generation, the difference between the sales price and the marginal cost of the fuel was originally called dark spread DS. In Eq. (10.2) below, p_{el} denotes the sales price of electricity (in EUR/MWh; see Sect. 12.2.3), while the purchase price of coal p_{coal} (given in EUR/MWh fuel) is divided by the fuel efficiency ω of the coal-fired power plant,

$$DS = p_{el} - \frac{p_{coal}}{\omega}. \tag{10.2}$$

Therefore, the higher the fuel efficiency of coal-fired generation, the cheaper is coal as a fuel. However, it is not a clean fuel; accordingly, the so-called clean dark spread CDS is calculated by adding $\alpha \cdot p_{CO2}$, the cost of CO_2 emission rights required for generating electricity to the efficiency-adjusted price of coal,

$$CDS = p_{elek} - \left(\frac{p_{coal}}{\omega} + \alpha \cdot p_{CO_2}\right). \tag{10.3}$$

The factor α represents the amount of CO_2 emissions (in tons) associated with the generation of one MWh of electricity. Among other things, it also depends on the fuel efficiency ω of the power plant. The (clean) dark spread is defined for power stations running on natural gas in an analogous way.

Since the marginal cost of electricity generation comprises more than the (efficiency-adjusted) price of the fuel and the cost of CO_2 permits, $CDS > 0$ is a necessary (but not sufficient) condition for a power station fueled by coal or natural gas to be viable in the long term (see Sects. 1.2.1 and 12.2.2). For German power stations fueled by hard coal, this condition was mostly met during the period from 2000 to 2014 (see Fig. 10.7). Indeed, the wholesale price of electricity moves largely in parallel with that of coal and the cost of CO_2 emission permits, the two major components of marginal cost. In view of the low own-price elasticity of the demand for electricity, an increase in marginal cost results in an almost commensurate increase in the market price (see Sect. 1.2.1). Thus, a higher CO_2 price drives up the wholesale price of electricity. This is even true of the period from 2005 to

10.3 Markets for Emission Rights

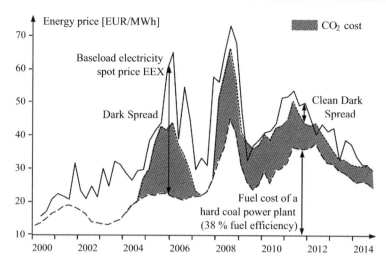

Fig. 10.7 German (clean) dark spread between 2001 and 2014

2007, when the German government gave emission rights to electricity generators for free (CO_2 prices represented an opportunity cost for plant operators). As argued in Sect. 10.3.1, generators expected the market for emission rights to be short by the end of the first ETS trading period, causing their price to be positive up to 2007, when it became clear that the market would be long.

These observations suggest that the price of electricity and the marginal cost of coal as given by Eq. (10.3) may be driven by a common stochastic trend. In fact, the 169 monthly day-ahead electricity prices p_{el} and the marginal cost of German coal-fired power stations (with an assumed fuel efficiency of 38%) turn out to be stationary after differentiation with respect to time (see Sect. 9.3.2). Therefore, the two time series are integrated of order one, and the appropriate statistical tests do not reject the following cointegration equations,

$$\text{Baseload electricity price} \quad p_{el\_base} = 1.31 \cdot \left(\frac{p_{coal}}{\omega} + 0.88 \cdot p_{CO_2}\right);$$
$$\text{Off-peak electricity price} \quad p_{el\_offpeak} = 1.09 \cdot \left(\frac{p_{coal}}{\omega} + 0.88 \cdot p_{CO_2}\right). \tag{10.4}$$

According to the first equation, the CDS for German baseload power traded on the spot market was 31% of marginal generation cost (see Sect. 12.2.3). Since baseload capacities are also needed to meet peak load demand, whose own-price elasticity of demand is particularly low (see Filippini 2011), this high value is intuitive. It also implies that an increase in the price of CO_2 emission rights can be passed on to buyers more than proportionally ($1.15 = 1.31 \cdot 0.88$). By way of contrast, the *CDS* reduces to 9% for off-peak power, whose own-price elasticity of demand is higher. Accordingly, a higher price of CO_2 emission cannot be fully passed on to buyers ($0.96 = 1.09 \cdot 0.88$).

According to Fig. 10.7 *DS* and *CDS* have declined during the observation period. This is the likely consequence of successful efforts by the regulator designed to reduce the market power of German generators as well as the growing importance of renewable electricity generation, which both put pressure on wholesale electricity prices. While the clean dark spread was still positive most of the time up to 2014, it was no longer sufficient to justify investment in coal-fired power plants (see Sect. 12.3.3 for a discussion of capacity investment in deregulated markets for electricity). It is important to note that this situation cannot be attributed to the EU-ETS, as higher CO_2 prices can be passed on just about one-to-one to the purchasers of electricity on the wholesale market, as shown above.

10.3.3 Coal Perspectives

Prices for CO_2 emission rights have been quite low in recent times (see Fig. 10.6 again). They thus do not create an economic incentive to develop clean coal technologies that would allow stabilizing and reducing greenhouse gas emissions while using the abundant global coal resources. In addition, coal-fired electricity generation has average fuel efficiencies below 35%. If it could be raised to 45% (the value characterizing modern power stations), global CO_2 emissions from this source could be reduced by 25%. Given that global CO_2 emissions amounted to an estimated 14.8 bn tons in 2013 (IEA 2016), the reduction would be at least 3.7 bn tons per year.

However, at CO_2 prices above 50 to 70 EUR/tons, analysts predict that carbon capture would become an attractive option for operators of coal-fired power plants. The following alternatives are being discussed.

- Post-combustion capture: The CO_2 is washed out of the flue gas after combustion. A retrofitting of existing power plants is possible, but with the downside of reduced fuel efficiency.
- Pre-combustion capture: CO_2 is removed from coal (and fossil fuels more generally) before combustion. One option is to use integrated coal gasification technologies (IGCC) such as Fischer-Tropsch synthesis which produces so-called synthesis gas under high temperature and pressure. The gas is a mixture of hydrogen H_2, carbon monoxide CO, carbon dioxide CO_2, and smaller amounts of other gaseous components, such as methane CH_4. The so-called water-gas shift reaction uses the remaining CO and water H_2O as inputs that are converted into H_2 and CO_2. By capturing and separating the CO_2, the remaining H_2-rich fuel can be used in combustion processes without any greenhouse gas emissions.
- Flue gas capture: Coal is burned using pure oxygen O_2 rather than air. The flue gas contains only steam and CO_2, which can easily be separated.

For these technologies to be environmentally friendly, a release of the captured CO_2 into the atmosphere must be avoided. Apart from non-energetic uses of CO_2, a solution widely discussed is underground storage (carbon capture and storage CCS). This technology is being applied on a large scale in advanced oil and gas extraction, with exhausted gas fields serving as storage locations. Yet carbon-capture technologies are generally far from being mature, a state of affairs unlikely to change as long as the price of CO_2 emissions remains low.

References

Böhringer, C., & Rutherford, T. (2000). *Decomposing the cost of Kyoto. A global CGE analysis of multilateral policy impacts*. Mannheim: Zentrum für Europäische Wirtschaftsforschung ZEW.

BP. (2014). *BP statistical review of world energy*. Retrieved from www.bp.com/statisticalreview/

Bretschger, L. (2015). *Greening economy, graying society*. Zurich: CER-ETH Press.

Capoor, K., & Ambrosi, P. (2006). *State and trends of the carbon market 2006*. Washington: The World Bank.

EEA. (2015). *SOER 2015–The European environment—State and outlook 2015*. Copenhagen: European Environment Agency.

EU Commission. (2003). Directive 2003/87/EC Establishing a Scheme for Greenhouse Gas Emission Allowance Trading Within the Community and Amending Council Directive 96/61/EC. Brussels. *Official Journal of the European Union, L 275*, 32–46.

Fachagentur Nachwachsende Rohstoffe. (2005). *Basisdaten Bioenergie Deutschland (Basic data on bioenergy in Germany)*. Gülzow. Retrieved from www.nachwachsende-rohstoffe.de/

Filippini, M. (2011). Short- and long-run time-of-use price elasticities in Swiss residential electricity demand. *Energy Policy, 39*(10), 5811–5817.

IEA. (2016). *World energy outlook special report 2016: Energy and air pollution*. Paris: International Energy Agency/OECD.

IPCC. (1990). *Climate change: A key global issue. Overview and conclusions*. Geneva, Nairobi: World Meteorological Organization, United Nations Environment Programme.

IPCC. (2014). *Climate change 2014 synthesis report*. Geneva, Nairobi: World Meteorological Organization, United Nations Environment Programme. Retrieved from www.ipcc.ch/report/ar5/

Nordhaus, W. D. (1994). *Managing the global commons. The economics of climate change*. Cambridge, MA: MIT Press.

Nordhaus, W., & Boyer, J. (2000). *Warming the world: Economics of global warming*. Cambridge, MA: MIT Press.

Stern, N. (2006). *The economics of climate change*. Cambridge: Cambridge University Press.

Umweltbundesamt. (2005). *Emissionsfaktoren und Kohlenstoffgehalte (Emission Factors and Carbon Contents)*. Berlin: Deutsche Emissionshandelsstelle. Retrieved from www.dehst.de/

Uranium and Nuclear Energy

11

The peaceful use of nuclear energy began in the 1950s with the assumption that it would make electricity abundantly available at low cost. However, mistrust of this energy technology has been salient from its beginnings. After the nuclear catastrophe of 1986 in Chernobyl, Ukraine, public acceptance of nuclear energy plummeted in industrial countries even though the Chernobyl reactor was of a very different design from those common in Western models. The following issues are addressed in this chapter:

- What are the risks of accidents in nuclear power plants from a technical perspective?
- What are the dimensions of potential damages?
- What type of risk assessment does the economic model lead to in the case of nuclear power?
- What insurance premiums are to be expected if nuclear risks are to be internalized?
- Are the risks of nuclear power plants insurable at all?

If a reassessment of nuclear power is taking place today, it is because greenhouse gas emissions and the need for an active climate protection policy combine with concerns regarding energy supply security. Such a reassessment gives rise to an additional set of questions:

- How long are uranium reserves expected to last?
- What are the costs of uranium fuels, and what are their major components?
- Is the industrial structure of the uranium market competitive or rather monopolistic?

Finally, there are issues such as the secure final disposal of radioactive waste as well the dangers of proliferation of nuclear fuels for military purposes. These aspects are touched on briefly in this chapter, while the comparative efficiency of nuclear power plants in electricity generation will be discussed in Sect. 12.2.

The variables and symbols used in this chapter are:

A	Activity of a radioactive substance
av	Pratt-Arrow measure of (absolute) risk aversion
D_k	Damage associated with damaging event k
D_{PSA}	Damage according to the probabilistic safety analysis (PSA)
$E[D]$	Expected overall damage (accident value)
μ	Expected loss at the individual level
N	Number of atoms not yet disintegrated/decayed
POP	Number of individuals exposed to an accident risk
R	Risk assessment
σ^2	Variance of damage
$T_{1/2}$	Half-life of radio activity
U	Utility
W	Wealth
w_k	Probability of occurrence of damage scenario k, per year

11.1 The Foundations of Nuclear Technology

The technical application of nuclear power is based on the discovery of Albert Einstein at the beginning of the twentieth century, stating that mass can be transformed into energy. Energy extraction from mass could 1 day become possible through the fusion of light atoms (for example, hydrogen) to heavier atoms (for example, helium). In contrast, contemporary nuclear power generation uses fission of rather heavy atoms (with an uneven number of neutrons) into lighter atoms. The most important milestones in the development of nuclear technology are listed in Table 11.1. The 'Atoms for Peace' speech of 1953 epitomizes the significant governmental support for nuclear technology. Initially motivated by military interests, later made available for civilian purposes, the large-scale application of light-water technology (which dominates the present electricity generation of nuclear power plants) would not have materialized.

In nuclear power plants, thermal energy produced by nuclear fission is used to activate a Carnot process (see Sect. 2.2.2). The most widespread commercial reactor type is the light-water reactor (LWR), which comes in two common variants. In the boiling water reactor, steam with a pressure of about 70 bar and a temperature of 290 °C is led directly to a steam turbine. Having done its work, the steam cools down to become water. In the pressurized water reactor, there are two cooling circuits, one of them separated from the nuclear reaction. A pressure of 150–160 bar in the primary cooling circuit prevents the vaporization of the water, which is conducted into a steam generator. There, it is cooled down before returning to the nuclear reactor. The steam generator produces saturated steam, which drives

11.1 The Foundations of Nuclear Technology

Table 11.1 Milestones for the development of nuclear power

1896	Discovery of radioactivity by Antoine H. Becquerel
1897	Separation of radium from uranium by Marie and Pierre Curie
1938	Proof of the technical feasibility of nuclear fission by Otto Hahn and Fritz Strassmann
1941	First demonstration of the chain reaction by Enrico Fermi
1945	Dropping of atomic bombs on Hiroshima and Nagasaki (both in Japan)
	Development of the nuclear fusion bomb
1953	'Atoms for Peace' speech by President Dwight D. Eisenhower, who offered to share nuclear power technology with countries who are willing to abandon the development of nuclear weapons
1970	Non-proliferation treaty of nuclear weapons, monitored by the International Atomic Energy Agency (IAEA) in Vienna (Austria)
1979	Accident of the nuclear reactor Three Mile Island in Harrisburg (United States)
1986	Chernobyl catastrophe (Ukraine)
2011	Reactor accident in Fukushima (Japan)

a steam turbine for the generation of electricity in a secondary cooling circuit. This separation of the nuclear from the conventional cycle constitutes a safety feature.

About 90% of the 440 nuclear reactors in operation worldwide are of the LWR type. Installed capacities of a block vary between 300 and 1600 MW, compared to 8 MW of the wind turbine with the highest performance as of 2016. In many cases, several blocks are combined to form a nuclear site. Total installed net capacity of nuclear power plants reaches 370,000 MW worldwide, representing 14% of thermal power plant capacity. In 2014, nuclear power plants generated almost 2.6 mn MWh of electrical energy (16% of global power generation, with Europe accounting for 3.3 mn MWh). Particularly in the 1980s, electricity generation through nuclear power plants boomed in response to the two oil price shocks of 1973 and 1979. However, the Chernobyl accident of 1986 caused most Western countries to impose a moratorium or at least slow down on new power plant construction. Until recently, the increase in nuclear energy production since 1990 has been mainly the result of a more efficient operation of existing reactors in the United States and in Europe.

11.1.1 Radioactivity

The radioactivity of a substance is measured by the amount of radioactive decay per second (Becquerel). With N_t being the number of atoms not yet disintegrated, radioactivity A_t is equal to

$$A_t = \frac{\ln(2)}{T_{1/2}} \cdot N_t \quad (11.1)$$

with $T_{1/2}$ denoting the so-called half-life time at which the radioactivity of a substance is halved.

Three types of radioactivity can be distinguished.

- α radiation (helium nuclei): An α particle usually provides an amount of energy between 0.005 to 0.006 eV (electronvolt; 1 eV = 1.6 · 10^{-19} J). This type of radiation is short-range only so it can easily be shielded, e.g. using a sheet of paper.
- β radiation (electrons): The energy of β particles lies in the range of 0.0001–0.002 eV and can be absorbed by a metal plate with a thickness of a few millimeters.
- γ radiation (photons, i.e. quants of electromagnetic radiation): γ radiation derives from the excess energy produced by nuclear decay in the fission processes (which also gives rise to α or β radiation). Its energy lies in the range of 0.0001 and 0.005 eV. Shielding from it is technically demanding and requires heavy materials such as lead or concrete.

To account for these differences, one distinguishes between the energy dose (Gray, Gy) and the radiation equivalent dose (Sievert, Sv). The latter attributes a weight of 1 to β and γ radiation but of 20 to α radiation in order to reflect its particular biological harmfulness. In Europe, average natural radiation exposure of the human body is around 0.002 Sv per year. In addition, medical exposure through x-ray diagnostics in particular amounts to the same magnitude (Table 11.2).

The energy of the emitted particles is absorbed by the surrounding matter. Thereby the atoms of these substances become ionized, causing a temperature increase. The ionization of living cells can change and even destroy them, resulting in radiation sickness. Inside the cell nucleus, radiation can also cause mutations and genetic damage.

With regard to the living body, a distinction is made between external and internal radiation. Internal radiation is particularly dangerous, because it is related to the absorption of radioactive substances by the organism and thus to a continuous exposure to radiation. The health impacts depend on the organ accumulating the radioactive substances and on the duration of exposure.

Human beings experience radiation sickness from a short-term equivalent dose of 0.5 Sv onwards, while cell mutations can already occur at a much lower value. The living organism has the ability to partly repair damages caused by radioactive radiation, provided overall radioactive exposure does not exceed certain limits. As

Table 11.2 Radioactivity units

Feature	Unit		Description
Activity	Becquerel	Bq	1 decay per second
Energy dose	Gray	Gy	Energy absorbed by matter (J/kg)
Equivalent dose	Sievert	Sv	Biologic impact of the energy absorbed by the matter (J/kg)
	Rem	= 0.01 Sv	Outdated unit

there is no possibility of determining these limits experimentally, one falls back on the assumption that natural radioactive radiation is tolerable, neglecting large geographical differences.

11.1.2 Uranium as the Dominant Fuel for Nuclear Power

Due to its easy fissionability, the uranium isotope ^{235}U is the most important nuclear fuel. The raw material is natural uranium ore, which consists of the isotope ^{238}U (99.29%) and the isotope ^{235}U (0.71%). The uranium isotope ^{235}U can be split into lighter atoms by bombarding it with slow and low-energy neutrons. Fission of one ^{235}U nucleus releases $3.2 \cdot 10^{-11}$ J of heat (a consequence of the so-called mass defect). With each fission, two or three new neutrons are created which induce the decay of further ^{235}U-nuclei in the guise of a chain reaction. With the help of moderators, the neutrons are slowed down. In the LWR, the moderator is natural water, which is also used for discharging the heat produced by nuclear fission from the reactor vessel.[1] The chain reaction is controlled and can be stopped using so-called control rods made of cadmium that partially absorb the neutrons.

Producing uranium fuel is technically complex and associated with risks of radiation. Uranium mining constitutes the first step of the production chain. The extracted uranium oxide (U_3O_8, so-called yellowcake) has a uranium concentration of 60–85%. To achieve the required degree of purity of 99.95%, the uranium ore is dissolved in nitric acid, filtered, treated with chemical solvents, and reconverted into uranium oxide.

In order to maintain the chain reaction in light-water reactors, concentration of ^{235}U isotopes in the nuclear fuel needs to be increased from 0.71% to 3 to 4%.[2] For this enrichment process, uranium oxide has to be converted into the gaseous uranium hexafluoride UF_6, which is channeled to gas centrifuges. At this point the separation of ^{235}U from 238 U isotopes proceeds by taking advantage of a difference in their molecular mass. It takes place in so-called separative work units (SWUs) and requires 50 kWh/kg of electricity. The enriched uranium hexafluoride is chemically reconverted into uranium oxide powder UO_2, to be processed to uranium fuel rods.

According to Table 11.3, the production cost of uranium fuel is 1880 USD/t UO_2 as of 2016. One kilogram uranium oxide powder UO_2 generates about 3400 GJ of heat (944.6 MWh heat), equivalent to about 315 MWh of electricity. Thus, the fuel cost of nuclear power amounts to 5.97 USD/MWh or 5.43 EUR/MWh, a rather low figure compared to fossil power plants (e.g. 40 EUR/MWh for gas-fired power plants).[3]

---

[1]Other possible moderators are heavy water D_2O or graphite ^{12}C; in this case, the chain reaction also proceeds using natural uranium.

[2]For nuclear weapons an enrichment level of >90% is necessary. Thus, weapons-grade material can be converted to nuclear fuel by blending it with depleted uranium.

[3]A currency exchange rate of 1.1 USD/EUR is assumed for 2016.

Table 11.3 Unit cost of uranium fuel production

Process	Quantity per kg fuel (kg)	Average price (USD/kg)	Average price (USD/tons UO$_2$)
U$_3$O$_8$ mining	8.9	97	862
Conversion	7.5	16	120
Enrichment	7.3 SWU[a]	82	599
Fuel assembly for production	1	300	300
Total			1880

[a]SWU: Separative work units; data source: WNA (2016)

11.1.3 Nuclear Waste

Table 11.4 provides an overview of the transformation of 100 t of uranium fuel during a 3-year period of use in a nuclear reactor. Only part of the isotope ^{235}U is split into lighter materials that can be used for generation. In addition, radioactive plutonium is produced from the isotope ^{238}U, which partly decays during the 3-year period, releasing heat.

Unlike the source material, used nuclear fuel is highly radioactive. It produces large amounts of residual heat (around 250 MW$_{th}$ in a nuclear power plant of 1400 MW$_{el}$ capacity) even after the reactor is turned off. This heat has to be dissipated to prevent destruction of the reactor containment, causing the release of radioactive material into the environment.

Usually, nuclear fuel rods are removed from the reactor after a 3-year period of use. At that time, the rods contain about 35 different chemical elements with about 300 radioactive isotopes. After their removal, the spent rods are first stored in a water basin for several decades before being transferred to a reprocessing facility or a final waste deposit. During interim storage, short-lived isotopes lose most of their radioactivity. In contrast, plutonium isotopes (so-called transuranium isotopes) with their long half-life represent a source of long-term nuclear radiation. Table 11.5 shows the time profiles of the respective sources of radioactivity.

During the reprocessing of used nuclear fuel rods, plutonium and unspent uranium isotope 235 U are removed, to be used in the production of new fuel rods which are of the mixed oxide (MOX) type. As a consequence, radioactivity of the remaining nuclear waste diminishes over time, thus reducing the cost of final waste disposal. On the other hand, reprocessing poses considerable safety challenges. It is also much more expensive than the direct disposal of nuclear waste, even when crediting the nuclear fuel recycled. Therefore, direct disposal of nuclear waste is the preferred alternative in many countries.

For a classification of radioactive waste, besides radioactivity the heat arising from radioactive decay is also of importance. Given that the increase in temperature should not exceed 3 °C for geophysical reasons, about 95% of the volume of waste can be stored in a final deposit. This value includes waste associated with the later demolition of the power plant.

11.1 The Foundations of Nuclear Technology

Table 11.4 Inventory of 100 tons uranium fuel after 3 years in a light-water reactor

Input	Reaction	Output (after 3 years)
3300 kg ^{235}U	(no reaction)	756 kg ^{235}U
	Capture of neutrons	458 kg ^{236}U
	Fission	2100 kg fission products
96,700 kg ^{238}U	(no reaction)	94,200 kg ^{238}U
	Breeding reaction	900 kg plutonium Pu
	Capture of neutrons, α, β decay	70 kg Np, Am, Cm
	Fission	1500 kg fission products of Pu

Source: Staub (1991)

Table 11.5 Radioactivity of 100 tons uranium fuel and waste

| Isotope | Before usage | Years after removal of waste from the nuclear reactor | | | |
		1	100	1000	100,000
	(10^{12} Bq, i.e. decays per second)				
Uranium ^{238}U	44	43	43	43	43
Uranium ^{235}U	10	2	2	2	2
Plutonium ^{238}Pu	–	430,000	190,000	0	0
Plutonium ^{239}Pu	–	40,000	40,000	40,000	2335
Plutonium ^{240}Pu	–	70,000	70,000	50,000	2
Plutonium ^{241}Pu	–	13,700,000	70,000	0	0
Plutonium ^{242}Pu	–	200	200	200	167
Krypton ^{85}Kr	–	20,400,000	30,000	0	0
Strontium ^{90}Sr	–	17,400,000	1600,000	0	0
Cesium ^{134}Cs	–	37,000,000	0	0	0
Cesium ^{137}Cs	–	30,200,000	3,100,000	0	0
Neptunium ^{237}Np	–	46	46	46	44
Americium ^{241}Am	–	44,400	38,200	2150	0
Americium ^{243}Am	–	1000	1000	828	0.08
Curium ^{245}Cm	–	1400	1400	1200	0.1

Source: Staub (1991)

However, the remaining 5% of radioactive substances (being isotopes) contain 99% of the radioactivity, calling for a staggered system of artificial and natural barriers in geologically suitable final deposits for highly radioactive waste. Exposure to radiation at the surface should not exceed the limit of 0.1–0.3 millisievert (10–30 millirem) per year. At present, no final storage facility satisfying this requirement is in operation anywhere around the globe, implying that the cost of storage can only be estimated. According to the World Nuclear Association, it is in the range of 1 EUR/MWh generated electricity (in the case of direct waste disposal) and 1.50 EUR/MWh (after reprocessing). At a maximum, this amounts to one-fourth of the production cost of uranium fuel.

To finance the final disposal of radioactive substances and the dismantling of nuclear power plants after their shutdown, plant operators often accrue reserves themselves or pay a certain amount of money per MWh to a public fund designed to cover the future cost of waste disposal and plant dismantling. National governments decide which of the two modalities applies, which differ in terms of their cost implications for nuclear power. Although this creates scope for distortion of competition in the energy industry, the European Commission has so far abstained from issuing a directive aiming at harmonization.

11.2 Uranium Market

The Nuclear Energy Agency of the OECD and the International Atomic Energy Agency (IAEA) of the United Nations publish a statistical compilation of global uranium reserves in biannual intervals, based on data provided by about 20 - uranium-producing countries (see Nuclear Energy Agency 2014). Taking into account that for a resource to become an economically relevant reserve, its sales price must at least cover the cost of extraction, several cost levels are distinguished. For instance, at a unit cost of 130 USD/kg U_3O_8 (a rather high value compared to extraction cost in 2016 according to Table 11.3), known uranium reserves are about 5.9 mn tons.

Global demand by nuclear power plants currently amounts to roughly 50,000 tons of natural uranium per year (see Table 11.6). If this figure is compared to recoverable uranium reserves, a static range of more than 100 years can be inferred.

Per MW of power plant capacity, the natural uranium requirement equals about 160 kg on average per year (compare this to the 250,000 tons of hard coal per MW and year required by a typical coal-fired plant). More advanced reactors are likely to have an even lower specific uranium requirement. The Swedish Oskarshamm·3 reactor with 1400 MW installed capacity may serve as an example. Following the repeal of the nuclear phase-out decision in Sweden, it was retrofitted to generate between 0.8 and 1.3 mn MWh electricity per ton of ^{235}U, depending on mode of operation. This means that its uranium requirement may be as low as 18 g/MWh, 30% below the global average cited in Table 11.6. This reduction results from an increase in thermal efficiency and a higher yield in ^{235}U-combustion, due to an enrichment of the uranium fuel to more than 4% ^{235}U.

Figure 11.1 compares the development of global military and civilian demand for uranium with that of global extraction. Between 1950 and 1970, production

Table 11.6 Global uranium demand for power generation in 2014

	Capacity	Energy
Global nuclear capacity	300,000 MW	1900 TWh
Specific ^{235}U demand	0.0124 tons/MW	1.95 tons/TWh
^{235}U demand	3700 tons/a	
Natural uranium demand	49,000 tons/a	
Specific natural uranium demand	0.16 tons/MW and a	26 g/MWh

Data source: Nuclear Energy Agency (2014)

11.2 Uranium Market

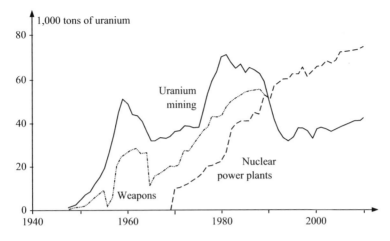

Fig. 11.1 Uranium supply and demand (source: Gerling et al. 2005)

consistently exceeded global demand, something one is unlikely to observe in a competitive market. A plausible explanation is governmental stockpiling for military purposes (note that the pertinent time series ends after 1990). Even with the advent of nuclear power plants in the late 1960s, excess production continued for two decades. Nevertheless, the price of natural uranium rose to more than 80 USD/kg during the second half of the 1970s due to expectations of a rapid expansion of global nuclear power capacities.[4] Again, governmental stockpiling played a role as well, by the U.S. Atomic Energy Commission who initially was the only supplier of enriched uranium in the western world. Westinghouse/Toshiba, the leading producer of nuclear power plants at the time, reinforced the price increase by purchasing uranium beyond its short-term requirements.

However, expectations of a bright future for nuclear power were dashed in 1979 when the accident at the pressurized water reactor of Three Mile Island (Pennsylvania, United States) occurred—with global uranium production reaching an all-time high just then. The drop in demand caused uranium production and price to fall, the latter to a level below 40 USD/kg. Pressure on price further intensified during the 1990s, when traders started selling Russian nuclear fuel on the world market. U.S. American and European restrictions of imports from Russia could not prevent a collapse to about 20 USD/kg, even though many uranium mines abandoned their production at the time. While weapons-grade uranium became available for civilian use, there was still a shortfall of uranium supply relative to current requirements of nuclear power plants.

Only after 2003 did this shortfall result in a hefty increase in the price of natural uranium. The price hike by a factor four is comparable to that in crude oil prices

---

[4]In U.S. statistics, the natural uranium price is specified in USD/lb (pound). A kilogram corresponds to a mass of 2.205 lb.

after 2000 (see Sect. 8.3). Reduced uranium exports of Russia and a series of accidents in uranium mines and processing plants contributed to this price explosion. While an acceleration of global uranium exploration and development has been observed lately, comparatively high prices are likely to persist because these investments take 5–7 years to affect production.

Uranium production is heavily concentrated regionally, with only five countries accounting for three-fourths of it, namely Canada (28%), Australia (23%), Kazakhstan (9%), Nigeria, and Russia (8% each). The United States, just like China, produce their own uranium oxide but need imports to meet their demand. France, Japan, Germany, and Great Britain are entirely dependent on imports.

Corporate concentration is marked as well, exceeding that in crude oil and coal markets. At the level of natural uranium extraction, the four largest companies currently have a joint market share of more than 60%. These are Cameco (Canada, 20%), Rio Tinto (Australia, 20%), Areva (France, 12%), and BHP Billiton (Australia and Great Britain, 9%).

At the level of uranium enrichment, the U.S. government allowed private possession of uranium only after 1968, and state monopolies have in fact persisted since then. The largest ones currently are the Russian TENEX (32% market share), the United States Enrichment Company (U.S. Department of Energy, 17%), and the French Areva (15%)—all government-controlled. Only the production of fuel rods has a competitive industry structure.

This heavy governmental involvement is the likely reason that with the exception of French Areva, there are no vertically integrated companies along the nuclear value chain in the western world. In fact, economic conditions (factor-specific assets, high transaction costs, and high supplier concentration) would favor such an industry structure (see Sects. 8.2.1 and 9.3.1). In spite of its consolidation during the 1990s, the industry is unlikely to become more vertically integrated in future in view of governmental reservations in particular against private uranium enrichment.

Operators of power plants are the customers of the producers of nuclear fuel. Even at a historically high price of 130 USD/kg natural uranium, their variable fuel costs are very low compared to coal-fired and gas-fired power plants (see Sect. 12.2.2). The cost of fuel being such a small part of the total, still higher uranium prices would not make them lose their competitiveness. In addition, most nuclear power plants are almost fully amortized, while fossil power plants are likely to be burdened by the cost of avoiding CO_2 emissions in the near future.

11.3 Risk Assessment of Nuclear Energy

Risks associated with nuclear power are of three types. First, abuse of nuclear fuels (enriched uranium, plutonium) for military and terrorist purposes needs to be prevented effectively. Second, secure final waste disposal of radioactive substances needs to be guaranteed for a long period of time. Third, incidents in nuclear power plants must not lead to the release of large quantities of radioactive substances.

11.3 Risk Assessment of Nuclear Energy

All three risks are borne only in part by the operators of nuclear power plants—and ultimately by the consumers of electricity. Therefore, they constitute external effects of a stochastic nature. Economic efficiency in the management of such risks calls for an amount of preventive effort such that its certain marginal cost equals the expected value of marginal utility (for a discussion of this condition as well as ways to attain it, see Sect. 7.3), for example by imposing an internalization tax (so-called Pigou tax; see Fig. 7.4 in Sect. 7.3.1). However, such policy measures require knowledge of both the marginal cost and marginal utility schedules. Both of these schedules are extremely difficult to estimate.

While economists generally are in favor of internalization through price ('the polluter pays' principle), they tend to prefer legal rules and norms in this instance to deal with the risks cited above.

- Theft and abuse of nuclear fuels (enriched uranium, plutonium) for military and terrorist purposes: To decrease this risk, a surveillance system for nuclear power, enrichment, and reprocessing plants was created by the International Atomic Energy Agency IAEA. However, only countries who have ratified the Treaty on the Nonproliferation of Nuclear Weapons of 1970 submit themselves to this surveillance. Furthermore, even after ratification some countries have been conducting fairly advanced clandestine nuclear weapon programs. This demonstrates that fully-fledged surveillance is not possible in the long run. Finally, nongovernmental organizations increasingly possess both the financial means and knowledge necessary to acquire and use nuclear weaponry. The proliferation of nuclear weapons is thus difficult to prevent in the long run, calling for the consideration of additional instruments in security policy. However, this issue is hardly related to the civilian use of nuclear power; indeed, countries without commercial nuclear power have been able to acquire nuclear weapons in the past. Thus, even a global phasing-out of nuclear power would not entirely eliminate the risk of proliferation.
- Final disposal of radioactive waste from nuclear power plants: Spent fuel remains highly radioactive over a period of 100,000 years (see Sect. 11.1.3, particularly Table 11.5). There are technical procedures and geological deposits that prevent release of radioactivity into the biosphere even beyond periods that humans are able to foresee. However, if a discharge of radioactivity should occur far in future, neither plant operators, nor insurance companies, nor governments can be held liable. A possible solution could be the conversion of radioactive waste into less dangerous substances through irradiation with neutrons and protons (so-called artificial nuclear transmutation). However, at present not even commercial pilot projects are under way anywhere in the world.
- Incidents in nuclear power plants: This risk category constitutes a different case. The peaceful use of nuclear power is based on the precondition that the release of radioactive substances is limited to an amount corresponding to the natural level of radioactivity. Permanent adherence to this precondition can be verified during the life of a nuclear power plant; given normal operation, it is satisfied. However, a severe incident can lead to the release of very large quantities of radioactive

substance. There are mechanic and electric systems designed to prevent this. While they are characterized by a great deal of redundancy, they may fail with a very small probability. The following section is devoted to the estimation of this probability.

11.3.1 Probabilistic Safety Analysis of Nuclear Power Plants

Probabilistic safety analysis (PSA) is a procedure to determine the annual probability with which a particular system may fail. In the case of a nuclear power plant, the system should prevent the release of the plant's radioactive inventory (the so-called source term). PSA also seeks to quantify the corresponding damages in monetary units.[5] This method, originally developed by Rasmussen et al. (1975), has become the most common procedure to calculate the operational risk of nuclear power plants (U.S. Nuclear Regulatory Commission 1991).

The results of a probabilistic safety analysis are k loss scenarios with their estimated annual probabilities of occurrence w_k and the respective damages D_k. For the case of the nuclear power plant Mühleberg in Switzerland, seven loss scenarios with an increasing source term are distinguished in Table 11.7.

The so-called expected loss is given by

$$E[D] = \sum_k D_k \cdot w_k. \qquad (11.2)$$

Expected loss $E[D]$ is a measure of financial risk commonly used in insurance; in the present context, it indicates the safety-related risk of a nuclear power plant. It is

Table 11.7 Accident scenarios for the Mühleberg nuclear power plant (Switzerland)

Source term (% of inventory)	Damage D_k (mn EUR)	Modeled frequency per year w_k	
		Given low release rates	Given high release rates
0	0	0.999992	0.9.99868
0.0005	4	$5.00 \cdot 10^{-6}$	$1.00 \cdot 10^{-4}$
0.5	4353	$1.00 \cdot 10^{-6}$	$2.00 \cdot 10^{-5}$
5.0	91,905	$1.30 \cdot 10^{-6}$	$6.67 \cdot 10^{-6}$
15.0	178,965	$4.00 \cdot 10^{-8}$	$3.33 \cdot 10^{-6}$
30.0	417,555	$1.00 \cdot 10^{-8}$	$1.00 \cdot 10^{-6}$
70.0	765,794	0	$1.00 \cdot 10^{-6}$
$E[D_{PSA}]$ (mn EUR)		0.135	2.480
Standard deviation (mn EUR)		118	961

Data source: Ott and Masuhr (1994, p. 83ff)

---

[5]This means that a value needs to be assigned to a (statistical) human life (see Sect. 7.4).

11.3 Risk Assessment of Nuclear Energy

plant-specific, depending on reactor type, safety technology employed, and reactor site (because of weather conditions and population density in its vicinity). Since radioactive inventory increases with plant capacity, $E[D]$ is usually related to the annual amount of electricity generated, a very large quantity. For this reason, the values shown in Table 11.8 are just fractions of U.S. cents per kWh.

These values (see Table 11.8) are often used as a measure of the external cost of operation imposed on society by nuclear power plants because most of the damage is suffered by individuals who have no economic relationship with the plant. They are so small that the internalization of these stochastic externalities through a Pigou tax (see Sect. 7.3.1) would not affect the competitiveness of nuclear power vis-à-vis other power generation technologies.

For many engineers and physicists associated with nuclear technology, the lack of acceptance of nuclear energy-related risks by large parts of the population seems irrational. They turn to psychologists, sociologists, political scientists, and philosophers with the request to scientifically analyze the seemingly irrational behavior of specific social groups. However, this request emanates from a neglect of standard economic theory. For simplicity, let damage be measured in terms of the number of premature deaths D occurring with probability w. There is a choice between technologies which differ with regard to these two parameters. One of them is a coal-fired plant that causes 20 premature deaths due to air pollution with probability $w = 0.05$, resulting in $E[D] = 1$ (the actual probability is much closer to $w = 1.00$, but this would complicate calculations). Another is the LWR; with probability $w = 10^{-5}$, it causes the death of 100,000 persons, resulting also in $E[D] = 1$ (both values are on the high side but simplify calculations). Now engineers and physicists associated with nuclear technology typically argue that the two technologies (and in fact all technologies and their combinations with the same expected loss of $E[D] = 1$) should be viewed as equivalent. In Fig. 11.2, they are all on the same hyperbolic locus (note that $w \cdot D = 1$ implies $w = 1/D$), constituting the feasibility frontier. Coal-based generation is represented by point C, the nuclear alternative, by point N.

Yet people have preferences regarding the choice of technology. Let there be just two types of people, I and II. Their preferences are depicted by indifference curves, along which expected utility is constant. The direction of preference is indicated by arrows which point to the origin since ($w = 0, D = 0$) constitutes the

Table 11.8 Expected loss of nuclear power plants

Author	Year	Expected loss(U.S. cents/kWh)
Friedrich/Voss	1993	0.006–0.041 (Germany)
Ott/Masuhr	1994	0.0007–0.12 (Switzerland)
CEPN	1994	0.00018–0.013 (France)
PSI/ERI	1994	0.0012 (Mühleberg, Switzerland)
PSI/ERI	1994	0.0014 (Peach Bottom, United States)
PSI/ERI	1994	0.0069 (Zion, United States)

Data source: ExternE (2003)

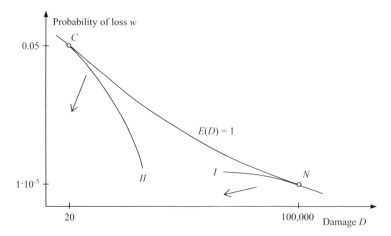

Fig. 11.2 The feasibility locus $E[D] = 1$ and two indifference curves

best imaginable situation for both types. This implies that for type *I*, the tangency point *N* is the optimal choice, involving exclusive reliance on nuclear power but no use of coal. For type *II* however, generation of electricity should optimally be by coal only.

Neither type *I* nor type *II* is irrational. The concavity of their indifference curves (more easily discernible for type *I*) indicates that when they have to accept a higher number of deaths, they both need to be compensated by an increasingly marked reduction in the probability of occurrence—a very intuitive assumption. However, type *I* would be willing to trade off a small decrease in the number of deaths *D* in return for a very small increase in the probability *w* only. For instance, he or she may have most relatives and friends living in the vicinity of the power plant, creating a particular interest in the survival of relatively few individuals. By way of contrast, type *II* would be willing to trade off the same decrease in the number of deaths *D* against a substantial increase in *w*. This type may have relatives and friends living spread out all over the world; only his or her survival is at stake. Note that sociological surveys are unlikely to identify the difference between the two types because they fail to confront respondents with the trade-off involved. If asked, "Do you find an energy-generating technology that may kill 100,000 people acceptable?", they will of course say 'No'. They may respond differently if made aware that the alternative is a technology that kills 20 people with a much higher probability (in reality, almost with certainty).

11.3.2 Risk Assessment According to the (μ, σ^2) Criterion

From an economic point of view, an internalization tax equal to the value of the expected loss as given by Eq. (11.2) would not bring about the welfare maximum in relation to the use of nuclear power. Recall that the appropriate condition states that

11.3 Risk Assessment of Nuclear Energy

the marginal cost of effort undertaken for risk prevention should be equal to its marginal utility in terms of risks reduction. However, marginal cost of effort is not directly related to expected loss while marginal utility is a subjective quantity. If a market for the prevention of nuclear risk existed (including the purchase of insurance coverage by private households), one would know that buyers' marginal utility is at least as high as the observed market price. Equivalently, their marginal willingness to pay (WTP) would be at least as high as the market price. Since no such market exists, one has to look for other ways to measure WTP.

A first approach is the so-called (μ, σ^2)-criterion which is popular for describing the behavior of risk-averse investors in capital markets. Its mathematical formulation can be traced back to Pratt (1964) and Arrow (1974) and amounts to a version of expected utility theory (see Sect. 3.5). According to it, the willingness of person i to pay for risk avoidance (denoted by R_i) is given by the expected loss μ_i the person is exposed to plus a surcharge that depends on the variance σ_i^2 of the possible loss and the individual's degree of subjective risk aversion av_i,

$$R_i = \mu_i + \frac{av_i(W_i)}{2} \cdot \sigma_i^2 \quad \text{with} \quad av_i(W_i) = -\frac{U_i''(W_i)}{U_i'(W_i)}. \quad (11.3)$$

The so-called coefficient of absolute risk aversion av_i depends on $U_i'(W_i)$, the curvature of the individual's risk utility function $U_i(W_i)$ which is a function of assets at risk W_i. In the context of the risks associated with nuclear power, willingness to pay of course importantly reflects concerns for health and survival. However, note that these concerns can be integrated by making the $U_i(W_i)$ function dependent on the state of health, see Zweifel and Eisen (2012). For marginal utility, one has $U_i'(W_i) > 0$, while the second derivative $U_i''(W_i)$ depends on the individual's risk preference. If $U_i''(W_i) > 0$, the individual is risk-seeking, if $U_i''(W_i) = 0$, he or she is risk-neutral. However, for a risk-averse individual, the second derivation is negative,

$$U_i''(W_i) < 0. \quad (11.4)$$

This implies that the person values a loss of assets more heavily than an equally probable gain of the same amount. From Eq. (11.3), one therefore has $av_i(W_i) > 0$ given risk aversion but $av_i(W) = 0$ given risk neutrality.

At the macroeconomic level, willingness to pay for the avoidance of nuclear risk R corresponds to individual values R_i summed up over the population POP exposed to the risk,

$$R = \sum_{i=1}^{POP} \mu_i + \sum_{i=1}^{POP} \frac{av_i(W_i)}{2} \cdot \sigma_i^2. \quad (11.5)$$

In the following, all persons POP are assumed to be exposed to the same loss with expected value μ and same variance σ^2 and to exhibit the same degree of risk aversion $av(W) > 0$. Thus, Eq. (11.5) reduces to

$$R = POP \cdot \mu + POP \cdot \frac{av(W)}{2} \cdot \sigma^2. \tag{11.6}$$

Although commonly used in transitions from the microeconomic to the macroeconomic level, assumptions of this type are admittedly not very realistic. In fact, they cut the social evaluation problem down to the willingness to pay of a representative individual for the avoidance of risk. However, such simplifications are helpful as a first step to estimate the magnitude of an aggregate willingness to pay value.

For an empirical implementation of Eq. (11.6), a value for the coefficient of absolute risk aversion $av(W)$ characterizing a society is needed. One way to infer a society's degree of risk aversion is to analyze the share of its assets it chooses to insure. This was done by Szipiro (1986) for a number of industrial countries.[6] Applying his estimate to the Swiss population, Zweifel and Nocera (1994) derived $av(W)$ to be between $5 \cdot 10^{-5}$ and $7 \cdot 10^{-5}$ per CHF. Using the 1994 conversion rate of 1.61 CHF/EUR, one obtains an interval for $av(W)$ of

$$8.1 \times 10^{-5} \text{per EUR} < av(W) < 11.3 \cdot 10^{-5} \text{ per EUR} \tag{11.7}$$

Although these are very small values, when multiplied with the variance of aggregate loss (which is huge), the surcharge over expected loss $POP \cdot \mu$ in Eq. (11.6) becomes sizable. Therefore, the view of engineers and physicists that expected loss is sufficient for assessing the risk of energy-related technologies is refuted (see Sect. 11.3.1).

This insight can be deepened by taking up the notion, touched upon in Sect. 11.3.1, that people do not care about their own health and survival only but also about that of relatives and friends. The results of the probabilistic safety analysis applied to the Swiss nuclear power plant Mühleberg (see Table 11.7) may serve as the point of departure. By dividing expected loss $E[D]$ by the number of persons POP exposed to the risk, one obtains an estimate of expected loss at the individual level,

$$\mu_i = \frac{E[D]}{POP}. \tag{11.8}$$

Now assume that people not only consider their own expected loss μ_i, but also that of 100 other persons μ_j, with $j \neq i$ (e.g. relatives, neighbors, friends, colleagues). Let their risk utility function be of the logarithmic type (it qualifies

---

[6]From an ethical point of view, one could argue that the use of market results is inadmissible when dealing with human life and health. This issue is discussed in Sect. 7.4.

11.3 Risk Assessment of Nuclear Energy

because $U'_i(W_i) > 0$ and $U''_i(W_i) < 0$. After taking into account altruism, expected loss $\mu_{i,alt}$ thus becomes

$$\mu i, alt = (1 + \ln(100)) \cdot \frac{E[D]}{POP} = 5.6 \cdot \mu i. \qquad (11.9)$$

In total, the individual evaluation of the damage increases by the factor 5.6 in contrast to calculations with the formulas (11.2) or (11.7).

Finally, the variance of potential damages σ^2 needs to be estimated. At the individual level, it is given by

$$\sigma i^2 = \sum_k \left(\frac{D_k - E[D]}{POP} \right)^2 \cdot w_k. \qquad (11.10)$$

To take into account altruism again, it has to be scaled up by the factor $(1+\ln(100))^2 = 5.6^2$ to become

$$\sigma i, alt^2 = 5.6^2 \cdot \sum_k \left(\frac{D_k - E[D]}{POP} \right)^2 \cdot w_k. \qquad (11.11)$$

Returning to aggregate values, one sees that Eq. (11.6) needs to be modified by simply inserting the factors 5.6 and 5.6^2, respectively, resulting in

$$R = 5.6 \cdot \mu + 5.6^2 \cdot \frac{av(W)}{2} \cdot \sigma^2. \qquad (11.12)$$

Using the interval (11.7) for $av(W)$ and the Mühleberg data for low and high release rates (see Table 11.7), respectively, one obtains willingness-to-pay values between 3.3 mn and 247.0 mn EUR per year.

Up until now the fact has been ignored that nuclear contamination persists over long periods (at least many decades) when estimating willingness to pay (even though probabilities w_k are given as frequencies per year). However, due to the long-term impact of nuclear contamination, insurance companies do not need to provide the entire sum of total remuneration payments immediately. Instead, they can distribute remuneration payments over a relatively long period (following the distribution of damages over time). Assuming a uniform distribution of damage over a period of 30 years, the variance of potential damages σ^2 becomes

$$\widehat{\sigma}^2 = \sum_k \left(\frac{D_k}{30} - \frac{E[D]}{30} \right)^2 \cdot 30 \cdot w_k = \frac{1}{30} \cdot \sigma^2. \qquad (11.13)$$

In contrast to variance σ^2, average aggregate damage μ remains constant. Therefore, the estimation for the aggregate willingness to pay R (Eq. (11.12)) can be adjusted using Eq. (11.13) to become

$$\widehat{R} = 5.6 \cdot \mu + 5.6^2 \cdot \frac{av(W)}{2} \cdot \frac{\sigma^2}{30}. \qquad (11.14)$$

In 1994, the Swiss population was about 7 mn. Using the data for the Mühleberg plant provided in Table 11.7 and applying Eq. (11.14), one can estimate adjusted aggregate willingness to pay,

$$0.8 \text{ mn EUR}/\text{a} < \widehat{R} < 21.7 \text{ mn EUR}/\text{a}. \qquad (11.15)$$

Dividing these figures by the annual electricity production in the Mühleberg plant (about 2500 mn kWh), willingness to pay is bounded by 0.0003 and 0.0087 EUR/kWh. To the extent that financial reserves of plant operators are insufficient for the payment of possible nuclear damages, these figures also represent the external cost of nuclear power. With figures this low, the introduction of internalization taxes would not affect the competitiveness of nuclear power.[7]

Even though estimated external effects can be internalized through taxes on nuclear power, the population still rejects nuclear energy in many cases. An explanation of this could lie in an incorrect estimation of willingness to pay using the (μ, σ^2)-criterion which assumes variance of damage to be finite. It is questionable whether this assumption is correct when assessing risks associated with the current generation of nuclear plants. However, this might change with improvements of the safety technology in future reactor generations.

11.3.3 Risk Assessment Based on Stated Preferences

The (μ, σ^2)-criterion presented in the previous section constitutes an attempt to base risk assessment as far as possible on objective quantities. However, in the determination of willingness to pay (WTP) for risk reduction, $av(W)$ enters, a subjective parameter. Moreover, values of $av(W)$ derived from e.g. insurance data may not be applicable to the present context, where not only survival but also the health of relatives and friends are at stake. In this situation, determining WTP through experiments may be worthwhile. A popular alternative is the discrete choice experiment, in which participants repeatedly choose between two alternatives, one of them typically the status quo. The status quo is described by a set of attributes, while the alternative features attribute levels that vary in the course of the experiment. If one of these attributes is the price to be paid, WTP values for the other attributes (and hence for the alternative as a whole) can be inferred using econometric methods. Admittedly, discrete choice experiments measure only stated preferences rather than preferences revealed through actual choices in markets.

---

[7]Since 2003, electricity consumers in Germany and Austria connected to a low-voltage grid have been paying an environmental tax of about 0.021 EUR/kWh, which however does not differentiate between power plant types, and thus lacks an incentive effect.

11.3 Risk Assessment of Nuclear Energy

However, a market for nuclear risk reduction (e.g. insurance against risks of nuclear power) does not exist for private households.

A discrete choice experiment designed to measure WTP for a reduction of financial risk emanating from nuclear power was conducted by Schneider and Zweifel (2004), involving 500 Swiss participants. In accordance with the theory of consumer demand developed by Lancaster (1966), the product 'electricity' was described by five attributes,

- Financial damage per household in case of a severe accident;
- Problem of final nuclear waste disposal solved/not solved;
- Average number of power interruptions per year;
- Coverage ratio of liability insurance to be purchased by nuclear plant operators for payment of damages to households;
- Price of electricity at the household level.

The damage probability does not appear as an attribute here; this is supposed to prevent the danger of inconsistent statements made by the participants. In many former experimental designs, it was noticed that the interviewees gave inconsistent answers when probabilities changed (the so-called Allais paradox).

As is well known, the slope of an indifference curve indicates how much the individual considered is willing to sacrifice of one good (attribute, respectively) in return for obtaining one unit of the other. In the present context, the slope of the indifference curve through the status quo shows how much disposable income (through paying a higher price for electricity) a respondent is willing to sacrifice in return for a higher degree of financial protection through a higher coverage ratio in plant operators' liability insurance. Therefore, respondents' repeated choices between the status quo and an alternative permit the experimenter to identify their indifference curves and with them, their marginal WTP in the neighborhood of the status quo.

Schneider and Zweifel (2004) estimated a value of 0.0012 EUR/kWh as the marginal WTP of the Swiss population for an increase of liability coverage from 0.55 bn EUR (the status quo) to 1.2 bn EUR per nuclear plant. They also found that marginal WTP decreased with the coverage ratio, as predicted by economic theory (see Fig. 11.3, with a linearized function for simplicity). Moreover, it reached zero at 100% coverage, which is intuitive because there is no financial risk anymore at that point. Most importantly, cumulated marginal WTP between 0.55 and 1.2 bn EUR clearly exceeded the estimated cost of a corresponding extension of liability coverage. Marginal utility can therefore be said to be at least as high as marginal cost, justifying the extra preventive effort from an efficiency perspective.

Maximum damage has been estimated to reach (and even exceed) 100 bn EUR. Using this value, one obtains willingness to pay of 0.092 EUR/kWh for the increase of liability coverage from 0.55 to 1.2 bn EUR as the integral of the marginal WTP schedule (see Eq. (11.16)),

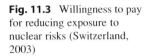

Fig. 11.3 Willingness to pay for reducing exposure to nuclear risks (Switzerland, 2003)

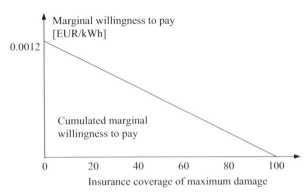

$$0.0012 \cdot (100 - 0.55)/(1.2 - 0.55) \cdot 0.5 = 0.092 \text{ EUR/kWh}. \quad (11.16)$$

This is a lot more than the 0.0087 EUR/kWh derived from the (μ, σ^2)-criterion. If nuclear power plants had to pay an internalization tax of this magnitude, they would not be competitive anymore on the market for electricity generation. Yet Schneider and Zweifel (2004) cite an estimate according to which additional insurance coverage up to even more than 1.2 bn EUR could cost as little as 0.007 EUR/kWh. Still, the result of this discrete choice experiment reflects the prevalent non-acceptance of nuclear energy, at least in Switzerland.

At the same time, the experiment provides evidence that 100% liability coverage does not represent the optimum amount of internalization when it comes to the risks of nuclear power.[8] For efficiency, insurance coverage should be such that its marginal cost (the additional insurance premium) equals to marginal willingness to pay. According to the authors, this equality would be reached through a fivefold increase of coverage, from 0.55 bn to 2.75 bn EUR.

In some countries, liability insurance coverage is not provided by insurance companies but mutually by nuclear plant operators. In the United States in particular, there is the so-called joint and several liability rule which mandates all operators to contribute to the payment of damages caused by one of them. In Germany, nuclear liability has three layers which in combination approximate the optimal amount of coverage as calculated by Schneider and Zweifel (2004):

- Private liability insurance (limit of 260 mn EUR per accident);
- Joint and several liability among plant operators (2244 bn EUR of liquid assets);
- Liability of plant owners including their holding companies with their total assets (amount unknown but huge).

Yet in spite of such an extremely high degree of coverage, acceptance of nuclear power in Germany is limited, evidenced by its government's decision to exit from

---

[8]The bankruptcy risk of a company with limited liability is not fully borne by its owners but in part also by society.

nuclear (as part of the so-called *Energiewende*) in response to the Fukushima accident of 2011 in Japan. Clearly, acceptance cannot be attained by internalization of the risks associated with nuclear power alone. In the end, the crucial factor will be the population's belief whether or not security of electricity supply and mitigation of greenhouse gas emissions can be achieved without nuclear power plants.

References

Arrow, K. J. (1974). *Essays in the theory of risk bearing*. Amsterdam: North Holland.
ExternE. (2003). *External costs. Research results on socio-environmental damages due to electricity and transport* (ExternE project). Luxemburg.
Friedrich, R., & Voss, A. (1993). External costs of electricity generation. *Energy Policy, 21*, 114–122.
Gerling, P., Rempel, H., Thielemann, T., & Thoste, V. (2005). Energie hat ihren Preis (Energy has its price). *Commodity Top News 22*. Hannover: Bundesanstalt für Geowissenschaften und Rohstoffe. Retrieved from www.bgr.de/b121/commo.html
Lancaster, K. (1966). A new approach to consumer theory. *Journal of Political Economy, 74*, 132–157.
Nuclear Energy Agency. (2014). *Nuclear energy data 2014*. Paris/Vienna: OECD-NEA/IAEA.
Nuclear Regulatory Commission. (1991). *Severe accident risks: An assessment for five U.S. nuclear power plants* (NUREG-1150). Washington.
Ott, W., & Masuhr, K. P. (1994). *Externe Kosten und kalkulatorische Energiepreiszuschläge für den Strom- und Wärmebereich (External costs and imputed price surcharges for electricity and heating)*. Bern: Bundesamt für Konjunkturfragen.
Pratt, J. W. (1964). Risk aversion in the small and in the large. *Econometrica, 32*, 122–136.
Rasmussen, N., et al. (1975). *Reactor safety study – an assessment of accident risk in U.S. commercial nuclear power plants*. WASH-1400 Report of the Nuclear Regulatory Commission. Washington: U.S. Government Printing Office.
Schneider, Y., & Zweifel, P. (2004). How much internalization of nuclear risk through liability insurance? *Journal of Risk and Uncertainty, 29*(3), 219–240.
Staub, P. (1991). *Kernreaktoren und Radioaktivität (Nuclear reactors and radioactivity)*. Zürich: Institut für Wirtschaftsforschung.
Szipiro, G. G. (1986). Measuring risk aversion: An alternative approach. *Review of Economics and Statistics, 86*, 156–159.
WNA. (2016). *World nuclear performance report 2016*. London: World Nuclear Association.
Zweifel, P., & Nocera, S. (1994). Was kostet die Vermeidung von Atomrisiken? Fundierte Grundlagen zur Bewertung externer Kosten (Prevention of nuclear risk at what price? Sound principles for evaluating external cost). *Neue Zürcher Zeitung*, 274/1994, 25.

Markets for Electricity 12

The electric value chain consists of the following elements: generation, wholesale trade, transmission, distribution, marketing, and metering. In many countries around the world, vertically integrated utilities used to assume all of these functions similar to the vertically integrated companies in other energy sectors (see Sect. 8.2.1). For several reasons, the European Union has mandated the electric industry to unbundle the grid from its other activities along the value chain (see Sect. 13.2.4). Therefore, it seems reasonable to structure the economic analysis of power markets accordingly. In this chapter the economic aspects of electricity generation and sales are discussed, whereas Chap. 13 is devoted to the economics of transmission and distribution.

For the time being, storing electricity is practically impossible in view of its cost. Therefore, electricity generation and electricity consumption must be synchronized continuously. In order to secure the supply of electrical energy for all customers, it is necessary to permanently maintain an amount of capacity in power generation which exceeds the maximum load.

Starting in the 1990s, the electricity industry (especially the generation sector) has been liberalized in many countries. This move, combined with the growing share of electricity from renewable sources and distributed generation, has led to a major transformation that continues to this day. Based on the experience gained from these recent developments, the following issues are addressed in this chapter:

– How might electricity markets work in a competitive business environment, although power has to be delivered through a single grid?
– What does generation dispatch look like in a competitive market?
– What are the particularities and pricing mechanisms of power exchanges?
– How can sufficient investment in backup and excess capacities be secured?
– How can the abuse of market power in the generation market be prevented?
– What are the possibilities to manage the transformation to 'green' power generation?

The variables used in this chapter are:

C	Total cost
Cap_{el}	Installed electric capacity
C_{fix}	Total fixed cost
c_{mc}	Marginal unit cost
c_{var}	Variable unit cost of power generation
CF	Cash flow (contribution margin)
CS	Consumer surplus
dz	Normally distributed stochastic variable
FP	Forward premium
h	Full-load hours per year (capacity factor $= h/8760$)
κ	Reversion rate characterizing a mean reversion process
Inv	Investment expenditure
L	Lagrange function
λ	Lagrange multiplier
Π	Profit
p	Wholesale price for electricity fed into the grid (day-ahead prices with subscripts, p_{peak}, $p_{off\text{-}peak}$, p_h, p_s)
p_F	Price of electricity forwards or futures
p_{gas}	Natural gas price
p_L	Long-term equilibrium price
p_{end}	End user price for electricity
Q	Generated or sold electric energy (in MWh)
σ	(Annualized) Volatility
$Skew$	Skewness of the distribution of a stochastic variable
$Std.dev$	Standard deviation of a stochastic variable
t	Present time
T	Future delivery period
u	Error term of an econometric estimation
Var	Variance of a stochastic variable
ω	Fuel efficiency of power plants

12.1 Features of Electricity Markets

Electric power is based on the directed movement of electrons. Key parameters are the rate of electrical charge measured in amperes (A) and the electrical voltage (V), which determines the force ensuring the flow of electric charge. The product of the two is electric power measured in kilowatts (kW) or megawatts (MW).[1] By multiplying electric power by a time unit (e.g. 1 h), one obtains electric work

---

[1] For combined heat and power plants, a distinction is made between thermal capacity (measured in MW_{th}) and electric capacity (measured in MW_{el}).

12.1 Features of Electricity Markets

measured in kilowatt-hours (kWh) or megawatt-hours (MWh), respectively (see Sect. 2.1.1).

As the supply of electricity is characterized by constant frequency and voltage, electric power and electric work are homogeneous products from a physical point of view. From an economic point of view, however, electricity is not so homogeneous, as evidenced by prices that exhibit both substantial fluctuations over time and differences between geographical areas. Economic heterogeneity is a core aspect of the economic analysis of electricity markets, to be discussed in Sect. 12.2.

12.1.1 The Consumer Surplus of Electricity

Electricity has particular features that no other energy source can offer:

- Electricity is the energy source with maximum exergy. Thus, electric applications, such as electric motors, have higher energetic efficiencies than fossil-energy applications.
- The laws of thermodynamics impose no limit on energy density. Therefore, electricity can be used to produce extremely high temperatures.
- Being the energy of an electromagnetic field, electricity is a virtually mass-free energy source. It therefore has excellent switch-on/switch-off properties, a basic requirement for signal processing and transmission.
- With the exception of electric smog and some heat and noise emissions, the environmental impact of electricity at the point of use is negligible.

As a result of these properties, substitutability of electricity by other energy sources is rather limited (e.g. in the case of light) and sometimes even impossible (e.g. in the case of information technology) as shown by Praktiknjo (2014). Thus the own price elasticity of electricity demand is rather low. Many kilowatt-hours would even be purchased at a price which exceeds current levels by a factor of 50. From an economic viewpoint, this implies that electricity markets are characterized by a very high consumer surplus (CS). This high consumer surplus becomes particularly evident when it is lost because of blackouts (so-called value of lost load (VOLL), see Praktiknjo 2013). To recoup part of it, consumers may eventually resort to auto-generation of electricity even if the associated cost exceeds the electricity price delivered by the grid.

The aggregate demand function $Q(p_{end})$ relates consumption to the end price paid by consumers. It can be transformed to become the inverted demand function $p_{end}(Q)$ which describes the end price as a function of quantity. Consumer surplus CS can be calculated for each market constellation (p^*_{end}, Q^*) by either one of the two following integrals

$$CS = \int_{p^*_{end}}^{\infty} Q(x)\,dx = \int_0^{Q^*} p_{end}(x)\,dx - p^*_{end} \cdot Q^* \qquad (12.1)$$

Both integrals reflect the area bounded by the price paid p^*_{end} and the demand function Q. The first integral measures this area as the accumulation of quantities as long as the marginal willingness to pay as expressed by the demand function Q exceeds the price p^*_{end} actually paid. The second integral represents the marginal willingness to pay of consumers cumulated over all quantities up to Q^* minus their effective payments $p^*_{end} \cdot Q^*$.

12.1.2 Non-storability of Electricity

As with many other goods and services, the demand for electricity is subject to daily, weekly, and seasonal fluctuations. Typical daily load profiles for northern countries are shown in Fig. 12.1. Winter demand (with daily peaks during the evening hours) is usually higher than summer demand (with daily peaks around noon). During typical spring and autumn days, load profiles differ as well. In southern regions, they may look quite different because of a lower demand for heating but higher demand for cooling.

Facing fluctuating demand, suppliers would ideally try to pursue the following strategies:

- Storing in times of low (off-peak) demand and withdrawing in times of high (peak) demand;
- Varying service quality using interruptible contracts and other load management measures;
- Price differentiation designed to shift demand from peak to off-peak periods.

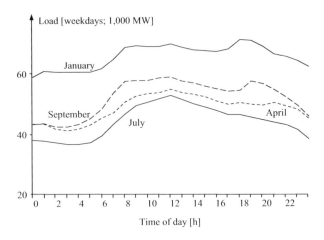

Fig. 12.1 Daily electricity load profiles

12.1 Features of Electricity Markets

Even though all of these strategies are to some extent employed (particularly for serving industrial customers), daily load curves are far from being levelized. There are two reasons for this. First, using currently available technologies, large-scale power storage is not economically viable yet.[2] Second, there has not been a roll-out of smart meters on a massive scale. Smart meters are capable of quasi-continuous metering as well as bidirectional communication between customer and utility. Thus, they are necessary for the introduction of interruptible contracts and flexible time-of-use tariffs or—more ambitiously still—real-time pricing.[3]

Today, power retailers mostly offer uniform tariffs, where price is independent of time and actual state of the market. With a growing share of intermittent generation (e.g. wind and solar), flexible tariff structures will become even more useful. However, their introduction conflicts with the way power is retailed. Presently, retail customers are characterized by and supplied according to a predefined standard load profile (SLP). In a SLP, a theoretical annual consumption of 1 MWh is proportionally distributed over all $365 \cdot 25 \cdot 4 = 35{,}040$ quarter hours of a year. After multiplication by the total annual electricity demand of the customer, the SLP determines the amount of electricity the retail supplier will have to provide during each quarter hour. This system offers an efficient way for dealing with customers who shift their supplier by enabling the transfer of crucial information, though it excludes effective load management.

12.1.3 Power Market Design Options

Before their liberalization, most electricity markets were organized as closed concession areas in which the regulator allowed retailing to be performed by a single utility only. In addition, these local and regional retailers were allowed to sign long-term and exclusive contracts with upstream power generators. According to these contracts, utilities had the exclusive right to deliver electricity to the retail company in the concession area. Directly supplying final electricity users was prohibited. As a result, all final users were obligated to purchase electricity from a single retailer, precluding competition between generators. In return, distributors were not allowed to refuse any customer seeking grid connection. In addition, electricity prices in excess of regulated tariffs were disallowed, while large industrial customers benefitted from special purchase agreements at prices below the regulated tariff.

These state-guaranteed regional monopolies were quite instrumental in establishing a safe and reliable electricity infrastructure covering even remote areas. Investments could easily be financed provided the regulator approved

---

[2]Economic viability of pump storages is highly dependent on geographical circumstances. Also, a lithium battery with a mass of 1 kg can currently store no more than 1 kWh of electricity.

[3]In a sense, electricity is still "too cheap to meter". This may change if smart meters become available at lower cost.

sufficiently high tariffs. Yet without the pressure of competition, utilities often had no incentive to invest in an efficient way, resulting in high cost and hence high regulated prices. Economic theory predicts that competition between generators and market access of independent power producers significantly reduces cost of operating an electricity system. In the European Union, another important motivation for promoting competition by liberalizing power markets was the intention of the European Commission to create a single power market across Europe.

In addition, vertically integrated utilities are not necessarily natural monopolies. According to Christensen and Greene (1976), potentials for economies of scale had been exhausted in large vertically integrated utilities in the United States. Thompson and Wolf (1993) support this finding which suggests that only the transmission and distribution parts of the electricity value chain represent a natural monopoly, where competition would cause inefficiency (see Sect. 13.2.1). Liberalization efforts should therefore focus on the other parts of the value chain, in particular generation, trading, and marketing, while regulating grid access in a way that competition among generators (and retailers) becomes possible (see Sect. 13.2).

These insights leave a choice between several (partly) liberalized market design options.

- Single buyer market: All electricity must be offered to a single buyer (usually government-managed). According to Hunt (2002), long-term contracts are required because there are not enough buyers for achieving full competition. The single buyer calculates the minimum cost dispatch such that the aggregate load demanded is always met by the least expensive combination of available capacities. However, supply-side regulation is still necessary to prevent generators from manipulating their bids (see Sect. 12.2.6). Retailers and other affected customers have no alternatives other than to buy all electricity from the single buyer since bilateral contracts between generators and consumers are prohibited. This market design permits incumbent retailers to keep their monopolistic market positions. Additionally, the single buyer may allocate side payments to stimulate investment in reserve capacity if deemed necessary.
- Mandatory power pool: All generated electricity must be offered to a pool, which serves as an exchange for retailers and other affected customers, who are permitted to submit individual bids to satisfy their power needs. The pool operator calculates the market-clearing price, which is applicable for all buyers and sellers. Bids are based on load forecasts which may reflect demand-side management designed to reduce fluctuations and with them cost (see Sect. 12.1.2). Again, manipulation of bids can occur, calling for price regulation.
- Free wholesale competition: Power can be traded either through bilateral long-term contracts (forward and future contracts with physical settlement) or anonymously through an exchange. This model offers more flexibility to sellers and buyers than a mandatory power pool. However, optional participation in the exchange may result in reduced liquidity and higher volatility of wholesale prices.

– Fully liberalized market with retail competition: This is the most sophisticated design option because it gives also small customers the right to freely choose their supplier. They are no longer 'captive customers' in the hands of their original contractual partner. Retail companies can enter the market without physical assets, allowing them to gain market share with innovative products. However, because load forecasting errors are unavoidable, an independent balancing mechanism needs to be in place. Each of the participating companies needs to have a contract with the system operator comprising the obligation to follow grid codes, report load schedules, and purchase balancing power in the event of deviations from the schedules. Yet experience shows that many small customers are reluctant to change supplier. Margins are usually small in the retail business because all retailers purchase electricity at more or less the same wholesale prices. Many authors (e.g. Stoft 2000, p. 26ff; Bhattacharyya 2011, p. 713ff) therefore argue against the benefits of retail competition. However, the European Electricity Market Directives 96/92/EC, 2003/54/EC, and in particular 2009/72/EC mandate the implementation of this design in the European Union (see European Commission 2009a, b).

12.2 Electricity Generation

As a consequence of the virtual non-storability of electricity and the limited availability of load management measures, power generators need to continuously adjust their production in order to balance supply and demand. In this section, the basic generation technologies to accomplish such a task are presented. The discussion also addresses the economic implications of the fact that the portfolio of generation capacities is fixed, at least in the short run. A third topic is the balancing of supply and demand as currently accomplished in the European Union and how it differs from procedures employed in non-liberalized markets.

12.2.1 Types of Power Generation Technologies

Most power plants generate electricity according to the principle of magnetic induction. Their electric side consists of a stator (a coil) and a rotor (a rotating electromagnet). The generator produces alternating current (AC), with a specified frequency (50 Hz in Europe) and an electric voltage between 6 and 21 kV. For the propulsion of the generator, kinetic energy is supplied by turbines using thermal energy from combustion processes. Other types of power plants use hydropower and wind power as a source of kinetic energy. Still another approach is to use electrochemical processes such as those characterizing photovoltaic cells and fuel cells. These devices produce direct current (DC) that needs to pass through an inverter before being fed into public grids, which operate with AC. Table 12.1 shows some key properties of several generating technologies.

Table 12.1 Typical properties of generating technologies

	Fuel efficiency ω (%)	Investment outlay Inv (EUR/kW)	Useful life T (years)	Fuel cost (EUR/MWh$_{el}$)
Steam turbine				
– Hard coal 700 MW	38–46	1250–1800	40	25–45
– Lignite 700 MW	35–43	1350–1900	40	15–25
– Nuclear 1400 MW	36	2400–5000	40	10–15
Gas turbine 200 MW	28–42	450–700	20	75–100
CCGT with 300 MW	>58	680–900	30	50–70
Hydropower 100 MW	80–90	1500–4000	50–80	–
Wind power onshore	40–50	1000–2500	20	–
Photovoltaics 1 MW	8–13	2000–4000	40	–
Fuel cells (<100 kW)	30–50	Rather high	~5	60–120

- Steam turbine power plants are based on a thermal cycle (see Sect. 2.2.2, particularly Fig. 2.1). The heat from burning fossil fuels is used to transform water into high-temperature and high-pressure steam. The steam is fed to a turbine, where it expands, generating rotational energy that drives the generator. The residual heat dissipates through a steam condenser into the environment. Up to 46% of the thermal energy contained in the fuel (which comprises fossil and nuclear energy sources) can be converted into electricity. Solar thermal and geothermal power plants work according to the same thermodynamic cycle.
- Gas turbine power plants are based on the combustion of a gaseous fuel in the turbine. In the cold part of the turbine, a mix of gas and air is compressed and fed to the combustion chamber. There, the mix is ignited to produce high temperatures and pressures. In the hot part of the turbine, the mix expands, generating rotational energy that drives the generator. Depending on pressure and temperature, thermal efficiencies of up to 42% can be reached (also known as Carnot efficiency).
- Combined-cycle gas turbines (CCGT) use both gas and steam technologies. The exhaust gas from a gas turbine is directed to a waste heat boiler where it is used to produce steam that in turn powers a turbine. In this way, combined-cycle power plants can reach fuel efficiencies of more than 60%.
- Hydropower plants transform the kinetic energy from flowing water into rotational energy. Run-of-river plants use vertical drops amounting to only a few meters, storage power plants of up to several 100 m. While storage power plants

use the potential energy of the water collected in an (artificial) mountain lake only once, pump storage power plants are able to reuse the water several times to generate electricity. They collect the water in a lower basin and pump it back into an upper basin using cheap excess power. While run-of-river plants produce electricity more or less continuously, storage and pumped storage power plants are preferably used to cover peak demand.
- Wind power plants use the kinetic power of wind to drive a generator. Like hydropower stations, they make do without fuel, resulting in low variable cost and no greenhouse gas emissions. However, their production crucially depends on wind speed. As shown in Fig. 12.2, wind speed is a random variable characterized by a high degree of skewness. In addition, wind turbines require wind speeds in excess of 3 m/s but below 14 m/s to be able to generate power, resulting in a characteristic performance line that levels off at 14 m/s. Moreover, its capacity factor is usually below 30% in the case of onshore plants, while offshore plants can even reach capacity factors of up to 50%. The capacity factors of wind power plants have an impact on their average generation cost (the higher the capacity factor, the lower average cost, see Sect. 3.1, particularly Table 3.1).
- Photovoltaic power generation is based on electrochemical transformation of sunlight into a DC of electrons that is usually converted to AC. Like wind power, photovoltaics represent an environmentally friendly but intermittent way of power generation. Its capacity factor lies between 10% and 25%. Recently, the unit cost of the modules has strongly declined, leading to growing shares of photovoltaic capacity worldwide.
- Fuel cells produce an electron current from hydrogen and oxygen. In a proton exchange membrane (PEM) fuel cell, hydrogen flows over an anode and is split

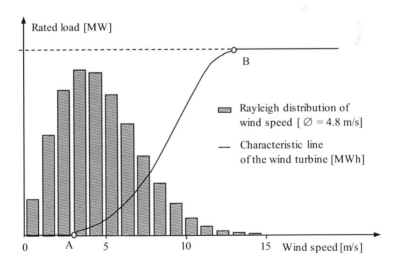

Fig. 12.2 Wind speed and electricity generation from wind turbines

into protons and electrons using a noble metal (e.g. platinum) as catalyst. A membrane (PEM) separates anode and the cathode. At the cathode, oxygen reacts with protons and electrons to form water. With a process temperature below 100 °C (so-called cold combustion), a PEM fuel cell can be operated quite dynamically.

Levelized cost of electricity (LCOE or average production cost, respectively) mainly depends on the cost of fuel as well as on the annualized investment outlay in combination with the rate of capacity utilization. A power plant with a rated capacity of 1 MW_{el} could theoretically generate $24 \cdot 365 = 8760$ MWh of electricity per year. However, for maintenance work already, no generator is able to operate at full load during all 8760 h of a year. Furthermore, there are economic reasons why power plants might operate at low capacity factors (defined as the ratio of actual output over potential output in a year). Figure 12.3 compares levelized cost of two selected generation technologies, natural gas and hard coal, as a function of the number of full load hours. Due to their relatively high investment outlay per unit of installed capacity, levelized cost of hard coal-fired plants is higher than that of gas-fired plants at low rates of capacity utilization. However, beyond 3000 h of operation, its relatively low fuel cost (see Table 12.1) begins to drive levelized cost below that of a gas-fired plant. Accordingly, coal-fired power plants usually are more efficient for covering base load demand (>5000 full-load hours p.a.), while gas-fired ones are generally used to cover peak load demand.

12.2.2 Power Plant Dispatch in Liberalized Markets

Power plant operator seeking to maximize profits will generate electricity to the point where their (short-term) marginal cost is still covered by the extra revenue from selling it (see Sect. 1.2). Given a perfectly competitive market, the extra

Fig. 12.3 Levelized costs of electricity depending on capacity utilization

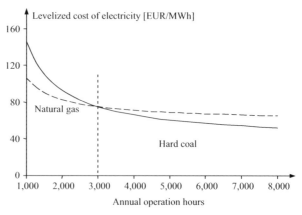

12.2 Electricity Generation

revenue equals the market price. Depending on the type of plant, marginal cost comprises the following components:

- The fuel cost incurred to generate an additional unit of electricity depends on fuel prices and (inversely) on fuel efficiency. Thus, modern, highly efficient power stations usually have lower marginal cost compared to older, less efficient facilities. Furthermore, all power plants are characterized by technical conditions (such as degree of utilization and temperature) for maximum energy efficiency. Deviations from these conditions cause efficiency losses and hence higher fuel consumption. This also includes additional fuel consumption caused by shut-on and shut-off processes as thermal power stations need to be heated up before being able to generate electricity.
- In the European Union, fossil fuels used for power generation are subject to CO_2 emission allowances. Therefore, the marginal cost of electricity generation also depends on the quantity of carbon dioxide emitted by the power station to produce one unit of electricity as well as on the CO_2 market price (see Table 10.5).

As discussed in Sect. 12.1.3, one needs to have functioning markets in order to introduce competition at the level of generation. In the European Union, the most important one is the spot market which is equivalent to the day-ahead market.[4] Products traded on this market are deliveries of power for specific hours of the following day as well as blocks of these contracts. The European Power Exchange (EPEX) constitutes the most liquid day-ahead market in Europe. It is of the uniform price auction type in that all bids and asks for a given hour are collected and aggregated to form an hourly supply and an hourly demand curve. At the close of trading, the exchange calculates the hourly market-clearing price (MCP), which is determined by the intersection of the two curves. Market participants are informed whether their bids and asks are accepted or not. All accepted bids and asks receive (pay, respectively) the same MCP.

Assuming perfect competition, the optimal strategy of each supplier is to ask the (short-term) marginal cost of the power plant. This causes the aggregate supply curve to reflect the so-called merit order as shown in Fig. 12.4. During off-peak hours (typically during night and weekend hours), the hourly price $p_{off\text{-}peak}$ is low, covering only the marginal cost of power plants with low marginal cost such as lignite and hard coal power plants. Therefore, it is these plants that will be dispatched, while the higher-cost plants remain offline. During peak hours (defining peak demand), the price p_{peak} is sufficiently high to cover the marginal cost of higher-cost production units such as oil-fueled and gas-fueled power plants.

Depending on market design, generators may be allowed to sign long-term contracts with retailers, causing them to offer only part of their generation capacity on the spot market. This is the case for many European countries, e.g. Germany. For

---

[4]In the United States, the day-ahead market is not regarded as a spot but rather a futures market.

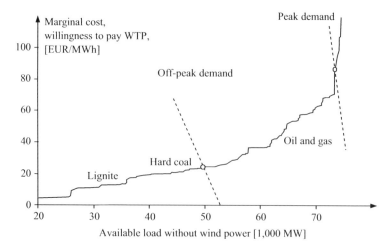

Fig. 12.4 Price formation on the electricity spot market

this reason, only 30–50% of total power generated in Germany is sold on the spot market. Furthermore, participation of foreign suppliers and customers is limited due to constraints concerning available interconnector capacities.

As shown in Table 12.1, generators using renewable energy sources have rather low marginal cost (with the exception of biogas). If these generators were to offer their capacities under competitive conditions making them sell their power at marginal cost, hydropower, wind, and photovoltaic would be prioritized in the merit order dispatch. Their increasing production thus shifts the position of the other power generators with higher marginal costs in the merit order to the right. As long as demand remains unaffected, this causes the market-clearing price to fall, an effect known as the 'merit order effect of renewables'.

12.2.3 Properties of Day-Ahead Power Prices

Hourly day-ahead power prices are relatively volatile due to low price elasticities of the demand and supply function in a number of situations. This volatility is also reflected in daily averages of hourly prices which are at the focus of the following analysis. For reasons that will become clear below, daily average prices are studied separately for peak and off-peak periods.[5]

Part of the day-ahead price fluctuations can be explained by calendar effects and is therefore predictable. For risk management, only the non-predictable part of price fluctuations is relevant. The following regression equation relates (the natural logarithm) of average daily peak and off-peak prices to predictable and non-predictable variables:

---

[5] According to the definition of the European Power Exchange, peak hours are the 12 h between 8:00 and 20:00 from Monday to Friday, while the remaining times are off-peak hours.

$$\ln p_t = c_0 + c_1 \cdot Friday + c_2 \cdot Saturday + c_3 \cdot Sunday + c_4 \cdot PublicHoliday$$
$$+ c_5 \cdot School\ vacation + c_6 \cdot Christmas\ time + c_7 \cdot \ln p_{F,t-1} + u_t$$
(12.2)

The first six independent variables are dummy variables that take on either the value '0' if the observation does not fall in the pertinent category or the value '1' if it does. Variable no. 7, $\ln(p_{F,t-1})$, represents (the natural logarithm of) the peak price (the off-peak price, respectively) of the derivative traded on the previous day. Its coefficient incorporates the effects of fuel prices, prices of CO_2 allowances, and other influences impinging on the average day-ahead price. The unpredictable component is accounted for by u_t, the error term of the ordinary least-squares (OLS) estimation.

The results from Eq. (12.2) can be used to calculate the adjusted day-ahead prices p_t^* that include only the non-predictable component of the variation in price, with $\hat{u}_t$ symbolizing the estimated residual of the OLS regression,

$$\ln p_t^* = c_0 + \hat{u}_t + c_5 \cdot mean(\ln p_{F,t-1}).$$
(12.3)

Depending on the price elasticities of demand and supply, small variations in power demand and supply may lead to major price fluctuations during peak periods while having little impact during off-peak periods (see the example of Fig. 12.4). In the past, this difference could be observed regularly, as indicated by the histograms of day-ahead prices between 2003 and 2005 in Fig. 12.5: While the frequency distribution of peak prices is skewed to the left (indicating price spikes), that of off-peak prices is roughly symmetric.

However, at that time, market shares of volatile wind power and photovoltaic were still small. In the meantime, their share exceeds 20% in several countries and may occasionally rise to over 50%, depending on weather and power demand conditions. As noted above, the merit order effect of renewables shifts the aggregate supply curve (see Fig. 12.4) away from the origin to the right. In addition, the relevant section of the merit order curve becomes more price-elastic, which serves to reduce the frequency of upward price spikes. Finally, renewables in combination with so-called must-run capacities[6] may even generate more electricity than demanded at the given price. During these periods, price turns negative, implying that plant operators have to pay money in order to get rid of their power. This negative price reflects the so-called cycle-cost (for the shut-off and shut-on process) of the plant.

Another important property of day-ahead power prices is their so-called mean reversion. This property states that deviations between the actual spot market price p_t and the steady-state price p_L tend to be eliminated over time.[7] This can be formalized as

---

[6]Must-run capacities are generators with contracts for so-called control power (see Sect. 13.1.3) and combined heat and power plants during the heating period.

[7]Accordingly, the residuals of Eq. (12.2) are highly auto-correlated.

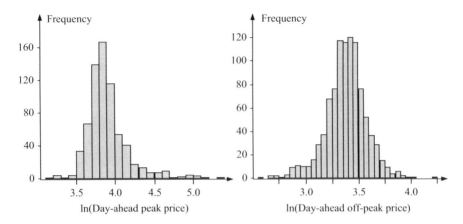

Fig. 12.5 Histogram of adjusted day-ahead power prices. Data source: EEX (May 2003 to December 2005)

$$\ln\left(\frac{p_{t+1}}{p_t}\right) = \kappa \ln\left(\frac{p_{L,t}}{p_t}\right) \cdot dt + \sigma dz \text{ with } 0 < \kappa < 1. \quad (12.4)$$

If the (adjusted) spot market price p_t is larger than the equilibrium price $p_{L,t}$, the logarithm on the right-hand side becomes negative, leading to a price reduction in the time interval dt according to the reversion rate $0 < \kappa < 1$. Obviously, the converse holds if the spot market price is below the equilibrium price. Estimates of κ suggest that mean reversion does not take more than two weeks in the day-ahead power market. The second term in Eq. (12.4) captures the impact of stochastic fluctuations. While textbook economics assumes dz to be normally distributed (so-called random Brownian motion), the histograms of Fig. 12.5 indicate this not to be true.

12.2.4 Intraday Markets

Because electricity cannot be stored, all market participants must close their open positions (typically every quarter of an hour) with reference to a specific execution period. A position is open if actual demand or supply differs from the contracted (or forecast) quantities. These forecasts depend on many parameters and must regularly be revised whenever new information becomes available. In particular, such a revision becomes necessary when retailers attract or lose new customers.

An important cause of forecasting errors is intermittent electricity generation from wind power and photovoltaics. Even the most sophisticated day-ahead forecasts of aggregate supply regularly exhibit errors. In view of the large installed capacities of these plants, these errors can exceed several thousand MW.[8] However,

---

[8] Average day-ahead wind forecasting errors (measured by the root of mean squared error RMSE) are presently in the range of 6–7%.

12.2 Electricity Generation

hour-ahead forecasts are much more accurate compared to day-ahead forecasts. Therefore, intraday markets that allow trades until one hour before execution are well suited to close gaps between day-ahead and intraday forecasts. There are two types of intraday markets:

- Pool-type intraday markets re-use the schedules and bids that have been submitted for day-ahead scheduling. Close to real-time delivery, the optimal dispatch of power plants is recalculated.
- Intraday markets can also consist of bilateral trades on energy exchanges without being institutionally linked to a day-ahead market. This is the model used in most European countries.

However, bilateral intraday markets usually have limited liquidity, particularly if characterized by continuous trading. Nevertheless, observed intraday price volatility does not appear excessive compared to day-ahead price volatility. The reason is arbitrage transactions by some operators of conventional power plants. On the one hand, when more renewable energy is offered than predicted by the day-ahead forecast, they may reduce their own generation, substituting it with electricity from renewables purchased on the intraday market. Of course, they only do this if their own cost saving exceeds the current price of electricity on the intraday market. On the other hand, when supply from renewables falls short of prediction, these operators step up their generation if possible. In both cases, the marginal cost of the respective conventional plant determines the intraday market price provided the market is efficient. Gaps between supply and demand that remain after close of trading on the intraday market must be balanced by the responsible system operator during the delivery period (see Sect. 13.1). Eventually, intraday prices converge to expected prices for balancing power prices (real-time prices).

12.2.5 Portfolio Management

A distinction can be made between companies that initially have long positions (net suppliers) and companies that initially have short positions (net demanders). Power generators without final customers belong to the first group, while retailers without their own generation capacities belong to the second. Both groups are exposed to a substantial risk of price volatility on the day-ahead markets (see Sect. 12.2.3).They can hedge this risk by concluding long-term contracts where prices are usually agreed upon contract conclusion and settlement occurs in the future, at time of delivery.

There exist two basic types of such derivatives: forwards and futures. Forwards (also called over-the-counter contracts) are bilateral contracts tailored to the needs of the two parties. However, with the establishment of liquid day-ahead markets and informative spot market prices, futures can be established as an alternative to forwards. Futures are standardized contracts traded and cleared through exchanges (see also Sect. 8.3.3). The most important power future is the year-ahead base contract, which is defined by 1 MW of electricity to be delivered in each of the 8760 h of the coming year. Similarly the year-ahead peak contract is defined for all peak hours of the following year. Settlement can occur either physically or financially. In the case of physical settlement, the seller delivers the contracted amount of electricity to the exchange at the specified time. In the case of financial settlement, there is no physical delivery. Moreover, a payment is made amounting to the difference between the hourly day-ahead price and the agreed future price (so-called contract for differences). This allows financial speculators from outside the electricity industry to participate in risk hedging.

Portfolio management refers to the optimal combination of different contracts. Risk-averse generators and retailers have to decide whether to use long-term contracts (forwards and futures) to close positions or to trade on the spot market instead. However, prices of long-term contracts often differ from expected spot market prices. The difference between the current forward price $p_{F,t}(T)$ for delivery in period T and the expected spot price $E_t[p_T]$ of this period,

$$FP_t(T) = p_{F,t}(T) - E_t[p_T]. \tag{12.5}$$

is referred to as the forward premium. The forward premium can be positive or negative. In the case where the forward price is higher than the expected spot price, the market is said to be in contango; otherwise, it is in backwardation. A contango situation implies that retailers are more risk-averse than generators and therefore pay the forward premium to generators. Under backwardation the opposite is the case.

According to John Maynard Keynes, backwardation should be the dominant case in speculative markets because producers, being less diversified in terms of their assets, are usually more interested in hedging price risks than customers (see Hicks 1939, 135–140). Besembinder and Lemmon (2002) developed this idea further. In their model all market participants are risk-averse and buy forward contracts in order to maximize the linear combination of expected profit and associated variance (so-called Bernoulli criterion, see Sect. 3.5). In electricity wholesale markets, participants are exposed to cost risks and revenue risks. Since the revenue risks of producers equal the cost risks of retailers, this risk is netted out at the market level. Consequently, the forward premium depends only on

- the revenue risk of the retailers,
- the cost risk of electricity generators.

According to the authors, the forward premium is therefore given by

$$FP_t(T) = d_0 + d_1 \cdot Std.dev(p_s) + d_2 \cdot Skew(p_s) \quad \text{with} \quad d_1 < 0 \quad \text{and} \quad d_2 > 0. \tag{12.6}$$

Among other things, this equation implies that peak load forward premiums should be larger than off-peak forward premiums because the skewness of peak prices exceeds that of off-peak prices (see Fig. 12.5). However, empirically testing it is challenging because the forward premium depends on the expected spot market price, which cannot be directly observed using market data.

With power market liberalization and the introduction of free wholesale markets and retail competition, efficient portfolio management has become an important asset for market participants. In the case of Germany, retailers and eligible final customers secure 80–90% of their power needs either through their own generation or through forwards and futures. This leaves less than 20% of demand to be covered by transactions on the spot market. However, during times when supply from renewables is high, purchases by conventional generators are needed to achieve balance. If the spot price falls to a level below the short term marginal generation cost (STMGC), it is efficient for generators to become buyers rather than sellers of electricity.

12.2.6 Market Power

Up to this point, the analysis of power prices proceeded on the assumption of perfect competition among power plant operators, implying that no single generator is able to drive the wholesale price above the competitive level (Mas-Colell et al. 1995). Perfect competition thus requires a rather large number of independent generators, but in reality a relatively small number of power companies dominates the market, providing them with leeway to fix prices above marginal cost.

There is a manifold of models designed to explain the supply behavior in oligopolistic markets. Some models assume simultaneous decisions, others, sequential decisions by competitors. Since day-ahead prices result from single uniform auctions, assuming sequential decision-making does not seem to be appropriate here. A more relevant distinction is whether the strategic variable of generators is quantity or price. The first case is called Cournot competition, the second, Bertrand competition.

Focusing on Cournot competition, one finds that the analysis becomes rather complex unless simplifying assumptions are made. One assumption is that a predetermined number of n generators have the same cost function with identical fixed cost C_{fix} and constant marginal cost c_{mc}, where Q_i is the quantity of electricity produced by generator i.

$$C(Q_i) = C_{fix} + c_{mc} \cdot Q_i \tag{12.7}$$

This assumption implies that all generators use the same technology in each market segment (i.e. peak, off-peak). As a consequence, the optimal rate of production is the same across generators.[9]

In addition, a linear inverse demand function is assumed, with the market price p depending on the supply of all n producers, $Q_1, Q_2, \ldots, Q_n$.

$$p(Q_1, Q_2, \ldots, Q_n) = b_0 - b_1 \sum_{i=1}^{n} Q_i \quad \text{with} \quad b_0, b_1 > 0. \tag{12.8}$$

Profit Π_i of company i is therefore equal to

$$\Pi_i = \left(b_0 - b_1 Q_i - b_1 \bar{Q}_i\right) Q_i - \left(C_{fix} + c_{mc} \cdot Q_i\right) \quad \text{where} \quad \bar{Q}_i = \sum_{j \neq i} Q_j \tag{12.9}$$

indicates the sum over the (optimal) supplies of all other companies.

Under perfect competition (with $p = c_{mc}$), market size Q_s would be equal to

$$Q_S := \frac{b_0 - c_{mc}}{b_1}. \tag{12.10}$$

This benchmark quantity can be used in the first-order optimality condition of the profit function (12.9). Taking its first derivative with respect to Q_i, setting it to zero, and solving, one obtains

$$Q_i^* = \frac{1}{2b_1}\left(b_0 - b_1 \bar{Q}_i^* - c_{mc}\right) = \frac{1}{2}\left(Q_S - \bar{Q}_i^*\right) \quad (i = 1, \ldots, n). \tag{12.11}$$

This implies

$$Q_i^* = Q_S - Q^* \quad \text{because of} \quad Q^* = \sum_{j=1}^{n} Q_j^*. \tag{12.12}$$

Therefore, each oligopolist takes the competitive market volume as the point of departure and deducts the (optimal) quantities supplied by everyone. However, given the common cost function (12.7), the optimal generation of all n companies is equal. Cournot competition thus leads to the following optimum for all generators,

$$Q_i^* = \frac{Q_S}{n+1}, \quad \text{with overall market size} \quad Q^* = \sum_{i=1}^{n} Q_i^* = \frac{n}{n+1} Q_S. \tag{12.13}$$

---

[9] If oligopolists have differing cost functions, it can be shown that the one with the most favorable cost function has the highest market share in equilibrium.

12.2 Electricity Generation

This shows that the total quantity produced in equilibrium falls short of the competitive benchmark. The oligopolistic market price is given by

$$p^* = b_0 - b_1 Q^* = \frac{1}{n+1}((n+1)b_0 - nb_1 Q_S) = c_{mc} + \frac{b_1 Q_S}{n+1} \qquad (12.14)$$

As expected, the oligopolistic equilibrium price exceeds the competitive one, given by marginal cost c_{mc}. The markup decreases with the number of generators.[10] This shows that incumbent generators have an incentive to prevent market entry by newcomers. If permitted by antitrust law, they may also try to reduce the number of competitors, e.g. through horizontal mergers.

According to Eq. (12.14), the price markup over marginal cost c_{mc} depends on the slope $b_1 > 0$ of the inverse demand function (12.8). It decreases with the own price elasticity of electricity demand. Therefore, elastic demand is an effective instrument against market power of generators.

In order to obtain a more realistic depiction of market power in the case of electricity, the assumption of constant marginal cost has to be dropped. In Sect. 12.2.2 (see Fig. 12.4) it is shown that the merit order of power generation is basically a non-linear and convex function, which can be approximated by

$$c_{mc} = a_0 + a_1 Q^{a_2} \quad \text{with} \quad a_0 > 0, \quad a_1 > 0 \quad \text{and} \quad a_2 > 1. \qquad (12.15)$$

If marginal cost increases exponentially with the rate of production Q as assumed here, the withdrawal of a generating unit from the day-ahead market leads to a relatively high increase in prices. On the one hand, capacity withholding eliminates the contribution margin of the plant that is not operating. On the other hand, the operator receives higher contribution margins from its remaining plants. In general, the additional contribution margins overcompensate the losses if the price effect and the remaining capacities of the operator are sufficiently high. This effect is usually stronger during peak than off-peak hours. The key point is that withholding strategies can be attractive even for generators with only moderate market shares. Therefore, competition authorities see a need to supervise spot markets for electricity.

However, it can be argued that wholesale power prices would be at competitive levels even though the generation industry is concentrated and in the absence of regulation.

- A first argument is theoretical by nature. Should generators use price instead of quantity as strategic variable, the market is said to be in Bertrand competition. Assuming equal cost functions for all generators, this gives rise to the so-called Bertrand paradox. If an oligopolist asks a price above its marginal cost, it risks

---

[10] In the case of monopolistic competition with $n = 1$ (amounting to a monopoly), the optimal solution corresponds to the profit-maximizing solution derived in Sect. 1.2.2.

losing the market if competitors ask marginal cost prices. Therefore, no price markup is expected under Bertrand competition.
- The other arguments are empirical by nature. With an increasing market share of renewables, the merit order flattens (a_2 in Eq. (12.15) becomes close to one). This reduces the profit potential of withholding capacity.
- Under free wholesale competition, generators are not only on the supply side but also on the demand side of the market (see Sect. 12.2.5). In fact, generators on the demand side do not benefit from price markups. Indeed, they would rather prefer low prices. As a consequence, regulation of day-ahead prices in free markets is less urgent than in pool-type markets which constrain generators to be suppliers only.
- As will be shown in Sect. 12.3.2, a price equal to marginal cost may be insufficient for calling forth investment in generation capacities. Therefore, strict (marginal) price regulation of the day-ahead market may cause a need to implement an additional mechanism for creating revenue that makes investing in power capacities attractive, thus securing future electricity supply.

12.3 Power Plant Investments

12.3.1 Power Plant Investments in Regulated Markets

Before market liberalization, power generation and retail were organized in closed concession areas without competition. The concession usually entailed three obligations:

- Potential customers must be connected to the grid provided this is economically viable;
- Customers must be supplied at a politically regulated tariff;
- The concessionary must pay a fee to the jurisdiction where it operates the grid.

Under these conditions, investment planning is straightforward. First, the monopolistic utility forecasts the so-called ordered load duration curve for each year of the planning period by ordering the $24 \cdot 365 = 8760$ h according to the expected load (see Fig. 12.6).[11] The load duration curve is not predetermined but can be modified by measures of demand-side management, such as peak shaving and load shifting.

The second step of the monopolistic planning process is to match predicted demand with existing supply. In order to do so, the area below the duration curve is filled by rectangles representing each available power plant whose height indicates the rated load and whose width corresponds to the expected load factor. Power

---

[11]Note that this is nothing but a frequency distribution with frequencies depicted on the x-axis rather than the y-axis.

12.3 Power Plant Investments

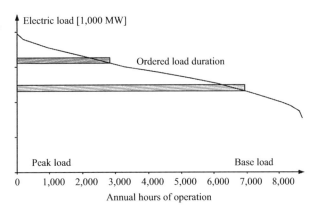

Fig. 12.6 Load duration curve and planning of power plant investments

plants designed for an operation with less than 3000 h per year are peak load units while plants designed for more than 6000 annual operating hours are base load units (depending on their cost structures, see also Sect. 12.2.1, in particular Fig. 12.3). This planning step also takes into account power plants that will be retired during the planning period.

Finally, the need for investing in new power plants is signaled by failure of the area below the ordered load curve to be entirely covered by the existing power plants, including a predetermined reserve margin. To finance the required investments, the regulator may allow a tariff surcharge. In principle, this could result in less rather than more revenue, depending on the own price elasticity of demand. However, this elasticity is usually relatively low in absolute value in the case of electricity, implying that the quantity demanded falls by a small amount only.

Evidently, regulators need to know how high investment in capacity and the associated surcharge should optimally be. The pertinent theory was developed by economists, notably Boiteux (1956), Steiner (1957), and Kahn (1970). Its starting point is the marginal willingness to pay (WTP) for electricity, with WTP for off-peak power distinguished from WTP for peak power. In Fig. 12.7 both schedules of marginal WTP for off-peak power are falling with quantity, reflecting two demand functions. For simplicity, current production and capacity are depicted on the same x-axis. By deducting marginal cost of current production, one obtains marginal WTP specifically for capacity, one for the off-peak and another for the peak segment. They are nonlinear because marginal cost of current production is assumed to be increasing. Note that marginal WTP for capacity is zero at $Q_{0,off-peak}$ for consumers in the off-peak segment and at $Q_{0,peak}$ for consumers in the peak load segment. Assuming non-rivalry in consumption across the two segments, one can combine the two marginal WTP schedules vertically to form a total marginal WTP schedule as a function of quantity and hence capacity Q. Aggregation is vertical rather than horizontal (as in the case of a private good) because a given capacity is at the disposal of peak as well as off-peak consumers, thus amounting to a public

Fig. 12.7 Optimal investment in generating capacity

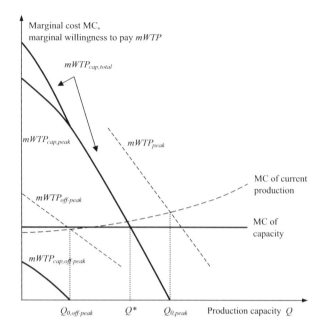

good. After vertical aggregation, one obtains total marginal WTP for capacity, which coincides with the peak load segment between $Q_{0,peak}$ and $Q_{0,off\text{-}peak}$. Below $Q_{0,off\text{-}peak}$, marginal WTP of off-peak consumers kicks in.

Optimal capacity is indicated by Q^*, where total marginal WTP for capacity equals its marginal cost (which is assumed to be constant for simplicity). If existing capacity is below this optimum, Q^* indicates the efficient amount of investment. In the case depicted in Fig. 12.7, only consumers in the peak load segment optimally pay for the extra capacity because marginal WTP of off-peak consumers does not enter the determination of Q^*. However, if the marginal cost of capacity were (much) higher, the optimum would shift to a point below $Q_{0,off\text{-}peak}$. There, the two consumer groups would have to contribute to the cost of capacity expansion according to their marginal WTP. Needless to say, estimating marginal WTP is difficult for the regulator since consumers have an incentive to understate it. Finally, note that the total price paid for electricity exceeds the marginal cost of its current production. Consumers are made to also cover the cost of capacity expansion, which is to be regarded as a fixed cost once the investment has been made. This constitutes a deviation from the rule "price equals marginal cost" which causes a welfare loss. The regulator may seek to minimize this welfare loss by applying so-called Ramsey pricing, to be discussed in Sect. 13.2.2.

One of the aims of electricity market liberalization is to permit effective competition in the generation segment of the electricity value chain. Once competition is established, the market determines optimal generation prices, as explained in Sect. 12.2.2. Thus the regulator should restrain from imposing prices (including Ramsey pricing) on the generation industry. However, regardless of how electricity

12.3 Power Plant Investments

competition is organized, the grid will always constitute a natural monopoly and therefore needs to be regulated. Therefore, even though the theory of optimal regulation and Ramsey pricing is not relevant for the liberalized generation segment, they will remain relevant for the grid segment of the electricity value chain (for further discussion, see Chap. 13).

12.3.2 Power Plant Investment in Competitive Markets

Sufficient generation capacities are a key condition for a safe and reliable electricity supply. Yet the discussion in Sect. 12.2.6 shows that by withholding capacity, generators can drive up wholesale prices. This opportunity militates against investing in additional capacity even though it may be indispensable for supply security in future. Independent power producers—if admitted as newcomers—may close the gap provided economic opportunities exist. In this case, incumbents risk loss of market share if they abstain from investing in an attempt to limit generation capacities. Therefore, no systematical underinvestment is to be expected if generation markets are both competitive and open.

The economic theory of investment laid out in Sect. 3.5 can also be applied to power plants. Investment in a new generation unit can be assessed by comparing expected cash flows or contribution margins and capital expenditures. Figure 12.8 shows the (expected) ordered price duration curve consisting of the 8760 hourly day-ahead prices p_h in a particular year of the planning period. The power plant will be running as long as this helps to recover user cost of capital, i.e. as long as its marginal cost (variable unit cost c_{var}, respectively) is below the sales price p_h. The

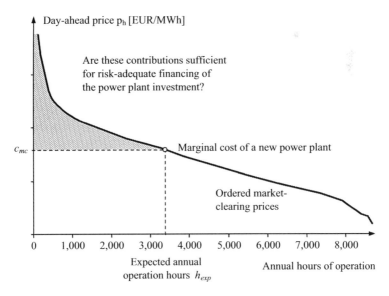

Fig. 12.8 Annual price duration curve

equality of the two determines the expected number of operation hours h_{exp} in that year. In Fig. 12.8, annual cash flow is therefore graphically displayed by the hatched area, it is given by

$$E[CF] = \sum_{h=1}^{h_{exp}} E[p_h] - c_{var}. \qquad (12.16)$$

Clearly price spikes contribute to cash flow, making investment in capacity attractive. Therefore, by suppressing price spikes the regulator weakens incentives to invest in new generation capacities.

Since day-ahead power prices vary from year to year, the calculation according to Eq. (12.16) must be repeated annually, using the respective hourly price forecasts. To reflect the riskiness of day-ahead prices, their frequency distribution should be estimated as well, possibly by means of Monte Carlo simulation.

In view of this distribution, investors can decide whether they want to hedge the price and cost risks by selling power and purchasing fuel and emission allowances using long-term contracts. If forward and futures markets for electricity, natural gas, coal, and emission rights are sufficiently liquid, power plant investments can be assessed using parameters gleaned from these markets:

– Spark spread for gas plants $= p_{F,electr} - (1/\omega_{gas}) \, p_{F,gas}$. This is the difference between the peak load electricity future and the gas future corrected by the fuel efficiency of the gas plant ω_{gas}.
– Clean spark spread for gas plants. This is derived from the spark spread by subtracting the cost of CO_2 allowances for gas-fueled power generation (see Sect. 10.3).
– Dark spread for coal plants $= p_{F,electr} - (1/\omega_{coal}) \, p_{F,coal}$. The dark spread is the difference between the base load electricity future and the coal future corrected by the fuel efficiency of the coal power plant ω_{coal}.
– Clean dark spread for coal plants. This is derived from the dark spread by subtracting the cost of CO_2 emission rights for coal-fueled power generation (see Sect. 10.3).

In the absence of liquid forward and futures markets, these spreads need to be estimated using forecasting methods. Once investors have estimates of the clean spreads, they can assess the viability of a new power plant by comparing the spreads with the annual user cost of capital.

An extension to this approach is based on real options theory (see Sect. 3.6). For instance, a gas power plant can also be interpreted as a call option on electricity with a strike price equal to the marginal cost of production. Once a new unit is available, the plant operator exercises this option whenever the clean spark spread is positive, producing as much electricity as possible. The interpretation of power plants as real options implies that their value exceeds the value of the underlying (i.e. the net present value of cash flows) by an option premium. This option premium increases with the volatility of cash flows and hence expected volatility of hourly spot prices (see Sect. 3.6). This again highlights the importance of spot market price spikes for investment in power plant under competition.

It is reasonable to assume that a period of low investment in generating capacity leads to tight electricity supply, and thus higher spot and futures prices in both the base load and the peak load segment. If sufficiently large, the price increase creates an investment signal which ends the period of insufficient investment. However, one problem remains. Only if the time lag between the decision to invest and completion of the investment is sufficiently short does the market mechanism guarantee a stable long-term power supply.[12] Otherwise, long-term price fluctuations combined with swings in supply may result.

12.3.3 Capacity Markets

The discussion of the preceding section raises the question of whether a liberalized electricity market is able to continuously secure power supply by calling forth sufficient investment in generating capacity. As electricity cannot be stored at reasonable cost given the present state of technology, safe and reliable power supply requires both excess and reserve capacity. Excess capacity is needed to cover unexpected surges in demand, while reserve capacities are required to make up for scheduled and unscheduled power plant outages. Some additional capacity is required for supplying so-called regulation power and other grid services, in particular so-called redispatch of generation in case of grid bottlenecks (see Sect. 13.1). Overall, reserve margins of about 10% of maximum load are usually assumed to be necessary to secure electricity supply at any time (known as system adequacy).

Arguably, system adequacy has a public good characteristic in the absence of smart grids because a single generator who contributes to it cannot easily prevent others who do not pay from reaping its benefits. In a monopolistic market with exclusive concession areas, the regulator requires the utility to secure system adequacy and allows a surcharge of tariffs to finance it. However, a competitive power market may fail to provide a sufficient reserve margin, calling for a separate mechanism for financing it. Several such mechanisms have been developed:

---

[12] At the beginning of market liberalization, long-term power contracts were seen as an obstacle for competition. In contradistinction with the United States, European markets at the time were characterized by excess capacities which prevented planning for new investment from being an issue. Once these excess capacities in Europe are gone, long-term contracts could prove to be an indispensable tool for relieving investors of part of their risk, inducing them to add generating capacity. An alternative would be governmental guarantees, subsidies, and other types of market intervention.

– The system operator (independent system operator [ISO] or regulated transmission system operator [TSO]) purchases capacities that are needed for supplying balancing power. Plant operators receive capacity payments determined by pay-as-bid auctions (see Sect. 13.1.3).
– In a fully liberalized market with retail competition, (potential) demand-side participants (often represented by so-called balancing group managers) have to purchase balancing power from the system operator in charge. If the imbalances are large, the regulator may fine participants (the balancing group manager, respectively). In extreme situations the system operator can prohibit them to use the grid (see also Sect. 3.6.1).
– Special over-the-counter capacity markets are created, designed to provide back-up power in case of plant outages. Demand importantly originates with operators of small cogeneration plants.
– In some countries, the regulator purchases (or mandates the system operator to purchase) emergency capacities that are released if the system threatens to collapse. The regulator has to decide the amount of capacity to be purchased, possibly through a public auction where bidders commit to supplying it in all circumstances. Since emergency capacities cannot be offered on the regular day-ahead market, this mechanism causes an increase in regular wholesale power prices. Conversely, when emergency capacities are in use, peak prices are under pressure. Obviously, the regulator needs a criterion for releasing emergency capacities, and this criterion determines the maximum hourly peak load price. Once again, public intervention therefore reduces price spikes (i.e. the slope of the price duration curve), undermining incentives to invest especially in peak power plants.

The importance of price spikes for the capacity market can be illustrated using Fig. 12.9. It shows a simplified merit order and two levels of demand. Point

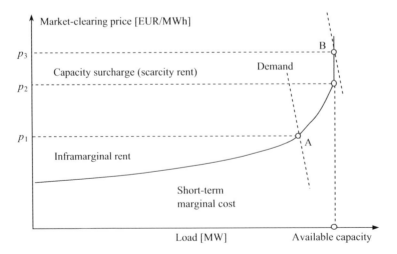

Fig. 12.9 Scarcity rent for capacities

A corresponds to a regular market situation in which the marginal cost of the last plant that is available (i.e. excluding the reserve margin) determines the market-clearing price p_1. Plants with lower marginal cost (to the left) also receive the price p_1, earning a so-called inframarginal rent. The last unit in the merit order has marginal cost equal to p_2. However, if the combined capacity of all power plants is insufficient to cover demand as in the case of point B at the capacity limit, the market-clearing price spikes, exceeding marginal cost by ($p_3 - p_2$). This difference is the so-called capacity rent, reflected by a capacity surcharge.

If the situation depicted by point B occurs frequently, investment in generation capacity is stimulated, as discussed in Sect. 12.3.2. Note that while at point B of Fig. 12.9 the price exceeds marginal cost of any plant in the merit order, it is not the result of market power. In liberalized markets the wholesale power price can—and must from time to time—exceed marginal cost. In these situations, the regulator may come under public pressure to intervene, with the consequence that the electricity market on its own (so-called "energy only market") is unable to generate sufficient revenues for financing investment in capacity. To correct this failure (often referred to as "missing money problem"), capacity payments to power generators may be introduced, which may be financed by a general electricity levy.

However, a decentralized design is possible for a capacity market as well in the following way. Retailers and eligible industrial customers are mandated to hold capacity certificates if they wish to purchase peak load electricity at the wholesale market price. The supply side comprises generators, customers with interruptible loads, and owners of electricity storage devices. The capacity price is high if capacities are hardly sufficient to meet demand but it can be zero in times of weak demand and excess capacity. While a decentralized capacity market requires a lot of control and supervision by the regulator, it can do without a central planner who determines the necessary capacity.

In systems with a high market share of intermittent renewable energy sources, still another concept could be implemented. It is based on the choice by customers regarding their desired quality of electricity supply. Some types of contract could provide lower quality by allowing the retailer to cut supply during one or more hours per day if wind or photovoltaic electricity generation is in short supply (usually during evening hours). Contracts of this type would certainly spur innovation on the demand side. They also might well be less expensive than the holding of costly backup generation capacities.

References

Besembinder, H., & Lemmon, M. (2002). Equilibrium pricing and optimal hedging in electricity forward markets. *Journal of Finance, 57*, 1347–1382.
Bhattacharyya, S. C. (2011). *Energy economics. Concepts, issues, markets and governance.* London: Springer.
Boiteux, M. (1956). Peak load pricing. *Journal of Business, 33*(2), 157–179.
Christensen, L. R., & Greene, W. H. (1976). Economies of scale in U.S. power generation. *Journal of Political Economy, 84*, 655–676.

EU Commission. (2009a). Directive 2009a/72/EC of 13 July 2009a Concerning Common Rules for the Internal Market in Electricity and Repealing Directive 2003/54/EC. Brussels. *Official Journal of the European Union, L 211*, 55–93.

EU Commission. (2009b). Directive 2009b/73/EC of 13 July 2009b Concerning Common Rules for the Internal Market in Natural Gas and Repealing Directive 2003/55/EC. Brussels. *Official Journal of the European Union, L 211*, 94–136.

Hicks, J. R. (1939). *Value and capital*. Oxford: Oxford University Press.

Hunt, S. (2002). *Making competition work in electricity*. New York: Wiley.

Kahn, A. (1970). *The economics of regulation*. Cambridge, MA: MIT Press.

Mas-Colell, A., Winston, M. D., & Green, J. R. (1995). *Microeconomic theory*. Oxford: Oxford University Press.

Praktiknjo, A. (2013). *Sicherheit der Elektrizitätsversorgung. Das Spannungsfeld von Wirtschaftlichkeit und Umweltverträglichkeit (Security of electricity supply. The tension between economic efficiency and environmental compatibility)*. Wiesbaden: Springer.

Praktiknjo, A. (2014). Stated preferences based estimation of power interruption costs in private households: An example from Germany. *Energy, 76*, 82–90.

Steiner, P. O. (1957). Peak loads and efficient pricing. *Quarterly Journal of Economics, 71*(4), 585–610.

Stoft, S. (2000). *Power system economics. Designing markets for electricity*. New York: Wiley.

Thompson Jr., H. G., & Wolf, L. L. (1993). Regional differences in nuclear and fossil-fuel generation of electricity. *Land Economics, 69*(3), 234–248.

Economics of Electrical Grids 13

The electrical grid connects generators and customers. Without it, no electricity market is possible. For enabling competition among generators and retailers, third party access to the electrical grid must be assured on terms that are transparent and nondiscriminatory. From an economic point of view, electrical grids represent both a natural monopoly and an essential facility. This confers a dominant market position upon vertically integrated utilities and power grid operators that may be abused. To prevent this and the concomitant welfare losses, power grids need to be regulated.

Another issue is the network characteristic of the electrical grid. For reasons of economic efficiency, it links many countries on the European continent. The associated grid externalities require grid operators to provide system services according to common rules and standards, among others control power (also called regulation power) to keep demand and supply in continuous balance.

This chapter addresses the following questions:

- What are the economic reasons motivating grid integration?
- What are economically efficient approaches to the provision of grid services?
- What are economically efficient grid tariffs?
- What are the economic benefits and costs of unbundling?

How should interconnectors be efficiently managed?
The variables used in this chapter are:

C	Total cost
CS	Consumer surplus
c	Average cost $(= C/Q)$
c_{mc}	Marginal cost
e	Effort into cost reduction
g	Simultaneity factor
h	Full-load hour per year
L	Lagrange function

λ   Lagrange multiplier
Π   Profit
p   Price for grid use
Q   Amount of distributed electricity (in MWh)
RPI   Retail price index
SR   Sales revenue
W   Macroeconomic welfare
X   Efficiency factor

13.1 Grid Properties and System Services

13.1.1 Electrotechnical Aspects

The transmission and distribution of electrical energy is carried out through integrated electrical grids. With few exceptions, power lines are in alternating current (AC) operation (in contrast to direct current (DC)). AC lines deliver three-phase current with common voltage amplitude but with a phase difference of one-third of the period by combining three wires. Therefore, the sum of the three electric currents is always zero. The direction of electron flux alternates periodically with the target frequency of 50 hertz (Hz) in the European power grid with a tolerance of ±0.15 Hz. In an interconnected AC grid, frequencies are synchronized, resulting in uniform oscillation.

Depending on the voltage level of the power line, one distinguishes between:

- Extra-high voltage grid (220,000–380,000 V) for long distance transmission;
- High-voltage grid (35,000–10,000 V) for interregional transmission;
- Mid-voltage grid (1000–30,000 V) for regional distribution;
- Low-voltage grid (220–380 V) for local distribution.

Since transmission and distribution entails losses that increase with distance, it is efficient to site generation as closely as possible to the point of use electricity. Indeed, the average transmission distance of electricity is below 100 km, with the consequence that transmission and distribution losses are below 5% of delivered electricity, the major part occurring in the low-voltage grid (see Table 13.1). However, according to Ohm's law, loss is inversely related to voltage, making long-distance transmission through extra-high voltage lines economically more viable.

Neglecting the use of electrical grids for telecommunication, power grids are factor-specific assets, meaning that they are exclusively used for delivering electric power from generators to consumers. Many types of infrastructure such as gas grids, water pipes, and railways are factor-specific assets. However, the electrical grid has a particularity which sets it apart from all other such assets: The current flow cannot be limited to one line of the grid. According to Kirchhoff's laws, the

13.1 Grid Properties and System Services

Table 13.1 Average power transmission and distribution losses in Germany, in percent

	RWE energy	ESAG Dresden	SWM Munich
Extra-high voltage grid	1.0		
Transformation extra-high/high voltage	0.5		0.2
High-voltage grid	0.5	0.9	0.3
Transformation high/mid voltage	0.6	0.4	0.4
Mid-voltage grid	1.6	2.0	0.3
Transformation mid/low voltage	1.7	0.8	1.3
Low-voltage grid	4.5	3.7	2.3

Average power losses in percent of the delivered power in each voltage level
Source: Müller (2001)

current flow along a single line of a network depends on its electric resistance relative to all other paths that connect points of entry and exit. Thus electric currents always use all lines of an integrated network regardless of who owns them. Individual power lines can be separated from the grid for repair or to prevent damage from overload, but from an economic point of view, the integrated electrical grid is an indivisible good.

At the end of nineteenth century, electricity was initially supplied in local insulars. While the technical feasibility of long-distance power transmission was demonstrated in the 1880s, it took until in the 1920s and 1930s for nationwide electrical grids to develop in the United States and Europe. This development was fostered by supportive 'eminent domain' legislation weakening property rights of landowners affected by a power line. With the creation of the Union for the Coordination of Transmission of Electricity (UCTE) in 1951 which is now the European Network of Transmission System Operators for Electricity (ENTSO-E), grid interconnection and synchronization spread across Europe. An integrated grid offers the following advantages in terms of economic efficiency[1]:

- In case of power plant failures, customers can be supplied from distant power plants, permitting local providers to reduce their backup capacities. This is equivalent to an insurance-like pooling effect.
- The aggregation of regional load profiles results in a more uniform load, enabling power plants to operate more regularly. This is a positive externality, the so-called network externality (David 1987).
- Power plants that supply larger volumes thanks to enlarged service can be scaled up, resulting in lower unit cost of generation (economies of scale). However, recent technological change seems to have diminished scale economies in generation (Thompson and Wolf 1987), modifying the relative economic benefit of integrated power grids.

---

[1]The high-voltage networks in Europe are typically designed according to the $n-1$ criterion. This means that supply of all customers is still ensured, provided that a single resource (power plant, power line, transformer station) has failed.

– On the other hand, the development of offshore wind and other location-specific generation capacities has led to a renaissance of integrated power grids, with high-voltage direct current (HVDC) technology being used for reducing transmission losses in long-distance transmission.

Without access to the grid, no independent power producer can deliver electricity to customers and no retail customer can shift to a more efficient supplier. Therefore, the key condition for liberalization of electricity markets (see Sect. 12.2) is mandatory third party access to the grid on transparent and discrimination-free terms. Beginning in the 1990s, this condition was satisfied in several industrial countries.

13.1.2 Services to Be Provided by Electrical Grid Operators

When a customer purchases power from another generator rather than from the local utility, the electricity always comes from the nearest power plant connected to the grid. Currents in the integrated grid change only if generators lose (gain, respectively) customers, causing them to reduce (increase) generation. This is a consequence of non-storability (see Sect. 12.1.2). Similar requirements hold for retailers and eligible industrial customers with access to the wholesale power market who are expected to draw exactly the amount of electricity from the grid as contracted with their supplier. The electricity market is in equilibrium if all purchasing contracts are executable with the grid transmission and distribution capacities available.

In Europe, the synchronized integrated grid is divided into control areas where a single transmission system operator (TSO) has the responsibility for reliable and secure grid operation. A high quality of supply requires that all TSOs meet the technical rules and standards set up by the European Network of Transmission System Operators for Electricity (ENTSO-E).

Each TSO needs information to perform this task, which comes from retailers and eligible customers (also balancing group managers) who seek access to the grid. The data to be provided one day ahead comprise planned aggregate volumes of electricity fed into and withdrawn from all grid connecting points in their respective control areas. They typically cover for time intervals no longer than 15 min (see Sect. 3.6.3).

Based on this information, the TSO is obliged to provide the following services[2]:

– Frequency control (secured by so-called spinning reserve and control power);
– Voltage control (secured by compensating so-called reactive power);

---

[2]In some countries, the transmission operator is only responsible for the high and extra-high-voltage grid, whereas the mid and low-voltage power grids are controlled by distribution system operators (DSO).

- Black-start capacities for grid restoration after blackouts (secured by contracts with suitable generators);
- Compensation for transmission losses (which can be substantial in wholesale electricity purchases);
- Redispatch of generators in case of congested grid lines[3];
- Cross-border interconnection management;
- Balancing fluctuations in the supply of electricity produced from renewable sources (if required by the regulator).

While conventional power stations are mostly connected to the high-voltage grid controlled by the TSO, most of the distributed generation capacities are connected to mid- and low-voltage networks controlled by distribution system operators (DSOs). The DSO secures stable operation of the distribution grid, in particular voltage control. Grids of this type are not designed for large-scale transmission. They may even become obsolete with the implementation of smart grids.

13.1.3 Markets for Control Power

Due to the non-storability of electricity in the electrical grid, demand and supply for power must be equal within each control area. However, due to stochastic demand and supply fluctuations, permanent divergences between them occur that must be balanced by a system operator (TSO or ISO). Unexpected fluctuations arise both on the demand side (e.g. due to meteorological conditions) and supply side (e.g. power plant outages). The resulting imbalances can be recognized by deviations from the target frequency of 50 Hz (in Europe). Excess demand causes frequency to drop below 50 Hz, indicating that a positive amount of balancing power is needed. Excess supply causes it to rise above 50 Hz, calling for a negative amount of balancing power.

In Europe, the TSO has the obligation to provide balancing power to grid users which it procures on transparent and competitive markets for control power (also called regulation power); see Fig. 13.1. The TSO calls for combined tenders, specifying both volume and price, at given intervals. Control power is assured by three levels of reserve capacity:

- The primary reserve (historically also known as spinning reserve), which is automatically activated within 15 s and delivered simultaneously by committed suppliers. These suppliers are compensated for the capacity that must be available for both upward and downward regulation.
- The secondary reserve must be available within 30 s to 5 min. Auctions for it are multivariate because suppliers offer prices for both capacity (availability) and

---

[3]Redispatch means to change the power plant schedule by reducing generation in front of and increasing generation behind a grid congestion.

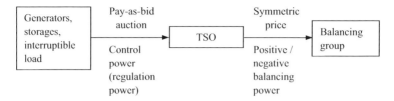

Fig. 13.1 Control power and balancing power

energy (work). Eventually, bids with the lowest prices for capacity are selected. Suppliers are activated by the TSO following the merit order based on the contracted prices for energy. A distinction (also in terms of prices) is made between positive and negative regulation power.
- The tertiary reserve (also called minute reserve) is used to substitute secondary reserves when necessary. It must be available within 15 min upon request of the TSO and is remunerated in a similar fashion as the secondary reserve. Again, a distinction between upward and downward capacities is made.

Prices for both capacity and energy are based on the pay-as-bid principle rather than according to the highest accepted bid (uniform pricing) as in the day-ahead market (see Sect. 12.2.2).

The procurement of balancing power entails additional cost of capacity and energy. The cost of capacity is charged to customers as a flat transmission grid fee. The cost of energy delivered is assigned to the parties seeking access (in the guise of so-called balancing groups) according to their individual discrepancies between registered and realized power (see Sect. 3.6.3). The energy cost depends on the total amount of balancing energy needed which corresponds to the sum of all discrepancies (with correct signs). The price of balancing energy is constant and equal to the average price of control energy supplied to the TSO with a time interval for pricing of 15 min (real-time pricing). There are no price spreads between positive and negative deviations. If this price is positive, balancing groups who exhibit net excess energy receive this price for supplying it, while parties who show net deficits have to pay this price.

13.2 Regulation of Grid Fees

In view of Kirchhoff's law, users of the grid lack control over the route electricity takes in the grid. Thus, the relevant concept is the extra cost caused by admitting an extra MW for transmission regardless of points of entry and exit. Grid fees based on this concept evidently facilitate competition among generators and have been favored by the European Union for this reason. In addition, the EC Directive 2003/54/EG on the single European electricity market establishes that access fees may be charged on the exit side, not on the entry side of the grid. Consequently, power consumers are charged for access to the grid according to the voltage level,

13.2 Regulation of Grid Fees

with those connected to the low-voltage grid having to pay for all higher voltage levels. These fees are collected by the distribution grid operator, who transfers them to the respective operators managing the higher-level grids.

13.2.1 The Grid as an Essential Facility

The electrical grid is a natural monopoly, which means that the cost function that links transmission and distribution expenditure to quantity transmitted is sub-additive. Sub-additivity implies that combining grid assets of K system operators with transmission Q_k and costs $C(Q_k)$ respectively reduces the overall cost of supply, i.e.

$$C\left(\sum_{k=1}^{K} Q_i\right) < \sum_{k=1}^{K} C(Q_i). \tag{13.1}$$

Given a natural monopoly, it is therefore cost-effective to merge transmission units of a common region to become a single unit rather than having two or more separate companies compete with their grids. A sufficient (but not necessary) condition for a natural monopoly is that average cost be below marginal cost. This condition holds for power grids, at least given the current state of technology. Artificially injecting competition into the transmission and distribution industries is also near impossible because of high barriers to entry for newcomers especially in countries with already sufficient transmission and distribution capacities.

In addition, an electrical grid also constitutes an essential facility. Without it, generators cannot supply their customers unless they are located right next to the power plant. This gives vertically integrated utilities and power grid operators a dominant market position, which they may abuse by denying independent power producers access to the grid or charging them excessive fees. The result is an artificial limitation of supply that causes a welfare loss (see also Sect. 1.2.2). For this reason power grid operators must be regulated. The economic theory of regulation provides concepts and models for governments who seek to set access fees for grids in an optimal way.

13.2.2 Optimal Grid Fees

In the interest of welfare maximization, the price for access to a network should be equal to marginal cost, the so-called first-best solution. The regulator may be tempted to impose marginal cost-pricing. But the grid being a natural monopoly, its marginal cost is below average cost. Therefore, a price equal to marginal cost fails to generate enough revenue to recover total cost (see point A in Fig. 13.2). In this case, public regulation needs to find a second-best solution (Demsetz 1968).

Fig. 13.2 The electrical grid as a natural monopoly

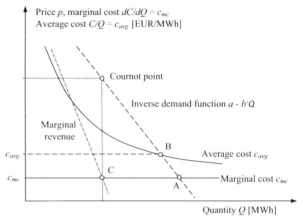

The classical proposal is to let the monopolistic network operator charge a price that covers average cost, including an appropriate return on the capital employed (so-called cost-plus regulation). However, this solution is problematic. Frist, since price depends on average cost, incentives to minimize cost are undermined. Second, there is a welfare loss because some customers who are willing to pay a price in excess of marginal cost are not served (those with a demand between points A and B of Fig. 13.2).

Both of these concerns are addressed by a split tariff, which amounts to price discrimination according to marginal willingness to pay (WTP):

- Customers with marginal WTP in excess of average cost cavg pay a price equal to cavg;
- Customers with a marginal WTP between marginal cost cmc and average cost cavg pay a price equal to cmc.

Therefore, the split tariff ensures that all customers whose willingness to pay is sufficient to cover the marginal cost of service are served. The utility breaks even since up to point B, its average cost is covered by the revenue obtained from costumers with high willingness to pay, whereas the extra quantity provided between points B and A is priced in a way to recover the additional cost.

Obviously, identifying customers with high marginal WTP is difficult. In addition, actually using this information for pricing is prohibited by the European directive on the common market for electricity (European Commission 2009a, b), which stipulates discrimination-free and transparent access to the grid. By prohibiting any kind of price discrimination in the use of grids, it in fact makes the introduction of split tariffs impossible.

Another approach is the two-part tariff:

- The first part of the tariff makes all costumers pay a price equal to the marginal cost of transmitting or distributing electricity. It preserves incentives for

13.2 Regulation of Grid Fees

efficiency because by lowering marginal cost, the network operator can generate more profit.
– The second part of the tariff makes up for the shortfall in revenue. It is a separate price for access to the grid, which transfers part of the consumer surplus (given by the area below the demand function but above the marginal cost function) to the network operator. This part of the tariff is tricky because the network operator has a clear interest in appropriating as much consumer surplus as possible, beyond the amount necessary to break even. Moreover, the break-even point itself depends on the location of the average cost function, which is under the operator's control. Finally, consumers have a weakened incentive to invest in energy efficiency because the capacity fee does not depend on their consumption.

Yet several customers may use the same grid capacity if they do not call on it during the same period (see Sect. 12.3.1). To account for this, the capacity ordered is multiplied by a simultaneity factor $0 < g(h) < 1$, which is a function that increases with the so-called annual usage time h.[4] Annual usage time is an indicator of the probability that a grid customer orders grid capacity at peak load time. An example of such a function is

$$g(h) = \begin{cases} 0.1 + \dfrac{0.6 \cdot h}{2,500} & \text{for } h \leq 2,500 \\ 0.58 + \dfrac{0.42 \cdot h}{8,760} & \text{for } h > 2,500 \end{cases} \quad (13.2)$$

A distinction can be made between off-peak and peak usage of the grid. Therefore, grid companies can be regarded as monopolistic companies with $k = 2$ products or segments. In order to avoid arbitrary allocation of cost between the two segments, regulators may use the Ramsey pricing model. This model calculates a price vector (p_1, p_2) that maximizes net welfare (gross welfare W minus cost C),

$$\max_{Q_1, Q_2} (W(Q_1, Q_2) - C(Q_1, Q_2)) \quad (13.3)$$

subject to the constraint that total revenue must cover cost,

$$\sum_{k=1}^{2} p_k \cdot Q_k - C(Q_1, Q_2) \geq 0. \quad (13.4)$$

A crucial assumption is that the production cost as well as demand for one two products is independent of production cost and demand for the other (see Laffont

---

[4]The annual usage time h [h/a] is calculated by dividing annual amount of energy transmitted [MWh/a] by maximum capacity demanded [MW] during the pertinent period. Maximum capacity demand is measured over a fixed time unit (usually 15 min).

and Tirole 1993: p. 250 for the case of nonzero cross price elasticities for demand, involving so-called super-elasticities).

If the regulator does not want to grant the network operator any excess revenue the constraint (13.4) becomes an equality. Thus, the optimization problem can be solved using the Lagrangian approach,

$$L = \left(W(Q_1, Q_2) - C(Q_1, Q_2)\right) + \lambda \left(\sum_{k=1}^{2} p_k \cdot Q_k - C(Q_1, Q_2)\right) \to \max! \quad (13.5)$$

Here, $\lambda > 0$ denotes the Lagrangian multiplier which indicates how strongly goal attainment would suffer if cost where to exceed revenue. If gross welfare is equated to consumer surplus CS (see Eq. (12.1)), one has

$$\frac{\partial W}{\partial Q_i} = p_i, \quad i = 1, 2. \quad (13.6)$$

With this in hand, the first-order conditions of the Lagrangian function read

$$\frac{\partial L}{\partial Q_i} = (p_i - c_{mc,i}) + \lambda \left(\sum_{k=1}^{2} \frac{\partial (p_k \cdot Q_k)}{\partial Q_i} - c_{mc,i}\right) = 0. \quad (13.7)$$

The sum in Eq. (13.7) contains terms which pertain to cross-price elasticities, which however are neglected in keeping with the assumption of independent demands. Therefore, this sum can be written as

$$\sum_{k=1}^{2} \frac{\partial (p_k \cdot Q_k)}{\partial Q_i} = \frac{\partial p_i}{\partial Q_i} \cdot Q_i + p_i. \quad (13.8)$$

The following optimality condition for the price p_i results,

$$\frac{p_i - c_{mc,i}}{p_i} = -\frac{\lambda}{1+\lambda} \cdot \frac{1}{\eta_i} \quad \text{with} \quad \frac{1}{\eta_i} = \frac{\partial p_i}{\partial Q_i} \cdot \frac{Q_i}{p_i} < 0 \quad (13.9)$$

Here, η_i is the own price elasticity of demand. The price p_i resulting from Eq. (13.9) is called the Ramsey price.

According to Eq. (13.9), the Ramsey price contains a surcharge over marginal cost. It increases with λ, the so-called shadow price of a constraint, in the present case constraint (13.4) that ensures the recovery of total cost. Furthermore, the surcharge decreases with the absolute value of the own price elasticity of demand η_i. If customers in a particular market segment respond strongly to an increase in the grid fee (as is typical for off-peak customers) a surcharge over marginal cost entails a large welfare loss. On the other hand, there are market segments where the price elasticity is low (typically peak customers). Following the optimality condition, these customers should bear a larger proportion of the grid cost than off-peak customers.

For the practical application of Ramsey pricing, regulators need to have detailed knowledge of the current cost of the grid (backward-looking) as well as the future cost associated with efficient grid services (forward-looking). A large number of operational and economic parameters must be assessed as well:

- How much physical (and hence financial) capital is required for efficient operation of the grid?
- What standards of quality (e.g. interruption duration) must the grid operator guarantee?
- Is the network operator to be allowed to include the cost of future expansions of the grid in the fee?
- What method of depreciation is to be applied to grid assets (e.g. procurement cost or replacement cost)?
- What is the so-called rate base, i.e. the allowable share of equity?
- What is the allowable rate of return on equity?

There is the definite possibility that the regulator answers these questions in a way that conflicts with the assessment of the grid operator. In the case of private grid ownership, the specifications of the regulator in fact determine the company's decision to invest, blurring the division of responsibilities between the two. Eventually, the result may be a nationalization of electrical grids because it vests managerial responsibility unambiguously with the government. However, such a decision will always entail long-term consequences for economic efficiency.

13.2.3 Incentive Regulation

Another critical issue of all public regulation is the asymmetry of information between regulator and the regulated firm (the grid operator in the present context). Grid operators have detailed knowledge concerning potential for efficiency improvement and tendencies in demand that is unavailable to regulators. This is an instance of the principal-agent problem, where a principal lacks the information for controlling the agent's effort, who can therefore pursue its own interests. All the principal can do in this situation is to structure the contract in a way as to provide the best possible incentives to the agent, at least in expected value. In the present context, grid operators may use their informational advantage to obtain grid fees in excess of the level justified by minimum cost regardless of the regulation method chosen:

- Under rate-of-return regulation (also known as cost-plus or markup regulation), grid operators are granted a fixed markup on proven cost. This type of regulation creates an incentive to increase cost, notably by employing capital in excess of

the economically efficient amount. This is the so-called Averch-Johnson effect (see Averch and Johnson 1962).
- Under price-cap regulation, the regulator sets a maximum grid fee. In this case, the incentive is to increase profit by reducing investment. Therefore, price-cap regulation results in underinvestment, thus hurting grid reliability in the long term.
- Under revenue-cap regulation, the regulator sets the maximum revenue. Revenue-cap regulation gives rise to an incentive to increase profit by minimizing costly grid services.

Whatever the approach of the regulator, its objectives may fail to be achieved, notably economically efficient and reliable grid operation. The popular response to this failure is tighter control and increased sanctions. However, such a response often is not helpful because supervision and compliance are not without cost themselves, resulting in an increase in the macroeconomic cost of electrical grids.

This dilemma has spawned the concept of incentive regulation, which was developed by Stephen Littlechild, who later became the first regulator of the electric industry in the United Kingdom (see Beesley and Littlechild 1989; Laffont and Tirole 1993, Chap. 4). According to this concept, regulation should be compatible with the incentives of the regulated firm. Applied to grid operators, it calls for letting them earn higher profits for a few years if they increase efficiency more than required by the regulator. After this grace period, however, they must pass the benefits from efficiency gains to their customers in the form of lower fees.

Incentive regulation determines the time path of a selected indicator, e.g. maximum allowable sales revenues SR, in the following way during a specified period,

$$SR_t \leq SR_{t-1} \cdot \left(1 + RPI_{t-1} - X_{general} + X_{individual}\right). \quad (13.10)$$

In this formula, RPI_{t-1} denotes the percentage change in the index of retail prices over the previous period, $X_{general}$, a required rate of productivity increase, calculated over all grid operators, and $X_{individual}$, a required rate of productivity increase, applied to an individual grid operator.

According to Eq. (13.10), an operator's revenue may increase with the general rate of inflation. There are two extensions, however. The first is a deduction reflecting the rate of productivity increase in the industry. The second is designed to raise the bar for grid operators who have been lagging behind, forcing them to catch up with the rest. Conversely, grid operators who improve productivity $X_{individual}$ by more than $X_{general}$ can benefit from an increase of their allowable revenue, permitting them to earn higher profits. In this way, incentive regulation seeks to conserve incentives for dynamic productivity improvement. Grid operators can retain excessive profits, but only temporarily because the regulator adjusts the formula (13.10) at the end of a specified period. At that point, costs and profits are examined, which are (close to) their true values, providing information that would usually not be accessible to regulators.

13.2 Regulation of Grid Fees

In practice, this approach suffers from its exclusive focus on cost-efficiency. Reliability and other quality dimensions of supply aspects are not considered. Security of supply is defined here as the capability of the power transmission and distribution system to continuously maintain the flow of electricity in case of unforeseen disruptions. To account for this aspect, the incentive regulation formula (13.10) can be extended to include a bonus for high-quality grid operation which is usually based on the value of lost load (see Praktiknjo 2013). An indicator of quality is the predicted number of grid customers that can still be supplied if one element of the grid (e.g. power line, transformer, control room) fails (this constitutes the so-called n−1 criterion). Rather than this ex-ante indicator, most regulators use ex-post indicators. These include

- SAIDI: System Average Interruption Duration Index;
- SAIFI: System Average Interruption Frequency Index;
- CAIDI: Customer Average Interruption Duration Index.

Usually, these indicators reflect quality deficits only with a time lag. While insufficient maintenance reduces cost immediately, the quality of grid services deteriorates only in the medium term. Conversely, expenditure on investment and maintenance increases grid cost instantly but has a positive effect on quality with a lag.

13.2.4 Unbundling

The term 'unbundling' means undoing the vertical integration that has been characterizing the electric power industry for the past century. Its objective is to open up the market to competition between generators and to traders who are independent of both generators and distributors. However, pursuing this objective through unbundling is not without opportunity cost because the efficiency advantages of vertical integration mentioned in Sect. 12.1.3 are lost. Nevertheless, the EU Directive 2009/72/EC (European Commission 2009a) stipulates that large utilities must be at least legally unbundled, resulting in independent business units for generation, transmission, and distribution (see Table 13.2). For the time being, unbundling in terms of ownership is not required. Alternatively, grid ownership can remain within the integrated company, in return, operation of the transmission network is to be transferred to an independent system operator (ISO).

An example of the unbundling of the grid is the PJM (Pennsylvania—New Jersey—Maryland Interconnection) market in the northeastern United States, which serves an area of 13 states with 51 mn grid customers. In addition to providing the usual grid services, an independent system operator (ISO) determines transmission prices at each node where power can be fed in and taken out (so-called nodal pricing). Every 5 min and at every node (approaching a real-time market), the locational price is determined by the marginal cost of the last power plant which has to be connected to the grid in order to cover the load forecasted by the ISO without

Table 13.2 Unbundling concepts

Accounting	Informational	Management	Legal	Ownership
Separate accounts for different lines of business	Confidential treatment of sensitive data within the line of business	Division of business units into separate departments	Legal separation of business units	Spin-off and sale of grid
Regulatory requirements concerning financial statements	Separate use of information by lines of business	Functional separation of staff	Regulatory requirements concerning (in-)admissible relationships between business units	No grid ownership permitted for power plant operators
		Financial auto-nomy of departments		Possibly state ownership

violating any grid restrictions. Furthermore, the ISO performs the economically efficient dispatching of power plants using data such as maximum power gradient (i.e. the speed with which the plant can be brought up to required output), minimum uptime and downtime, and start-up and shut-down cost. Power plant operators act according to the price signaled by the ISO, which reflects the shadow price (i.e. the value of the Lagrangian multiplier) pertaining to the constraint,

$$Generation = Load. \qquad (13.11)$$

This shadow price is part of the solution of an optimization problem. Power plant operators are free to not respond to this price signal, speculating to be able to extract higher capacity prices in a later period. The price signaling activities of the ISO are financed in analogy to the market for balancing power in Europe (see discussion in Sect. 13.1.3).

13.3 Economic Approach to Transmission Bottlenecks

According to Kirchhoff's laws, the transmission of electricity between a generator and a so-called load sink uses all available routes. This can lead to loop flows across linked control areas of a grid, giving rise to congestion. As a result, intended trades cannot be executed simultaneously, forcing the (independent or transmission) system operator (ISO or TSO, respectively) to modify individual delivery schedules.

The left-hand side of Fig. 13.3 illustrates such a situation. A generator (indicated at the top left) seeks to transmit 8 MW to a customer (indicated at the bottom left). The direct connection (dashed) has a capacity of 4 MW only. However, the

13.3 Economic Approach to Transmission Bottlenecks

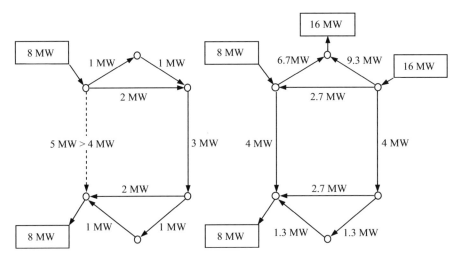

Fig. 13.3 Reverse flow and the elimination of a grid bottleneck

intended transmission would trigger a power flow of 5 MW in the dashed line, resulting in system failure.

The system operator (ISO or TSO) can avoid congestion in this example, by ordering an additional delivery between two indirectly affected grid nodes (see right-hand side of Fig. 13.3). The additional delivery of 16 MW creates an indirect counterflow of 1 MW on the congested line. As a consequence, the net demand placed on this link is reduced to 4 MW, equal to its capacity.

This is but one of several options for dealing with grid bottlenecks. Other options are the following.

- Rationing: This amounts to capping the amount of power that can be transmitted during a given period. If rationing is imposed frequently, grid customers begin to weigh the value of lost load caused by it against the value of purchasing and operating emergency backup units. They cannot be expected to undertake the investment for the elimination of a notorious network bottleneck themselves. Such an investment would benefit all other grid customers, creating a positive external effect. Therefore, this is up to the grid operator, who can be induced by the regulator to initiate the necessary investment e.g. by granting increased grid fees.[5]
- Explicit auctioning of temporal capacity rights on critical segments of the grid (see Hogan 1993): A company who has acquired capacity rights is allowed but not required to use these rights at its discretion. This gives it potential for abuse by not exercising them, thus blocking transmission by competitors. In this way,

---

[5]For the elimination of transborder grid bottlenecks, the European Commission envisages subsidizing investments as part of its Trans-European Networks program.

regional market areas can be insulated from international competition. A solution to this problem is for the grid operator to be able to withdraw capacity rights from non-users, applying the principle "use it or lose it". The elimination of grid bottlenecks could in principle be financed using the proceeds of these auctions.
- Implicit auctioning of capacity rights: In the absence of a grid bottleneck between two market areas, price differences between them can be removed by merging the two (so-called market coupling). If the local power exchanges cooperate, demand in the more expensive area can in part be met by supply from the low-cost market area until the price difference disappears. However, grid capacity between the two market areas may not be sufficient for price equalization. In this case, the participating power exchanges may aim at maximum possible price equalization by ensuring that power flows from the low-price area to the high-price one.
- Market splitting (nodal pricing): Grid bottlenecks may also occur within a single control area. They can be overcome by temporarily dividing the control area into separate market areas and ensuring that each of them has market prices that balance regional demand and supply. In the area with a high market price, customers pay a surcharge on the price that would prevail if the control area were integrated. This constitutes extra revenue for the generators. Conversely, customers in the area with a low market price benefit from a low price, while generators achieve less revenue. Eventually, the price differences incentivize investment in generation capacity in the high-cost area and investment in grid capacity between the low-cost and high-cost region, both alleviating future congestions. This model has been implemented in Scandinavia for years, ensuring that bottlenecks are managed efficiently by Nord Pool, the Scandinavian power exchange.

Implicit auctioning and market splitting make efficient handling of grid bottlenecks possible, suggesting that they are likely to become more common in future. However, they too fail to provide an answer to the question of how to create economic incentives for completely eliminating grid bottlenecks. In principle, a grid bottleneck hurts economic efficiency if investment in its removal is less costly than the present value of the price differences caused by it. As a result, grid operators have usually no reason to make such an investment (eliminating price differences and thus potential for arbitrage activities) unless the regulator provides them with appropriate incentives (e.g. granting a higher return on equity or exemptions from regulation imposing nondiscriminatory access to the grid).

References

Averch, H., & Johnson, L. (1962). Behavior of the firm under regulatory constraint. *American Economic Review, 52*, 1052–1069.
Beesley, M., & Littlechild, S. (1989). The regulation of privatized monopolies in the United Kingdom. *Rand Journal of Economics, 20*(3), 454–472.

References

David, P. A. (1987). Some new standards for the economics of standardization in the information age. In P. Dasgupta & P. Stoneman (Eds.), *Economic policy and technological performance* (pp. 206–239). Cambridge: Cambridge University Press.

Demsetz, H. (1968). Why regulate utilities? *Journal of Law and Economics, 11*(1), 55–65.

EU Commission. (2009a). Directive 2009a/72/EC of 13 July 2009a Concerning Common Rules for the Internal Market in Electricity and Repealing Directive 2003/54/EC. Brussels. *Official Journal of the European Union, L 211*, 55–93.

EU Commission. (2009b). Directive 2009b/73/EC of 13 July 2009b Concerning Common Rules for the Internal Market in Natural Gas and Repealing Directive 2003/55/EC. Brussels. *Official Journal of the European Union, L 211*, 94–136.

Hogan, W. W. (1993). Markets in real electric networks require reactive prices. *Energy Journal, 14*(3), 171–200.

Laffont, J. J., & Tirole, J. (1993). *A theory of incentives in procurement and regulation.* Cambridge, MA: MIT Press.

Müller, L. (2001). *Handbuch der Elektrizitätswirtschaft (Handbook of the electricity industry).* Berlin: Springer.

Praktiknjo, A. (2013). *Sicherheit der Elektrizitätsversorgung. Das Spannungsfeld von Wirtschaftlichkeit und Umweltverträglichkeit (Security of electricity supply. The tension between economic efficiency and environmental compatibility).* Wiesbaden: Springer.

Epilogue   14

While Chaps. 1–7 are dedicated to overarching issues and systemic relationships, Chaps. 8–13 of this book turn to the individual markets for energy. Starting from the pertinent constraints imposed by the laws of science and engineering, the discussions revolve around respective costs, supply and demand, forms of competition, and resulting prices, taking account of peculiarities that shape consumer preferences. In an attempt to keep the analysis reasonably simple, the existence of the respective other markets and prices prevailing on them have been taken as given, thus abstracting from the interdependencies between the several energy markets. In addition, the question why politicians want to see certain market outcomes rather than others, e.g. by subsidizing renewables or prohibiting the use of fracking technologies, remains mainly unanswered.[1] In that sense, energy policy is outside the scope of this book.

This is not to deny that energy markets are very much influenced by policy. This becomes particularly apparent when considering the call formulated at several international conferences and summits to practically cease all greenhouse gas emissions by the middle of this century. Yet the implementation of this call would have consequences for energy markets of a magnitude exceeding anything observed during the past 100 years—a period certainly not devoid of turmoil concerning energy.

Using some of the insights obtained in this book, it may be worthwhile to speculate on what a future decarbonized energy system might look like. One possibility is technological change with a focus on electricity with renewable fuels, short- and long-term storage of power, and its transmission between continents. Developments of this type would foster the use of electricity in markets that up to now have been relying on fossil energy sources, be they solid, liquid, or

---

[1] Answers to this question would require a good deal of so-called public choice theory, a branch of economics that analyzes the behavior of voters, politicians, and public officials (see e.g. Buchanan and Tullock 1962).

gaseous. The expanded use of electricity need not be direct, in the guise e.g. of battery-powered vehicles or heat pumps. Rather, it might also be indirect, through a transformation of renewable electricity into other final energy sources (known as sector coupling, e.g. power-to-heat, power-to-gas, and power-to-liquid). The advantage of this scenario is that at least part of the existing infrastructure can be used in future.

Another alternative is to substitute fossil energy sources by derivatives of biomass. However, this would call for the development of new technologies designed to reduce land requirements. Otherwise, competition between 'biomass for energy' and 'biomass for food' is likely to render this solution to the greenhouse gas problem unacceptable. Another option is carbon capture and storage (CCS) and carbon capture and use (CCU). In both cases, the carbon dioxide (CO_2) released is filtered from the gases associated with the combustion of fossil fuels. Obviously, CCS and CCU make sense only if the release of CO_2 into the atmosphere can be permanently prevented. The CCS technology amounts to the use of suitable geological formations for this purpose. However, available capacities are likely to fall short of the quantities of CO_2 that have been accumulating during decades. In response to this challenge, ongoing research is focusing on CCU technologies, which enable CO_2 to be stored in e.g. cement and other building materials. Evidently, for CCU to contribute to climate protection, the quantities of CO_2 usable in the production of these materials must be huge.

Whether or not the aim of an emission-free energy industry can be attained in the foreseeable future also depends on the decisions taken by the international climate conferences and summits. However, at the time being an agreement implementing the most efficient instrument (from an economic perspective) appears to be beyond reach: a global, nondiscriminatory CO_2 tax. In the short term, such an internalization tax is apt to trigger low-cost avoidance efforts, notably directed at improving energy efficiency and the substitution of coal by natural gas. Yet for attaining the objective of climate neutrality, the long-term impacts of a CO_2 tax are even more important. By credibly committing to it, the international community would create incentives to invest in innovation that brings about climate neutrality.[2]

To attain the goal of climate neutrality, breakthrough innovations in one or several of the fields cited above need to occur within a rather short period of time. However, one should abstain from trying to identify the one innovation that will win this technology race based on the current state of knowledge.[3] Historical experience suggests that a mix of innovations is likely to emerge. Following the portfolio theory developed by Markowitz (1952) expounded in Sect. 3.5.1 of this book, there might be an optimal mix of technology to achieve climate neutrality

---

[2] As argued by Hayek (1960, p. 32), information about potential innovations is distributed among a multitude of agents in an economy, who moreover have an interest in keeping it to themselves rather than sharing it with a policy maker.

[3] The same holds for predicting with any precision the costs of realizing ambitious scenarios of climate protection within this century.

from a cost-benefit perspective. However, such an assessment requires reliable data on all technologies and especially on the cost of CO_2 mitigation associated with them. But evidently such data is unavailable for future innovations by definition.

In sum, energy policy in general and climate policy in particular will continue to be subject to (often unpredictable) changes. Therefore, this book limits itself to the analysis of the several markets for energy and their way of functioning. Possibly, some of them may disappear altogether in future. As long as there is a need for commercial sources of energy, however, there is also a need for markets on which they can be traded. This implies that basic influences such as preferences governing demand, (marginal) costs and technological breakthroughs governing supply, their interaction governed by various degrees of competition, and politicians' motivations for intervening in markets will not change in a fundamental way. This remains true even if elements of central planning should again supersede energy markets. One should never forget the most important message of energy economics, which is that consumers and producers will continue to pursue their own objectives!

References

Buchanan, J. M., & Tullock, G. (1962). *The calculus of consent: Logical foundations of constitutional democracy*. Ann Arbor: University of Michigan Press.
Hayek, F. A. (1960). *The constitution of liberty*. Chicago: Chicago University Press.
Markowitz, H. M. (1952). Portfolio selection. *Journal of Finance, 12*, 77–91.

Index

A
Achnacarry agreement, 174
Adaptive expectation, 98, 187
Adjustment time, 99, 100
Agriculture, 19
Alcohol, 169
Allais paradox, 265
Alternating current (AC), 275, 298
Altruism, 263
Ampere, 270
Ancillary service, 300
Anergy, 17
Annual usage time, 305
Annuity, 79
Antitrust Act, 171, 173, 174
API grade, 160
Arbitrageur, 190
Arrow paradox, 11
Asset pricing, 53
Associated natural gas, 202, 204
Atomic Energy Commission, 255
Augmented Dickey-Fuller test, 219
Averch-Johnson effect, 308

B
Backstop technology, 120
Backup capacity, 294
Backwardation, 191, 284
Backward integration, 202
Balancing group, 300
Balancing power, 60–62, 283
Barrel, 20
Base load, 278
Becquerel, 249
Benchmark crude, 183
Bernoulli criterion, 50, 284
Bertrand competition, 285, 288
Bertrand paradox, 288

Bio methane, 203
Bio natural gas, 203
Biodiesel, 169, 171
Biogas, 202
Biomass, 228
Biomass gasification, 170
Biomass to liquid, 169, 170
Black-Scholes formula, 59
Black-start, 301
Blending, 169
Boiling water reactor, 248
Bottom-up approach, 65, 154
Brent, 161
British Thermal Unit, 20
Brundtland report, 131

C
Call option, 55, 293
Calorie, 16
Capacity factor, 39, 278
Capacity rent, 295
Capacity rights, 223
Capital intensity, 39
Capital recovery factor, 40
Capital user cost, 40, 209
Carbon capture and storage, 244
Carnot efficiency, 22, 276
Cartel, 178, 206
Cash flow, 46
Cash margin, 193
Churn rate, 217
Clean coal, 244
Clean dark spread, 242
Clean spark spread, 242
Clearing, 53, 183
Cluster risk, 216
CO_2 concentration, 236
Coal equivalent, 20

Coal to liquid, 169
Coase theorem, 145
Cobb-Douglas production function, 136
Cointegration, 190, 203, 219
Coke, 231
Cold combustion, 278
Combined cycle gas turbine, 22, 216, 276
Combined heat and power, 203
Commercial energy, 24
Commodity, 172
Competition
　atomistic, 4
　perfect, 6, 278
　policy, 173
Compliance, 308
Concession, 202, 289
Concession fee, 289
Condensate, 167
Conjoint analysis, 156
Consistency, 71
Consumer surplus, 271
Contango, 191, 192, 284
Contingent valuation, 156
Contract for differences, 284
Contracting, 85–87
Contribution margin, 39, 292
Control area, 300
Control power, 301
Control variable, 124
Convenience yield, 54, 191
Conversion plant, 167
Cookery, 200
Cooperation, 179
Coordination, 6
Cost of carry, 190
Cost of conserved energy, 80
Cost of ownership, 69
Cost plus regulation, 304
Coulomb force, 17
Counterparty risk, 53, 183
Cournot competition, 285
Covariance, 51
Crack spread, 193

D
Dark spread, 242, 293
Day-ahead market, 279
Decision tree analysis, 58
Density, 200
Depletion midpoint, 163

Derivatives, 55, 190
Differential rent, 121
Direct current (DC), 275, 298
Discount factor, 39
Discounting, 39, 123
Discount rate, 40, 44
Discrete choice, 264, 265
Dispatch, 278–280
Distillation, 167
Distribution system operator, 301
Diversification, 50, 216
Double marginalization, 208
Drift, 59
Dubai Crude, 161
Dutch disease, 139

E
Economies of scale, 172
Efficiency, 77
Efficiency factor, 22, 77
Efficiency principle, 24
Efficient allocation, 6
Efficient market hypothesis, 183
Elasticity, 136, 306
　Allen, 105
　cross price, 96
　income, 92
　price, 95
　short-term, 99
　of substitution, 104, 133
　super, 306
Electricity supply curve, 279
Eligible customer, 300
Emission, 144
Emission allowance, 227, 237, 279
Emission trajectory, 236
Endothermic process, 18
Energy balance, 23–28
Energy density, 132
Energy efficiency, 78
Energy ellipse, 161, 200
Energy intensity, 92, 93
Energy only market, 295
Energy payback time, 28
Energy savings, 79
Energy service, 27
Enhanced oil recovery, 164
Enrichment, 252
Enthalpy, 20
Entry point, 217

Index 321

Entry-exit system, 222
Environment liability, 152
Enzyme, 170
Equilibrium, 5, 96, 219
Equilibrium model, 34
Equivalent dose, 250
Error correction model, 219
Error correction term, 190
Essential facility, 303
Essential good, 7
Estimated ultimate recovery, 112
European Power Exchange, 280
Exergy, 1, 17, 78, 271
Exit point, 217
Exothermic process, 18
Expectation error, 122
Expected loss, 258
Exploration cost, 115
External cost, 12, 144, 259
  marginal, 146
External effect, 144

F

Factor-specific investment, 173
Factor specificity, 197, 206, 298
Final energy consumption, 24, 26
Fischer-Tropsch synthesis, 229, 244
Fixed feed-in tariff, 42
Fixed proportions production
  function, 32, 34
Flue gas capture, 244
Forward, 54, 283
Forward premium, 284
Fracking, 115, 166, 201
Fraction, 167
Fuel cell, 277
Fuel switching, 217
Full load operation, 278
Fundamental analysis, 185
Future, 283

G

Game theory, 178, 206
Gas hub, 216
Gas storage, 216
Gas to liquid, 169
Gas turbine power plant, 276
Goodness of fit, 101
Grandfathering, 237
Graphite, 251
Gravitation, 16

Gray, 250
Gray energy, 28, 34
Grid access, 221
Gross Domestic Product, 97
Gross energy, 23
Gross production, 32
Gumbel distribution, 73

H

Habit persistence hypothesis, 98
Half-life time, 249
Hamiltonian function, 125
Hartwick consumption trajectory, 133
Hartwick rule, 134, 135, 138
Harvesting factor, 28
Heat equivalent, 16
Heating degree day, 224
Heavy oil, 166
Hedge, 53
Hedonic price approach, 156
Henry Hub price, 217
Hertz, 298
High-pressure pipeline, 205
Holdup problem, 206, 210
Hotelling price trajectory, 118, 120
Hotelling rule, 126
Human capital, 138
Hydro cracking, 167
Hydrogen, 168, 203, 248
Hydropower, 276
Hysteresis, 99

I

IIA assumption, 73
Immission, 144
Incumbent, 287
Independent power producer, 291
Independent system operator, 309
Industrial firewood, 228
Information asymmetry, 84
Input/output table, 29
  energy, 30
Integrated grid, 299
Interconnector, 280
Interest arbitrage, 84
Internal rate of return, 40
International Energy Agency, 179, 185
International Monetary Fund, 186
Intraday market, 283
Investor/user problem, 83
Ionization, 250

Isocost line, 103
Isoquant, 102, 107

J
Johansen test, 220

K
Kilowatt, 16, 270
Kirchhoff's laws, 298
Kurtosis, 184

L
Lagrange function, 124, 148, 306
Lagrange multiplier, 118, 148
Least-cost planning, 80
Leontief multiplier, 32
Leontief production function, 32, 34
Levelized cost of electricity (LCOE), 278
Levelized costs, 42, 278
Liability insurance, 150, 266
Life-cycle assessment, 28
Light-water reactor, 248, 249, 251, 253
Lignite, 228
Liquefied natural gas, 211
Load duration curve, 289
Load profile, 272
Logit model, 70
    multinomial, 72
    nested, 73
Log-normal distribution, 59
Long position, 182, 283
Long-term contract, 216
Lorenz curve, 91
Lower heating value, 20, 77, 200, 217

M
Magnetic induction, 275
Marginal abatement cost, 237
Marginal cost, 4
Marginal cost of generation, 278
Marginal rate of substitution, 104
Marginal supplier, 4
Market area, 222
Market-clearing price, 279
Mass defect, 251
Market failure, 9, 147
Market power, 130, 285–288
Mean reversion, 281
Market splitting, 312

Megajoule, 16
Megawatt, 270
Merit order, 279, 287
Methane hydrate, 201
Minute reserve, 302
Missing money problem, 295
Mixed oxide, 252
Monopoly, 8
    regulated, 52
Monte Carlo simulation, 58, 292
Multi-criteria evaluation, 10
Must-run capacity, 281
Myopia, 48, 83

N
Nash equilibrium, 208
National Balancing Point (NBP), 217
Nationalization, 180, 181, 307
Natural monopoly, 303
Netback price, 215
Net energy, 27
Net present value, 39
Newton, 16
Nodal pricing, 312
Nonproliferation treaty, 257
Non-stationarity, 219
Norwegian Pension Fund, 139

O
Off-peak period, 280
Ohm's law, 298
Oil equivalent, 20
Oil future, 190
Oil sands, 166
Oligopoly, 285
Opportunity cost, 5, 124, 243
Option, 54
Organization of Oil Exporting Countries
    (OPEC) basket, 178
Over-the-counter contract, 183
Ownership probability, 68
Oxidation, 18

P
Paper barrel, 113
Pareto efficiency, 6
Pareto optimum, 77, 144, 235
Payback time, 42
Peak demand, 279
Peak load, 278

Peak oil hypothesis, 164, 189
Peak period, 280
Peak shaving, 289
Persistence, 82
Phillips-Perron test, 219
Photovoltaics, 277
Pigouvian tax, 151, 235
Pipe-in-pipe competition, 205
Pit gas, 227, 232
Plutonium, 252
Policy failure, 11
Pooling, 299
Population growth, 90
Portfolio management, 284
Post-combustion capture, 244
Posted price, 174, 178
Poverty trap, 7
Power, 16
Pre-combustion capture, 244
Present value factor, 40
Pressure, 20, 22, 205
Pressurized water reactor, 248
Price differentiation, 272
Price duration curve, 292
Price return, 184
Price spike, 292
Primary energy, 23
Principal-agent problem, 180, 307
Prisoner's dilemma, 178
Probit model, 70, 72
Process analysis, 66
Process chain analysis, 28
Producer surplus, 4
Profit center, 172
Proliferation, 257
Property right, 115, 130, 145
Public good, 294
Purchasing power parity, 94
Put option, 55, 59

Q
Quad, 20

R
Radiation sickness, 250
Radioactive exposure, 250
Radioactivity, 257
Ramsey consumption trajectory, 132
Ramsey price, 290, 305, 306
Ramsey rule, 126–128
Random Brownian motion, 184, 282

Random utility model, 70
Random walk, 183
Rapeseed oil methyl ester, 169
Rate of return, 50
Rate-of-return regulation, 307
Real option, 85, 293
Real price of energy, 95
Real-time pricing, 273, 302
Rebound effect, 82
Redispatch, 301
Refinery gas, 167, 199
Regulation power, 301
Renewable energy, 52, 131
Reprocessing, 252
Reserves, 112
Resources, 112
Retail price index, 308
Return on investment, 40, 44
Reversion rate, 282
Revolution
 industrial, 2
 Islamic, 178
 Neolithic, 2
Risk aversion, 50, 284
 individual, 261, 262
Risk free interest rate, 51, 53

S
Sales revenue, 38
Scarcity rent, 119, 134
Scenario, 187
Secondary energy, 23
Securities and Exchange Commission, 113
Self-fulfilling expectation, 122
Sensitivity analysis, 58
Separative work units, 252
Settlement, 183, 190
Shadow price, 124, 148, 306
Shale gas, 201
Shale oil, 166
Shephards lemma, 106
Short position, 182, 283
Sievert, 250
Slurry, 166
Smart grid, 301
Smart meter, 273
Social discount rate, 48
Solar radiation, 131
Sour crude, 161
Sovereign wealth fund, 139, 140
Spare capacity, 185
Spark spread, 293
Spinning reserve, 301

Spot market, 279
Spread, 193
Standard cubic meter, 20
Standard deviation, 50
Standard load profile, 273
Standard price approach, 153, 236
State variable, 124
Static range, 116
Steam coal, 231
Steam engine, 21
Steam reforming, 18
Steam turbine power plant, 276
Stochastic variable, 69, 184
Stock adjustment hypothesis, 98
Strategic petroleum reserve, 179
Sub-additivity, 303
Substitution principle, 24
Sufficiency, 79
Sunk cost, 206
Supply security, 7, 209, 216, 294, 309
Surface mining, 231
Sustainability, 8, 48, 131
Sweet crude, 161
Swing producer, 178
Synthesis gas, 244
System adequacy, 294

T
Take-or-pay contract, 214
Technological change, 107, 138, 162
   Hicks-neutral, 108
Temperature, 22, 221
Therm, 20
Thermodynamics, 17
Third party access, 221
Time-of-use tariff, 273
Time preference, 44
   pure, 48
   social, 48, 123
Time series analysis, 219
Title Transfer Facility (TTF), 217
Tons of oil equivalent, 20
Top-down approach, 65
Trading period, 239
Transaction cost, 82, 146, 172, 183
Translog cost function, 105
Transmission losses, 298
Transmission system operator, 294, 300
Transmutation, 257

U
Unbundling, 269
Underground mining, 232
Underlying, 55, 59
Upper heating value, 20, 200, 217
Upstream, 202
Uranium, 251
Uranium hexafluoride, 251
Uranium price, 255
Usable natural gas extraction, 202
Use it or lose it, 223
User cost, 119
   capital, 103
Utility, 4, 70

V
Value change, 79
Value of lost load, 271, 309, 311
Variance, 50, 261
Vega, 61
Vertical foreclosure, 172
Vertical integration, 171, 210
Vintage model, 67, 109
Volatility, 59, 61, 184, 221
   annualized, 59
   implicit, 62
Voltage, 270
Voluntary agreement, 150

W
Weibull distribution, 73
West Texas Intermediate, 161
Wiener process, 59, 60
Willingness to pay, 156, 261, 290, 304
Wind power, 277
Wobbe number, 199
Work, 16

Y
Year-ahead price, 284
Yellowcake, 251
Yield, 52, 170
Yom Kippur War, 177

Z
Zeebrugge, 217